The Correspondence Of The Late Charles Earl Grey With His Majesty King William Iv. And With Sir Herbert Taylor From Nov. 1830 To June 1832: The Reform Act, 1832. Edited By Henry Earl Grey. In 2 Volumes...

Charles Earl Grey

Nabu Public Domain Reprints:

You are holding a reproduction of an original work published before 1923 that is in the public domain in the United States of America, and possibly other countries. You may freely copy and distribute this work as no entity (individual or corporate) has a copyright on the body of the work. This book may contain prior copyright references, and library stamps (as most of these works were scanned from library copies). These have been scanned and retained as part of the historical artifact.

This book may have occasional imperfections such as missing or blurred pages, poor pictures, errant marks, etc. that were either part of the original artifact, or were introduced by the scanning process. We believe this work is culturally important, and despite the imperfections, have elected to bring it back into print as part of our continuing commitment to the preservation of printed works worldwide. We appreciate your understanding of the imperfections in the preservation process, and hope you enjoy this valuable book.

THE REFORM ACT, 1832

LONDON
PRINTED BY SPOTTISWOODE AND CO.
NEW-STREET SQUARE

THE REFORM ACT, 1832

THE CORRESPONDENCE

OF THE LATE

EARL GREY

WITH

HIS MAJESTY KING WILLIAM IV.

AND WITH

SIR HERBERT TAYLOR

FROM NOV. 1830 TO JUNE 1832

EDITED BY HENRY EARL GREY

IN TWO VOLS.—VOL. I.

LONDON
JOHN MURRAY, ALBEMARLE STREET
1867

Bot. 234 n9 7/1

PREFACE.

During the whole of my father's administration he carried on a constant correspondence on public affairs with the King. Nothing of importance was done by the Government without being fully explained to His Majesty in the letters addressed to him by his Minister; while in those written by the King, or by his order, his opinions on the various questions brought under his notice, and the objections he sometimes felt to the advice offered to him, were stated without reserve. These objections again were met, and the policy of his confidential servants was defended when necessary, in the answers returned to him. This correspondence is now in my possession, and having applied for, and obtained, Her Majesty's gracious permission for that purpose, I have determined to publish so much of it as took place between my father's accession to office on the 22nd of November, 1830, and the passing of the Reform Act in the beginning of June, 1832. My principal object in doing so is to make the difficulties of the memorable struggle by which that great measure was carried, better understood than they have been.

None of the accounts of this struggle hitherto published can, I think, be regarded as satisfactory. Many of them are disfigured by misstatements, and misrepresentations arising from prejudice and passion on one side or the other; and even those which are written with commendable fairness are not free from serious errors, into which the authors have been betrayed by the want of sufficiently full and trustworthy information. In the interest of historical truth it is desirable, that the authentic record of the opinions and feelings of two of the principal actors in these remarkable transactions, furnished by their own letters written at the time, should be accessible to future historians. And this is also due to the memory of the late King and of my father, as the conduct and motives of both have been the subject of no little misrepresentation, which the light thrown upon them by these letters will help to dispel. With regard to my father, all that it becomes me to say is, that none who knew him can doubt that his letters only describe his real feelings in expressing so constantly, and so strongly, his sense of the responsibility imposed upon him by the post he held, his conviction that a Reform in the House of Commons was absolutely necessary for the welfare and even for the safety of the nation; and that it was, therefore, his duty to omit no exertion, and to shrink from no sacrifice in order to effect it; while he considered it no less his duty to preserve the fundamental principles and the character of our Constitution untouched in any amendments of it he might help to introduce. These feelings

PREFACE. vii

and opinions, together with a very strong attachment to the King and devotion to his service, are to be traced in all his letters, and never ceased to guide his conduct through all the difficulties with which he had to contend.

As to the King, I think no impartial reader of his correspondence can fail to form from it a higher estimate of his character than that which is commonly received. His earnest desire to do what he believed to be his duty, his readiness to listen to those in whom he placed confidence,* and to consider their arguments even when most opposed to the opinions of his early life, are constantly shown in his letters. His determination never to allow his personal convenience or predilections to stand in the way of any arrangements proposed by his Ministers;—his consideration for them, and desire to spare them unnecessary labour, and to facilitate the performance of their duties;—his disinterestedness as shown by his refusal to make use of a sum of money to which he thought (though as it proved without reason) that his right might be doubtful,† and by the manner in which he acquiesced in the somewhat ungracious refusal of an outfit to the Queen,‡ are also most honourable to him. Even upon such matters as the apprehended interference of the House of Commons with respect to the Duchy of Lancaster, the attempt to take away existing Pensions, and the reduction of the salaries charged on the Civil

---

* See Sir H. Taylor's letter, No. 76.
† See letters, Nos. 46 and 48.   ‡ Nos. 65 and 67.

List, though he expressed himself very strongly, it will be seen that his anxiety was never for his personal interests, but for the dignity and authority of the Crown. For maintaining these he considered himself responsible not only to his successors, but also to the nation, justly believing the nation to be deeply concerned in not allowing the position of the Sovereign to be lowered. Above all, his perfect honesty and truthfulness, and the sense he uniformly showed of its being his duty as a Constitutional King to give his unreserved support to his Ministers so long as they continued in his service, yet without ever becoming a partizan, are worthy of all admiration, especially when it is remembered that, before his accession to the throne, this duty had been by no means distinctly recognized even in principle, and had often been very openly disregarded in practice. His determination to give his full support to his Ministers did not however, as it will be seen, prevent him from pointing out to them any objections to which he thought the measures they recommended to him were open, nor from exercising his judgment as to accepting their advice. The letters supply abundant evidence of the conscientious industry with which he must have laboured to make himself master of the public questions of the day, so as to be able efficiently to perform in this respect his duty as Sovereign.

And considering what were the ideas and opinions which his education, his early years passed in the court of George the Third, and his whole subsequent life, were calculated to form, it is matter of just surprise that he should have been found so equal to the arduous duties of Royalty in the very difficult times in which he was called upon to undertake them; that so much good sense should be displayed in his remarks upon public affairs; and that he should so generally have been right in his final judgment upon the practical questions he was required to decide. Even upon the great question on which he differed from his Ministers, and which led to their resignation,—the proposed creation of Peers after the defeat of the Government in the House of Lords on Lord Lyndhurst's motion in May, 1832,—there seems to me to be no just ground for the censure often thrown upon the King. A very large creation of Peers for the purpose of carrying the Reform Bill would have been so great an evil, even in the judgment of those who advised it, that nothing but the dread of still greater evils would have induced them to propose it. It was natural, therefore, that the King should have shrunk from taking such a step, and should have thought it better to throw upon the Opponents of Reform the responsibility of endeavouring to form a new Administration to carry on the government of the country, in the circumstances created by their victory in the House of Lords. Nor can it be doubted that the result of the King's decision proved that it was far the best for the nation that he could have adopted. If he had accepted the advice his Ministers were compelled to offer him, even the large creation of Peers they contemplated might have been insufficient to enable them to carry the Bill satisfactorily through the Committee. And it would certainly have provoked a bitter and determined resistance in all the farther stages of the Bill, not only from those who had all along been its uncompromising enemies, but also from those who, with Lords Harrowby and Wharncliffe, had voted for its second reading, though they had opposed the former measure. The powerful party of the Opposition thus re-united, and not improbably reinforced by some of those who had hitherto voted for Reform, but who would have been alienated by the violence of the means taken to coerce the House of Lords, would have obstinately fought every detail of the Bill in Committee. To overcome this resistance, the Government might have been driven to a further creation of Peers. But even this expedient, destructive as it would have been to the character of the House of Lords and the balance of the Constitution, would have been of little avail to cut short a struggle which might have been almost indefinitely prolonged, and which would have excited such fierce passions both in the House and out of doors, that it is impossible to conjecture to what acts of even revolutionary violence they might have led.

All these dangers and evils, which might probably have ensued from His Majesty's adopting the advice offered to him, were avoided by the signal failure of the Opposition to form an Administration, when the opportunity of doing so had thus been given to them, owing to the overwhelming expression of indignation which the attempt called forth, both in the House of Commons and in the country. A conviction (which probably nothing else would have produced) was thus forced upon them of the absolute necessity for their acquiescing in the passing of the measure.

In addition to the interests of historical truth, and to the object of doing justice to the late King and to my father, another reason for the publication of these letters is to be found in the circumstances of the present time. Parliament has now again to consider what was so justly called, in 1831, 'the perilous question of Reform.' It will not, therefore, be without advantage, that the arduous nature of the conflict by which Reform was then achieved, should be recalled to the minds of those who are old enough to remember it, and should be brought clearly under the notice of those who are too young to have a personal recollection of it, by a correspondence in which it is so vividly described. The events of those days are full of instruction for the present time. We may learn from them, on the one hand, that an absolute resistance to political changes, when the state of opinion and of the country requires them, is full of danger; and tends not to prevent changes from being accomplished, but to render it impossible that they should be as well considered, and as carefully framed, as they ought to be. On the other hand we may also learn, that when a change in the Constitution has to be carried, in spite of the determined resistance of the strongest party among the actual holders of political power, by the force of popular excitement, this force, when once called into full action, is indeed irresistible, but is most dangerous from its being so difficult to control or direct. Hence both men of Conservative opinions and those who desire Reform, but desire also that the principles of our Constitution should be maintained, and that the country should not be exposed to the fearful risk of revolutionary violence, ought equally to draw from the experience of 1831-2 the conclusion, that it is their duty and their interest to endeavour to prevent Parliamentary Reform from again becoming the subject of a fierce party strife. And this is only likely to be accomplished by dealing with the question in a spirit of conciliation and mutual concession, with the view of carrying such amendments of our Constitution as may be found, after dispassionate deliberation, to be best calculated to promote not party objects, or the gratification of popular passions, but the true welfare of the nation at large.

Such are the reasons which have led me to resolve on publishing these letters, believing that, after the lapse of six-and-thirty years since the earliest of them were written, there is no valid objection to their being given to the world. It may be proper for me to add some further explanation with regard to the letters themselves, and to the manner in which they have been prepared for publication. Very few of the King's letters (only two or three short ones in the whole collection) are in his own handwriting. This arose from the difficulty he had in writing, owing to a rheumatic affection in his hand.* His Majesty's letters were generally written for him, from his verbal instructions, by his private secretary, Sir H. Taylor, and he signed them after they had been read over to him and approved. A large proportion of the letters, however, it will be observed, were addressed to or written by Sir H. Taylor; but these letters are in fact no less a part of the correspondence between the King and my father than those which are so in form as well as in substance.

My father's letters, which were intended for the King's information, were often addressed to Sir Herbert Taylor, because they could be written in less time and with somewhat greater freedom than when the formal style had to be used, which was invariably adopted by his confidential servants in writing to the King himself. These letters (as Sir Herbert mentions more than once) were always shown to the King: in answering them the same form was naturally adopted, and Sir Herbert wrote in his own name; but, except in a very few instances in which he distinctly mentions that he is speaking for himself, and without authority, his letters professed to convey the King's views and opinions; nor can there be any doubt of their having done so correctly, from the complete identity his Ministers always found between those stated in Sir H. Taylor's letters on behalf of the King, and those expressed verbally by His Majesty himself, in the frequent audiences in which he was accustomed to discuss public affairs with them,

* See Sir H. Taylor's letter of January 23rd, 1831, No. 57, vol. i. p. 78.

and in which he showed the deep and intelligent interest he took in what was going on.

Perhaps it may be thought that this mode of carrying on the correspondence between the King and his Ministers must have given more influence than was right to His Majesty's private secretary; and, undoubtedly, it might have been attended with much inconvenience, if the post had been held by a person capable of abusing the great trust reposed in him. But Sir H. Taylor stands far above any such suspicion; and though it is scarcely possible that so able a man could perform the duties confided to him without exercising some influence over the mind of the King, it was my father's conviction that this influence was only used for the purpose of allaying the feelings of irritation created at times in His Majesty's mind, and of smoothing any difficulties that arose between him and his Ministers. I have often heard my father express his admiration of the manner in which Sir H. Taylor acquitted himself of the very difficult and delicate duties of his situation, and say that if the office of Private Secretary to the King had been held by a less honourable and high-minded man, the difficulty of carrying on the government would have been very greatly increased.

Perhaps Sir Herbert Taylor was too fond of writing, and thus added inconveniently to the labour imposed upon my father by his office. The necessity of returning full replies to the long letters so constantly addressed to him, of which, on some occasions, two and even three were received in a single day, was a very serious

PREFACE.

increase to the burthen of the Prime Minister's business, which must at any rate, in such times, have been very heavy; but this inconvenience was more than compensated by the opportunity his correspondence with the King afforded, of meeting objections to the conduct of the Government which had arisen in His Majesty's mind, or been suggested to him by others, before they had become too deeply rooted to be removed. This was the more important, because there were persons having access to the King, who were eager to avail themselves of every opportunity of endeavouring to injure his Ministers in his opinion, and there was always a danger that such attempts might succeed, though it will be seen in the correspondence, that His Majesty checked them as far as he could.

My father's own letters were almost invariably written without any draft or rough copy, generally in great haste, frequently amidst constant interruptions: some of not the least important were written by him from the room where Cabinets had been held, before his colleagues had left him, in order that they might be shown to them before being sent. The Cabinet Minutes were generally written in the same manner, the originals in his own handwriting being usually sent to the King, and copies made for himself by his private secretary.

In preparing this correspondence for publication, I have omitted as many as I could of the letters of which the interest seems to have passed away. But, perhaps, the omissions on this ground are fewer than might have been desirable, from my having often found it difficult to make them, without destroying the connexion of the letters, and also because some, which are of little interest in other respects, are not without value, as throwing light on the relations existing between the King and his Minister. I have also omitted nearly all the letters, or parts of letters, in which the conduct or character of individuals, or their claims on the favour of the Crown, are discussed, because in such discussions there was necessarily much that would give pain to the persons referred to, or to their surviving friends and relations. Almost the only exception I have made from this rule is in the case of the letters relating to the grant of Lord de Saumarez's peerage. These I have not omitted, because I think they are honourable to the King and to his Minister, and contain nothing to wound the feelings of the family of Lord de Saumarez. The King, in the first instance, refused to allow this peerage to be granted, not from personal dislike to the officer recommended to him, but because he erroneously believed that Sir J. Saumarez had, on an important occasion, so failed in the performance of his professional duty, as to make it improper that this honour should be conferred upon him. My father thought it his duty, in justice to a distinguished officer, to combat this opinion of the King's, which he did much more strongly in conversation than in writing. At length, though with much difficulty, he succeeded in convincing His Majesty that he had been mistaken, when the King at once withdrew his refusal, which had been most acutely felt by Sir James Saumarez as a slur on the high character he so justly bore in the Navy.

While I have endeavoured to show all due respect to the feelings of individuals, I have not thought it right, on this ground, to omit even severe remarks on the public, as distinguished from the private, conduct of those who took an active part in political affairs at the time. To have done so would have destroyed much of the value of the correspondence, especially as a record of the motives and considerations which determined the measures of the Ministers. And though, in some of his letters, my father used strong language, and, perhaps, may have occasionally taken a more unfavourable view of the conduct of his political opponents than he might have adopted, when looking back at it, after the heat of the struggle was over, every candid reader will make allowance for warmth of expression in letters written in a time of so much excitement, and with so little leisure for weighing the force of the words he used. I may be permitted to add, that while I believe so severe a political contest was never carried on, without some things being said and done by all the prominent actors in it, which, upon reflection, they must have regretted, much less allowance is required on this score for any undue severity in my father's judgment of his political opponents, than for the conduct on their part that provoked his censure.

I have also thought that it would not be right for me to omit expressions of opinion, on the part either of the King or my father, which may possibly jar on the minds of many readers of the present day. Such omissions would be inconsistent with historical truth;

nor do I think that a full and fair record of their opinions and feelings as expressed by themselves at the time, can be otherwise than honourable to both William IV. and his Minister in the eyes of all candid judges, notwithstanding the great change which has since taken place in the ideas commonly accepted in the world on many political questions.

Besides the omissions I have considered it advisable to make in printing this correspondence, there are a good many occasioned by some letters not having been copied, or the copies having been lost. Among these are the greater part of the letters written by my father to the King to inform him of the proceedings of the House of Lords. After every debate of importance, however late he might get home, or however much he might be fatigued, my father never omitted writing to the King an account of what had taken place, before going to bed. But his private secretary was rarely in attendance when he returned from the House of Lords, and he did not usually think it necessary to have letters of this kind sent back to him to be copied, so that they have not in general been preserved. A few letters are also missing, which from the importance of the matters they relate to must certainly have been copied, though no copies of them are now to be found. I have pointed out one or two cases of this kind in notes. I have, however, avoided adding more notes than I have considered indispensable, being anxious that the writers of the letters should speak for themselves without comment from myself. The notes I have given are therefore strictly confined to statements of fact which have seemed to me to be wanted for a clear understanding of the correspondence. I have even abstained from calling attention to those cases in which these letters, if carefully read, supply a decisive contradiction of erroneous statements which have been confidently put forth, as to what happened on some important occasions.

Letters written in the manner I have described those of my father to have been (and though with somewhat less force the remark applies to those of the King and Sir H. Taylor, which were also often written in haste), cannot be expected to be free from obscurities and inaccuracies of expression which would no doubt have been corrected had the letters been revised by the writers; but I have not thought myself at liberty to make even the slightest correction, except in cases where the mistake is quite obviously a mere slip of the pen.

I have only to add that I have confined this publication to the letters written from the time of my father's accession to office till just after the passing of the Reform Act. I find no correspondence of the slightest consequence between my father and the King in the few days which intervened between the resignation of the former Ministers and the completion of the new Administration. This, I believe, is to be accounted for by the fact, that almost all my father's communications with the King respecting the proposed arrangements were made verbally: if any letters were written on the subject, they must have been lost or destroyed. I have not continued the publication beyond the giving of the Royal Assent to the English Reform Bill, except by the insertion of two or three letters which, though later in date, belong to the preceding discussions, partly because it was unnecessary to go further for my object of throwing light on the struggle for Reform, partly because it might not as yet be quite convenient to publish the correspondence that took place on some of the questions that arose in the two last years of my father's administration, after the subject of Reform had been disposed of. I have included in this collection all the letters written in the period it embraces, except those omitted for the reasons I have mentioned, because the struggle for Reform was much affected by the discussions on other public questions which arose during its progress.

GREY.

HOWICK: *December,* 1866.

CONTENTS
OF
THE FIRST VOLUME.

1830.

NO.		PAGE
1.	Earl Grey to the King, Nov. 23, enclosing Cabinet Minute as to measures to be adopted for restoring peace in the country	1
2.	The King to Earl Grey, Nov. 23, in reply, approving proposed measures. Remarks respecting Militia and Police	3
3.	The King to Earl Grey, Nov. 26. Will see Lord Grey. His Ministers to understand His Majesty's convenience is never to interfere with his attention to public business	5
4.	The King to Earl Grey, Nov. 27, suggesting arrangements respecting Ordnance department	6
5.	Earl Grey to the King, Nov. 27. Change in constitution of Ordnance department would require time for consideration	8
6.	The King to Earl Grey, Nov. 27. His Majesty does not wish to embarrass Lord Grey	8
7.	The King to Earl Grey, Dec. 1. Alarm excited by Lord Holland's observations respecting the Duchy of Lancaster. The King's jealousy of Parliamentary interference with respect to it	9
8.	Earl Grey to the King, Dec. 1, reassuring His Majesty as to the intentions of his Ministers with respect to the Duchy of Lancaster	12
9.	The King to Earl Grey, Dec. 1. His Majesty's satisfaction with Lord Grey's letter	14

CONTENTS OF

NO.		PAGE
10.	Sir H. Taylor to Earl Grey, Dec. 2. Outfit for the Queen, enclosing copy of letter to the Duke of Wellington respecting it	11, 15
11.	Earl Grey to Sir H. Taylor, Dec. 3. Reply to the above	16
12.	Sir H. Taylor to Earl Grey, Dec. 4, enclosing copy of the Duke of Wellington's letter	17
13.	Cabinet Minute, as to measures for restoring tranquillity	18
14.	The King to Earl Grey, Dec. 4, approving measures proposed	19
15.	Sir H. Taylor to Earl Grey, Dec. 7. Purchase of Jewels for Queen Charlotte, precedent for outfit to Queen	19
16.	Sir H. Taylor to Earl Grey, Dec. 10. The King proposes that Mr. Stanley should be returned for Windsor	20
17.	Sir H. Taylor to Earl Grey, Dec. 19, enclosing letter from Sir H. Blackwood, asking for appointment in the Ordnance	21
18.	Earl Grey to Sir H. Taylor, Dec. 20. Reply to the above. Arrangements proposed with reference to Ordnance department	21
19.	Earl Grey to Sir H. Taylor, Dec. 21. Ordnance arrangements. Notice in the House of Commons as to Duchy of Lancaster. Account received of Mr. O'Connell's entry into Dublin. Trades Union at Manchester	23
20.	Earl Grey to the King, Dec. 21. Archbishop of Canterbury's proposal of a form of prayer. Deanery of Chester. Ordnance arrangements	25
21.	Sir H. Taylor to Earl Grey, Dec. 21. King's approval of Ordnance arrangements. Appointments in the Household. Hardship of depriving Naval Officers holding such appointments of their half-pay	26
22.	Sir H. Taylor to Earl Grey, Dec. 22. Notice of Motion in the House of Commons, respecting Duchy of Lancaster. Mr. O'Connell's entry into Dublin. Trades Union assemblages. Application to the King for a loan. Suggestion as to giving greater accommodation to Charles X. in Holyrood House	28
	(*Enclosure.*) The King to Earl Grey, Dec. 22. Approves proposal submitted to him. Duchy of Lancaster	29
23.	Earl Grey to Sir H Taylor, Dec. 22. Application for a	

THE FIRST VOLUME. xxiij

NO.		PAGE
	Peerage. Case of Naval Officers holding Naval appointments. Ordnance and Household appointments. Mr. Stanley advised to abandon scrutiny and petition against Mr. Hunt's return for Preston. King's offer of Windsor	30
24.	Sir H. Taylor to Earl Grey, Dec. 23. The application for a Peerage. Case of Naval Officers in the Household. Lord Falkland's appointment. Mr. Stanley's proposed return for Windsor	32
25.	Earl Grey to the King, Dec. 23. Appointment of Captain Duncan as Storekeeper of the Ordnance. Militia to be embodied: Ballot required, and Council necessary. Better accounts from manufacturing districts. Less good from Ireland. Adjournment of the two Houses not to extend beyond the 4th of February . . .	35
26.	The King to Earl Grey, Dec. 24. Approves Captain Duncan's appointment. Militia and Yeomanry. Council at Brighton. Accounts from Ireland and manufacturing districts	35
27.	Sir H. Taylor to Earl Grey, Dec. 24. Invitation to the Pavilion. Question as to amending Act of Parliament respecting half-pay of Naval Officers	36
28.	Sir H. Taylor to Earl Grey, Dec. 25. Transmits paper on the Militia, by Sir R. Jackson	37
29.	Earl Grey to the King, Dec. 30, enclosing Minute of Cabinet as to state of Ireland, and measures to be taken	39
30.	Sir H. Taylor to Earl Grey, Dec. 30. Reasons for preferring an augmentation of the regular Army to embodying the Militia	40
31.	The King to Earl Grey, Dec. 31. Approving of measures proposed by the Cabinet. Necessity of caution as to the Militia	42

1831.

32. Earl Grey to the King, Jan. 11. Reasons for not having written to His Majesty for some days. Conduct of the Government in Ireland. Arrangements respecting the

NO.		PAGE
	command of the troops in Ireland, and the seat for Windsor. Preparation of measures for Parliament	43
33.	The King to Earl Grey, Jan. 12. Approves of proposals submitted to him. His confidence in his Ministers, and especially in Lord Grey	46
34.	Sir H. Taylor to Earl Grey, Jan. 12. Lord Grey's longer silence then usual not taken amiss by His Majesty. King's health good. His anxiety as to proceedings in Parliament, and the maintenance of the authority of the Government, and his sense of the importance of Lord Grey's services. Mr. Hunt's failure	47
35.	Earl Grey to the King, Jan. 12. Resignation of Chief Baron. Usual pension to him, and appointment of Lord Lyndhurst to succeed him. Convicts at Winchester, except two, recommended to mercy. Two fires in Wiltshire	49
36.	The King to Earl Grey, Jan. 13. Approves proposals submitted to him	51
37.	Earl Grey to Sir H. Taylor, Jan. 13. Gratified by letters received. News from Ireland not pleasant; but confidence that difficulties may be overcome. King's anxiety as to what may happen in Parliament reasonable. The perilous question that of Parliamentary Reform. Hopes before long to submit measure to His Majesty. With his sanction little fear of carrying it. Alternative an afflicting one	51
38.	Earl Grey to the King, Jan. 13. Gratitude for His Majesty's letter. Encloses letters from Lord Lieutenant of Ireland and Lord Ponsonby. Remarks upon them	52
39.	Sir H. Taylor to Earl Grey, Jan. 14, enclosing King's answer. His Majesty's feelings about Reform, and his confidence in Lord Grey	54
40.	The King to Earl Grey, Jan. 14. Returns letters from Lord Anglesey and Lord Ponsonby. His Majesty's opinion as to Ireland. The payment of the Roman Catholic Clergy. Belgium	55
41.	Earl Grey to Sir H. Taylor, Jan. 14. Encloses anonymous letter respecting Sir W. Fremantle and Sir A. Barnard. Sends a book brought by M. de Choiseul	57

NO.		PAGE
42.	Sir H. Taylor to Earl Grey, Jan. 15. Returns anonymous letter sent to him with a statement in refutation of it	60
43.	Earl Grey to the King, Jan. 15. His Majesty's opinions respecting Ireland and Belgium. Possible necessity of proposing to suspend Habeas Corpus Act in Ireland. Importance and difficulty of paying the Roman Catholic Priests there. Duchy of Luxemburg. Opinion respecting it expressed to the Prince of Orange	64
44.	Earl Grey to Sir H. Taylor, Jan. 15. Expression of the King's confidence gratifying. Fear that His Majesty may think Lord Grey's views as to the Parliamentary Reform required too extensive. Measure ought to be one on which the Government can stand. Disadvantage of discussing the subject in such difficult times; but unavoidable. Consequences that would follow from attempting to postpone it	65
45.	Sir H. Taylor to Earl Grey, Jan. 16. Great interest taken by the King in the correspondence respecting Reform. His Majesty's apprehensions. Lord Grey's communications have gone far to allay them. Opinions of the King on the subject	66
46.	Sir H. Taylor to Earl Grey, Jan. 16. Question, whether certain sums should be paid into the Privy Purse. Hopes his letter about Reform will be satisfactory. Has encouraged His Majesty to broach the subject instead of brooding over it	68
47.	Earl Grey to the King, Jan. 17, encloses letter from Lord Anglesey, with list of persons proposed for appointment as Lords-Lieutenants of Irish counties	69
48.	Earl Grey to Sir H. Taylor, Jan. 17. Right of the King to the money adverted to in Sir Herbert's letter. Parliamentary Reform	70
49.	The King to Earl Grey, Jan. 17. Persons proposed for office of Lord-Lieutenant in Irish counties. Approves Proclamation against seditious meetings and proceedings against Messrs. O'Connell and Steel. Measures for the improvement of Ireland	71
50.	Sir H. Taylor to Earl Grey, Jan. 18. The King has been	

NO.		PAGE
	pleased with letters respecting money arising from hereditary revenues and Parliamentary Reform . . .	72
51.	Earl Grey to Sir H. Taylor, Jan. 19. Answer respecting anonymous letter satisfactory; but no doubt of imprudent conversation at the Speaker's, and belief of the Opposition that a blow may be struck at the Government through the Court. Pamphlet on the late Revolution in France	73
52.	Earl Grey to Sir H. Taylor, Jan. 20. Measures for augmenting Naval force	74
53.	Sir H. Taylor to Earl Grey, Jan. 21. King approves measures proposed. Arrest of Mr: O'Connell . .	75
54.	The King to Earl Grey, Jan. 21. Death of Lord Sydney. Duke of Sussex to succeed him as Ranger of Hyde Park	75
55.	Earl Grey to the King, Jan. 22. Duke of Sussex accepts Rangership. Neutrality of Belgium . . .	76
56.	Sir H. Taylor to Earl Grey, Jan. 22. The King's annoyance at the Secretary-at-War's contemplating the reduction of the Riding establishment. Recommends it to Lord Grey's protection	77
57.	Sir H. Taylor to Earl Grey, Jan. 23. Accounts for delay of King's answers to last letters. King only signs his letters. The appointment of the Duke of Sussex. Neutrality of Belgium	78
58.	Earl Grey to Sir H. Taylor, Jan. 24. The Riding establishment. Belgium. Count Flahault's arrival from Paris. Conversation with him. Plan of Reform has been under the consideration of the Cabinet. Lord Grey proposes to submit it to the King personally. Thanks to His Majesty for giving the Guelphic Order to General Grey	79
59.	The King to Earl Grey, Jan. 24. Rangership of the parks. Communications from Lord Melbourne and Lord Palmerston	82
60.	The King to Earl Grey, Jan. 24. Guelphic Order given to General Grey. The Grand Cross of the Bath will be so on a fitting opportunity	83
61.	Sir H. Taylor to Earl Grey, Jan. 25. Expresses the King's satisfaction that the plan of Reform will soon be ready to	

NO.		PAGE
	be submitted to him. Invites Lord Grey to the Pavilion. The Riding establishment. The King's eagerness on such questions. Affairs of Belgium, and choice of a Sovereign for that country	84
62.	Earl Grey to the King, Jan. 25. Explanation as to his letter respecting the Order given to General Grey. Renewed acknowledgments for King's approval of the services of his Ministers. Letter from Lord Anglesey. Ecclesiastical appointments in Ireland. Application from Captain Campbell for office of Groom of the Bedchamber	86
63.	The King to Earl Grey, Jan. 26. Letter respecting Guelphic Order to General Grey. Union of bishoprics. Approves contemplated ecclesiastical appointments in Ireland. Situation of Groom of the Bedchamber . .	88
64.	Earl Grey to the King, Jan. 27. Letter from Lord Anglesey. Lord Grey's opinion as to Mr. O'Connell. Groomship of Bedchamber	90
65.	Earl Grey to Sir H. Taylor, Feb. 3. Anxiety for the King's observations on the proposed measure of Reform. Reference to his interview with His Majesty on the subject. The Queen's outfit. Lord Grey's disappointment at being obliged to abandon the proposal . .	91
66.	Earl Grey to Sir H. Taylor, Feb. 4. Disposition of both Houses on re-assembling. Letter from Lord Anglesey. Choice of a Sovereign for Belgium	92
67.	Sir H. Taylor to Earl Grey, Feb. 4. Queen's outfit. Feeling of Their Majesties with respect to opposition made to it	93
68.	The King to Earl Grey, Feb. 4. Statement of His Majesty's opinions on Parliamentary Reform, and on the measure proposed by his Ministers . . .	94
69.	Earl Grey to the King, Feb. 5. King's letter on the measure of Reform gratifying. The question of Ballot. The county franchise. The census of 1821 a sufficient basis for the measure	105
70.	Sir H. Taylor to Earl Grey, Feb. 5. Lord Anglesey's letter. Probable opposition to Reform. Belgium. Renewal of Princess Sophia's appointment as Keeper of Greenwich Park	107

xxviii   CONTENTS OF

NO.		PAGE
71.	Sir H. Taylor to Earl Grey, Feb. 6. Lord Althorp's statement in the House of Commons as to outfit for the Queen	109
72.	The King to Earl Grey, Feb. 6. Parliamentary Reform: points referred to in Earl Grey's letter	110
73.	Earl Grey to Sir H. Taylor, Feb. 7. Apology for deferring answer to the King's letter. Satisfactory accounts from Paris. Pensions on the Civil List	112
74.	Earl Grey to Sir H. Taylor, Feb. 8. Sends papers for the King. Corrects the King's impression as to views of the other members of the Cabinet respecting Ballot. Proceedings in the House of Commons respecting Pensions	114
75.	Sir H. Taylor to Earl Grey, Feb. 8. The Queen's language on the refusal of an outfit. The King's approval of course taken respecting Belgium. His feelings on the question of Pensions, and towards Lord Grey. His Majesty's character	115
76.	Earl Grey to the King, Feb. 8. Reform: sanguine hopes of carrying it through Parliament with His Majesty's support. Lord Grey participates in painful impression made on the King by disposition shown by the House of Commons. Things seem to be taking a better turn owing to Lord Althorp's firmness on the question of Pensions; but a very unfortunate feeling exists on this subject	118
77.	Sir H. Taylor to Earl Grey, Feb. 9. The King's strong feeling on the question of maintaining existing pensions	119
78.	The King to Earl Grey, Feb. 9. No excuse was necessary for Lord Grey's delaying his answer to former letter. His Majesty surprised he is able to write so fully. The King satisfied with explanations on Reform Bill. Lord Grey has acted wisely in bringing the subject forward without delay. Misconception as to opinions of other members of the Cabinet on Ballot. Pensions on the Civil List. His approval of Lord Althorp's conduct on this question. Difficulty that may arise from it. Necessity for a high tone upon it; but does not object to checks on abuse for the future	121
79.	Lord Grey to Sir H. Taylor, Feb. 11. Outfit to the Queen.	

NO.		PAGE
	State of feeling on this and similar questions in the House of Commons and in the country. Letter from Lord Anglesey. Lord Grey going to Claremont	124
80.	Sir H. Taylor to Earl Grey, Feb. 12. Lord Anglesey's letter. The King's remarks on the state of feeling respecting Pensions. Windsor election	126
81.	Earl Grey to the King, Feb. 14. The Budget. Satisfactory meeting at Lord Althorp's. Abandonment of proposed tax upon Transfers. Mr. O'Connell's withdrawal of plea of Not Guilty on first counts of indictment	127
82.	Earl Grey to Sir Herbert Taylor, Feb. 15. Every thing had passed off well the previous evening in both Houses. Opposition to Lord Duncannon in Kilkenny	129
83.	The King to Earl Grey, Feb. 15. Changes in the Budget. Lord Anglesey's communications gratifying to His Majesty	130
84.	The King to Earl Grey, Feb. 19. Case of Representative Peers of Scotland and Ireland becoming British Peers	131
85.	Earl Grey to Sir H. Taylor, Feb. 21. Proceedings of the Committee on the Civil List. State of public opinion on the subject. Prince Talleyrand and Madame de Dino. Indictment against Cobbett. Asks to see His Majesty	132
86.	The King to Earl Grey, March 3. Question as to proceedings of Committees of House of Commons being constitutional. Lord Saye and Sele's appointment	134
87.	The King to Earl Grey, March 3. Progress of debate on Reform in the House of Commons. Effect produced by the measure out of doors	135
88.	Earl Grey to the King, March 4. Legal question shall be submitted to Law Officers. But inquiry of Committee rests on other grounds. Lord Saye and Sele cannot accept appointment.	136
89.	Sir H. Taylor to Earl Grey, March 4. Appointment of Lord of Bedchamber left to Lord Grey, to mark His Majesty's determination to support his Government. Reform: the King's feelings on the question	138
90.	The King to Earl Grey, March 4, acknowledging Lord Grey's report of proceedings in both Houses. Lord Saye and Sele's communication overlooked	140

CONTENTS OF

NO.		PAGE
91.	Earl Grey to Sir H. Taylor, March 4. Less favourable report of prospects of Reform Bill in the House of Commons. Country more and more favourable . .	141
92.	The King to Earl Grey, March 4. Proceedings of Committees of the House of Commons on Salaries and the Civil List. His Majesty's anxiety with regard to them increased by their connexion with the Reform Bill. His Majesty's reasons for agreeing to that measure; but bound to maintain the dignity of the Crown. Hence his communications. What he regards as details of Civil List, which ought to be exempt from the interference of the House of Commons	143
93.	Sir H. Taylor to Earl Grey, March 5. King regrets grounds for apprehending failure of the Reform Bill. Aware of its serious consequences, but prepared to encounter them	146
94.	Earl Grey to the King, March 5. Explanation as to intentions of the Committee on the Civil List . .	147
95.	Sir H. Taylor to Earl Grey, March 6. Reasons for the King's jealousy of proceedings of Committees of the House of Commons	148
96.	The King to Earl Grey, March 6. Reductions in the Civil List made by the Committee	148
97.	The King to Earl Grey, March 7. Progress of debate on Reform in the House of Commons. Proceedings in the House of Lords. Acceptance of Mr. Wynn's resignation of office of Secretary-at-War. Appointment of Sir H. Parnell to be Secretary-at-War	150
98.	The King to Earl Grey, March 7. Opinion of the Chancellor and Law Officers as to proceedings of Committees of the House of Commons	152
99.	The King to Earl Grey, March 8. Postponement of Lord Wharncliffe's motion in the House of Lords .	153
100.	The King to Earl Grey, March 9. Progress of the debate in the House of Commons	153
101.	Earl Grey to Sir H. Taylor, March 19. Defeat of the Government in the House of Commons on the Timber Duties. Its bad effect. Still confident of majority for Reform Bill on second reading. Doubt as to carrying	

NO.		PAGE
	it through the Committee. Course to be taken to be considered by Cabinet. Question as to a dissolution of Parliament. What are the King's feelings upon it?	154
102.	Earl Grey to the King, March 19. Defeat of the Government in the House of Commons; how caused; its probable consequences. Cabinet summoned to consider it	155
103.	The King to Earl Grey, March 20. His regret for what had occurred. His determination to support the measure of Reform unaltered, and his confidence in his Ministers unabated. Would lament the fall of his Government. Hopes that means to avert it may be found without a dissolution, to which he could not consent. Reasons for objecting to it. The state of the country. His earnest desire not to lose the services of Lord Grey and his colleagues	156
104.	Earl Grey to Sir H. Taylor, March 20. Determination of Ministers to carry on the government, notwithstanding the vote of the House of Commons. Remarks upon it. Prospect of defeat in Committee on Reform Bill. Question as to dissolving Parliament does not yet arise	160
105.	Earl Grey to the King, March 20. Result of the Cabinet. Civil List Bill	162
106.	The King to Earl Grey, March 20. Satisfaction at the determination of Ministers to retain their offices. His determination to support them, provided he is not called upon to dissolve Parliament	163
107.	Sir H. Taylor to Earl Grey, March 20. Why he had shown Lord Grey's letters referring to a dissolution of Parliament to the King. His Majesty's feelings upon that subject and towards Lord Grey	165
108.	Earl Grey to Sir H. Taylor, March 21. Attendance of Lord Belfast and Colonel Cavendish on His Majesty may interfere with their being in the House of Commons for the division on the Reform Bill. Course said to be contemplated by the Opposition. Condemnation of it	167
109.	Earl Grey to the King, March 21. Grateful acknowledgments for His Majesty's approbation and support in bringing forward measure of Reform. The King's ob-	

jection to dissolving Parliament perceived by Lord Grey at Brighton. This led him to communicate with Sir H. Taylor. This not done without consideration of the state of the country and of Ireland. It was the personal act of Lord Grey; not a proposal only preparatory to one. Declaration of His Majesty's opinion commands respect of Ministers. Their wish to conform to it, but not to deprive them of privilege of submitting advice a painful necessity may require. Hope the necessity may not arise. Their feelings towards His Majesty. Lord Grey asks for audience . . . 169

110. Earl Grey to Sir H. Taylor, March 21. Pain occasioned to him by discussion on dissolution. Necessity of secresy as to His Majesty's opinions 173

111. Sir H. Taylor to Earl Grey, March 21. The King's anxiety about his answer to Lord Grey on the subject of a dissolution. Sir Herbert's opinion, that His Majesty's objection to the measure will prove final and conclusive 174

112. The King to Earl Grey, March 21. Full statement of His Majesty's opinion with respect to a dissolution, and the reasons for it 177

113. Earl Grey to the King, March 22. Debate in the House of Commons on the second reading of the Reform Bill . 184

114. Earl Grey to Sir H. Taylor, March 22, enclosing letter from Lord Durham. Three things to be impressed upon the King's mind 186

115. Sir H. Taylor to Earl Grey, March 23. Regret that he was not at liberty to show Lord Durham's letter to the King. The King's readiness to listen to all that is urged against his opinions. Sir Herbert's habit of submitting everything to him. Remarks on the three points insisted upon by Lord Grey 187

116. The King to Earl Grey, March 23. Rejoices that the second reading of the Reform Bill has been carried. Colonel Fox appointed Equerry 194

117. Sir H. Taylor to Earl Grey, March 23. Will show Lord Durham's letter and his own to the King. Removal from Household places of persons who had voted against the Reform Bill 195

NO.		PAGE
118.	Sir H. Taylor to Earl Grey, March 23. King's thanks for the communication of Lord Durham's letter . .	196
119.	Earl Grey to Sir H. Taylor, March 23. Remarks on Sir H. Taylor's letter of 22nd. His Majesty's manner to Lord Durham less kind than to his other servants. Injurious effect on the division of the report of the King's veto on a dissolution	197
120.	Sir H. Taylor to Earl Grey, March 24. Reasons for King's strong objection to dissolving Parliament. His Majesty's satisfaction at Lord Grey's having acknowledged his good faith and sincerity. Not displeased with Lord Durham's letter: his manner not intentionally cold to him. Reports of King's objection to a dissolution not from his want of caution	202
121.	Earl Grey to Sir H. Taylor, April 5. Moderation shown by France with respect to Austrian advance to Bologna. Hopes of maintaining peace. Polish war. Accounts from Ireland. Dinner at the Mansion House . .	207
122.	Earl Grey to Sir H. Taylor, April 6. His letter to General Kosciusko in 1814. Polish war . . .	209
123.	The King to Earl Grey, April 10. Lord Ponsonby's private letter. Affairs of Belgium	210
124.	Earl Grey to the King, April 11. Acknowledges His Majesty's letter. State of Ireland. Asks for an audience	213
125.	The King to Earl Grey, April 11. State of Ireland. Will see Lord Grey	214
126.	Earl Grey to the King, April 19. Letter from Lord Anglesey. General Gascoigne's motion on the Reform Bill. Expectation of favourable division . . .	214
127.	Earl Grey to Sir H. Taylor, April 19. Character of General Gascoigne's motion. Its success would destroy all hope of carrying the Reform Bill in the present House of Commons. Case of distress submitted to His Majesty. Impatience in the City for a visit from their Majesties	215
128.	The King to Earl Grey, April 19. State of Ireland. Approval of Lord Anglesey's conduct. Lord Grey's intimation of probable necessity for advising dissolu-	

NO.		PAGE
	tion. His Majesty's objections to the measure unaltered. Hopes the division on General Gascoigne's motion may relieve Ministers from the necessity of proposing it. His Majesty's satisfaction with the manner in which they have carried on the business of the country. His hope that the further discussion of the Reform Bill might have been postponed	218
129.	Sir H. Taylor to Earl Grey, April 19. Lord Grey's letter had been seen by the King. His Majesty distressed by the part of it relating to a dissolution	220
130.	Sir H. Taylor to Earl Grey, April 19. Captain ———'s application. Demands on the Privy Purse	221
131.	Earl Grey to the King, April 20. Gratitude for the expression of His Majesty's confidence. Division on General Gascoigne's motion adverse to the Government. Cabinet summoned	223
132.	The King to Earl Grey, April 20. His Majesty's concern at the result of the division. Will see Lord Grey	224
133.	Minute of Cabinet, April 20. Advice to dissolve Parliament	224
134.	The King to Earl Grey, April 20. Must further consider his decision on the advice submitted to him	226
135.	Earl Grey to the King, April 20. Ministers do not wish to press for earlier decision than consistent with His Majesty's convenience and mature consideration	226
136.	The King to Earl Grey, April 21. Full statement of His Majesty's reasons for acquiescing in a dissolution, notwithstanding his objections to the measure. Relies upon his Ministers resisting measures to extend the principle of the Reform Bill. Urges their consenting to modifications which may conciliate opponents without impairing the measure	227
137.	Earl Grey to Sir H. Taylor, April 21. Gratitude for the King's kindness. Cabinet to meet at 12	233
138.	Sir H. Taylor to Earl Grey. King gratified by Lord Grey's letter, and desires that he will himself be the bearer of the answer of the Cabinet to his communications	233
139.	The King to Earl Grey, April 21. Will see Lord Grey	

	PAGE
next day at half-past 11, and hold a Council at 12. Note explaining circumstances under which this letter was written	234
Earl Grey to Sir H. Taylor, April 24, enclosing antedated Minute of Cabinet	236
The King to Earl Grey, April 24. Review of past proceedings and correspondence relating to the Reform Bill. The King's sentiments on the subject, and on the state of affairs	239
Earl Grey to the King, April 25. Intention of the Ministers to revise the provisions of the Reform Bill; but must not detract from its efficiency. Evils that would follow from consenting to do so . . .	247
The King to Earl Grey, April 25. Acknowledges Cabinet Minute on His Majesty's letter of the 21st .	248
Sir H. Taylor to Earl Grey, April 26. Lord Mayor's invitation to be accepted for the 20th of May . .	248
Earl Grey to the King, May 2. His Majesty's disapproval of the Lord Mayor expressed to Lord Melbourne. Lord Grey concurs in it. Ireland more tranquil. Dispatches from Lord Granville	249
The King to Earl Grey, May 3. Conduct of the Lord Mayor. Regrets the City being again disappointed as to Royal visit. Information from Lord Granville satisfactory. His Majesty sends paper which appears treasonable. Passages in it recommending assassination of the Emperor of Russia	250
Sir H. Taylor to Earl Grey, May 3. King's health a sufficient reason for his not going to the City . .	252
Earl Grey to Sir H. Taylor, May 3. Placard attributed to the Lord Mayor a fabrication. City invitation. No contest in Northumberland.	253
Sir H. Taylor to Earl Grey, May 3. Fabricated placard. The King's indignation. His Majesty persists in declining City invitation. Northumberland election . .	254
Sir H. Taylor to Earl Grey, May 6. Progress of the elections. King's refusal of City invitation final. Presentation of kettle drums to Life Guards . .	255
Earl Grey to Sir H. Taylor, May 6. Regret at the	

NO.		PAGE
	King's determination respecting the City. The elections. Deaths of Sir Joseph Yorke and Captains Bradby and Young	256
152.	Sir H. Taylor to Earl Grey, May 7. Lord Melbourne to communicate the King's decision respecting the City to the Lord Mayor. The Elections. Accident to Sir Joseph Yorke	257
153.	Earl Grey to Sir H. Taylor, May 7. Lord Melbourne has written to the Lord Mayor. Elections. Grant of Lodge in Richmond Park to Lord and Lady Errol. Mode of giving orders for it. Hopes a different one will be taken in future	258
154.	Earl Grey to Sir H. Taylor, May 8. The elections. Bad effect produced by the King's declining City invitation. Pains taken to create a belief that His Majesty is really adverse to the measure of Reform	259
155.	Sir H. Taylor to Earl Grey, May 8. The elections. Mode of giving the King's commands as to the grant of the Lodge in Richmond Park	260
156.	Earl Grey to the King, May 9. Communications with the Lord Mayor. Letters from Lord Lieutenant of Ireland. Proposes appointments to the Privy Council in Ireland. List of returns. Lord Grey will attend His Majesty	261
157.	The King to Earl Grey, May 13. Objection to Portuguese refugees residing at Gibraltar	262
158.	Earl Grey to the King, May 14. His Majesty's letter has been communicated to Lord Goderich, and instructions will be sent accordingly to the Governor of Gibraltar	263
159.	The King to Earl Grey, May 15. His Majesty's feelings as to the propriety of excluding Spanish or Portuguese refugees from Gibraltar. They have been strengthened by his apprehension of the revolutionary spirit in France and Belgium	264
160.	The King to Earl Grey, May 17. Full statement of His Majesty's views of the state of public opinion with reference to Reform, and his apprehensions as to the spirit that prevails among the people	265

THE FIRST VOLUME. xxxvii

NO.   PAGE

161. Sir H. Taylor to Earl Grey, May 21. The Lord Advocate's letter. King's neck doing well . . . 270

162. The King to Earl Grey, May 23. Account from Ireland. His Majesty will not delay further giving the Blue Riband to Earl Grey 271

163. The King to Earl Grey, May 28. His Majesty's anxiety at the prospect of renewal of Parliamentary discussions on Reform. Reference to his former letters. Earnest recommendation to his Ministers to endeavour to moderate opposition to the Bill by modifications not inconsistent with its principle 272

164. Earl Grey to the King, May 29. Reply to the above. Explanation of Earl Grey's opinions, and of the past conduct of the Ministers with respect to Reform. Principles which will govern Lord Grey's conduct for the future 276

165. The King to Earl Grey, May 29. Further discussion of the same subject. His Majesty has never urged a departure from the principle of the Bill . . . 281

166. Earl Grey to Sir H. Taylor, May 29, enclosing Cabinet Minute on the preceding letters 284

167. Earl Grey to Sir H. Taylor, June 6. Return of Scotch Representative Peers. Votes of Peers connected with the Court. The Government deprived of support it ought to command. Satisfactory effect of Special Commission in Clare and Limerick. Unfavourable accounts from Merthyr Tydvil. Belgium. Distress in the west of Ireland. Battle of Ostrolenka . . 286

168. The King to Earl Grey, June 7. Election of Scotch Representative Peers. Notice of Lord Grey's remarks on the position of the Government as affected by the Court. His Majesty's earnest wish for the success of the Bill, but his apprehensions as to a collision between the two Houses 289

169. Sir H. Taylor to Earl Grey, June 7. Preceding letter dictated by the King. Accounts from Ireland and Glamorganshire. Belgium 294

170. Earl Grey to the King, June 7. Gratitude for His Majesty's confidence and favour; but avowed hostility

		PAGE
	of persons connected with the Court diminishes the strength of the Government in the House of Lords. The Reform Bill. Alterations suggested in it. House of Lords. Hope that a hostile amendment will not be carried the first day of the Session. Accounts from Merthyr Tydvil and from Ireland	295
171.	Earl Grey to Sir H. Taylor, June 7. Reasons for writing the preceding letter. No knowledge of the plans of the Opposition. Does not doubt they will try to thwart the Administration. Sends letter pressing demands on the Government	298
172.	Sir H. Taylor to Earl Grey, June 8. Probable that the Bishops will not be inclined to contend against a sweeping majority of the House of Commons . . .	299
173.	The King to Earl Grey, June 18. Returns draft of Speech with remarks	300
174.	The King to Earl Grey, June 22. His Majesty is glad no amendment to the Address was moved in the House of Lords	300
175.	Sir H. Taylor to Earl Grey, July 2. Communication from the Duke of Cumberland. Question as to Coronation	301
176.	Sir H. Taylor to Earl Grey, July 5. Debate in the House of Commons. Question in the House of Lords as to the Coronation. The King going to Lord Hill's breakfast	302
177.	Earl Grey to the King, July 12. Proposed proceedings respecting the Coronation. Vacancies in the Order of St. Patrick. Acceptance by Government of Belgium of the propositions of the Conference . . .	303
178.	The King to Earl Grey, July 12. Approves proposed proceedings as to Coronation. Acceptance of Belgian Government, and prospects of French elections satisfactory	304
179.	Earl Grey to Sir H. Taylor, July 16. Expenditure in Lord Chamberlain's department. . . .	305
180.	Sir H. Taylor to Earl Grey, July 17. Reply to the above	306
181.	The King to Earl Grey, July 17. Arrangements re-	

specting Prince Leopold's annuity on his becoming King of the Belgians. Colonelcy of 5th Dragoon Guards	308
182. Earl Grey to the King, July 18. Explanations respecting Prince Leopold. Alarming account of Earl Spencer's health. Hostilities between French squadron and Portuguese	309
183. The King to Earl Grey, July 19. Reply to the above .	311
184. Earl Grey to the King, July 19. Better account of Lord Spencer. Tithe Bills in the House of Lords. Communication as to Prince Leopold's intentions well received in the House of Lords	312
185. The King to Earl Grey, July 29. Message for increased provision for the Duchess of Kent and Princess Victoria. New Ministers in Belgium	313
186. Earl Grey to the King, July 3. Manner of passing the Bill for the Queen's dower	314
187. Earl Grey to the King, Aug. 5. Letter from the King of Belgium. Orders for squadron to assemble in the Downs. Proceedings of the Conference. State of Dutch and Belgian armies	314
188. The King to Earl Grey, Aug. 5. Crown to be worn by the Queen at the Coronation. The King's letter to Lord Melbourne on the state of the country, and augmentation of the army	316
189. The King to Earl Grey, Aug. 5. Affairs of Belgium .	316
190. Earl Grey to the King, Aug. 5. Crown for the Queen. Increase of the Army. Discussion in the House of Lords about Portugal. Lord Granville's dispatches. Acknowledges King's letter respecting Belgium. Hopes of an arrangement	320
191. The King to Earl Grey, Aug. 6. Belgian affairs. Debate in the House of Lords about Portugal . .	322
192. Sir H. Taylor to Earl Grey, Aug. 6. The King will be glad to see Lord Grey. His Majesty much pleased by the decided course taken by his Government in the Belgian business	323
193. Earl Grey to the King, Aug. 9. Account of debate in the House of Lords on Lord Londonderry's motion on Belgium	324

NO.		PAGE
194.	Earl Grey to Sir H. Taylor, Aug. 12. Baronetcy of Sir J. Macgregor. Conversation in the House of Lords respecting Coronation. Dutch army ordered to retire. Orders in consequence to Sir E. Codrington to return to Portsmouth. Marquis of Queensbury to be Lord of the Bedchamber. Baron Stockmar's letter to Lord Durham	326
195.	Sir H. Taylor to Earl Grey, Aug. 13. Sir James Macgregor's baronetcy. The Coronation. Communications from the Hague. Lord Queensbury's appointment. Letter of Baron Stockmar. Hanoverian Resident at Vienna	328
196.	Earl Grey to Sir H. Taylor, Aug. 14. Marquis of Queensbury's appointment. Apology for not attending levee. Letter of Hanoverian Resident at Vienna. Letter from Lord Granville. The Coronation	329
197.	Sir H. Taylor to Earl Grey, Aug. 15. Lord Granville's letter. Lord Queensbury. The Coronation. Professions of the French Government. Necessity of insisting on withdrawal of French troops from Belgium	331
198.	Earl Grey to the King, Aug. 18. Letters from the King of the Belgians. Instructions to Lord Granville. Duke of Bedford unable to carry the sceptre at the Coronation	333
199.	Sir H. Taylor to Earl Grey, Aug. 21. Question of brevet or other boon to the Army and Navy on the Coronation	334
200.	Earl Grey to the King, Aug. 22. Communication to the House of Commons respecting the Coronation through the Speaker. Settlement on the Queen. Brevet. Dispatch to Sir C. Bagot respecting retreat of Dutch army. Duke of Saxe Weimar and Lord William Russell. Lords-Lieutenants proposed for Irish counties	336
201.	The King to Earl Grey, Aug. 23. Reply to the above	337
202.	Earl Grey to Sir H. Taylor, Aug. 26. Interview with the Duke of Wellington respecting Belgian fortresses. Coronation. Letter from Archbishop of Canterbury. A Naval and a Military Peer to be made. Lord Howden proposed for the Army. Sir J. Saumarez for the Navy.	

NO.		PAGE
	His services. Objection of His Majesty on account of ships lost in the Baltic	338
203.	Sir H. Taylor to Earl Grey, Aug. 27. Homage of Bishops at the Coronation. Belgian fortresses. His Majesty approves of Peerage to Lord Howden for the Army. Sir J. Saumarez for the Navy still objected to . .	340
204.	Earl Grey to Sir H. Taylor, Aug. 28. Naval Peers. Sir J. Saumarez. Belgian fortresses . . .	342
205.	Earl Grey to Sir H. Taylor, Aug. 29. Belgian fortresses. Duke of Leinster's refusal of the Irish riband . .	343
206.	Earl Grey to Sir H. Taylor, Aug. 31. Affairs of Belgium and Holland. Interview with General Baudrand. Sentiments of French Government. Had not been able to attend levee. Going to Sheen. Hopes to see the King next week respecting promotions for the Coronation. Suggests, for the Navy, giving an Earldom to Lord Duncan. State of things in the House of Lords. Reported resolution of the Opposition . . .	345
207.	Sir H. Taylor to Earl Grey, Sept. 1. The King going to town. His Majesty's opinion respecting Belgium. King approves of making Lord Duncan an Earl. His regret at the state of things in the House of Lords; he is prepared to meet the difficulties that may arise .	347
208.	Sir H. Taylor to Earl Grey, Sept. 10, enclosing letter from King sanctioning the grant of a Peerage to Sir James Saumarez	349
209.	Earl Grey to the King, Sept. 11, acknowledging the above	350
210.	Earl Grey to Sir H. Taylor, Sept. 27. Death of Lord Durham's son. Asks to be excused from the levee. King's displeasure respecting the language of an officer about the House of Lords. Reasons for not noticing it as proposed by His Majesty	351
211.	Sir H. Taylor to Earl Grey, Sept. 27. Reply to the preceding letter	353
212.	Sir H. Taylor to Earl Grey, Sept. 27. His own condolence with Lord and Lady Durham. The King's feeling as to the language used about the House of Lords	355

xlii   CONTENTS OF

NO.
213. Earl Grey to Sir H. Taylor, Sept. 29. His thanks to the King for excusing his absence. Question as to the liability of an officer on full pay, but absent on leave, for a military offence. Living of Halesworth vacant by Dr. Whately's appointment to be Archbishop of Dublin; recommends Mr. Badeley for it . . . . .

214. Sir H. Taylor to Earl Grey, Sept. 30. The King approves the appointment of Mr. Badeley. His Majesty had seen Sir James Graham. Grounds of his objection to Admiralty Minute . . . .

215. Sir H. Taylor to Earl Grey, Oct. 4. Lord Waldegrave's resignation of his office of Lord of the Bedchamber .

216. The King to Earl Grey, Oct. 4. Acknowledges Lord Grey's account of the first night's debate in the House of Lords on the Reform Bill. Lord Hill's absence. Lord Durham . . . .

217. The King to Earl Grey, Oct 6. Acknowledges further report of proceedings in the House of Lords . .

218. The King to Earl Grey, Oct. 7. Further adjournment of the debate . . . .

219. The King to Earl Grey, Oct. 8. Acknowledges letter announcing the defeat of the Reform Bill in the House of Lords. His Majesty had anticipated this result. His apprehensions of a collision between the two Houses of Parliament. Difficulty of meeting the state of things. Retirement of Earl Grey and his colleagues would be a great evil. The King hopes it will not be proposed by the Cabinet . . . .

220. Earl Grey to the King, Oct. 8. Lord Grey has laid His Majesty's letter before the Cabinet. Their gratitude for his confidence, and desire for time to consider before deciding on their course. Lord Grey wishes to wait on His Majesty to explain his views . . . .

221. Earl Grey to Sir H. Taylor, Oct. 8. Monday would be the day that would suit him best for waiting on the King. The amount of the majority puts a further creation of Peers out of the question. Desire to admit of modifications in the Bill; but it was impossible. Carrying a measure not less efficient absolutely necessary .

NO.		PAGE
222.	The King to Earl Grey, Oct. 8. Propriety of Ministers taking time for consideration. Will see Lord Grey at any hour on Monday	367
223.	Sir H. Taylor to Earl Grey, Oct. 8. The King's confidence in the continued exertions of his Ministers. Suggests 3 o'clock on Monday for Lord Grey's seeing the King	367
224.	The King to Earl Grey, Oct. 9. Sends Colonel Napier's speech for Lord Grey's consideration. Proposes that he should be struck off the half-pay list if the report is accurate	368
225.	Sir H. Taylor to Earl Grey, Oct. 10. Lord Howe's resignation of the office of Lord Chamberlain to the Queen. His Majesty will not prorogue Parliament in person	370
226.	Earl Grey to the King, Oct. 11. Transmits Minute of Cabinet. His gratitude for the King's kindness and confidence. Lord Howe's resignation. Parliament may be prorogued at the end of the week. Hopes the King will reconsider his determination not to prorogue it in person	371
227.	Earl Grey to Sir H. Taylor, Oct. 11. His anxious hope that the King may be induced to prorogue Parliament in person. Good effect produced by Lord Althorp's declaration of the previous evening in the House of Commons. Note explaining what this declaration was, with a letter respecting it, from Lord Grey to one of his colleagues	374
228.	The King to Earl Grey, Oct. 12. Acknowledges Cabinet Minute. His Majesty's satisfaction at the readiness of his Ministers to continue in his service. His sense of the feeling that induces them to do so. His assent to their proposal that a new Bill should be brought forward. Recalls their attention to his letter of the 24th of April. Hopes that modifications of the measure which may reconcile opinions may be found. Will prorogue Parliament in person. His reason for having been unwilling to do so	376
229.	The King to Earl Grey, Oct. 17. His desire that the Speech from the Throne may not increase excitement.	

NO.

Great evil of a second rejection of a Reform Bill by the House of Lords. Whatever can irritate the majority should be avoided. Quotation from Lord Bolingbroke

230. Earl Grey to the King, Oct. 17. Reply to the above. Review of what had taken place with respect to Reform since his accession to office . . . .

231. The King to Earl Grey, Oct. 18. Further discussion of the same subject. Reference to Lord John Russell's letter to the Chairman of the Birmingham meeting .

232. Sir Herbert Taylor to Earl Grey, Oct. 20. Remarks on the draft of the King's Speech on proroguing Parliament

233. The King to Earl Grey, Oct. 26. Plan for building a barrack in the Birdcage Walk Proposed boon to the subaltern ranks of Army and Navy. Pay of Officers of the Blues . . . . . .

234. Earl Grey to the King, Oct. 27. Reply to the above. Satisfactory dispatches from Sir C. Bagot and Sir R. Adair . . . .

235. Earl Grey to Sir H. Taylor, Oct. 28. Letter from Archbishop of Canterbury respecting prayer on account of Cholera. Appointment of trustees for the Queen .

236. Sir H. Taylor to Earl Grey, Oct. 29. Answer to the above. Applications in consequence of the death of Sir G. Naylor . . . . . .

237. Earl Grey to Sir H. Taylor, Nov. 1. Riots at Bristol. Measures proposed in consequence. A Council required. Cabinet Minute enclosed . . . .

238. Sir H. Taylor to Earl Grey, Nov. 1. King will come next day at 3, to St. James's, for a Council . .

239. Earl Grey to Sir H. Taylor, Nov. 3. Outrages stopped at Bristol. Good conduct of the troops. Inefficiency of civil authorities. Cabinet on intended meeting at White Conduit House. Satisfactory accounts from Sir R. Jackson and Major Mackworth . . .

240. Sir H. Taylor to Earl Grey, Nov. 4. Answer to the above. The King's opinion respecting the Political Unions—as to members of them serving as special constables. Employment of Pensioners at Bristol. Objection to the employment of the Militia . .

NO.		PAGE
241.	Earl Grey to Sir H. Taylor, Nov. 6. Notices issued by Magistrates as to the intended meeting under the advice of the Law Officers. The meeting abandoned. Measures for preserving peace successful; but importance of settling the question of Reform. Opposition to this measure has caused the extension of the Political Unions. The danger of their becoming permanently established. Remedy, the passing of the Reform Bill. Employment of Pensioners. Necessity for effectual organisation of Civil Power. Hopes no addition to military force will be required	402
242.	Sir H. Taylor to Earl Grey, Nov. 7. Lord Grey's letter had been satisfactory to the King. Remarks on the objects of the Agitators and Political Unions, and probable effect upon them of passing the Reform Bill	405
243.	Earl Grey to Sir H. Taylor, Nov. 7. Assemblage at White Conduit House. Views of the Government as to seditious proceedings. Letters from Lord Durham, from Brussels. Case of English cholera at Sunderland	408
244.	Earl Grey to Sir H. Taylor, Nov. 8. Political Unions—how far connected with the Reform question	410
245.	Sir H. Taylor to Earl Grey, Nov. 8. State of things in London. Political Unions. Good effect of Lord Durham's advice in Belgium. Cholera	412
246.	Earl Grey to Sir H. Taylor, Nov. 10. Correspondence between the King and the Duke of Wellington. Lord Grey's letter to the Duke. Real cholera at Sunderland	413
247.	Sir H. Taylor to Earl Grey, Nov. 11. The Duke of Wellington's statement as to arming of Political Unions	414
248.	Earl Grey to Sir H. Taylor, Nov. 11, returning correspondence with the Duke of Wellington. Opinion respecting it. Cabinet on Canada. Progress of cholera at Sunderland	415
249.	The King to Earl Grey, Nov. 13. His Majesty, in his correspondence with the Duke of Wellington, desired to convey the impression of his confidence in his Ministers. His trust that they will not allow the formation of armed bodies contrary to law	417

xlvi CONTENTS OF

| NO. | | PAGE |

250. Sir H. Taylor to Earl Grey, Nov. 13. Correspondence with the Duke of Wellington. The King's opinion respecting Canada and the United States . . . 419
251. Sir H. Taylor to Earl Grey, Nov. 15. The King is glad he did not delay answering the Duke of Wellington's letter; in future, the reply to any similar communication will be a simple acknowledgment. Hopes medical report from Sunderland may show the alarm about cholera to have been a false one 421
252. Sir H. Taylor to Earl Grey, Nov. 16. Reported contract for firearms at Birmingham. Another letter to His Majesty from the Duke of Wellington. The King's opinion as to representation of Metropolitan districts. Further account from Sunderland satisfactory; also that of the proceedings of the Conference . . . 422
253. Earl Grey to Sir H. Taylor, Nov. 18. Correspondence of the King with the Duke of Wellington. Possible inconvenience of His Majesty's expressing opinions on public matters to others than his confidential servants. Political Unions. Character of that at Birmingham —difficulty of dealing with it. Representation of Metropolitan districts. Belgian affairs. Worse accounts from Sunderland. Barracks in the Birdcage Walk. Captain Lyons can give the best information respecting Greece 423
254. Sir H. Taylor to Earl Grey, Nov. 19. Correspondence with the Duke of Wellington. Political Unions. Metropolitan representation. Lord Palmerston's able management of Conference on Belgium. Cholera. Barracks in the Birdcage Walk. Captain Lyons . 428
255. Earl Grey to Sir H. Taylor, Nov. 19, encloses Cabinet Minute, recommending that Parliament should be called together. Council required. Necessary for the King to come to London. Opinion of the Law Officers as to the illegality of the proposed organisation of the Birmingham Union 431
256. Sir H. Taylor to Earl Grey, Nov. 20. The King will go to London for the Council. His Majesty will be glad to see Lord Grey when he wishes it, but is unwilling

NO.		PAGE
	to call for his attendance. His Majesty pleased with the opinion of the Law Officers	433
257.	Earl Grey to Sir H. Taylor, Nov. 22. Proposed arrangements as to another Council for the King's Speech on opening Parliament. Hope that Proclamation ordered the day before will have a good effect. Nothing yet done as to illegal organisation of Political Unions. Mr. O'Connell's scheme of Union. Advantage of his being brought over by the meeting of Parliament. Importance of early settlement of the Reform question. Desire of Ministers to conciliate the opponents of the Bill. Is to see the Bishop of London, Archbishop of Canterbury, and Lord Wharncliffe. Hopes the next discussion of the question in the House of Lords may have a more fortunate issue. If the next Bill should be rejected, serious consequences that must follow .	435
258.	Sir H. Taylor to Earl Grey, Nov. 23. The King will hold a Council at St. James's on the 5th of December. His approval of the Proclamation. Concurs in Lord Grey's opinion as to Mr. O'Connell. The King sensible of the importance of settling the question of Reform. His confidence in Lord Grey and his colleagues. He would lament the loss of their services: is therefore glad of the communication with Lord Wharncliffe. Hopes as to communications with the Archbishop of Canterbury and Bishop of London. Thinks the Duke of Wellington could not have been consulted by Lord Wharncliffe. Letter from the National Political Union	438
259.	Earl Grey to Sir H. Taylor, Nov. 25. Answer to the above. Has received written communication from Lord Wharncliffe: it is less encouraging. Cabinet on Reform to be held next day. Conversation with Bishop of London most satisfactory: from the Archbishop of Canterbury has got nothing definite. Effect that would be produced by the expression of His Majesty's opinion. The King's satisfaction with the Proclamation has given him pleasure. Its good effect. Meaning of the declaration of the National Union. Looks forward to	

CONTENTS OF THE FIRST VOLUME.

NO.		PAGE
	speedy dissolution of these Unions if Reform can be carried. Bill for plate ordered by the late King	442
260.	Sir H. Taylor to Earl Grey, Nov. 27 The King's remarks on the communications with the opponents of the former Reform Bill. City meeting. The King's regret that he cannot exert his influence with either Spiritual or Lay Peers in favour of the Reform Bill. Effect of the Proclamation. Bill for plate	446
261.	Earl Grey to Sir H. Taylor, Nov. 28. Acknowledges the preceding letter. Sends letters from Dr. Fenwick respecting cholera at Sunderland, and from Lord Lismore respecting Ireland	449
262.	Sir H. Taylor to Earl Grey, Nov. 29. Reply to the above. The King desires advice as to an application for a subscription for the Paisley Weavers	450
263.	Earl Grey to Sir H. Taylor, Nov. 30. Interview with Lord Wharncliffe. Discussion with him of his proposed alterations in the Reform Bill. Excuse for deferring consideration of other matters referred to him by His Majesty. P.S. Note received from Lord Wharncliffe putting an end to all hope of agreement	451
264.	Sir H. Taylor to Earl Grey, Dec. 1. King desires him to defer replying to the part of Lord Grey's letter relating to the Reform Bill and his communication with Lord Wharncliffe	457
265.	Earl Grey to Sir H. Taylor, Dec. 2. Sends rough draft of Speech for the opening of Parliament. Captain Lyons. Article in the 'Standard'	458
	Appendix A. Report on Reform by Lord Durham, Sir James Graham, Lord John Russell, and Lord Duncannon	461
	Appendix B. Minute of Conversation between Lord Grey and Lord Wharncliffe, Nov. 16, 1831	464
	Appendix C. Lord Wharncliffe's Plan for the Alteration of the Reform Bill, Nov. 23, 1831.	471

THE CORRESPONDENCE OF EARL GREY

WITH

KING WILLIAM IV.

No. 1.

Earl Grey to the King.

Berkeley Square, Nov. 23, 1830.

EARL GREY has the honour of submitting to your Majesty the minutes of a Cabinet, held last night at Earl Grey's house. Your Majesty's servants are to meet again to-day, at three o'clock, to take into further consideration the mode of executing the measures resolved upon, as stated in the above minute; upon which Earl Grey hopes to be able further to inform your Majesty when he has the honour of waiting on your Majesty, in obedience to your Majesty's commands, to-day, at four o'clock. All which is most humbly submitted by Your Majesty's most dutiful subject and servant,

GREY.

(Enclosure.)

PRESENT:

The Lord Chancellor.
The Lord President.
The Lord Privy Seal.
The Duke of Richmond.
The Earl of Carlisle.
Earl Grey.
The Viscount Melbourne.
The Viscount Palmerston.
The Viscount Goderich.
The Viscount Althorp.
The Lord Holland.
Sir James Graham.
The Right Hon. C. Grant.

1. A Proclamation to be issued to warn all persons engaged in illegal acts, of the danger of their proceedings, and of the determination of the Government to exert all their powers to suppress unlawful assemblies and acts of outrage. To exhort the Magistrates and others to use the utmost vigour in the execution of their duties, and to offer a reward for the detection of all offenders.

2. To address a Circular Letter to all Lords-Lieutenants to use the utmost diligence and vigour in assembling the civil power, and immediately directing it to the suppression of all acts of violence; and suggesting to all Lords-Lieutenants who, from any circumstances, are unable personally to use the exertions required in such an emergency, to appoint Vice-Lieutenants to repair to the disturbed parts of their respective counties, and to exercise the powers of Lords-Lieutenants, for the purposes above stated.

3. In the foregoing, to be enclosed the form of a circular to be addressed to the Magistrates to exhort them to act with vigour, to inform them of the powers vested in them for this purpose, and the security afforded

them by the law in the exercise of these powers; warning them at the same time that any remissness in the discharge of their duty will incur His Majesty's severest displeasure. To enclose in this circular the plan adopted by the Duke of Richmond in Sussex, with an account of the success attending its execution.

4. To communicate with the Commander-in-Chief for the purpose of sending officers into the disturbed parts of the country, to communicate with the Magistrates, and to form plans for the distribution and exertion, both of the civil and military power.

5. To inquire at Chelsea Hospital respecting the number and residence of discharged soldiers receiving pensions, with a view to forming them into bodies for the protection of the public peace. To consult with the Commander-in-Chief on this point.

6. To direct all the depositions which have been received either at the Home Office, or by the Solicitor to the Treasury, to be laid before His Majesty's Law Officers, requiring them to take the same into their immediate consideration, and to report their opinion thereon as to the expediency of instituting prosecutions in any cases on which there may be proof sufficient to obtain convictions.

No. 2.

The King to Earl Grey.

St. James's, Nov. 23, 1830.

The King acknowledges the receipt of Earl Grey's note of this day, and the accompanying minute of a Cabinet held last night.

His Majesty approves in general of all that is therein submitted for his consideration, sensible as he is that the present state of the country imperiously calls for every possible demonstration of firmness in the resolution of his Government, for the utmost vigour and energy in its measures, and for promptness and decision in the execution of these measures. There is one point only, that contained in Art. 5 of the minute, on which His Majesty considers it necessary to observe more particularly. His Majesty has reason to believe that what is therein suggested, has, at various times, engaged the attention of his late Government, that the necessary information will prove to have been collected, and arrangements to have been proposed by Sir Henry Hardinge, and possibly to a certain extent carried into effect in Ireland, upon a principle more or less applicable to the state and circumstances of this country. The King conceives that great discrimination will be necessary in assembling for the preservation of the public peace, otherwise than in military bodies subject to military discipline, men whose habits may, unless brought under close control and restriction, be considered little calculated to promote the object with a view to which it is proposed to assemble them. At any rate it appears to His Majesty, that military officers should be sent to the points at which they may be assembled in counties or districts, to inspect them before they are formed into bodies; and to ascertain whether their physical and *moral* qualifications shall justify their being employed *as protectors of the public peace.*

Another point upon which the King had spoken to Sir Robert Peel, is the occasional augmentation, for any particular emergency, of the metropolitan police; and the expedient which suggested itself, appeared to His Majesty a very simple one. Namely, that the men constituting the permanent police should each be required to give in the names of one or more residents within their respective districts, efficient men of good character, and well affected, for whom they would be responsible, and whose names should be enrolled as assistants or subsidiary policemen, to be brought by them to the station of assembly, when required, upon which occasion they should be sworn in as special constables, and should receive pay while so employed. The King suggests these as general ideas for the consideration of Lord Grey, but does not consider it necessary to enter into further details. WILLIAM R.

No. 3.

The King to Earl Grey.

St. James's, Nov. 26, 1830.

The King acknowledges the receipt of Lord Grey's letter, and will be glad to receive him at three this day, or at any other hour that may suit him. His Majesty indeed wishes it to be clearly understood by Lord Grey and the other members of his Government, that he will never suffer any engagement or his convenience to interfere with the attention which His Majesty considers to be due to public business. His Majesty has learnt with satisfaction, that Mr. Chas. Wynne has accepted the office of Secretary at War.

WILLIAM R.

No. 4.

The King to Earl Grey.

St. James's, Nov. 27, 1830.

The King, aware as he is of the difficulties which have arisen with respect to the appointment of a Master-General of the Ordnance,* is induced to communicate to Earl Grey, for his consideration, what has occurred to him upon the subject. However averse His Majesty has ever been, upon principle, to the idea of breaking up an old established public department of considerable extent and importance, and which has been conducted with great ability and respectability, and with acknowledged efficiency in its various branches; much as His Majesty dislikes even the appearance of yielding to clamours for reform, which have often been, and may still be, urged by individuals who, in their eagerness for reductions, do not take the trouble of making any distinction between that which is useful and necessary, and that which is wasteful and superfluous, or who may be altogether incapable of forming a correct judgment upon the subject,—the King is not less alive to the objection of maintaining a high and important establishment upon a footing inconsistent with the character so long attached to it. Yet, such would be the effect of placing at the head of the Ordnance Department any individual of rank in the

---

* The arrangement originally proposed to the King, and approved by him, was that the Duke of Richmond should be Master-General; but this appointment did not take place, owing to an objection made to it by the Commander-in-Chief, on the ground of the Duke's rank in the army not being sufficiently high.

service, or station in the country, inferior to those who have hitherto presided over it, or of placing the military parts of it in hands not of the military profession. Under these circumstances, His Majesty would not feel disinclined to sanction an arrangement which has been frequently suggested, and which he has reason to believe would be by no means unpalatable to the corps of Royal Artillery and Royal Engineers. Namely, to place these corps and the millitary arrangements of the Ordnance Department under the Commander-in-Chief, with a Major-General of each corps on the staff, through whom the details of the service should be carried on, and who would report to, and receive their orders and instructions from, the Commander-in-Chief. The Barrack Department to be placed under the superintendence of the Quartermaster-General, subject also to the control of the Commander-in-Chief. The accounts of the military branches to be thrown into the War Office. The Civil Departments of the Ordnance might form a distinct establishment, and be regulated by a Board, similar to the Navy Board, and might be responsible to the Treasury for their expenditure.

His Majesty believes that the actual constitution of the Ordnance Department, and the division of business into civil and military, would facilitate the execution of this arrangement. WILLIAM R.

No. 5.

Earl Grey to the King.

Berkeley Square, Nov. 27, 1830.

Earl Grey has had the honour of receiving your Majesty's most gracious letter of this day's date. He will not fail in his duty to give the most anxious attention to the very important suggestions of your Majesty, with a view to a new regulation of the Ordnance Department. But he humbly submits to your Majesty, that so great and extensive a change would require much time for inquiry and consideration, and that it might be inconvenient to leave, during the interval, so important a branch of the public service under officers who held their appointments only till their successors shall be named.

Earl Grey therefore humbly entreats your Majesty to allow him to proceed in his endeavours to fill the offices of the Ordnance according to the present mode, in the hope that he may shortly be able to recommend to your Majesty some officer of suitable rank and character to be at the head of that department, under whose care and management any regulations that may be found to be more beneficial for its future constitution, may be carried into effect.

All which, &c. GREY.

No. 6.

The King to Earl Grey.

St. James's, Nov. 27th, 1830.

The King has this moment received Earl Grey's letter, and does not delay to assure him that his only motive in suggesting what had occurred to him, was to satisfy Earl Grey that he would not object to any arrangement of the Ordnance Department which might relieve him from a difficulty; but His Majesty has not the most distant wish to embarrass him by the communication of any suggestion, and he is perfectly satisfied that Lord Grey's arrangements will be such as must receive his approbation. WILLIAM R.

No. 7.

The King to Earl Grey.

St. James's Palace, Dec. 1, 1830.

The King is induced to make this confidential communication to Earl Grey, as to the head of his Government, and the individual on whom he rests his hopes of support, in consequence of some hints thrown out by Lord Holland, when His Majesty placed in his hands the seals of the Duchy of Lancaster, and of some further observations which he made to him yesterday, which His Majesty cannot deny to have occasioned to him considerable alarm and uneasiness, as threatening an invasion of those rights and privileges which he is in duty bound to maintain, and to transmit unimpaired to his successors. It appeared to be, in the contemplation of Lord Holland, not only to admit of the threatened interference by Parliament in the concerns of the Duchy of Lancaster, but even to promote it, and His Majesty cannot but apprehend that the idea of submitting them for investigation to a committee of the House of Commons has been entertained.

To such a course His Majesty conceives that he would be justified in objecting most strenuously, as being inconsistent with, and in violation of the especial and hereditary rights which, as Sovereign of this country, he possesses in the Duchy of Lancaster, and as tending to lower his dignity and authority, and to bring his name into contempt.

The King hopes he may be mistaken, and that the apprehensions raised by Lord Holland's expressions may be groundless, but lest this should not be the case, he deems it necessary thus early to notice them to Earl Grey, as it is his anxious wish to avoid the possibility of any discussion with his Government, which should be at variance with his earnest desire to continue to it his unqualified countenance and support. His Majesty is convinced that Lord Grey will agree with him that the value of that support, more especially in such times as the present, will depend in great measure upon the estimation in which His Majesty's character may be held in the country, and that nothing is more likely to shake it, nothing more calculated to lessen the benefit which his Government may derive from it, than any act which shall create the impression that His Majesty is disposed tamely to submit to invasions of his just rights, and to surrender privileges which have not hitherto been questioned.

These are the grounds of his present communication to Earl Grey. They are personal as connected with the integrity of his possession in the Duchy of Lancaster, they are public as affecting his character as Sovereign of this country, and its influence upon the opinions and feelings of his subjects in these critical times ; and

His Majesty is satisfied that Earl Grey will give him credit for the importance which he attaches to the maintenance of both.

Earl Grey cannot be surprised that the King should view with jealousy any idea of Parliamentary interference with the only remaining pittance of an independent possession which has been enjoyed by his ancestors during many centuries, as their *private* and *independent estate*, and has now, as such, lawfully devolved upon him in right of succession. That he should feel that any successful attempt to deprive the Sovereign of this independent possession will be to lower and degrade him into the state and condition of absolute and entire dependence, as a pensioner of the House of Commons, to place him in the condition of an individual violating or surrendering a trust which had been held sacred by his ancestors, and which he is bound to transmit to his successors.

The King cannot indeed conceive upon what plea such a national invasion of the *private* rights, and such a seizure of the *private* estates of the Sovereign could be justified. It cannot be founded upon any principle of retrenchment, for if such be the object, if it be thought fit or becoming to reduce the resources of the Sovereign in a greater degree than has already been effected by the surrender of certain allowances, an equivalent reduction in the grant of that portion of the Civil List revenue which is appropriated to His Majesty's Privy Purse would naturally have occurred to those who may wish to curtail the attributes of Royalty.

The King has entrusted the *guardianship* of this, his ancient private estate and inheritance, to one of his confidential servants, who, upon his installation into the office of Chancellor of the Duchy, took a solemn oath that 'all things that may serve for the weal and profit of the King's Highness, his "*heirs and successors*" (that is in relation to the Duchy of Lancaster), and for the good rule and governance of the said Duchy, he would well and truly do and fulfil to his cunning and power.' And His Majesty has fair reason to expect that a pledge so solemnly taken will be fulfilled, and that he will be supported in his assertion of these *private* rights, not only of himself, but of his heirs and successors, as they have devolved upon him, *separate* from all other his possessions *jure coronæ*, and consequently as his separate personal and private estate, vested in His Majesty, by descent from Henry VII., in his body *natural*, and not in his body *politic* as King.

The King, in his desire to put Earl Grey in full possession of the view he takes of this question, has been drawn into much greater detail than he had contemplated.   WILLIAM R.

No. 8.

Earl Grey to the King.

Berkeley Square, Dec. 1, 1830.

Earl Grey has had the honour of receiving your Majesty's confidential and most gracious communication of this day's date.

It is with the deepest regret that Earl Grey learns from your Majesty, that some observations had fallen from Lord Holland, on the occasion of receiving from your Majesty the seals of the Duchy of Lancaster, and again yesterday, which had occasioned to your Majesty considerable alarm and uneasiness, as threatening an invasion of those rights and privileges, which your Majesty feels yourself in duty bound to maintain and transmit unimpaired to your successors. Earl Grey will lose no time in communicating with Lord Holland on this subject, and humbly requests permission to show him your Majesty's most gracious letter.

Earl Grey will not allow himself to doubt that a satisfactory explanation will be the result of this communication. Earl Grey, in the meantime, begs leave to assure your Majesty, that it has never been in his contemplation to sanction, still less to propose to Parliament, any interference in the concerns of the Duchy of Lancaster, nor is he aware that any idea of submitting them for investigation to the Committee of the House of Commons has been at any time entertained; and Earl Grey can have no hesitation in adding, that any consideration of the state of your Majesty's hereditary possessions in the Duchy of Lancaster, unless recommended by your Majesty's gracious and voluntary condescension, would be exposed to all the objections which your Majesty has so forcibly stated.

In conclusion, Earl Grey begs further to assure your Majesty, that it will always be his most anxious wish to prove himself not undeserving of the confidence with which your Majesty has been pleased to honour him, as it is also his bounden duty to resist any attempt to invade your Majesty's acknowledged personal rights, and to maintain unimpaired the honour of your Majesty's crown.

All which, &c. GREY.

No. 9.

The King to Earl Grey.

St. James's, Dec. 1, 1830.

The King hastens to assure Lord Grey of the sincere satisfaction which he has derived from the perusal of his letter just received, and that every expression of it confirms not less than it justifies the confidence which His Majesty had reposed in Earl Grey, and his conviction that he would find in him a steady supporter of the honour of his crown, and of His Majesty's acknowledged personal rights, against any attempts that might be made to assail them. His Majesty cannot have the least objection to Earl Grey's showing his letter to Lord Holland.

WILLIAM R.

No. 10.

Sir H. Taylor to Earl Grey.

St. James's, Dec. 2, 1830.

My dear Lord,—The King has honoured me with his commands to acquaint your Lordship, that in his conversation with you yesterday on the subject of the Civil List, His Majesty omitted to remind your Lordship of the question of a sum of money for the outfit of the Queen.

I have the honour to enclose for your Lordship's information, the copy of a letter His Majesty ordered me to write to the Duke of Wellington on this subject, and to add that upon subsequent reference to the Queen's Treasurer, the outfit was found to exceed 25,000l.

I have, &c.

H. TAYLOR.

(Enclosure.)

Sir Herbert Taylor to the Duke of Wellington.

St. James's Palace, Nov. 15, 1830.

My dear Lord Duke,—With reference to what the King said to your Grace yesterday, respecting a sum of money for the outfit of the Queen, His Majesty has this morning directed me to acquaint you, that it does not appear from the inquiry he has been able to make, that any sum of money was issued to the late Queen Charlotte, or to her Treasurer for that purpose, upon her arrival in England; but that everything had been prepared, equipages, horses, liveries, even to her trousseau, and it is presumed at the charge of the public; for it cannot be supposed that King George III. provided for all this out of his privy purse, any more than for the purchase of Her Majesty's jewels, which, from the directions in her will, appear to have cost 50,000*l.*

The Queen's outfit in the Stable Department alone will amount, as far as I can learn, to nearly 20,000*l.* and if this and the further sum that may be required, are to be provided by herself out of the annual income, she will start with a heavy debt, and will not be able to maintain her establishment on the scale upon which it has been formed, which is not larger than that of the late Queen Charlotte. His Majesty, therefore, trusts that your Grace will have the goodness to take this matter into your serious consideration, with a view to relieve the Queen from the difficulty in which she would be placed, by the omission of an adequate provision on the score of outfit.

I have, &c. H. TAYLOR.

No. 11.

Earl Grey to Sir H. Taylor.

Berkeley Square, Dec. 3, 1830.

My dear Sir,—I received your letter at too late an hour to answer it last night. I beg you will assure His Majesty that what he said to me (I believe the first time that I had the honour of being admitted to his presence) on the subject of an outfit for the Queen, had not escaped my observation. It will be my anxious desire, in the arrangement of the Civil List, to meet so reasonable and so necessary a demand; and I am not without sanguine hopes that I shall be able, with the assistance of my colleagues, to provide for it. But I will not conceal from you that I have considerable difficulties to encounter from the jealousy of the House of Commons on this subject, and from its not having been adverted to by my predecessors in office. I hope, however, that His Majesty will give me credit for a most anxious wish on this and on every other occasion, to do everything in my power to perform, in the way that may be most agreeable to His Majesty, the duty which I owe both to him and to Her Majesty the Queen.

I am much obliged to you for sending me the copy of the letter which you wrote, by His Majesty's command, to the Duke of Wellington. Would there be any impropriety in my requesting to see the answer to it, if there was one?

I am, &c. GREY.

No. 12.

Sir H. Taylor to Earl Grey.

St. James's, Dec. 4, 1830.

My dear Lord,—I have now the honour to send your Lordship the Duke of Wellington's answer to my letter respecting the outfit for the Queen. I was obliged to wait the return of my clerk, who had been sent to Windsor, and then found that the Queen, to whom the King had given the letter, had not returned it.

I forgot to mention to your Lordship, that the King had expressed himself perfectly satisfied with your letter on the subject, and quite sensible of the difficulty which may occur.

I have, &c. H. TAYLOR.

(Enclosure in No. 12.)

The Duke of Wellington to Sir Herbert Taylor.

London, Nov. 15, 1830.

My dear General,—The result of my enquiry respecting the outfit for Queen Charlotte has been exactly what His Majesty had anticipated. We cannot find the trace of any expenditure on this head. However, the Chancellor of the Exchequer and I will endeavour, if possible, to obtain some money to aid, at least, in defraying this expense.

Believe me, yours most sincerely,

W.

No. 13.

At a Cabinet Council, held at the Foreign Office,

December 4, 1830.

PRESENT:

The Lord Chancellor.
The Lord President.
The Lord Privy Seal.
The Duke of Richmond.
The Earl of Carlisle.
The Earl Grey.

The Viscount Melbourne.
The Viscount Palmerston.
The Lord Holland.
The Lord Goderich.
The Right Hon. C. Grant.

It was agreed that a Circular Letter, a copy of which will be submitted to your Majesty by the Viscount Melbourne, should be addressed to the Magistrates, cautioning them against concessions which might bear the character of intimidation and weakness, and exhorting them to increased activity and vigour.

That, for the preservation of the peace of the country, additional measures should be taken for the establishment of a Constabulary Force, and, where necessary, of Corps of Yeomanry.

That a Special Commission should be sent to Buckinghamshire, in addition to that already directed to be sent to Wilts, Hants, and Berks.

That orders should be issued to the Admiralty to send two sloops of war to the Tyne, for the protection of that and the neighbouring ports, in case the present insurrectionary spirit, of which there are as yet, happily, no symptoms, should extend to that important district.

No. 14.

The King to Earl Grey.

St. James's, Dec. 4, 1830.

The King approves of the measures proposed in the Minute of Cabinet which Earl Grey has sent him. His Majesty is very sensible of the objections, both on the score of alarm at home, and the effect abroad at this period, of resorting to any measure of military augmentation. He conceives, however, that the existing establishments might be completed, whereby alone an addition of 7000 or 8000 men would be made to the regular army in the United Kingdom.

WILLIAM R.

No. 15.

Sir H. Taylor to Earl Grey.

St. James's, Dec. 7, 1830.

My dear Lord,—A question having arisen as to the right of the late Queen Charlotte to dispose by her will of jewels given to her by the King George III. upon her marriage, and which His Majesty purchased for 50,000*l*., I was ordered by the King to apply to the Treasury for information required by Lord Lyndhurst to guide his opinion on the subject; and I have recently received from Mr. Stewart a minute, of which I have the honour to enclose a copy by His Majesty's commands; and from which it would appear that the jewels were purchased out of the Civil List Revenue, and not with George III.'s private monies; and therefore would become, after Her Majesty's demise, the property of the Crown. This, however, is the point for legal decision. His Majesty's object in making this communication to your Lordship is, to show that there was a provision made for the outfit of the late Queen Charlotte, allowing jewels to constitute a part of the royal outfit; and that this may offer an argument in support of his consort's claim, although it is by no means intended that it should embrace any jewels, or articles of jewelry; the Queen's outlay, at starting, being almost exclusively limited to the charges in the department of her Master of the Horse.

I have, &c.   H. TAYLOR.

No. 16.

Sir H. Taylor to Earl Grey.

St. James's, Dec. 10, 1830.

My dear Lord,—The King has honoured me with his commands to acquaint your Lordship, that Sir William Freemantle, who has been with him since you left his Majesty, has readily consented to waive his desire to be brought into Parliament, and to represent Windsor. This affords to His Majesty an opportunity to mark, in the most unequivocal manner, his determination to give, in these critical times, the utmost support in his power to your Lordship and the present Administration, by offering his assistance in bringing Mr. Stanley in for Windsor, if he should lose his election for Preston; and His Majesty has ordered me to assure you that he avails himself of this opportunity with great satisfaction.

If Mr. Stanley should take advantage of this opening,

he had better communicate at once with Sir Hussey Vivian, in order that the agents at Windsor may be apprised, without delay, of the proposed arrangement. Having been member for Windsor, I may state that the expenses of the election will amount to about 1000*l*., and the annual subscriptions, charities, &c., to something less than 100*l*.

I have, &c.   H. TAYLOR.

No. 17.

Sir H. Taylor to Earl Grey.

Brighton, Dec. 19, 1830.

My dear Lord,—I am honoured with the King's commands to transmit to your Lordship the letter enclosed, which His Majesty has received from Vice-Admiral Sir Henry Blackwood. His Majesty orders me to add, that Sir Henry Blackwood has been very long known to him as an excellent man, and a very meritorious officer; but that it is by no means his wish on this, or any other occasion, to interfere with your Lordship's disposal of official situations.

I have, &c.   H. TAYLOR.

P.S.—His Majesty asked me whether I had received any further account of poor Lord Spencer and Lord Althorp.

No. 18.

Earl Grey to Sir H. Taylor.

Downing Street, Dec. 20, 1830.

Dear Sir Herbert,—I had the honour last night of receiving your letter, written by His Majesty's command,

and enclosing one to His Majesty from Sir H. Blackwood, soliciting the appointment of Surveyor-General of the Ordnance.

I beg you will assure His Majesty of my readiness at all times to obey his commands with respect to matters of this nature. But, availing myself of His Majesty's permission to submit to his consideration what may appear best calculated for the good of His Majesty's service, in the appointment to official situations, I have to request that you will communicate to him the opinion of Sir James Kempt as to the office in question.

After receiving the melancholy news of Sir R. Spencer's death, I lost no time in consulting with Sir James, as to the best manner of supplying the place which he had left vacant. Sir James has represented to me, that, since the annexation of the Barrack and the Store Departments to the Ordnance, the duties of the Surveyor-General have been very much connected with military arrangements and details; and a person who is not conversant with such matters would experience, Sir James apprehends, considerable difficulty in performing the duties at present assigned to the Surveyor-General. On the other hand, the superintendence and delivery of the stores which belong to the office of Storekeeper, which involve details connected with the naval service, might, it appears, be more advantageously committed to the care of an officer of that profession; and I should, on this account, wish to recommend that officers should, in future, be thus distributed:—Surveyor-General, an officer in the Army; Storekeeper, ditto, Navy. In this event, Col. Maberley, with His Majesty's approbation, would take the first, and a naval officer the second.

With respect to Sir H. Blackwood, having no knowledge of his qualifications as a man of business myself, I should wish to act entirely in obedience to His Majesty's opinion, if this arrangement would suit him; but he probably would not be willing to accept the place of second officer at the Board after the Master-General.

This office has given me more trouble and vexation than all the other appointments which I have had to make; and now a new difficulty has occurred with respect to Mr. Denison, who has been disappointed in his expectation (which he had announced as certain on Thursday last, when I proposed his appointment as Clerk of the Ordnance) of obtaining a seat in Parliament. It is now, therefore, my intention, understanding that I had His Majesty's permission to do so, to offer this office to Mr. Tennyson; and I trust that this matter will be finally arranged to-morrow.

I have nothing further to communicate that will not be transmitted from the other departments to His Majesty, to whom I beg you will offer the expression of my humble duty.

I am, &c. GREY.

No. 19.

Earl Grey to Sir H. Taylor.

Downing Street, Dec. 21, 1830.

Dear Sir,—I enclose in a separate cover a letter to the King, to which I am anxious to obtain an answer as soon as may suit His Majesty's convenience.

I was in hopes I should have been able to settle a

final arrangement of the Ordnance with Sir James Kempt, subject always to His Majesty's approbation, in time to communicate it by to-night's post; but he has not yet appeared, and I am now obliged to go to the House of Lords.

A motion was given notice of last night in the House of Commons, for an account of all the offices, &c., held under the Duchy of Lancaster. It was appointed for to-day, but I am in hopes it will be given up. If not, Lord Althorp (though I am afraid he will not be able to attend), Lord Palmerston, and Sir James Graham are prepared to meet it with the most determined resistance.

Lord Melbourne has received an account to-day of Mr. O'Connell's entry into Dublin on Monday evening, about six o'clock. He was met by a procession, prepared by the Union of Trades, of between five and six thousand people, who conducted him to his house in Merrion Square, from whence he addressed them, recommending, at the end of his speech, that they should disperse peaceably, which they did. I mention this lest Lord Melbourne should not have transmitted the account to His Majesty. From all other parts of the country the accounts are much the same as they have been lately; and I am sorry to say the large assemblages in the neighbourhood of Manchester, under the direction of the Trades Union, for the purpose of compelling a general resistance to the rate of wages offered by the master manufacturers, still continue.

I enclose a letter which has been sent to me for the King, the cover of which has been torn, in consequence of its sticking to the seal of the envelope.

I remain, &c. GREY.

No. 20.

Earl Grey to the King.

Downing Street, Dec. 21, 1830.

Earl Grey has the honour of transmitting for your Majesty's consideration, a letter which he has just received from the Archbishop of Canterbury, desiring him to take your Majesty's pleasure on the expediency of directing a Prayer to be prepared by the Archbishop, and used on Sundays and Holydays in all churches and chapels in England and Wales. This subject has been very much pressed upon Earl Grey from various quarters; and if your Majesty has no objections, he would humbly recommend that the Archbishop's proposal should be complied with.

As the deanery of Chester will become vacant on the consecration of the Bishop of Exeter, Earl Grey begs permission to submit to your Majesty, in consequence of a recommendation from Her Royal Highness the Duchess of Kent, that it may be right to confer this dignity on the Rev. Mr. Davys. This clergyman, as your Majesty is informed, has had the superintendence of the education of the Princess Victoria; and, from the testimony borne to his merits by the Archbishop of Canterbury and the Bishop of London, as well as from the important trust with which he is charged, Earl Grey ventures humbly to submit that he is a person on whom this mark of your Majesty's royal favour might be properly conferred.

Earl Grey has further to state to your Majesty, that in consequence of Mr. Denison not being able to procure a seat in Parliament, Lord Grey has offered the appointment of Clerk of the Ordnance to Mr. Tennyson, by whom it has been accepted, of which Earl Grey humbly solicits your Majesty's approbation. The other offices, with the exception of the Treasurer, the appointment to which of Mr. Creevey your Majesty has already been graciously pleased to approve, remain undecided upon, till Earl Grey shall have learnt your Majesty's sentiments on the communication made by him yesterday to Sir H. Taylor.

All which, &c.   GREY.

No. 21.

Sir H. Taylor to Earl Grey.

(Private.)   Brighton, Dec. 21, 1830.

My dear Lord,—I have had the honour of receiving your Lordship's letter of yesterday, and of submitting it to the King.

His Majesty orders me to assure your Lordship, that he entirely concurs in the view which you have taken of the appointments to the Board of Ordnance, and that he equally approves of the arrangements you propose, namely, that the office of Surveyor-General should be filled by a military officer, and that of the Principal Storekeeper by a naval officer. His Majesty fully sanctions the nomination of Lieut.-Colonel Maberley to the first, and of Mr. Tennyson to the clerkship of the Ordnance; and he desires your Lordship will use your discretion in the choice of the naval officer for the situation of Storekeeper. His Majesty has no reason to believe that Sir Henry Blackwood would object to it, but is ignorant what may be his qualifications as a man of business, though in his profession he has shown great zeal and intelligence; but His Majesty orders me to repeat that his application was referred to your Lordship, as would that of any other individual similarly circumstanced, and not with the most distant view of interfering with or embarrassing you in your arrangements, all which His Majesty knows to be directed to the advantage and efficiency of his service.

The King has honoured me with his commands to acquaint your Lordship, that he has named Sir Robert Otway a Groom of the Bed-chamber, in the room of poor Sir Robert Spencer; also that, having this day received the unexpected resignation of the Earl of Beverley, who was one of the Lords of the Bed-chamber, His Majesty has availed himself of this opportunity to carry into effect his wish to confer that situation upon his future son-in-law, Lord Falkland. The vacancy has occurred most opportunely, to enable His Majesty to make this wedding present to the young couple, and he is persuaded your Lordship will give him credit for such disposal of it.

The next vacancy will be filled by Lord Say and Sele. The King has ordered me to transmit to your Lordship, with reference to these household appointments, when filled by naval officers, the enclosed memorandum from Sir Henry Blackwood, with the copy of a letter I was directed to write to Mr. Barrow and his answer. A similar representation was received some time ago from Lord James O'Brien, and sent to Lord Melville, but not noticed. You will perceive that His Majesty considers the question deserving of attention.

I am happy to say that the King appears already the better for his removal to this place. All is quiet here and in the neighbourhood, and the trials at Lewes are proceeding without interruption.

I am sorry to trouble your Lordship with so long a letter, while your time must be otherwise so much engaged, and equally desirous that you should, upon these occasions, not be at the trouble of answering me yourself.

If you will have the goodness to put me in communication with your Private Secretary, it may relieve you from this additional labour.

I have, &c.   H. TAYLOR.

No. 22.

Sir H. Taylor to Earl Grey.

Brighton, Dec. 22, 1830.

My dear Lord,—I have the honour to enclose the King's answer to your Lordship's letter, and in which His Majesty has noticed your communication, through me, relative to the notice given in the House of Commons, of a motion for an account of all offices, &c., held under the Duchy of Lancaster, which communication gave His Majesty great satisfaction. I hope, however, that it will be given up. His Majesty had not received any report from Lord Melbourne, but was not surprised to hear that a procession had been prepared to meet Mr. O'Connell, upon his entry into Dublin. The King observed, that he would have been better pleased if this assembly of people had not dispersed quietly *at his bidding*, as the control which he has successfully exercised upon various occasions in this way appears to His Majesty the most striking proof of the influence he has acquired over a portion of the lower classes in Ireland.

His Majesty had not flattered himself that the assemblages in the neighbourhood of Manchester, under the direction of the Trades Union, would very soon subside; though, unpleasant as they are, they have never occasioned to him serious uneasiness, being satisfied that these proceedings are duly watched, and that they will, when necessary, be met with due firmness, and checked.

The letter which your Lordship enclosed for the King was of no importance, from an individual, having no claim, applying for a loan of 300*l*.

It has been suggested to the King that there is an apartment at Holyrood House hung with tapestry, in His late Majesty's time, which would be used more freely if this tapestry were removed, and might be conducive to the comfort of Charles X. and his family, who may possibly be rather cramped for room. His Majesty has ordered me to name this to your Lordship, for such notice as it may appear to you to merit.

I have, &c. H. TAYLOR.

(Enclosure.)

The King to Earl Grey.

Brighton, Dec. 22, 1830.

The King acknowledges the receipt of Earl Grey's letter of yesterday, enclosing one from the Archbishop of Canterbury, which he returns.

His Majesty highly approves of the Archbishop's

proposal, that a Prayer should be prepared by him, to be used on Sundays and Holydays, in all churches and chapels in England and Wales.

His Majesty concurs with Earl Grey in the propriety of conferring the Deanery of Chester, which will become vacant by the promotion of the Dean to the see of Exeter, upon the Rev. Mr. Davys, who appears to be well entitled to this mark of favour.

Earl Grey will have already learnt His Majesty's approval of the appointment of Mr. Tennyson to the clerkship of the Ordnance; and he hopes that the remaining arrangements of the Ordnance department will be finally completed to his satisfaction.

His Majesty is very sensible of Lord Grey's determination to resist any motion in the House of Commons with a view to interference in the concerns of the Duchy of Lancaster.

WILLIAM R.

No. 23.

Earl Grey to Sir H. Taylor.

Downing Street, Dec. 22, 1830.

Dear Sir,—I have to acknowledge the receipt of your two letters of the 20th and 21st, the first containing ——'s letters to the King, was not, owing to some mistake or accident, forwarded by the regular post, but came by a special messenger sent by the Post Office yesterday evening.

With respect to ——'s application, I have to request that you will represent to His Majesty, that I can have no right to object to any orders he may be pleased personally to give respecting this matter, but that I could not take it upon myself to recommend to His Majesty a compliance with ——'s request.

The very short time that must necessarily elapse before he will succeed to his ——'s title seems to render his immediate advancement to the peerage a matter of comparatively inferior importance to him. To his family it would give little additional consequence to that which they already possess as derived from the succession; and the creation of a new peer would be seized as a favourable opportunity by many who are pressing claims to that distinction, to renew their applications with increased urgency.

Sir James Graham had already mentioned to me the case of the officers of the Navy who hold appointments in His Majesty's household; and it appeared to me, that the provisions of the Act of Parliament, which is adverted to in Mr. Barrow's letter, opposed an insurmountable obstacle to their claims. There is also the difficulty of carrying any proposition of this sort into effect, without its being canvassed and objected to in the House of Commons; but I will have some further communication on this subject with Sir James Graham.

I have had great pleasure in receiving His Majesty's sanction of the appointments of Mr. Tennyson and Colonel Maberley as Clerk and Surveyor of the Ordnance, and will proceed, under the permission of His Majesty, to fill up the other appointments with the least possible delay.

I have been much gratified at learning that the King has been pleased to appoint Vice-Admiral Sir R.

Otway to be one of the Grooms of His Majesty's Bedchamber. May I be permitted to add, that the motives which have induced His Majesty to name Lord Falkland as the successor of Lord Beverley are such as must naturally have been expected to prevail in His Majesty's disposal of that office. For His Majesty's kind assurance that Lord Say and Sele will succeed to the next vacancy I feel most grateful.

I am sorry to say that Mr. Stanley's legal advisers, after having carefully examined the case on the spot, have advised him to discontinue the scrutiny: the same opinion is given against a petition. This seat, therefore, is lost; and, what is worse, Mr. Hunt has found his way into Parliament. If no other seat, therefore, can be found for Mr. Stanley, I must revert to His Majesty's kind offer of Windsor, in the event of its being vacated by Sir Hussey Vivian.

I remain, &c. GREY.

P.S.—I have read with the liveliest pleasure your account of His Majesty's improved health.

No. 24.

Sir H. Taylor to Earl Grey.

Brighton, Dec. 23, 1830.

My dear Lord,—I have had the honour to submit your Lordship's letter of yesterday to the King, who has ordered me to say that he entirely concurs in the view you take of ——'s application, which will be met in that sense.

His Majesty cannot so readily reconcile himself to the abandonment of the claim of the Officers of the Navy who hold or may hold appointments in his household, as the provisions of the Act of Parliament must totally disappoint and defeat his wish to confer upon them such marks of his personal favour and approbation.

To Lord Byron and Lord Napier, who are only captains, the situation of Lord of the Bed-chamber will continue to be an object, as they forfeit only 12s. per diem; but, to Lord James O'Brien, the salary offers little more than an equivalent for what he is obliged to give up; and Sir Henry Blackwood and Sir Robert Otway would lose so much by holding the situations of Grooms of the Bed-chamber, that they had better not retain them.

The King is much gratified by your Lordship's approval of his appointment of Lord Falkland to be one of the Lords of the Bedchamber. His Majesty has learnt with great regret that Mr. Stanley is under the necessity of discontinuing the scrutiny, and of abandoning the petition against the return of Mr. Hunt; but orders me to repeat that Windsor will be open to him whenever vacated by Sir Hussey Vivian. As it may be material that no time should be lost, His Majesty suggests to your Lordship the expediency of making some communication to Sir Hussey Vivian which may expedite his retirement, provided his appointment to the command of the Forces in Ireland shall be free from doubt, which your Lordship will learn from your communication with Lord Anglesey.

I have, &c.   H. TAYLOR.

No. 25.

Earl Grey to the King.

Downing Street, Dec. 23, 1830.

Earl Grey has humbly to acknowledge your Majesty's letter of yesterday, with your Majesty's gracious approbation of the several appointments which he had ventured to recommend to your Majesty.

Upon full consideration, and with the advice of Sir Thomas Hardy, Earl Grey has proposed to the Hon. Captain Duncan the appointment to the office of Storekeeper of the Ordnance, of which, if he accepts it, Earl Grey anxiously hopes your Majesty will approve.

At a meeting of your Majesty's servants yesterday, it was thought necessary that an addition should be made to the military force of the country, with a view to the internal state both of England and Ireland, but more particularly with respect to the latter. For this purpose it was agreed that Earl Grey should immediately submit to your Majesty the expediency of embodying the Militia, which can only be done by taking immediate measures for a new ballot. It was also thought right to accept any offers that may be made for raising Yeomanry Corps in those parts of the country where the spirit of insubordination appears to be most prevalent.

As the order for balloting for the Militia will require the sanction of your Majesty in Council, Earl Grey has further to submit that a Council should be held at Brighton, at such time as may suit your Majesty's convenience; for which purpose, Earl Grey, with such other Members of the Privy Council as, added to those who are now at Brighton, would form the necessary number, will attend your Majesty's commands.

Earl Grey is happy to inform your Majesty that the letters received this morning from Sir H. Bouverie and the Magistrates give a better account of the state of things in the manufacturing districts near Manchester. The letters from Ireland are unfortunately not of so favourable a description. The Marquis of Anglesey, from whom letters have been received after his arrival at Holyhead, was to make his entry into Dublin to-day.

Earl Grey has further to inform your Majesty that, upon further consideration, it has been thought better not to extend the adjournment of the Two Houses beyond Thursday, 4th February.

All which, &c. GREY.

No. 26.

The King to Earl Grey.

Brighton, Dec. 24, 1830.

The King has received Earl Grey's letter of yesterday, and assures him that he considers that no Officer of the Royal Navy can be better qualified than Captain Duncan for the office of Storekeeper of the Ordnance.

His Majesty is not surprised that his confidential servants should, with reference to the present internal state of the United Kingdoms, have come to the resolution of submitting to the King that the Militia should be immediately embodied, and that encouragement should be given to the increase of the Yeomanry force. His Majesty is aware that the number of the former, which requires to be completed by ballot, is about 10,000; and he trusts that the measure now contemplated will have, with the recruiting of the Army, the effect of giving employment to a portion of the misguided individuals who may probably require only a better direction to become useful and loyal subjects.

His Majesty will hold the Council here on Monday, at such hour as may suit Earl Grey after eleven. The Privy Councillors here are Lord Holland, the Duke of Sussex, and Lord John Townshend. Four more will, therefore, be required.

The King regrets that the reports from Ireland continue unsatisfactory. Those from the manufacturing districts, however disagreeable, have at no time occasioned to His Majesty the same uneasiness as those from some other quarters.   WILLIAM R.

No. 27.

Sir H. Taylor to Earl Grey.

Brighton, Dec. 24, 1830.

My dear Lord,—The King having replied fully to the letter which your Lordship addressed to him yesterday, I have only, in obedience to His Majesty's commands, to acquaint your Lordship that he will be glad if you and those other Members of the Privy Council who may come from London on Monday will dine with him; and that he can lodge your Lordship and one more at the Pavilion, should you stay the night, which His Majesty recommends your doing at this season.

The King, before he had received your Lordship's letter, had ordered me to state his wish that you would consider of the propriety and practicability of altering the Act of Parliament which affects Officers on half-pay holding situations in his household, so as to relieve them from, what appears to His Majesty, so unjust a penalty upon acceptance of marks of his personal favour; but as you will have the opportunity of communicating verbally with His Majesty upon this point, your Lordship may possibly consider it more advisable to drop the question until then, and I merely mention this to prepare you for it.

I have, &c. H. TAYLOR.

No. 28.

Sir H. Taylor to Earl Grey.

(Private.) Brighton, Dec. 25, 1830.

My dear Lord,—In consequence of the intention of embodying the Militia, I take the liberty of communicating *privately*, for your Lordship's consideration, a paper drawn up by Major-General Sir Richard Jackson, the Deputy-Quarter-Master-General, and the copy of a letter from myself to Sir Robert Peel, on the same subject. You will observe that they (Sir R. Jackson's at least) are applicable chiefly to a period of war, but still there are parts which may be deserving of attention at present.

I do not send them to Lord Melbourne, as Sir Richard Jackson very properly considers that he should have Lord Hill's sanction for bringing forward anything.

If your Lordship should deem this suggestion useful, I can return them to him, and desire him to give them to Lord Hill.

I have, &c.

H. TAYLOR.

No. 29.

Earl Grey to The King.

Downing Street, Dec. 30, 1830.

Earl Grey has the honour of submitting to your Majesty the Minute of the Proceedings of a Meeting of your Majesty's servants, held to-day at the Foreign Office.

The alarming nature of the accounts from Ireland could leave no doubt as to the necessity of providing, by the most effectual measures, for any exigency that may arise; but, upon the most material points referred to in the annexed minute, private communications have already been made to the Lord-Lieutenant of Ireland, both by Lord Grey and Lord Melbourne.

Lord Grey has the greatest satisfaction in adding, that the accounts received to-day from Manchester and the neighbouring district, as well as from other parts of the country, afford an increased hope that obedience to the laws, and consequent tranquillity, may soon be re-established.

(Enclosure in No. 29.)

PRESENT:

The Lord Privy Seal.	Lord Holland.
Earl of Carlisle.	Viscount Althorp.
Earl Grey.	Sir James Graham.
Viscount Palmerston.	The Right Hon. C. Grant.
Viscount Goderich.	

That, with a view to having such a disposable force as circumstances may require, it is necessary to render the Militia efficient with as little delay as possible. That, for this purpose, instructions should be sent to the Lords-Lieutenants of counties to proceed with a ballot without loss of time; and that, in the meantime, the staff and quota of the Militia now liable to serve, should be called out for the purpose of immediate training.

That instructions be sent to the Lord-Lieutenant sanctioning his proposal to set on foot corps of Yeomanry, avoiding, as much as possible, in the measures necessary for this purpose, any thing that may tend to revive or to prolong religious animosities and distinctions.

That, at the same time, it should be recommended to His Majesty's Government in Ireland, to take into their immediate consideration, and submit to His Majesty's Cabinet, such measures as may appear to be required for the removal of any grievances, either in the actual state of the law, or in the mode of its administration, which may afford just cause of complaint.

That, in particular, immediate attention should be paid to the state of education in Ireland, with a view to the remedy of any defects in the system now existing for that purpose, and to the introduction of such improvements as may appear expedient.

That it be further recommended to the Government of Ireland, to consider and report upon the expediency of discontinuing the present appointment of Governors in the counties, and substituting Lords-Lieutenants, as is now practised in England, in their stead.

No. 30.

Sir H. Taylor to Earl Grey.

(Private.)   Brighton, Dec. 30, 1880.

My dear Lord,—Your Lordship will, I hope, forgive my troubling you with a few remarks or suggestions on the subject of the augmentation of our Military force, either for internal security, or foreign purposes, as circumstances may require, the official situation which I held during nearly ten years having directed my attention to the question at various times and in various shapes.

I am ignorant to what extent it may be in contemplation to increase the military means, either by calling out the Militia partially, or by any addition to the Regular force; but I am convinced that the latter would be, not only the most efficient, but the cheapest; and it would have the advantage of being applicable to all purposes.

The actual establishment of our regiments of Infantry of the Line is 740 rank and file. The effectives had been lowered to 660; and the difference to be made up by recruiting is 6,720 upon 84 battalions (regiments in India not being included), besides a few hundreds to complete the Guards. This has been ordered and is in progress, and I will suppose the regiments to be complete to that establishment. The 84 battalions might be augmented to 1,000 rank and file each, which would give a total addition of 21,840 rank and file in the Line; and the Guards to 100 per company, 672 rank and file in the Guards; total, 22,512; without adding an officer, or any additional regimental staff, as the actual proportion of officers would be sufficient, if effective. All that would be required would be one additional sergeant and one corporal per company. Whereas the same number of Militia, forming at least 28 regiments, would require 84 field-officers, 280 captains, 560 subalterns, besides regimental staff of various descriptions, and a large proportion of sergeants, drummers, &c. The expense would be at least one-third more for the same number of firelocks, and the force would not be so efficient, nor so generally available.

I am aware that there may be objections to any augmentation of the Regular Army, which do not apply to the embodying the Militia in whole or in part; but I felt it to be my duty to state the relative advantages and cost; and although it may not be possible or expedient to take the question into consideration, as it applies to the English Militia, it may be deserving of attention with reference to the Irish Militia, especially as these are not raised by ballot, but are recruited; and as the formation of them may require as much time as would the raising nearly the same number of men for the Line, the Militia of Ireland being, as far as I recollect, somewhat more than 20,000 men. It is obvious that, in point of expense, efficiency, and general utility, an augmentation of 20,000 men to the Regular regiments would be far preferable to the embodying 20,000 Irish Militia into regiments; and there may be many other reasons which would render it a preferable measure.

I have thus ventured to submit these ideas for your Lordship's consideration, and I beg to add that I should not have done so, if I had not reason to believe that Lord Hill and the other military authorities would be found to concur in opinion, that the augmentation to the Line might be effected as I have suggested.

I have only further to request that your Lordship will not take the trouble of replying to this letter.

I have, &c.   H. TAYLOR.

No. 31.

The King to Earl Grey.

Brighton, Dec. 31, 1830.

The King acknowledges the receipt of Earl Grey's letter of yesterday enclosing a Minute of Cabinet.

His Majesty approves of all that is therein proposed, being satisfied that the accounts from Ireland and the general aspect of affairs fully justify his Government in taking, with the least possible delay, such measures as shall place at its disposal a force applicable to any exigency; and that it is not less essential to show a determination to maintain the peace of the country and to enforce obedience to the laws.

The King trusts that the Lords-Lieutenants and Deputy-Lieutenants of counties will be cautioned to scrutinise the ballots for the Militia as far as possible, so as to endeavour to exclude from its ranks men of dangerous and designing character, whose influence might prove very pernicious upon newly established corps, and before they shall have acquired habits of discipline and subordination. This caution appears to His Majesty the more important, as he fears that what is left of the staffs of the Militia will, after a lapse of fifteen years, prove in many instances very incapable and inefficient.

His Majesty approves of the instructions to be sent to the Lord-Lieutenant of Ireland, relative to calling into service corps of Yeomanry, and to the other essential objects noticed in the Minute of Cabinet; and he is glad to find that his confidential servants have adopted the suggestion conveyed by His Majesty to Earl Grey and to Viscount Melbourne, to recommend to the Government of Ireland to consider the expediency of substituting for the present appointments of Governors of counties, Lords-Lieutenants, as in England.

The King rejoices with Earl Grey in the favourable character of the recent reports from the manufacturing districts and other parts of England; and His Majesty has no doubt that perseverance in the firm and energetic course now pursuing will extricate these kingdoms from every difficulty and danger with which they are threatened. WILLIAM R.

No. 32.

Earl Grey to The King.

Downing Street, Jan. 11, 1831.

Knowing that your Majesty had been regularly apprised from the Home and Foreign Offices, of everything that it was necessary to communicate to your Majesty, with respect to those affairs which in our foreign relations, and in the circumstances both of Ireland and of this country, were of the most pressing interest, Earl Grey has forborne to trouble your Majesty with unnecessary letters; nor would he now have ventured to intrude upon your Majesty, had he not been apprehensive that your Majesty might be surprised at his continued silence.

Several Cabinets have been held, at which no formal resolutions have been taken, and which, relating chiefly to the negotiations respecting Belgium, and the proceedings of the Special Commission, will have been known in their results to your Majesty.

The private letters which have been received by Earl Grey from the Marquis of Anglesey add nothing to the information which has been more fully communicated to Lord Melbourne in his dispatches. They evince the same determination to maintain the dignity of your Majesty's crown, and the authority of your Government, by the adoption of the most vigorous measures, where they may be required, under the guidance of a due discretion. For the general conduct of your Majesty's Government, in this respect, Earl Grey cannot help anticipating your Majesty's most gracious approbation.

As it appears to be more agreeable to Sir John Byng to retain the command in Ireland till the expiration of the term at which such appointments have not unfrequently been changed, Lord Anglesey has been unwilling to press his resignation till the month of June. This might render it difficult for Sir Hussey Vivian to vacate his seat for Windsor at an earlier period, without having it to assign as a reason for doing so, that the duties of his new situation would be incompatible with the due performance of those with which he is charged as a Member of Parliament. To obviate this difficulty, it has been proposed that Sir Hussey Vivian should be immediately appointed a Lieutenant-General on the Staff in Ireland, with the assurance that the chief command will devolve upon him on the resignation of Sir John Byng. In the meantime his services as an experienced officer at the head of the Cavalry may be of great importance to the public service in any exigency that the state of Ireland may produce. Earl Grey has consulted Lord Hill on the propriety of this arrangement; and, if your Majesty has no objection to it, it will be made. Presuming that this may be sanctioned by your Majesty, Sir H. Vivian will be enabled to vacate his seat at the meeting of Parliament (as a new writ could not be issued during the Adjournment, it might be inconvenient that this should be done sooner), and Mr. Stanley, under your Majesty's gracious permission, may then be elected without further delay.

Earl Grey cannot conclude without praying your Majesty's indulgence for this long and perhaps not very necessary intrusion.

Your Majesty's servants are assiduously occupied in the preparation of the measures which it will be necessary to propose to Parliament; and which, so soon as they are sufficiently matured, Earl Grey will have the honour of submitting to your Majesty's consideration.

All which, &c. GREY.

No. 33.

The King to Earl Grey.

Brighton, Jan. 12, 1831.

The King acknowledges the receipt of Earl Grey's letter of yesterday, and assures him of his entire approbation of the arrangement proposed for placing Lieutenant-General Sir Hussey Vivian at once upon the Staff in Ireland, with a view to his succeeding Sir John Byng in the command of the troops there in June next. The former may thus vacate his seat at the meeting of Parliament, and Mr. Stanley may then be brought in for Windsor.

His Majesty is too sensible of Earl Grey's invariable attention to have felt surprised at not having recently received any communications from him, nor does His Majesty expect that he should address any to him unless Earl Grey should have occasion to do so upon questions and matters to which, as the head of the Government, he shall consider it necessary and expedient that he should more particularly call His Majesty's attention.

The King has been fully and regularly apprised of all that has been transacted in the various departments of the Government; and he has great pleasure in repeating to Earl Grey the assurance which he has, from time to time, given to Viscount Melbourne and to Viscount Palmerston, of his approbation of the measures which have been determined upon by his confidential servants, with respect to the domestic and external policy of the country, and of the satisfaction he has derived from the firmness and consistency of those measures, and the determination thereby manifested to maintain the dignity of the Crown and the authority of the Government at home, and to persevere in those efforts to which Europe has been hitherto mainly indebted for the preservation of peace.

The King cannot state this generally without expressing to Earl Grey more particularly, the confidence which His Majesty reposes in his integrity, his judgment and decision, and in his experience; and without assuring him that the manner in which he has discharged the duties of the important situation which His Majesty called upon him to fill, has amply realised the expectations which he had formed. His Majesty is satisfied that he may rely upon Earl Grey's strenuous support in his determination to resist all attempts which may be made to sap the established rights of the Crown, and to destroy those institutions under which this country has so long prospered, while others have been suffering so severely from the effects of revolutionary projects, and from the admission of what are called Radical remedies.

WILLIAM R.

No. 34.

Sir H. Taylor to Earl Grey.

(Private.) Brighton, Jan. 12, 1831.

My dear Lord,—I have had the honour to submit to the King your Lordship's letter of yesterday, as well as the enclosure which I beg to return.

Your Lordship may feel perfectly at your ease with regard to the interpretation put by His Majesty upon your silence, which had been accidentally longer than usual, as it is impossible for any person to be more satisfied than His Majesty is of your attention to him in the widest sense of the word; and he showed some anxiety that this should be strongly expressed in his answer to your Lordship's letter, as well as his approbation of the general measures of his Government which you direct, and the confidence which he reposes in you. Had His Majesty at any time dropped a hint that he had not heard from you for some days, I should have not lost a day in apprising you of it.

The King's general health is good, and his spirits are even. He appears to me to enter into the general situation of affairs at home and abroad with increasing interest, but without agitation and alarm, and nothing can be more firm than his language. I do not conceal however, from your Lordship, that he looks forward with more anxiety to the proceedings in Parliament than to any other circumstance; and that the evils and the mischief which may be met by the salutary exercise of the authority of a vigorous Government strike him as unimportant when compared with the possible admission of projects which may have the effect of permanently lessening the authority and resources of that Government, the maintenance of which His Majesty considers indispensable to the security of the country, and to its preservation from revolution. I venture to state this confidentially to your Lordship, and I am convinced that you will not mistake my motive. I will add that His Majesty's language to me has been invariably that of the confidence which he has at times so strongly expressed in his letters to you; and that he attaches the greatest importance to your Lordship's services at the head of his Government at this critical period, when he considers that the interests of the monarchy and the ancient institutions of the country would be in jeopardy, unless every exertion be made to uphold and maintain them. Your Lordship may indeed have drawn this inference from His Majesty's letters to yourself and to Lord Melbourne, and from the unequivocal desire he has shown to give the full weight of his name and influence in aid of your administration. I hope you will not think that I am exceeding the bounds of discretion in writing to your Lordship in these terms, or that I am guilty of any breach of that confidence which His Majesty is pleased to repose in me. I assure you that I should not feel the least objection to His Majesty's knowing that I have written this letter, or to his seeing it; but your Lordship will oblige me by considering it as addressed to yourself only.

The King has been pleased and amused at Hunt's failure, and hopes he may look upon it as a sign that the Radical mania is subsiding generally. The success in recruiting is satisfactory, considering that the detached parties of many corps had not reached their stations.

I have, &c. H. TAYLOR.

No. 35.

Earl Grey to the King.

Downing Street, Jan. 12, 1831.

Earl Grey has the honour of informing your Majesty, that he has this morning received a letter from the Lord Chief Baron of your Majesty's Court of Exchequer, requesting him to submit to your Majesty, his resignation of that office, and his application for the allowance of the usual pension.

Presuming on your Majesty's acquiescence in this request, Earl Grey ventures humbly to submit to your Majesty, having had the concurrence of the Lord Chancellor, that your Majesty's service cannot be more effectually promoted than by the appointment of Lord Lyndhurst to succeed to the office of Lord Chief Baron; which he trusts your Majesty will be graciously pleased to approve.

At a meeting of your Majesty's servants, it has been resolved to recommend to your Majesty's royal mercy, all the convicts left for execution at Winchester, with the exception of Cooper and Cook, the one having been proved to have been an active leader in the outrages which took place in Hampshire, and the other guilty of conduct marked by great personal violence.

No letters have been received to-day from any of the members of your Majesty's Government in Ireland; but Earl Grey grieves to add, that there are accounts of two fires in Wiltshire, one of which is supposed to have been occasioned by malice, the person whose property was destroyed having been a witness on one of the trials at Salisbury.

All which, &c. GREY.

No. 36.

The King to Earl Grey.

Brighton, Jan. 13, 1831.

The King has received Earl Grey's letter of yesterday, enclosing one from the Lord Chief Baron of the Exchequer containing the resignation of his office. His Majesty accepts it, and sanctions the grant to him of the usual pension. He also approves of the appointment of Lord Lyndhurst to the office of Lord Chief Baron.   WILLIAM R.

No. 37.

Earl Grey to Sir H. Taylor.

(Private.)   Downing Street, Jan. 13, 1831.

My dear Sir,—Nothing could be more gratifying to me than the King's letter of yesterday, and the private one by which it was accompanied from yourself: the latter you may be assured that I shall regard as strictly confidential.

The news from Ireland, as you will see by Lord Anglesey's and Mr. Stanley's letters, might be of a more pleasant description; but I feel a considerable confidence in our power to overcome all these difficulties, with a due mixture of prudence and resolution. The King's anxieties are reasonably directed to what may happen in Parliament. It is impossible for anybody to speak with confidence of the restoration of the influence and authority of the Government in the House of Commons. Much must be conceded to public opinion, and more perhaps may be forced upon us; but with such concessions as may satisfy all reasonable people, I will not abandon the hope of a successful resistance to all attempts inconsistent with the real security of the Government. The perilous question is that of Parliamentary Reform, and, as I approach it, the more I feel all its difficulty. With the universal feeling that prevails on this subject, it is impossible to avoid doing something; and not to do enough to satisfy public expectation (I mean the satisfaction of the rational public) would be worse than to do nothing. We are now occupied with the details of this measure, and I hope before long to be able to submit it to His Majesty. If what we shall have to propose shall obtain His Majesty's sanction, I should have little fear of carrying it through Parliament with the general approbation of the public, though not of the Radicals, whom nothing would satisfy but the complete adoption of their own extravagant and mischievous projects. If we should fail in this, I see nothing before me but an alternative of the most afflicting nature.

I am, &c.   GREY.

No. 38.

Earl Grey to the King.

Downing Street, Jan. 13, 1831.

Earl Grey feels that he would be wanting in the attention and gratitude due from him to your Majesty, if he were to delay offering to your Majesty his humble acknowledgments of the condescension and kindness manifested in your Majesty's most gracious letter of yesterday. To endeavour to deserve your Majesty's confidence and approbation, Earl Grey must ever consider as his first duty; and to have received so gratifying an exposition of them, is his best reward.

Earl Grey has the honour of enclosing for your Majesty's information two letters which he has this morning received from the Lord Lieutenant of Ireland and from Lord Ponsonby. The accounts contained in the first are certainly of a very distressing nature; and it probably may become necessary, not only to renew the Proclamation Act, which expires at the conclusion of this session, but to consider of the means of arming your Majesty's Government with further powers to repress the violence which Mr. O'Connell and his partisans are daily exciting.

If Lord Ponsonby's opinion of the increasing strength of the party of the Prince of Orange be correct, it is to be hoped that a beneficial effect may be produced by the letter which was sent yesterday by His Royal Highness as a declaration of the principles on which he would conduct the government, if it should be committed to his hands. But of everything relating to this matter, your Majesty will of course receive full communication from Lord Palmerston.

Earl Grey is persuaded that the establishment of the Prince of Orange in the Netherlands, to whatever inconvenience it may be subject, would now be, upon the whole, the easiest and most satisfactory solution of the difficulties which embarrass the election of a new sovereign.

All which, &c. GREY.

No. 39.

Sir H. Taylor to Earl Grey.

(Private.)   Brighton, Jan. 14, 1831.

My dear Lord,—I have the honour to enclose the King's answer to your Lordship's letter, and to acquaint you that I have considered it my duty to submit to His Majesty the whole of yours to me, convinced, as I am, that its contents could not prove otherwise than satisfactory to him, and particularly interesting, from the direct reference to the 'perilous' question of Parliamentary Reform. I need not tell your Lordship that it is that to which His Majesty more particularly alluded in recent communications, and that to which I adverted when I mentioned that he looked with uneasiness to the approaching proceedings in Parliament. His Majesty is not surprised that your Lordship should approach it with dread; that you should feel all its difficulties: nor is His Majesty blind or indifferent to public feeling, or to public expectation; but he believes these to be overrated by those who are such strenuous advocates for the measure of Parliamentary Reform—so eagerly bent upon carrying it, as to overlook all the objections and difficulties to which it is liable, and the danger attendant upon its agitation when there is so much of excitement and revolutionary feeling abroad, and when the general state of the country, its domestic and foreign contingencies require a strong Government, and one that shall not be placed at the mercy of individuals whose professed object it is to reduce the power of any Government and its resources. His Majesty is satisfied that your Lordship feels all this, and he is yet more satisfied that no one can be more strongly opposed in sentiment, in principle, in judgment, and firm solicitude for the preservation of the constitutional monarchy of this country, and for its welfare and security, to the wild and mischievous projects of the Radicals. His Majesty rests his confidence in your Lordship. He looks to you for the exertion of those high qualities which have secured to you that confidence in rescuing him from the difficulties in which His Majesty may be placed by the agitation of this perilous question; and His Majesty authorises me to assure you, that you will find him disposed to give a reasonable and dispassionate consideration to what you may have to propose, and anxious not to embarrass you by objections which can be considered frivolous or captious, or to arise from any other feeling than that which a correct sense of his duty must suggest to him.

I have, &c. H. TAYLOR.

No. 40.

The King to Earl Grey.

Brighton, Jan. 14, 1831.

The King acknowledges the receipt of Earl Grey's letter transmitting those from the Lord-Lieutenant of Ireland and Lord Ponsonby, which he returns.

His Majesty has never sought to disguise from himself the serious character of the accounts received from Ireland; but he had flattered himself that the firmness and energy displayed by his Government, and the better feelings and good sense of those classes which have an interest in the preservation of peace, and in the security of the country, would have opposed a more effectual check to the seditious proceedings of Mr. O'Connell and his adherents, and would ere this have had the effect of weakening his influence over those who are so strangely misled by him. Nor does His Majesty even now apprehend that such may not eventually be the case, or that the excitement which has been created in Ireland may not be got the better of without its producing violent collision. But Mr. O'Connell's obstinacy, his perseverance in mischief, and, unfortunately, his influence over a portion of the lower classes in Ireland are such, that it is impossible not to anticipate the necessity, not only of the renewal of the Proclamation Act, but also of arming the Government with further powers; and the King is inclined to admit the force of the observation, made by Lord Anglesey and Mr. Stanley, that proclamations may be so frequent as to become comparatively unimportant. Under these circumstances His Majesty conceives that his Government would be justified by what has passed, by what is notorious, and by the statement which they will be enabled to lay before Parliament, to resort even to the strong measure of proposing the suspension of the Habeas Corpus Act. The determination thus shown to face the evil in its fullest extent, and not to shrink from the responsibility attached to the exercise of so serious a power, and to its application, when it is called for and provoked by proceedings which are inconsistent with the security of the state, would, His Majesty hopes, not only go far to check the immediate mischief, but would produce a favourable impression upon the country at large; which has, at all times, shown itself disposed to approve acts of vigour and decision in responsible authorities, when sufficient ground has been shown for them. Nor does it follow, or has any reason been given to the country to imagine, that extraordinary powers, called for by a Government which has shown so much forbearance, will not be used with moderation and discretion.

The King has observed with satisfaction in Lord Anglesey's letter the expression of a strong opinion in favour of paying the Roman Catholic Clergy, as His Majesty's sentiments have always been in support of an arrangement of this nature, if it could be introduced; and as he is convinced that the sum applied to it would be returned with interest in the influence and other advantages it would secure to the Government.

Upon the subject of the establishment of the Prince of Orange in Belgium, and the view which the King has taken of what has been done and submitted to him, His Majesty refers Earl Grey to his letter of yesterday's date to Viscount Palmerston; and he will be very glad to learn that his opinion of the importance of annexing the Duchy of Luxemburg to Belgium, when placed under the sovereignty of the Prince of Orange, has met with Earl Grey's concurrence. WILLIAM R.

No. 41.
Earl Grey to Sir H. Taylor.

Downing Street, Jan. 14, 1831.

My dear Sir,—I last night received your letter enclosing one from the King, containing His Majesty's acceptance of the resignation of the Chief Baron, his approbation of the grant of the usual pension and of the appointment of Lord Lyndhurst, with respect to which all necessary measures have been taken. I cannot help enclosing for your private information an anonymous letter,* which I received last night. It would not have obtained from me more attention than other anonymous letters, had I not heard of a conversation, exactly corresponding with it, which had been held at the Speaker's, in a party at which Mr. Croker and Mr. Theodore Hook were present. It had also been reported to me, that several times there had appeared in 'John Bull,' a paper which I never see, details respecting the arrangements that were going on, which could not have been obtained except from persons who had accurate information respecting them. With this paper Mr. Hook is said to be connected: Mr. Croker is also said to write in it.

I am quite sure that the King would not allow of any such communications if he had the least suspicion of them; and I should hope that no persons in the situations of Sir W. Fremantle and Sir A. Barnard could

* Though this letter refers to an offensive and unfounded imputation upon two highly honourable men, I have not omitted it from the correspondence, because it appears from the subsequent letters that this imputation was refuted to my father's complete satisfaction; while the anonymous letter in which it was contained, and the explanation that letter called forth, are of importance as showing both the jealousy and suspicion not unnaturally felt by the supporters of the Government, of the many adherents of the opposite party who were about the Court, and also how fairly and honourably the King acted towards his Ministers. In retaining about his person those to whose society he was used, notwithstanding their political opinions, it will be seen that he took care not to allow this to interfere with his giving his full support to his Government.

be capable of the conduct imputed to them. But the circumstances attending this report are certainly somewhat extraordinary, and have induced me to entrust to you confidentially the statement as I have received it. In a case between equals I certainly should at once submit to the person, whose confidence might have been stated to be abused, the statement as I had received it, leaving it to him to do whatever might appear to him to be required upon it. But I feel that it would be improper for me, in every view that I can take of it, to trouble the King on such a matter. Perhaps I ought to add, that the conversation at the Speaker's was reported to me by Sir James Graham, to whom it had come from a person who was present. The accompanying book was brought to me to-day by M. de Choiseul, who came over with Charles X., and remains in town for the purpose of any communications that may be necessary with the Government. He says it was written under the eye of Charles X. He left with me, some time ago, a letter of introduction from the Duke of Wellington, but I had not seen him before.

I am, &c. GREY.

(Enclosure in No. 41.)

London, Jan. 12, 1831.

My Lord,—Your Lordship ought to know that two members of the King's household (Sir W. Fremantle and Sir A. Barnard) are in *constant communication* with Messrs. Croker and Hook; and that everything going on in the King's family, or court, is made known to these editors of 'John Bull.' It is a matter of surprise to many of your Lordship's old friends and supporters, that you should for one moment suffer such proceedings to go on, and that you should not have removed such persons from the household. Believe me, my Lord, that it is not safe, or reputable to your Government, to allow the persons alluded to, and such as them, to continue in office.

This hint is meant in the greatest kindness, every word of which I can prove.

Your sincere admirer, AN OLD FOXITE.

No. 42.

Sir H. Taylor to Earl Grey.

(Private.) Brighton, Jan. 15, 1831.

My dear Lord,—I beg to return the anonymous letter which your Lordship entrusted to me in your letter of yesterday, and to express my conviction that there is no foundation for what is therein stated, and that the Old Foxite is upon the wrong scent in ascribing to Sir Andrew Barnard and Sir William Fremantle the communication of anything to Mr. Croker and Mr. Theodore Hook, which might not be published anywhere. I have indeed never heard of them being much acquainted, or having more intercourse with them than I have myself, which amounts to nothing; and from long and intimate acquaintance with both Sir William Fremantle and Sir Andrew Barnard, I should consider either extremely unlikely to talk out of school, even if they had anything essential to tell. Sir William Fremantle has been, during a great part of his life, in habits of attendance upon, and communication with, the Royal Family; and I have never heard him accused of indiscretion, or traced anything to him; nor is he an eager politician. He has not been here during this visit of His Majesty to Brighton, and he was *here* during a considerable part of His Majesty's last residence in London. Sir Andrew Barnard is one of the most gallant and efficient officers in the Army, highly honourable and extremely popular. He is much in society, and his pursuits are those of cheerful society; but I believe him to be quite indifferent with respect to politics. I never hear him touch upon that topic, and much of his time here is taken up with the Queen's Band, of which he has undertaken the direction. I have indeed known him on service, in the late King's family and here, and have always considered him remarkable for his discretion and for his extreme caution as to interfering in any business not his own. I have no doubt he may be in the habit of meeting Mr. Croker and Mr. Theodore Hook, but I should very much doubt his mentioning what passes here unless it be connected with his *pet band*. I may add that I generally frank his letters, as well as Sir William Fremantle's when here, and should therefore be aware of any active correspondence with Mr. Hook. But, after all, there never was any Court from which and of which so little could be told, which every servant in the house, from the highest to the lowest, might not tell. Their Majesties are accessible at all hours; the apartments are open to everyone; there is no seclusion, no mystery, nothing to conceal. The King sees numbers of persons in the course of the day, and converses freely with them upon subjects on which they may give him information; but I am confident that, although he may listen to them, he never converses upon any matter which may be the subject of communication with his Government, or respecting ministerial or official arrangements in contemplation. Politics are never the subject of conversation at dinner, or at the evening parties; indeed, His Majesty professes not to allow it, and he never touches on the subject with the Queen, who indeed does not seem at all disposed to break through a rule so essential in such a society, and whose superior judgment and good sense would induce her to feel its importance, and to discourage any departure from it in others : even common articles of intelligence are not noticed otherwise than as conveyed in the newspapers. I have troubled your Lordship with these particulars, and more at length than may appear necessary, as I wished to put you in full possession of the course of things here upon a point to which you must naturally attach so much importance, especially when the Court circle and society are so extended and indiscriminate ; and you will easily conclude, from all I have said, that the anonymous letter has surprised me. It has, however, produced suspicions which may be wholly unfounded, and which I therefore beg to communicate very confidentially. Your Lordship will, I am certain, rather give me credit for than blame my anxiety to satisfy your mind upon this subject ; and I should feel much obliged to you if you would allow me to say to Sir A. Barnard and Sir W. Fremantle, that I have received or seen such a letter, without giving them any hint to whom it was addressed.

I am extremely obliged to your Lordship for sending me the French pamphlet, which I shall read with great interest and safely return to you. The King is not likely to peruse it, but I should think the Queen would like to do so.

I have, &c. H. TAYLOR.

P.S. I had almost forgotten to mention that, just before Their Majesties left Brighton in October last, I received an anonymous letter, stating that Mr. * * * *, the editor of the * * *, then here, had boasted at a dinner that I was in constant communication with him, verbal and epistolary, and that he received from me intelligence of all that passed at court. I had been unfortunately concerned with Mr. * * * * in the business of * * *; and had formerly seen and written to him on that subject; but I had avoided *all* communication with him since I came into my present situation, and had carried on such as was indispensable through my solicitor, Mr. Parkinson. I sent the latter a copy of the anonymous letter for the information of Mr. * * * *, who of course denied the truth of what it stated, and desired to see me; for which he made various attempts. But I declined the interview, as well as further written communications, upon the plea that, whether the charge in question was founded or unfounded, I had determined to hold no communication with the editor of a newspaper.

No. 43.

Earl Grey to the King.

Downing Street, Jan. 15, 1831.

Earl Grey has the honour of acknowledging your Majesty's letter of yesterday.

Earl Grey felt the greatest satisfaction and comfort in finding that your Majesty's sentiments with respect to what is passing in Ireland, and in the negotiations respecting the Netherlands, so entirely sanction those which he had himself entertained.

However painful the recourse to such a measure may be, it is impossible not to contemplate the necessity of proposing to Parliament a suspension of the Habeas Corpus Act, if the exercise of the powers now possessed by the Government should be found inefficient for the security of the former country. To attach the Irish priesthood to the Government by the ties of a common interest is also an object which their payment alone affords a reasonable hope of obtaining. An arrangement of this kind demands an early attention, and not the less because it is surrounded by considerable difficulties. Earl Grey had already stated to the Prince of Orange how much the settlement of the Netherlands would be assisted by the union of the Duchy of Luxemburg, saving the rights of the Germanic Confederation to that kingdom. Earl Grey repeated the same thing to His Royal Highness this morning, when he had another interview with him. But your Majesty is aware of the difficulties that have arisen in all the negotiations with the King of the Netherlands on this subject; and the Prince did not conceal his opinion, that there would be little chance of obtaining His Majesty's consent to such a cession of the Duchy.

All which, &c. GREY.

No. 44.

Earl Grey to Sir H. Taylor.

Downing Street, Jan. 15, 1831.

My dear Sir,—I have to offer you my best thanks for your letter of yesterday accompanying the King's. With the exception of what related to this matter, there was nothing in my letter to you which I could feel any objection in your placing before His Majesty, though perhaps it might have been more cautiously worded. Nothing can be more gratifying than the cordial expression of the confidence which His Majesty is so graciously pleased to place in me. It is my most anxious wish to prove that I am not altogether unworthy of it. But I fear he may think the view I take of such a measure as may be proposed with advantage on the subject of Parliamentary Reform too extensive. I have already expressed my opinion, that any measure for this purpose, to be useful, must be effectual. Anything that was not so would only leave a feeling of discontent, which would press for further concessions. The great desideratum therefore is, to make an arrangement on which we can stand, announcing our determination not to go beyond it. But to gain such a position our ground must be well and strongly taken. I am myself convinced that public opinion is so strongly directed to this question, and so general, that it cannot be resisted without the greatest danger of leaving the Government in a situation in which it would be deprived of all authority and strength. Under this impression I must naturally feel the greatest anxiety on a subject, which it is plain that His Majesty contemplates with so much apprehension and uneasiness. I am sensible, moreover, of all the disadvantage of entering upon the discussion of such a question, in a moment of so much difficulty and danger. It has often been my wish to find the means of postponing it. But the result of all my consideration has been, that an attempt to do so would be fatal to the character of the Government, and would lead to its dissolution under circumstances still more disastrous than those which would follow such a result, if His Majesty were unfortunately compelled, by a sense of duty, to withhold his assent from the measure which may be submitted to him by his Ministers.

I have written amidst too many interruptions and too hastily to enter fully into all the views presented by this important subject. But I was anxious to return an answer to your letter, and to put you in possession generally of my feelings upon it.

I am, &c. GREY.

No. 45.

Sir Herbert Taylor to Earl Grey.

(Private.) Brighton, Jan. 16, 1831.

My dear Lord,—I have had the honour of communicating your Lordship's letter of yesterday to the King, who ordered me to acquaint you, that he has taken extreme interest in the correspondence which has passed on the subject of Reform in Parliament, and all that is connected therewith; and that it has been satisfactory to him to have thus early learnt your Lordship's feelings upon the general question, before he was called upon to take it into more formal consideration: That it had naturally engaged his anxious thoughts and attention; and that he wished, as far as possible, to relieve his mind from the impressions made by early prejudices, and from the apprehensions raised by the opinions and reports occasionally conveyed to him, which might be more or less erroneous and unfounded. Your Lordship's communications have gone far to allay these apprehensions; they have proved in general satisfactory to His Majesty; and they have prepared his mind for the cool and deliberate consideration of the question, and for the discussion of its details.

His Majesty has authorised me to say, that he had felt convinced that your Lordship would have postponed the question if you could have done so, and that he is satisfied of the correctness of your judgment in not attempting it. That he agrees with you that the measure, to be useful, and to be secured, on its introduction, against a feeling of discontent which would press for further concessions, must be effectual; and aware as His Majesty is of the nature and extent of the concessions which some of the advocates for Parliamentary Reform are disposed to call for; and sensible as he is of the confusion and destruction by which they would be followed, His Majesty feels the importance of introducing the measure, if it must be introduced, as a measure of the Government, divested, as far as it may be possible, of all that is calculated to deprive the Monarchy of its legitimate rights and attributes, in its immediate or *progressive* operation, to cramp the exercise of the executive powers and functions of the Government, and to weaken the influence of the Aristocracy so essential to the maintenance of both. His Majesty is unwilling to anticipate the details of the measure further than to observe, that a strong ground of objection would, in his view of it, be removed, if it be not intended to propose that the duration of the period for which Members are returned shall be abridged, or that the number of Members be increased.

The King trusts that the sentiments which he has authorised me to express are neither unconstitutional nor arbitrary; and that they do not betray anything like obstinate adherence to prejudices which would be ill-suited to the times and to the circumstances under which he has been called to the sovereignty of this country.

I have, &c. H. TAYLOR.

No. 46.

Sir Herbert Taylor to Earl Grey.

(Private.) Brighton, Jan. 16, 1831.

My dear Lord,—I take the liberty of enclosing to your Lordship a letter, which General Wheatley has received from Mr. Dickie, and its enclosure, and of submitting for your consideration, whether, as the money therein mentioned had accrued previous to His Majesty's declaration to Parliament abandoning the hereditary rights from which it proceeds, His Majesty may not be advised to sign a warrant for the payment of it to his Privy Purse, to which he at present objects.

I hope the letter which I have been directed by the King to write to your Lordship on the subject of Parliamentary Reform, will prove satisfactory to you. It will account for communications which may have appeared to you to have been premature, as well as for the encouragement I do not deny to have given to His Majesty to *broach* the subject, feeling as I did the importance of not allowing him to brood over it in silence; or of the possible, though not probable, alternative of conversing with those who might feel disposed to suggest difficulties and objections of which the admission might prove very embarrassing to His Majesty's Government, whenever the question should be formally brought forward.

I am certain your Lordship will agree with me that, upon these occasions, it is no small matter to reconcile the feelings to the necessity and the expediency of the object which is to be brought forward, and of which the agitation may be apprehended.

The King has not acknowledged the receipt of your Lordship's letter of yesterday, as he considered it a reply to his own of the preceding day; but he desired me to assure you how satisfactory it had proved to him.

I have, &c. H. TAYLOR.

No. 47.

Earl Grey to the King.

Downing Street, Jan. 17, 1831.

Earl Grey, with his humble duty to your Majesty,

has the honour of enclosing a letter which he has received this morning from Lord Anglesey, with a list of the names of persons who, he thinks, might be eligible for the office of Lord-Lieutenant in the different counties of Ireland, with respect to whom Earl Grey will lose no time in making the necessary inquiries for your Majesty's further information.

All which, &c. GREY.

No. 48.

Earl Grey to Sir H. Taylor.

Downing Street, Jan. 17, 1831.

My dear Sir,—I have only a moment, having been incessantly occupied during the whole day, to acknowledge your letter of yesterday, and to return the enclosed.

The Lord Chancellor and Lord Althorp being here, though I had not the slightest doubt on the subject myself, I thought it better to take their opinion, and they concur with me in thinking that the money received from His Majesty's hereditary revenues, before his most gracious declaration, placing them at the disposition of Parliament, ought to be paid over to His Majesty's Privy Purse, upon a warrant from His Majesty for that purpose. I must, however, express the extreme satisfaction I have derived from the sentiments you have been instructed by the King to express on the subject of Parliamentary Reform, on which I shall soon have a fuller communication to make to His Majesty. In the meantime it may be satisfactory to His Majesty to know, that I had intended to propose to reduce the term for which Parliaments are elected to five years; and though I think such a provision would have some advantages, it is a point to which I attach comparatively inferior importance. As to the other, so far from having any view to increase the numbers of the House of Commons, a part of my plan will be to reduce them to 600.

I am, &c. GREY.

No. 49.

The King to Earl Grey.

Brighton, Jan. 17, 1831.

The King will not delay acknowledging the receipt of Earl Grey's letter of yesterday, enclosing one from the Lord-Lieutenant of Ireland, with a list of the names of persons considered by him to be eligible for the office of Lord-Lieutenant in the different counties in Ireland.

His Majesty has received, with great satisfaction, this early proof of Lord Anglesey's attention to a point to which His Majesty has attached great importance; and the list proposed by him appears in general unexceptionable.*

* * * * * * * *

The King has been much gratified by the perusal of Lord Anglesey's letter; and by the evidence it affords of the indefatigable zeal with which he directs the energies of his mind to the arduous and important task which has been entrusted to him.

* Here follow remarks upon the fitness of some of the persons whose appointment had been proposed, and suggestions for certain changes.

The issue of a Proclamation, more generally applicable to seditious meetings, appears to the King very judicious; and His Majesty rejoices that ground has offered for the prosecution of O'Connell, and that Steel is arrested. His Majesty will never withhold his approbation and his sanction from acts of vigour when they are called for; and it appears to him most important to assume and to maintain, in every measure of the Government, a firm attitude, at a period when the object of the factious and of the agitators is to set at defiance, or to bring into contempt, all Government and legal authority.

The King enters fully into Lord Anglesey's views and projects for the general improvement of Ireland. Upon the subject of paying the priests, His Majesty has already stated his sentiments, and he is glad to find that Earl Grey concurs in them. But His Majesty is firmly persuaded also, that the application of a large sum of money to the employment of the labouring and poorer classes of Ireland on public works, and more especially upon the improvement and the construction of roads (in the Connemara mountains for instance), would be a measure of the greatest wisdom and utility; and that its results would prove it to be one of the most economical measures which the Government could have devised and carried into effect.

WILLIAM R.

No. 50.

Sir H. Taylor to Earl Grey.

Brighton, Jan. 18, 1831.

My dear Lord,—I have been favoured with your

Lordship's letter of yesterday, and have had the honour of submitting it to the King. His Majesty was, as I believe I stated to you, not aware of the question which had arisen as to the money received from his hereditary resources, and the reference to you, as he had declined to sign all warrants on that account, but was not sorry I had made the reference to your Lordship, and was much pleased with its result.

His Majesty expressed himself yet more pleased with your Lordship's communication on the subject of Parliamentary Reform, and particularly with the information that part of your plan is to reduce the number of Members to 600.

I have, &c.   H. TAYLOR.

No. 51.

Earl Grey to Sir H. Taylor.

(Private.)   Downing Street, Jan. 19, 1831.

My dear Sir,—I have been so much pressed lately, that I have omitted answering your very kind and satisfactory letter, which you were so good as to write to me upon my communication of the anonymous letter which I sent to you a few days ago. I am quite satisfied that neither of the persons alluded to could lend themselves to anything of the kind imputed to them; and I never for a moment doubted, if such an attempt should be made, that His Majesty would have stopped it at once. There can, however, be no doubt that, at the party at the Speaker's, it was very imprudently and as incorrectly stated, that this mode of communication was open to them, and that they looked with confidence to its affording them the means of striking an effectual blow at the Administration on the question of Reform. For this boast, I need hardly add my conviction, that they had no better foundation than Mr. * * * for his, of an intimate correspondence with you. The pamphlet which I sent on the subject of the late Revolution in France was, at the desire of the Marquis de Choiseul, to be forwarded to the King. He gave me another copy for myself. I thought I had so explained the matter, but as you spoke of returning it, I must have omitted to do so.

I remain, &c. GREY.

No. 52.

Earl Grey to Sir H. Taylor.

Downing Street, Jan. 20, 1831.

My dear Sir,—The Cabinet dined with me yesterday, and, in consideration of the present aspect of affairs on the Continent, it was thought expedient that the Admiralty should put the men in the dockyards in full work, for the purpose of bringing forward the ships on which they are now employed with all possible expedition, and, particularly, of the largest class of frigates, of which, I am sorry to find, that at this moment, according to the returns we have obtained, the French appear to have a much greater proportion than we have. It was also thought necessary that some addition should be made to our Naval Force in the Mediterranean. This was not reduced into a formal Cabinet minute; but Sir James Graham was instructed to submit the matter to His Majesty, and, upon receiving His Majesty's sanction, to act accordingly.

I must refer you to the communications which will, of course, be made by Lord Melbourne, as to what has taken place at Dublin on the subject of Mr. O'Connell's arrest.

I am, &c. GREY.

No. 53.

Sir H. Taylor to Earl Grey.

(Private.) Brighton, Jan. 21, 1831.

My dear Lord,—I have had the honour of submitting your Lordship's letter of yesterday to the King.

The King has received from Sir James Graham the report of the proposed arrangements for giving greater activity to the works in the dockyards, and for strengthening the Naval Forces in the Mediterranean, which His Majesty highly approves; and he has learnt with great satisfaction from Lord Melbourne, the arrest of Mr. O'Connell and his associates.

I beg to enclose a letter from His Majesty, and I have, &c. H. TAYLOR.

No. 54.

The King to Earl Grey.

Brighton, Jan. 21, 1831.

The King does not delay acquainting Earl Grey, that he has this morning received the account of the death of Viscount Sydney. Having understood from Earl Grey in London, that he had intended recommending that the rangership of Hyde Park, &c., should be conferred upon the Duke of Sussex, His Majesty desires, if he should still entertain that wish, that he will himself communicate the proposed arrangement, and His Majesty's approval of it, to the Duke of Sussex. The King considers it right to add, that not a hint has escaped him on this subject to the Duke of Sussex, or to any other individual. WILLIAM R.

No. 55.

Earl Grey to the King.

Downing Street, Jan. 22, 1831.

Earl Grey, with his humble duty, has the honour of acknowledging your Majesty's gracious letter of yesterday.

Having heard yesterday morning of the death of Lord Sydney, Earl Grey, availing himself of the permission given to him by your Majesty, made an offer of the rangership of the Parks to His Royal Highness the Duke of Sussex.

A note has been this morning received from His Royal Highness, gratefully accepting this mark of your Majesty's favour.

As several interesting matters relating both to the foreign and domestic interest of your Majesty's kingdom will be laid before your Majesty by the servants to whom your Majesty has been pleased to entrust the departments to which they relate, Earl Grey will not trouble your Majesty unnecessarily by adverting to them; but he cannot help expressing an anxious hope, that your Majesty may be pleased to approve the proposition which has been adopted by the Conference, for the establishment of the future neutrality of Belgium.

All which, &c. GREY.

No. 56.

Sir H. Taylor to Earl Grey.

(Private.) Brighton, Jan. 22, 1831.

My dear Lord,—The King has been much annoyed by learning from Lord Hill, that it is in the contemplation of the Secretary at War to recommend the reduction of the Riding Establishment, and His Majesty has ordered me not to delay addressing your Lordship on the subject. It was formed by the late Duke of York, from a conviction of its utility and necessity towards introducing and maintaining in the British Cavalry a correct and uniform system of equitation, without which it is impossible to establish and maintain uniformity and precision of exercise and movement in Cavalry, which are so essential to its efficiency and its effect. The establishment has been kept up under successive Commanders-in-Chief, and under their immediate observation and inspection. A riding-house and a barrack and stables have been erected, and the importance and the utility of the establishment have been finally acknowledged by all commanding officers of regiments, although some *originally* viewed it with prejudice and jealousy, as interfering with notions of their own. His Majesty is perfectly acquainted with the merits of this establishment, and considers it deserving of the encouragement it has hitherto received.

The King, therefore, earnestly recommends it to your

Lordship's protection, as he does others which, like this, tend to the perfection and the efficiency of the Army and Navy, His Majesty being satisfied that efficiency is economy, and equally persuaded that your Lordship will agree with him, that the interests of the public will not be consulted by showing a saving in the Estimates, which is produced by a sacrifice of that which is not only essential but indispensable towards upholding the character and the efficiency of the service.

I have, &c.   H. TAYLOR.

No. 57.

Sir H. Taylor to Earl Grey.

(Private.)   Brighton, Jan. 23, 1831.

My dear Lord,—Your Lordship would have received by this evening's post the King's answer to the letter you addressed to him yesterday; and his answer to Sir James Graham would not have been delayed either, if, after I had despatched the letter for Lord Palmerston, I had not been seized with so violent a headache, that, after some ineffectual attempts, I was forced to give up writing the letters for the usual time of His Majesty's signing them, though they are now ready, and he will sign them to-morrow morning. You are, I believe, aware that, in consequence of the rheumatic affection in his hand, the King seldom uses his pen beyond signing. Indeed, I write all his letters for him, and as they have been very numerous lately, and others I receive in the course of the day average about fifty, I have, owing to a little indisposition, got on with difficulty.

The King's letter will inform you, that he entirely approves your communication to the Duke of Sussex, and that it has been in strict conformity to his verbal instructions to your Lordship. It will also express his entire approbation of the step which has been taken towards securing the future neutrality of Belgium, upon which subject His Majesty has written at great length to Lord Palmerston. I have never observed him take more interest in the construction and wording of a letter than upon this occasion, or more particular in his instructions for it; and, what is not usual, he made me read it *twice* over to him.

I have, &c. H. TAYLOR.

No. 58.

Earl Grey to Sir H. Taylor.

Downing Street, Jan. 24, 1831.

My dear Sir,—I have received your letters of the 22nd and 23rd, and I read with great regret that you had been suffering so severely from the headache.

I was rather sorry that any communication had been made to the King on the subject of the Riding Establishment by Lord Hill, without having spoken previously to me, which might have saved His Majesty the annoyance you state him to have experienced on this occasion. I have seen Lord Hill this morning, and have informed him that I entirely agree in the view taken by the King of this matter; and that I had written to Mr. Wynn to express to him my decided opinion that the establishment should be continued. The first I heard of any intention to reduce it was from your letter. Lord Hill,

I find, was to have seen Mr. Wynn upon it this morning; so that the matter was by no means settled; and upon my expressing to him a wish that, in the case of any difference arising with any of the other departments, as to anything connected with that of the Commander-in-Chief, he would in future have the goodness to communicate with me before making any reference to the King, he said that what had taken place on this occasion had arisen accidentally in conversation with His Majesty, and without any intention on his part of making a formal representation upon it.

I have been much gratified by hearing from you, that the King had been pleased to approve the last protocol, with respect to the future neutrality of Belgium, and still more by reading His Majesty's excellent letter to Lord Palmerston. The only point on which any doubt could be entertained as to the just and enlightened opinions of His Majesty is, that which relates to the free navigation of the Scheldt. On this Lord Palmerston will send, by this post, an explanation which, I trust, will prove satisfactory to His Majesty.

Count Flahault arrived last night from Paris. I have had a long conversation with him this morning. He has expressed, in the strongest terms, the anxious desire of the King of the French for the preservation of peace, and the danger which may be produced by the state of the Netherlands, if the Government cannot be settled at an early period on some permanent foundation. I professed, on the part of His Majesty, the same desire for the preservation of peace, and the same anxiety to secure it by a speedy termination of the Belgic question. The chief difficulty in the way of this is the choice of a sovereign. If the Prince of Orange cannot succeed, and M. de Flahault expressed an utter disbelief of the power of his party to re-establish him, some other choice must be resorted to. I confess I can see none that would be open to so few objections as Prince Charles of Bavaria. To this, I find, there are however objections of a personal nature on the part of the French King; such objections, surely, ought not to prevail. M. de Flahault, as Prince Talleyrand has done on several occasions, suggested a Prince of the Royal Family of Naples, who is nineteen. To such an arrangement it might perhaps be possible to submit for the sake of peace, but I confess I should not like it.

His Majesty's servants have been engaged in the consideration of a plan submitted to them by me, for effecting such a reform in the House of Commons as might be effectual for the removal of what is most complained of, without endangering the institutions of the country. Before the end of the week, I have a confident expectation that this very important and very difficult question may be brought into a shape in which I may be able to submit it to His Majesty's consideration;* and I shall be much obliged to you to request His Majesty's permission to take it myself to Brighton,

* The following extract from a letter written by my father the same day (Jan. 24th, 1831) to Lord Durham, will show that he had difficulties to contend with in obtaining the unanimous assent of the Cabinet to the plan of Reform submitted to the King.

' I find from Althorp that there is likely to be more difficulty than I thought about Reform. Upon his saying to Brougham that he was glad to find there was so great a concurrence of opinion, he answered that he had great objection to the abolition of the close boroughs; that they were by no means the worst parts of the representation; that there would be no means for getting seats for persons in the Government, &c.

that I may have an opportunity of affording to His Majesty any explanation he may require upon it. Sunday next is the day which I would propose for this purpose.

I shall also be obliged to you to communicate to His Majesty, with my humble duty, what I have done with respect to the Riding Establishment, as well as any other part of this letter which you may think material for His Majesty's information; and also to express to His Majesty my grateful sense of the honour he has done my brother, by conferring upon him the Grand Cross of the Guelphic Order. This, however, I have already done in my answer to Count Munster's letter. I write this in great haste, and must beg you to excuse inaccuracies.

I am, &c.   GREY.

No. 59.

The King to Earl Grey.

Brighton, Jan. 24, 1831.

The King acknowledges the receipt of Earl Grey's letter of the 22nd inst., and assures him of his entire approbation of his not having delayed to make the offer of the Rangership of the Parks to the Duke of Sussex, which he was fully authorised to do by the instructions he had received from His Majesty in the event of the vacancy. His Majesty rejoices to learn

&c. He had hinted at this in the general discussion, but I thought had been satisfied by my answer, that, whatever the inconveniences might be, these boroughs could not be maintained. On this point I cannot give way. If he persevere, he may throw us over with the King.'

that the appointment has proved so satisfactory to his brother.

His Majesty received with great interest the communications from Lord Melbourne and Lord Palmerston, and other heads of departments, whose zealous and able co-operation with Earl Grey, in the indefatigable and honourable discharge of the most arduous public duties, has proved uniformly satisfactory to him. He has communicated at some length to Lord Palmerston his sentiments upon the proposition which has been adopted by the Conference, for the establishment of the future neutrality of Belgium; and it is almost unnecessary that he should assure Earl Grey, that the proposition, and the principle on which it is founded, have received his entire approbation, however His Majesty may be inclined to doubt the good faith with which it may be entered into by France.

WILLIAM R.

No. 60.

The King to Earl Grey.

Brighton, Jan. 24, 1831.

The King trusts that Earl Grey has felt convinced that His Majesty had not lost sight of his intention to confer a mark of distinction upon General Grey, although immediate effect was not given to it; and as the Coronation may, from the general situation of affairs and the state of the country, be postponed to a remote, and possibly an indefinite, period (as indeed the King considers it may be most advisable under all circumstances to do), His Majesty purposes not further to delay giving the Grand Cross of the Guelph to General Grey, sincerely hoping that it will be received by him as a mark of his personal regard, and viewed by Earl Grey as a proof of His Majesty's desire to gratify, as far as he is now able, his feelings with respect to his brother. The King will rejoice to avail himself of a future opportunity of conferring upon him the Grand Cross of the Bath, when the regulations of that Order, which prescribe that no officer shall receive the Grand Cross unless he shall previously be a Commander, may be departed from without subjecting His Majesty to embarrassment.

WILLIAM R.

No. 61.

Sir H. Taylor to Earl Grey.

Brighton, Jan. 25, 1831.

My dear Lord,—I am honoured this morning with your Lordship's letter of yesterday, and have not delayed to submit it to the King, who read every part of it with great interest.

His Majesty was glad to hear that your plan for effecting a Reform in the House of Commons would be sufficiently matured towards the end of this week, to admit of your bringing it to him on Sunday, when his Majesty will have great pleasure in receiving your Lordship. It is, indeed, the day he would himself have proposed, and he concludes you will be here between three and four o'clock. You will find a room ready for you at the Pavilion. I need not add that His

Majesty looks forward to this communication with great anxiety.

The King learnt with great satisfaction that you objected, as he did, to the reduction of the Riding Establishment; and that you had expressed to Mr. Wynn your decided opinion that it should be continued. As far as I understood His Majesty, the communication was made to him by Lord Hill as a matter of information, in the course of conversation, not as a matter of complaint. But His Majesty takes up these things eagerly, as you may have observed heretofore. I may also express his sentiments strongly upon any occasion which concerns the *efficiency* of the Army, for which I had been *officially* contending during so many years.

The approbation which your Lordship has expressed of His Majesty's letter to Lord Palmerston, has been very gratifying to him. He has received Lord Palmerston's explanation on the subject of the free navigation of the Scheldt, and has replied to it, not with any intention of objecting to anything that has been done, but in order to account for his previous remarks. Your Lordship will perceive that His Majesty still thinks that Holland is, by the removal of the restrictions on the navigation of the Scheldt, placed in a situation less advantageous than that in which she stood before the French Revolution, or the union with Belgium, which has been dissolved; and that he considers that the latter is, in this respect, benefited by the present contract to the prejudice of Holland, and without any equivalent to Holland, though in the Fourth Article of the Eleventh Protocol, which admits of exchanges of territory, it is stipulated that the advantages shall be reciprocal.

His Majesty was also much pleased to hear that you had received from Count Flahault such satisfactory assurances of the anxious desire of the King of the French for the preservation of peace; which are to a certain degree confirmed by the more conciliatory and pacific tone of the despatches from Lord Granville, which His Majesty read this morning. He feels however, with your Lordship, that the Belgic question offers the greatest difficulty, and that its early settlement is a matter of the greatest importance.

The choice of a sovereign appears also to the King the chief impediment to that settlement, and he would regret very much the failure of the endeavour to obtain the nomination of the Prince of Orange. If, however, His Majesty's hopes with respect to him should be disappointed, he desires you will feel assured of his concurrence with you, that the Prince Charles of Bavaria would be preferable to a Prince of the Royal Family of Naples, though any objection on his part to the nomination of the latter would yield to His Majesty's earnest and anxious desire for the preservation of peace.

I have, &c.   H. TAYLOR.

No. 62.

Earl Grey to the King.

Downing Street, Jan. 25, 1831.

Earl Grey had not received your Majesty's most gracious letters of yesterday, when he wrote to Count Munster and to Sir Herbert Taylor, requesting them to offer to your Majesty his humble thanks for the distinction conferred by your Majesty on General Grey, by naming him a Knight Grand Cross of the Guelphic Order.

The gratifying and condescending manner in which this mark of your Majesty's favour has now been announced to Earl Grey by your Majesty's letter, demands a repetition of his sincere and dutiful acknowledgments; which are also called for by your Majesty's gracious expression of your wish to avail yourself of a future opportunity of conferring upon General Grey the Grand Cross of the Bath, when the regulations of that Order may be departed from without subjecting your Majesty to embarrassment.

To such embarrassment Earl Grey would, on no account, have your Majesty exposed, however anxious he may be to repair, what has appeared to him, an unjust exclusion of his brother (on his account) from a military distinction to which the late Duke of York thought him entitled; and for which, as Earl Grey has been informed, His Royal Highness sent in his name on the first establishment of the Order on its present footing.

Earl Grey has again to repeat his heartfelt satisfaction at the indulgent manner in which the services of his colleagues and himself have been received by your Majesty, and at your Majesty's gracious approbation of their conduct.

Though containing some matters with which it might be improper to trouble your Majesty, Earl Grey cannot help enclosing, for your Majesty's information, a letter from the Marquis of Anglesey, which he has received this morning, as it contains a very interesting account of what passed between Lords Cloncurry and Meath and Mr. O'Connell; and also a very satisfactory account of the confidence of the Attorney-General in the result of the prosecutions instituted against Mr. O'Connell.

An enquiry has been directed to be made respecting the union of the bishoprics, which were formerly united; and there are many examples of similar unions, one as late as in the year 1792. If this arrangement should not take place, Earl Grey is inclined to believe, if your Majesty should approve, the best appointment would be that of the Provost of Trinity College to the bishopric, and of Dr. Lloyd, as suggested by the Marquis of Anglesey, to the provostship; but, upon this, Earl Grey does not, at present, think himself at liberty to offer any definitive opinion.

In consequence of the presumed vacancy in the office of one of the Grooms of your Majesty's Bedchamber, by the death of the late Viscount Sydney, an application has been made to Earl Grey, to recommend to your Majesty the Hon. Captain Campbell, brother of the Earl of Cawdor, for that appointment; and Earl Grey hopes he is doing nothing improper in complying with this request, so far as humbly to lay it before your Majesty.

All which, &c.   GREY.

No. 63.

The King to Earl Grey.

Brighton, Jan. 26, 1831.

The King was aware that Earl Grey could not have

received his letter of the 24th inst., when he wrote to Count Munster and Sir Herbert Taylor on the subject of the Grand Cross of the Guelphic Order; and His Majesty rejoices to learn from Earl Grey's letter of yesterday, that his communication had proved so satisfactory to him.

The King was not ignorant that there had been instances of the union of bishoprics; and to show that His Majesty does not object to it on principle, he need only observe that he had himself given it as his opinion to the Duke of Wellington, and His Majesty is not quite certain that he did not mention it to Earl Grey also, that, whenever the arrangement could be made, the union of the bishoprics of Sodor and Man and of Chester would be beneficial. But it occurred to His Majesty that, at a period when Reform of every description is in vogue, and when there are rumours of projected reforms in the ecclesiastical institutions of the country, it might not be advisable to act upon a partial suggestion of Sir John Newport's, which could not embrace, and might, if carried into effect; embarrass, future and more general arrangements.

His Majesty is quite disposed to sanction Earl Grey's proposal, that, in the event of an immediate succession to the see of Cork, the Provost of Trinity should be the new bishop, and Doctor Lloyd should obtain the provostship.

The King desires Earl Grey will acquaint Captain Campbell that His Majesty will add his name to his list of candidates for the situation of Groom of the Bedchamber, and that he will be glad to bear his application in mind; but that the vacancy occasioned by the death of Lord Sydney had already been filled by Colonel Sir James Reynett, at the earnest request of the Landgravine of Homburg and the Duke of Cambridge.

WILLIAM R.

No. 64.

Earl Grey to the King.

Downing Street, Jan. 27, 1831.

Earl Grey, with his humble duty, has the honour of acknowledging your Majesty's most gracious letter of yesterday.

Earl Grey has now the honour of enclosing another letter from the Marquis of Anglesey for your Majesty's information, and feels assured that the information contained in it must prove satisfactory to your Majesty.

Before Mr. O'Connell's return to Ireland Earl Grey would have thought any terms, consistent with propriety, advisable, for preventing the agitation which has since taken place. But he now entertains more than a strong doubt, whether any attempt on the part of the Government, to conciliate a man who has done all the mischief in his power, would be either honourable or useful.

Earl Grey begs to offer his humble thanks for your Majesty's goodness in having placed Captain Campbell's name on the list of candidates for a future appointment to the office of one of the Grooms of your Majesty's Bed-chamber.

All which, &c.
GREY.

No. 65.

Earl Grey to Sir H. Taylor.

Downing Street, Feb. 3, 1831.

My dear Sir,—I last night received your letter of yesterday. I await, with great anxiety, the King's observations on the plan of Parliamentary Reform, which I had the honour of submitting to His Majesty on Sunday last. After what passed on that occasion,[*] I cannot doubt that they will be quite satisfactory.

I had some further conversation, yesterday, with —— on the subject, which has given me more pain than I can well express to you. He desired to take a short time to reconsider it. The result will be seen in the enclosed letter from him, which has greatly disappointed me. I cannot, in justice to His Majesty, indeed without disobedience to his commands, urge that a proposal should be made to Parliament under circumstances so disadvantageous. But I hope that, in making his statement of the Civil List, Lord Althorp will claim for His Majesty the gratitude so justly due to him, for

---

[*] In a letter to Lord Durham, dated Brighton, Jan. 31st, 1831, my father thus describes what passed in his interview with the King:—

'Within ten minutes after my arrival here I was introduced to the King, and he immediately entered into the consideration of our plan of Reform. He attended very minutely to every part of it, put questions wherever doubt occurred, and at the conclusion understood it perfectly. The result is most satisfactory. He approves entirely of the general view and effect of the measure, reserving to himself only the right of making such observations on the details as further consideration may suggest. He was particularly pleased with your report, and entirely concurred in the statement so clearly and powerfully made in it, of the necessity of doing something, and that that something should be effectual and final.' The report referred to will be found in the APPENDIX.

this new instance of his consideration for his people, in not making a claim sanctioned by precedent, and in itself both reasonable and just.*

I am, &c.   GREY.

No. 66.

Earl Grey to Sir H. Taylor.

Downing Street, Feb. 4, 1831.

My dear Sir,—The disposition of both Houses yesterday, upon the announcement of the measures to be brought forward by the Government, appeared very favourable. There were indications in some quarters of a strong opposition to the question of Reform, but this was to be expected; and if we are not greatly deceived in our estimate of numbers in the House of Commons, the result is not much to be feared. Mr. Hunt spoke four or five times. The account I hear of him is, that he is in appearance a good country gentleman, and that his manner of speaking with a strong provincial accent does not threaten much difficulty.

I enclose a letter from Lord Anglesey, the beginning of which the King might like to see. There are other

---

* This refers to a discussion which had arisen as to the propriety of proposing to the House of Commons, that a sum of money should be voted for an outfit to the Queen. My father and Lord Althorp were strongly of opinion that such a grant ought to be made, and nearly all the members of the Cabinet concurred with them; but the objection made to it by one of them was too decided to be overcome. It is right to add, that this objection appears to have been founded on an apprehension that proposing a grant for this purpose would have a bad effect in the House of Commons and on public opinion. From what afterwards occurred, it seems probable that this would have proved a correct anticipation, had the grant been asked for.

parts of it which it might not, perhaps, be proper for me to communicate to him, but this I leave entirely to your discretion. I feel a very confident expectation that the French Government will not consent to the choice of the Duc de Nemours. He and the Duke of Leuchtenberg being both put aside, I hope it may be possible to find a third candidate who may be sufficiently unobjectionable to be consented to for the sake of peace.

I am, &c. GREY.

No. 67.

Sir H. Taylor to Earl Grey.

(Private.) Brighton, Feb. 4, 1831.

My dear Lord,—I have not failed to read your Lordship's letter of yesterday to the King, as well as that from ——, which I beg to return. His Majesty is perfectly sensible of your Lordship's kind feeling on the subject of an allowance for the outfit of the Queen, and of your anxiety to remove the objection made by ——; and His Majesty desires I will convey to you his own and the Queen's acknowledgments for this feeling, which they are aware, also, that all have shared but ——, to whose proceedings, however, they are by no means disposed to assign any other motive than his conviction, that the introduction of this additional item might be productive of unpleasant discussion, notwithstanding the precedents which had induced His Majesty to start the question.

The King is, however, particularly anxious that not another word should be said on the subject, and that no allusion, direct or indirect, should be made to it by Lord Althorp in making his statement of the Civil List, as he does not wish to be considered as claiming the least merit for abandoning a claim to which an objection could possibly be urged.

The Queen has, unfortunately, greatly *exceeded* the proposed amount in her outfit, and His Majesty will make arrangements for reimbursing the amount to her out of his own income by instalments.

Your Lordship will, I hope, excuse the haste with which this is written. The King's long letter has taken up the greater part of my day.

I have, &c.   H. TAYLOR.

No. 68.

The King to Earl Grey.

Brighton, Feb. 4, 1831.

The King has too long been deeply impressed with the extreme importance of the question of Parliamentary Reform, which has so long engaged the attention of the public, and has recently been the subject of the serious deliberations of his confidential servants, not to have looked forward with great anxiety to the results of their deliberations, in the communications which were made to him on the 31st ult. by Earl Grey, 'The Report[*] on the state of the Representation, with a view to its thorough and effective Reform,' and of the three Bills attached to that Report, 'amending the Representation of England, Scotland, and Ireland,' with the accompanying explanatory documents.

[*] For this Report see Appendix A.

Although the King had felt willing to admit the necessity of engaging in this question, His Majesty would deceive Earl Grey, and his other confidential servants, if he were to disguise from them that his anxiety was not free from uneasiness, or that the apprehension of innovations fraught with danger, and proposed to be introduced at a period which other circumstances rendered so critical, did not greatly outweigh his expectations of advantage to the State and the country, from measures of which he had yet to learn the nature and the extent. These having, indeed, been produced, or at least hastened into discussion, more or less, by popular clamour, might prove of such a character as to call upon the King for an opposition to them of which the possible results would have been decidedly at variance with his general inclinations, and with his sense of the necessity of stability, and of cordial union in the councils of the nation.

Earl Grey cannot possibly be surprised that such should have been His Majesty's feeling, nor consider it as betraying any want of that confidence which induced him to call upon him for his able and valuable services, and to entrust him with the formation of the Administration, at a period of extreme national and general importance. That confidence has continued unimpaired, and it has been amply justified.

But His Majesty had, little more than four months after his accession to the Throne, been under the necessity of changing his Government—a Government to which he had given his strenuous and unqualified support—in consequence of the influence of that very House of Commons, of which, as the *popular* branch of the Legislature, it was to be understood that the power and influence should be further increased. He could not be ignorant, and was not ignorant, that some of those who had, in consequence of that change in the Government, been called to his councils were, more or less, committed in pledges on popular questions; and it was, therefore, natural that he should dread, independently of other sources of objection, the introduction into the House of Commons of such measures of Reform as would be likely to be rejected in the House of Lords, whence must arise a quarrel between these two branches of the Legislature, not upon a mere matter of form, not upon the enactment of a common law, but upon a matter affecting a main feature of the Constitution of the country upon a great popular question, and therefore to be viewed as a great national and political calamity.

Nor were these apprehensions groundless, either as they regard the objections which the King would have felt it to be his duty to maintain, or the opposition he would have anticipated in the House of Peers, supposing the Election by Ballot to have formed part of the Bill proposed to be introduced; for its adoption was actually proposed in the Report presented to Earl Grey, though positively rejected by him before he submitted it to His Majesty.

The King does not deny that he hails that rejection as removing an insuperable bar from his assent to the proposed measure; and he is induced thus pointedly to notice the proposal of introducing *Election by Ballot*, in order to declare that nothing should ever induce him to yield to it, or to sanction a practice which would, in his opinion, be a protection to concealment, would abolish the influence of fear and shame, and would be inconsistent with the manly spirit and the free avowal of opinion which distinguish the people of England. His Majesty need scarcely add that his opposition to the introduction of another, yet more objectionable, proposal,—the adoption of *Universal Suffrage*, one of the wild projects which have sprung from revolutionary speculation,—would have been still more decided.

In a question of such vital importance, possibly of greater moment, and more deeply affecting the general interests and welfare of the State than any (with the exception of the Emancipation of the Roman Catholics) upon which the Sovereign of this country has, for centuries past, been called upon to determine, the King feels that he would not do justice to himself if he were to omit stating his general view of the question as a subject of public discussion, and without immediate reference to the shape in which it is now submitted for his sanction, and to the explanations given to him by Earl Grey, which His Majesty acknowledges to have been ample and satisfactory on every point, and to have been offered without reserve or hesitation.

The King trusts that his general conduct will secure him against any inference that his opinions have arisen from an arbitrary disposition, have been conceived in the spirit of party, or that they have resulted from prejudice, other than that possibly which is produced by attachment to old institutions, under which England has so long enjoyed, and still enjoys, the benefits for which other countries are contending. But he wishes, by thus recording his opinions, to establish a clear understanding of the limits which a sense of his duty and the principles by which he considers he ought, as Sovereign of this country, to be governed, must affix to his admission of any proposals that may be made to him.

His Majesty is not disposed to deny the existence of defects in the system of the Parliamentary Representation; nor that it is natural, when defects exist, to wish to remove them: but he believes the evils to be more in theory than in practice, as shown by the mode in which the machine has worked; and the question is, Whether, in such a Constitution as that of these realms, the dangers of change may not be more to be dreaded and deprecated than the existence of defects; and whether the preservation of blessings we enjoy be not preferable to the prosecution of that which when acquired, after much difficulty and struggle, may grievously disappoint our expectations?

Great stress is laid upon the general opinion of the people, as being in favour of an extensive Reform; but His Majesty very much doubts whether there be sufficient ground for this conclusion. He cannot consider public meetings as a just criterion of the sentiments of the people. The objects of those meetings have, in general, been the promotion of discontent and the disturbance of the public peace; and those who have not felt inclined to encourage these objects have absented themselves from them, and have viewed with alarm proceedings which might affect their security and their property. On the other hand, those who have little or nothing to lose, naturally look for advantage to themselves from any change, and are callous to the prospect of its ruinous effects on the mass, as the prejudice cannot reach them. But even when such be not the motive of agitators, it may be questioned whether, in a country where so much freedom exists, Reform, which contemplates election by ballot and universal suffrage, be not a specious cloak for the introduction of Republicanism.

The influence which has been exercised by Peers in the representation, and which has become so much an object of vituperation, attaches to *property;* and it appears reasonable that it should in that sense be exercised by individuals who, having the larger stake, have the greatest interest in the maintenance of the security and prosperity of the country, and of the established order of things. It is natural that they should possess influence over those to whom their property enables them to give employment and subsistence; and it is desirable that an useful union should thus be promoted between the upper and lower classes of society, more especially as the means by which revolutionists chiefly strive to attain their ends is by the destruction of those links. Experience has indeed shown that their attacks are almost invariably levelled at the existing aristocracy, although the destruction of the monarchy may not always be their object.

The King conceives that the most strenuous advocates for Reform, those whose object it may be to introduce a preponderance of *popular* influence, will not be disposed to deny that the influence of the House of Commons has increased more than that of the Crown, or of the House of Peers; and the question is, Whether greater danger be not to be apprehended from its encroachments, than from any other evil which may be the subject of speculation; and whether it is not from this source that the mixed form of government of this country has to dread annihilation? Even now the House of Commons may at once disable the whole machine, and may, by a factious combination, stop the supplies; they may produce by a similar combination a degree of resistance which has been gradually placed more and more beyond the influence of the Crown and of the Government, and of which the effect, in the dissolution of the Government, may be instantaneous and unexpected. These manœuvres may be brought into play in rapid succession, and may totally deprive the executive authorities of their power of action, or suspend it at most critical periods, when the safety of the empire may depend upon the support to be given to that power of action. All this would seem to point out the inexpediency, not to say the insecurity, of rendering the House of Commons more *popular* than it already is in the materials of its composition, by the substitution of a representation of *numbers* for one of *property*. That *equilibrium* of the three estates, which it is so essential to preserve in their just and proper bearings relatively upon each other, would be destroyed. The House of Commons would acquire an undue preponderance in the scale; and the consequence, sooner or later, would be a democracy in its worst form.

The King has thus stated at length, and without reserve, the feelings and the sentiments with which he approached this perilous question; and he has been induced to do so from a desire that he should not be considered as having lightly and inconsiderately given his concurrence to the measure which has been submitted to him; and also because he felt that this full statement of the opinions he had entertained, and still entertains, would give greater value to his sanction of what had been proposed to him by Earl Grey, inasmuch as it would show that, serious as were his apprehensions and his objections, they have been removed by the nature and character of the proposed measure, and because the declaration of a sanction so obtained must convey to his Government with it the assurance of His Majesty's determination to afford to them his utmost countenance and support in the furtherance of this arduous and important undertaking. It must convince them that he is dealing fairly by them, and that he does not shrink from the responsibility of avowing his sentiments before his decision shall be called for by the results of the discussion which is approaching, when it might be supposed to rest upon the opinions and views of others. His Majesty's assent being given upon due and mature consideration of all the bearings of this question, ought, in his opinion, to be given in so unreserved a manner, as to secure his Ministers its full benefit.

The King does not consider it necessary to enter into the detail of the various provisions of the Bills, but will confine what he has still to say to some remarks upon the report made to Earl Grey which accompanied these Bills.

His Majesty admits the correctness of the principle, and the policy of 'not conceding so much only as might for the moment evade or stifle the demand for a more extensive alteration in the existing system;' and he considers it desirable 'to effect such a permanent settlement of the question as will no longer render its agitation subservient to the designs of the factious and discontented.' His Majesty concurs in the opinion offered in the report, that 'the plan of Reform ought to be of such a scope and description as to satisfy all reasonable demands, and remove at once and for ever, all rational grounds of complaint from the minds of the intelligent and independent portion of the community;' and he considers it most important that 'an effectual check should thus be opposed to that restless spirit of innovation, which aims in secret at nothing less than the overthrow of all our institutions, and even the Throne itself.'

His Majesty approves of the disfranchisement of all boroughs, the population of which amounts to less than 2000 inhabitants; and that those whose population amounts to less than 4000 should be deprived of one Member.

The King approves, for the reasons assigned in the report, of the extension of the elective franchise to all householders within the town, or borough and parish (in the latter class of boroughs as well as in those cities and boroughs where the right of voting is enjoyed by close corporations), who are entitled by the late act to serve on juries; those who are rated to the relief of the poor, or to the inhabited house-tax, at 20*l.* per annum; it being also understood that no person shall in future *acquire* a right of voting for a county by virtue of any property situated in any borough sending Members to Parliament.

He approves of granting representatives to all large and populous towns of more than 10,000 inhabitants, the right of voting to be vested in householders of 20*l*. per annum.

His Majesty approves of giving additional Members to counties whose population amounts to more than 150,000 inhabitants, dividing them into districts, leaving the forty shillings franchise as it now exists, but enfranchising leaseholders of 50*l*. per annum, and copyholders of 10*l*. per annum.

His Majesty approves of the proposals which have in view a diminution of the expense of elections, namely:

The enforcement of residence;

The registration of votes;

The increase of the numbers of polling-booths;

The shortening of the duration of the poll;

The taking the poll (in counties) in hundreds or divisions; and His Majesty is induced to waive his objection to shortening the duration of Parliament from seven to five years, in consideration of the shortening of the duration of the poll, and of the arrangements proposed in the Bills, which are calculated, not only to reduce the expense of elections, but to lessen the evils which have hitherto resulted from them. But, although the establishment of Septennial Parliaments is of recent institution, as compared with many other enactments connected with the Representation, His Majesty would not be sorry to learn that his Government had not found it necessary to persist in the proposed change of period.

The King is of opinion that, in an arrangement of which the foundation is the amount of population, it would be very desirable to remove all possibility of objection and doubt, with respect to the correctness of the returns of that population, and therefore that a new census should be taken, as the changes which may have occurred in the relative population, more especially of boroughs and cities, within the last ten years, may, in some cases, cause a material alteration of the numbers stated in the returns on which the arrangement is founded. A new census would also be desirable with reference to the ballots for the Militia.

His Majesty has abstained from objecting to one part of the arrangement—that which leaves the forty shillings franchise as it now exists; because he is aware that there might be considerable difficulty in raising it at once to 10*l.* per annum, which is proposed to constitute in future the qualification for the vote at any county election; but he owns that he would have been better satisfied by the introduction of a provision which should have abolished the forty shillings franchise.

Nor could such a provision be reasonably objected to as inconsistent with the constitutional principle on which the Representation was framed; as it must be considered that, when the right of voting was vested in forty shilling freeholders, the value of that sum far exceeded that which 10*l.*, or even four or five times that sum, bears in the present day. At any rate His Majesty trusts that the rates proposed in the Bills will not be lowered; and that it will be borne in mind that, in order to reconcile conflicting opinions, and to give due attention to the interests of all concerned, the principle adopted should embrace a representation of property as well as one of numbers.

WILLIAM R.

No. 69.

Earl Grey to the King.

Downing Street, Feb. 5, 1831.

Earl Grey presents his humble duty to your Majesty, and has the honour of acknowledging your Majesty's most gracious letter of yesterday.

The full exposition of your Majesty's feelings and opinions on the important question of Parliamentary Reform, concluding with the expression of your Majesty's approbation of the plan which, with the unanimous concurrence of his colleagues, Earl Grey has had the honour of submitting to your Majesty, is the more gratifying to him, as this assent has been given upon due ' and mature consideration of all the bearings of the question, and in such a manner as to secure to your Majesty's Ministers the full benefit of it.' It is unnecessary for Earl Grey to encroach upon your Majesty's time by a detailed reply to the various important points so distinctly stated, and so clearly and so powerfully discussed in your Majesty's letter. In the enlightened view taken by your Majesty of the whole subject, and of all the circumstances connected with it, Earl Grey has the happiness of being able to state that he entirely concurs; and he begs to repeat to your Majesty the assurance, that if he had not been convinced that a measure of this kind was imperiously called for by the circumstances of the times, and might be safely undertaken with a view to the security of your Majesty's crown and to the interests of your people, he never could have been induced to propose it to your Majesty.

On the question of the Ballot, the strong and decided

opinion expressed by your Majesty must operate as a command which Earl Grey feels himself bound to obey, objecting to it on the same grounds which are so forcibly stated by your Majesty. Earl Grey might otherwise, perhaps, have not felt himself at liberty to abandon all the benefits of the measure, if they could not have been obtained without yielding to a condition, which, condemning it as he does, Earl Grey thinks might be so far harmless as to be completely nugatory in destroying the influence against which it is intended to guard.

Earl Grey thinks it necessary to state to your Majesty. for fear of any misapprehension, that it is not proposed to limit the acquisition of a vote in counties in future to a freehold of the annual value of ten pounds. The forty shillings franchise it is intended to leave, as Earl Grey meant to explain to your Majesty, without alteration. There is no doubt that, estimating the value of money on a comparison between the period when this franchise was granted and the present day, a proposal for raising the votes for counties to a higher denomination than that of ten pounds might be contended for; but though in some respects it might be advantageous, Earl Grey is satisfied that the continuance of the forty shillings franchise will operate rather favourably than otherwise for the landed interest. With regard to your Majesty's suggestion of taking a new census, Earl Grey craves permission humbly to submit, that the time it would necessarily take would occasion an inconvenient delay, during which increased agitation and the propagation of dangerous theories might be apprehended; and further, that in taking a new census with a view to this professed object, there might be reason to apprehend that, in some instances at least, the accuracy of the new returns might be affected. The census of 1821 is sufficiently near the present time to afford a reasonable presumption, that it affords a tolerably just estimate of the present state of the population, which may be taken as a satisfactory basis for the principle on which the plan is formed, and without the possibility of a suspicion that any inaccuracy can have crept into it from interested motives.

Earl Grey cannot conclude this very imperfect acknowledgment of your Majesty's considerate and enlightened attention to this important question, without expressing the satisfaction and comfort which he has derived from so full and so candid an exposition of your Majesty's sentiments. He has the same acknowledgment to make with respect to every communication, whether written or personal, with which your Majesty has honoured him since his admission into your service, affording him the inestimable advantage of a full knowledge of your Majesty's views as to the measures which he brings before you; and a perfect security that, when once sanctioned by your Majesty, Earl Grey and the rest of your Majesty's Ministers will have your Majesty's full support in carrying them into execution.

All which, &c. GREY.

No. 70.

Sir H. Taylor to Earl Grey.

(Private.) Brighton, Feb. 5, 1831.

My dear Lord,—I have had the honour to receive and lay before the King your Lordship's letter of yesterday, and that enclosed from Lord Anglesey, which I return. I could feel no hesitation in reading the latter part to His Majesty after the communication he had made to you yesterday; and I am sensible of the satisfaction His Majesty derives from the unreserved manner in which your Lordship communicates with him, and of the importance of maintaining a confidence so happily established reciprocally.

The King naturally expects that there will be in some quarters a strong opposition on the question of Reform; but he trusts that it will prove limited as to numbers, when the measure is brought forward and its provisions are known.

Lord Palmerston mentions having shown you a letter from the King on the affairs of Belgium, and will probably show you one from me to him, of this date, with reference to it. I hope that His Majesty misconceived the Thirteenth Protocol, and the instruction to Lord Granville which accompanied it; and he could hardly bring himself to believe that the assent to the Duc de Nemours' election *had* been given, but, as I mentioned to Lord Palmerston, I was desired to read the documents three times to him, and he still retained his construction of them, in which I concurred.

The King has ordered me to say to your Lordship, that he forgot to request you would direct a warrant to be prepared *renewing* to the Princess Sophia of Gloucester the appointment of Keeper of Greenwich Park, by virtue of which H. R. H. holds the Ranger's house at Blackheath during His Majesty's pleasure.

I have, &c.   H. TAYLOR.

No. 71.

Sir H. Taylor to Earl Grey.

(Private.) Brighton, Feb. 6, 1831.

My dear Lord,—Although the King's answer to your Lordship's letter and to Lord Althorp's will not be ready to go by this day's messenger, I will not delay acknowledging the receipt of that with which you have favoured me, and acquainting you that His Majesty's reply will be perfectly satisfactory upon every point contained in both, and will convey his acquiescence in all you have submitted to him.

His Majesty was aware that my letter could not have reached you in time to prevent Lord Althorp's statement of what had passed on the subject of the outfit for the Queen, and he is very sensible of the kind feeling which suggested it. The disinclination shown in the House of Commons to have entertained any proposal to that effect, supposing it had been made, has however produced a very painful impression upon His Majesty, as has what passed respecting the Pension List. He has ordered me to make a general allusion to it in his letter to your Lordship, and to enter more largely into the subject in his reply to Lord Althorp.

Having to write and to copy these letters, I fear that they cannot go earlier than by the mail.

I have, &c. H. TAYLOR.

No. 72.

The King to Earl Grey.

Brighton, Feb. 6, 1831.

The King has been much gratified by the assurance conveyed in Earl Grey's letter of yesterday, that His Majesty's letter of the 4th instant, on the subject of the proposed measure of Parliamentary Reform, had proved so satisfactory to him, and by learning that Earl Grey entirely concurs in the view taken by His Majesty of the whole subject, and of all the circumstances connected with it. The King had indeed anticipated that concurrence in his sentiments from what had already passed between him and Earl Grey, and had not mistaken his feeling with respect to the introduction of the measure at this period.

With regard to the election by Ballot, the King has less hesitation in stating that he dreads the introduction of it under any modification, as Earl Grey has assured him that he objects to it upon the same grounds which have been stated by His Majesty; and as he fears that, however harmless its operation might seem to have been rendered, the inclination to the establishment of a preponderating popular influence of which so many proofs are daily afforded, would very soon defeat the endeavours to keep within due and safe bounds this and any other arrangements tending to the increase of that influence.

The King had, as it appears from Earl Grey's letter, mistaken one of the provisions of the Bill, as he imagined that although the existing forty shillings franchise would not be abolished, no vote in counties would be in future acquired by a freehold of the annual value of less than ten pounds. His Majesty is satisfied that this question has been well considered by Earl Grey, and is by no means disposed to object to the continuance of the forty shillings franchise, as Lord Grey considers that it will operate rather favourably than otherwise for the landed interest. Nor did His Majesty, by any observation conveyed in his letter of the 4th instant, mean to restrict his Government from lowering the qualification in cities and boroughs to ten pounds, if it should be found necessary to take this course, though His Majesty would, with Earl Grey, greatly prefer the higher qualification.

His Majesty leaves it to the discretion of Earl Grey to follow the course which he may consider most advisable with respect to the duration of the Parliament, though there may possibly be some advantage in introducing the usual term of seven years into the Bill, with a view to a compromise for five years.

His Majesty has given due consideration to Earl Grey's objections to taking a new census, with reference to the measure in contemplation, and is satisfied of their validity.

He must, upon this occasion, repeat to Earl Grey, that he may place full reliance upon His Majesty's firm determination to afford to him his utmost support towards the prosecution of his zealous, able, and honourable exertions for the service of his King and country, in a period of unexampled difficulty; and he acknowledges the satisfaction he derives from the unreserved communication which has been established between himself and his Government, alive as His Majesty is to the importance of it under circumstances which render the existence of any Government, and the maintenance of any authority, a question of so much difficulty and uncertainty.

His Majesty cannot conceal from Earl Grey, that he has received a very painful impression from the disposition shown in the House of Commons,* as reported by Viscount Althorp to himself, and as noticed in Earl Grey's letter to Sir Herbert Taylor; and he refers Earl Grey to the expression of his sentiments to Lord Althorp on the subject.

WILLIAM R.

No. 73.

Earl Grey to Sir H. Taylor.

Downing Street, Feb. 7, 1831.

My dear Sir,—I have been so long delayed at the Cabinet upon the Budget and other matters, that being now under the necessity of going to the House of Lords, I cannot by this night's post write to the King in acknowledgment of the very gratifying letter I have this morning received from him.

Will you have the goodness, therefore, to make my excuses to His Majesty for this omission. I must, on the same account, defer my answer to yours.

The King will have received from Lord Palmerston

---

* Apparently on the question whether persons in the enjoyment of pensions on the civil list could properly be deprived of them; but the letter to Sir H. Taylor referred to is missing.

the very satisfactory accounts we have received from Paris, of the measures taken by the French Government on receiving the news of the election of the Duc de Nemours. The sudden change of tone by M. Sebastiani is rather amusing. I attribute it to the receipt of dispatches in the meantime from Talleyrand and Flahault, stating the manner in which their communications had been received here.

* * * * *

The King's letter to Lord Althorp is irresistible both in feeling and argument. My own feelings on this subject are so strong, that if the House of Commons decides upon reducing the pensions,* I should be very much inclined to retire from the Government, if I did not think it might be injurious to His Majesty's interests. To His Majesty I owe a debt of gratitude which I never can repay; and my first wish must be, at what ever personal sacrifice short of that which would render my services useless, to devote myself entirely to his service.

I am, &c.   GREY.

---

* It is proper to explain, that while my father was of opinion that many pensions had in former years been improperly granted, he considered that to withdraw them from the persons in actual enjoyment of them, and upon whom they had been conferred in the exercise of a power given to the Sovereign by Parliament, and in accordance with a practice universally recognised at the time, would cause so much hardship to individuals, and be so substantially unjust, that it was his duty strenuously to maintain these existing pensions, though he was ready to consent to any regulations Parliament might consider necessary, to prevent abuses in granting them for the future. The pensions in question, I may add, had almost without exception been granted by Administrations to which my father had been opposed.

No. 74.

Earl Grey to Sir H. Taylor.

Downing Street, Feb. 8, 1831.

Dear Sir,—I have taken the necessary steps for issuing a warrant, in obedience to His Majesty's commands, for renewing to the Princess Sophia of Gloucester the appointment of Keeper of the Greenwich Parks. I send in a box, which will accompany this, copies of the Bill and papers respecting the proposed measure of Parliamentary Reform, which His Majesty desired to have; and I have also enclosed with them some alterations that it has been found necessary to make in the Irish Bill, which you will be easily able to insert in the original draft by means of the references. I have also enclosed the copy of the King's letter to Sir James Graham, which you wished to have returned to you.

In the King's letters on the Reform business, he has always spoken of the objection to the Ballot as if it had been made solely by me. I should be much obliged to you therefore, on any convenient opportunity, to explain the matter to him as it really is. This mode of election was not proposed, even by the framers of the report, as one to which they were themselves partial, but as a concession which would greatly facilitate the raising of the elective franchise in cities and boroughs, and that this would of itself diminish the evils which might be apprehended from the adoption of the Ballot. When it came to be discussed in the Cabinet, the objections to it were not more strongly stated by me than by the Chancellor, Lord Lansdowne, and others; and the decision in respect to it was taken by the whole Cabinet, though with an opinion still entertained by some, on the grounds which I have already stated, that it might be expedient.

I have the most satisfactory accounts of the impression made last night on the House of Commons by Lord Althorp's stout and manly expression of his decided opinion, that a reduction of the existing pensions would be contrary to all policy and justice. I had felt so much annoyed by what had previously passed on this subject, that I had directed Lord Howick to make a declaration to the same effect, as the best way of stating my feelings upon it; but this was rendered unnecessary by the effect of Lord Althorp's speech; and he very properly, in compliance with the advice of Sir James Graham, desisted from saying anything. I do hope, therefore, that we shall get through this very unpleasant business; but I am not by any means sure, that the fear of their constituents, and the disposition of great numbers in the House of Commons, may not bring it on us again. If this should happen, I am prepared to resist it, if His Majesty approves, at all hazard. I have not another moment.

I remain, &c. GREY.

No. 75.

Sir H. Taylor to Earl Grey.

(Private.) Brighton, Feb. 8, 1831.

My dear Lord,—I do not delay acknowledging the receipt of your Lordship's letter of yesterday, which I have read to the King.

* * * * * *

I cannot help telling you that no person could possibly express herself with greater good sense and good humour than the Queen did to me on the subject of the Outfit; giving to your Lordship the credit which is so justly due to you for your feeling upon it, and ascribing the disappointment, not to want of regard or consideration for herself, but to the temper of the times, which, she justly observed, seemed to have found its way into the minds of the representatives of the people.

Her Majesty will, of course, avail herself of the King's liberal offer to the extent only which may be beyond her own resources, and her means of avoiding embarrassment.

Your Lordship will learn from the King's letter to Lord Palmerston, how highly he approves of the whole course of his Government in the negotiation about Belgium, and how much he ascribes the altered tone of the French Government to the firmness and consistency of his own Government, and to the ability and dexterity with which the negotiation has been conducted by Lord Palmerston.

I have however, upon no occasion, seen His Majesty more pleased than upon learning that you approved of his letter to Lord Althorp, and that you did not seem to think that he had expressed his feelings too strongly. His Majesty was, indeed, persuaded that your Lordship entered into them from principle, and from the attachment of which, as well as zeal for his service and solicitude for the dignity of the Crown, you have given him ample proof. His Majesty observed that he was sensible that your Lordship could derive no satisfaction from being placed in the direction of Public Affairs in the present state and temper of the country, nor any comfort, except from the conviction that you are discharging a most important duty, though a very ungrateful one; but that he anxiously hopes that no circumstance arising out of this state of things, nor any other, will deprive him of the benefit of your services, and of your advice and support: That he considers that you are embarked in the same boat with him; and that he may rely upon your principles, and he hopes also upon the influence of your character, for support in his endeavours to maintain the Monarchy and the Aristocracy of the country, in that position which the Constitution has assigned to them, and to protect both against the encroachments which are daily attempted.

If any sovereign can hope to stem the revolutionary torrent, I think the King may. He is free from fancies and prejudices; he possesses firmness without obstinacy, and is therefore quite open to conviction upon points on which he may be advised by those whose judgment and principles he rightly appreciates, to concede so much as shall appear necessary and expedient, in order to conciliate, and to prevent greater mischief; and the general view he takes of subjects is disinterested, and at all times guided by an anxious desire to discharge correctly and honourably the duties of his high station, rather than by considerations of personal interest and personal gratification. While such are the principles and the motives which influence the conduct of the Sovereign, he can never embarrass his Ministers; and your Lordship will allow me to express a sincere hope, that the exertions of His Majesty and of his present Minister may long be combined for the welfare and interest of the country.

I have, &c.   H. TAYLOR.

No. 76.

Earl Grey to the King.

Downing Street, Feb. 8, 1831.

Earl Grey, with his humble duty to your Majesty, has in the first place again to entreat your Majesty to accept the excuse which he has already offered through Sir H. Taylor, for not having sooner acknowledged your Majesty's most gracious letter of the 6th inst.

It has given Earl Grey the greatest pleasure to find that his last communication respecting the proposed measure of Reform of Parliament has also met with your Majesty's approbation. With the assurance of your Majesty's support, Earl Grey is very sanguine in his hopes of being able to carry this important measure successfully through Parliament. For the gratifying exposition of your Majesty's continued confidence, Earl Grey can only offer in return the humble assurance of his increasing gratitude.

Earl Grey is not at all surprised that your Majesty should have received a very painful impression from the disposition shown in the House of Commons, as described in your Majesty's letter to him and Viscount Althorp. In that impression Earl Grey participates to the fullest extent, and has left no means in his power unemployed to arrest and check a feeling which would push economy to an extent that would be equally inconsistent with equity, and with the consideration which is due to your Majesty, and to the character of the Government.

From the accounts which Earl Grey has received of what passed in the House of Commons last night, things seem to be taking a better turn; and in consequence of the firm and honourable expression of his sentiments by Viscount Althorp, Earl Grey is willing to entertain the hope, that the House of Commons will not proceed to the unjust and unprecedented measure of meddling with existing pensions. But it cannot be concealed, not only that there is a very unfortunate disposition prevailing as to matters of this nature, but that this disposition is powerfully acted upon by the popular feeling, which has been excited by the publication of the Pension List, and the comments upon it in the public papers.

All which, &c. GREY.

No. 77.

Sir H. Taylor to Earl Grey.

(Private.) Brighton, Feb. 9, 1831.

My dear Lord,—I have the honour to enclose the King's answer to your Lordship's letter of yesterday, in which you will find His Majesty has noticed and replied to some parts of your letter to me, which I submitted to him.

His Majesty has entered so fully into the question of Reform, and the proceedings in the House of Commons with regard to the Pensions, in his letter to your Lordship and to Lord Althorp, that I need only repeat that all that has passed, so far as his Government is concerned, has been very agreable to him; and that the manner in which Lord Althorp has taken up and met what has been said on the latter subject, has in a great measure relieved Him from the uneasiness he felt. He seems, however, to be strongly impressed, as your Lordship appears to be, with the necessity of making a stand upon this question, which, in his opinion, involves the constitutional attributes of the monarchy, and the existence of the influence which connects the Sovereign with the Government; and his Majesty feels this the more strongly, as he cannot but view the attempt to carry the point as one feature of a systematic attack upon the power and prerogatives of the Crown. Great and *successful* pains have been taken to mislead and poison the public mind on the Pension subject. The whole principle has been wilfully misrepresented, for one of the objects of the provision was to enable the Sovereign to do *gratuitous* acts of kindness and benevolence. It was, I conceive, never intended, nor until this moment ever considered, that he was to be limited in these grants by reference to considerations connected only with public service. There may have been, and doubtless have been, abuses; and your Lordship will observe, that the King is by no means disposed to place those beyond the reach of future control and checks; but he dreads the idea of being called upon to visit the sins of his forefathers upon the objects of their favour and benevolence.

I believe I have correctly stated the King's feeling on this subject; but it must be very difficult to determine upon the nature of the check, or *where* it shall rest. If vested in the House of Commons, it would be in fact to make over to that body the Prerogative of the Crown; and the House of Commons is quite disposed to grasp at that, and at the whole executive power of the Government.

I have, &c. H. TAYLOR.

No. 78.

The King to Earl Grey.

Brighton, Feb. 9, 1831.

The King desires Earl Grey will feel assured, that it was unnecessary that he should make any excuse for not having replied on the following day to His Majesty's letter of the 6th instant, as His Majesty is too well aware of the pressure of his occupations at this period, to have expected an earlier communication. He must indeed add, that he is often surprised how Earl Grey can find time for all he does, and for the immediate and ample communications he makes to the King, or for His Majesty's information.

His Majesty repeats to Earl Grey, that he is perfectly satisfied with every explanation he has conveyed to him on the subject of the Reform Bills, since they were first submitted to His Majesty, including the alterations made in the Irish Bill this day received, which appear to him very judicious. The subject has, as before, engaged much of his thoughts; and he is more and more convinced that Earl Grey has acted most wisely in bringing it forward without delay; and that the provisions introduced in the Bills are well calculated to effect all that is correct and necessary, without entailing any of those evils which had been apprehended from the introduction of the measure by those who wished to have gone greater lengths.

The King notices, with very sincere satisfaction, what Earl Grey has said in his letter of yesterday to Sir Herbert Taylor, on the subject of Election by Ballot; as he does not deny that he had conceived it to be one of the propositions suggested by the framers of the report, and excluded by Earl Grey, and that His Majesty imagined that measure to have found other advocates in his Cabinet.

The King rejoices extremely to learn that he has in this laboured under a false impression, which he had admitted with concern; and he repeats, that although there may be grounds which may render some concessions expedient, he trusts that the object may be attained without introducing a measure which is admitted to be objectionable in principle, and which does not appear to him susceptible of any modification that can divest it of that objection.

All that Earl Grey has expressed in his letter to the King, and in his communications to Sir Herbert Taylor, with respect to the proceedings in the House of Commons and to His Majesty's notice of them, in his letter to Lord Althorp, has been very gratifying to His Majesty. He owns to Lord Grey that his feelings had been very strongly excited by the appearance of a disposition in the House of Commons, and by the apprehension of the possible success of an attempt to call upon him to reduce to the extent of more than one-half the *existing* pensions; and it was most satisfactory to him to learn, that he was not considered by Earl Grey to have expressed himself too strongly upon this occasion, and that his feelings corresponded with His Majesty's. The sentiments expressed by Viscount Althorp on the same subject, both in his communications to the King and in his observations to the House, have also given His Majesty great pleasure; and he has endeavoured to assure Lord Althorp how highly he approves of his gentlemanly and manly tone upon this occasion, as of the general course he is taking in the discharge of an arduous and, His Majesty fears, a very disagreeable task. Nor is the King less sensible of Earl Grey's kind and considerate feeling in desiring Lord Howick to make a declaration to the same effect, if it had been found necessary.

His Majesty is, however, sensible of the difficulty which may still arise from the discussion of this and other subjects, in the present temper and feeling of the House of Commons, as well as of the mischief which has been produced by the publication of the Pension List, and the comments upon it; and he feels the necessity of assuming and maintaining a high tone upon some of these points, in order to secure and encourage those who may be wavering, or who may mistake the intentions of his Government. Earl Grey will, however, do His Majesty the justice to believe, that he does not wish any feeling he may have expressed to be considered as conveying the least desire to contend for the continued exercise of any prerogative or influence, or for the uncontrolled power of dispensing favours which may be converted into *abuse*. His Majesty is not inclined to object to any checks which may be devised to prevent the *abuse* of that which the Constitution has given to the Sovereign, though he may reasonably protest against being debarred from the just and correct exercise of those rights which have been hitherto considered the prerogatives and the privileges of the Sovereign of this country, and which have always been deemed essential to the support of *any* Government.

WILLIAM R.

No. 79.

Earl Grey to Sir H. Taylor.

(Private.)   Downing Street, Feb. 11, 1831.

My dear Sir,—Having no particular communication to make to the King, I have abstained from troubling him with the repetition of my grateful feelings for all the kindness and condescension manifested in his letter of the 9th, which I had the honour of receiving yesterday. I trust to you, therefore, to make this acknowledgment, with a proper expression of my humble duty.

I have also to thank you for your letters of the 8th and 9th, which have, as usual, afforded me the greatest satisfaction. It was most gratifying to me to know that the painful communication I was under the necessity of making respecting the Outfit, had been received with so much considerate kindness by the Queen. Her remark on the temper of the times, and on its influence on the House of Commons, is most just. In truth a disposition to reduce the means in the possession of the Executive Government has prevailed, more or less, at all times, and has broken out at particular seasons, with more or less violence, as opportunity might offer or distress excite. Even in the middle of the last century, the House of Commons was occupied with motions and discussions such as these which we daily witness on the subject of Pensions. With respect to these, I receive, every day, additional proofs of the deep impression that has been made on the public mind. It is not only the clamorous part of the public that urges their reduction: men of sober character, and of the better orders of the community, including numbers of those who have hitherto supported Tory politics, join in the attempt. It has come to my knowledge within these two days, that many opulent merchants in the City of London had declined signing the resolutions in support of the Government, in consequence of our refusing to reduce the pensions. I believe the report of the Committee will be satisfactory, but I cannot have any assurance that the decision of the House will be in accordance with the opinion of Ministers. Nothing can be more just or more wise and liberal than the disposition expressed by His Majesty to concur in any useful and necessary provisions against future abuse; and I am made happy by the assurance that the conduct of Lord Althorp and myself on this matter has been viewed by him with approbation.

I enclose a letter from Lord Anglesey. I think what he says about the prosecutions will be satisfactory to His Majesty. O'Connell is, I believe, in a great fright; and I suspect that he is conscious of being in danger of discoveries which might lead to much more serious consequences than the present prosecutions.

* * * * *

Prince Leopold has been so good as to invite me to-morrow to Claremont, and to stay Sunday. If I can get away, I mean to take advantage of this opportunity to get a little rest and a little fresh air, which are very necessary to me.

I am, &c. GREY.

No. 80.

Sir H. Taylor to Earl Grey.

(Private.) Brighton, Feb. 12, 1831.

My dear Lord,—I have had the honour to receive your Lordship's letter of yesterday, and submit it to the King, as well as that from Lord Anglesey, which I beg to return. What his Lordship says on the subject of the prosecutions, and of O'Connell, has proved very satisfactory to His Majesty.

* * * * *

His Majesty readily admitted that the disposition to reduce the influence of the Crown, the power of the Executive Government, and, with both of course, the means of granting pensions, &c., had often prevailed; and he had not forgotten what passed in the House of Commons in the middle of the last century; but he observed that much had since been done towards reducing that power and influence, and towards throwing it into the scale of the House of Commons: That he had no objections to the reduction of that of the Crown, by the abolition of sinecures, the restricting of pensions, or the correction of any thing that could be called *abuse*, provided the equilibrium of the Three Estates could be maintained; but that he dreaded the Democracy, towards which he conceived the constitution of the country to be gradually approaching.

His Majesty was concerned to read what your Lordship says on the subject of the Pensions, and the feeling which prevails even among men of sober character and the better orders of the community; and he cannot account for it otherwise than by their mistaking the question, as he conceives it to be impossible that men of principle and of equitable feeling can expect that he or his Government should readily agree to the reduction of *existing* pensions.

Your Lordship will probably have learnt from Mr. Stanley that his election had been most satisfactory. Some of my friends at Windsor had anticipated difficulty, but I gave no credit to them.

I hope you have been able to get away, and that the weather will favour your visit to Claremont.

I have, &c. H. TAYLOR.

No. 81.

Earl Grey to the King.

Downing Street, Feb. 14, 1831.

Earl Grey having been detained late at the Cabinet on Saturday, was prevented writing to your Majesty before he left town for Claremont. Your Majesty, however, has been fully informed, both by Viscount Althorp and the Lord Chancellor, of all that passed in the House of Commons, on the discussion of the Budget on Friday last.

Yesterday a meeting was held at Lord Althorp's

house, of the principal Members of the House of Commons who support the Government. It was numerously attended, and the disposition manifested by them most satisfactory. It was agreed, however, in consequence of the impression made on the public against the proposed tax on transfers of property, that it would be necessary to give it up. This resolution has been confirmed, upon full consideration, by your Majesty's servants assembled in Cabinet this morning, and will be announced by Viscount Althorp to-day in the House of Commons. Earl Grey cannot but regret the necessity that compels your Majesty's Ministers to take this step, believing as he does the measure, which they have been thus obliged to abandon, to have been well calculated to promote the public advantage. Had it appeared to Earl Grey to be justly chargeable as a breach of public faith, he never would have consented to its being proposed; but not being able to regard it in this light, and thinking that, for the relief of the industrious classes of your Majesty's subjects, some contribution might justly be required from that interest, which alone, in the midst of general distress, has been enjoying increased advantages, to remit some of the most inconvenient taxes, he concurred most cordially in the plan proposed by Viscount Althorp for the accomplishment of that object. In this opinion it has been a great comfort and satisfaction to Earl Grey, to learn from Viscount Althorp that your Majesty concurred.

Earl Grey is happy to turn from this mortifying occurrence, to the satisfactory intelligence received this morning from the Marquis of Anglesey. As this will be communicated to your Majesty with all its details by Viscount Melbourne, Earl Grey will not trespass on your Majesty's time, further than to offer his humble congratulations on the complete vindication of the proceedings of your Majesty's Government in Ireland, by Mr. O'Connell withdrawing his plea of 'Not guilty' on the fourteen first counts in the indictment; and the proof it affords of his own consciousness, that the violation of the laws for which he had been arraigned could not be defended.

All which, &c. GREY.

No. 82.
Earl Grey to Sir H. Taylor.

Downing Street, Feb. 15, 1831.

My dear Sir,—Every thing went off last night as well as possible in both Houses. It is not pleasant to be under the necessity of making a retreat, but it was done, I am confident, without any loss of character, or of our future efficiency in the King's service. The feeling of the House of Lords was, according to all appearance, quite with me; so much so, that I have no doubt the measure would have been carried there without difficulty. I have nothing to-day from Ireland, except a short note from Lord Anglesey not worth sending.

* * * * * *

An opposition has been got up against Lord Duncannon* in the county of Kilkenny, of the result of which

---

* On his offering himself for re-election, after vacating his seat by accepting the office of First Commissioner of Woods and Forests.

there would, I am told, be no cause for apprehension, if it were not for the expense of the contest, which Duncannon is unable to meet, and with respect to which we have no means of assisting him, unless some of our rich friends could be induced to subscribe.

I am, &c. GREY.

No. 83.

The King to Earl Grey.

Brighton, Feb. 15, 1831.

The King has learnt with regret, though without surprise, from Earl Grey's letter of yesterday, that in consequence of the impression made upon the public against the proposed tax on transfers of property, his Government had determined to give it up. Earl Grey will have learnt from the King's letter to Viscount Althorp, that his opinion was favourable to this tax in every view of its character; and no one can be more thoroughly convinced than the King is, that Lord Grey is the last man who would propose any measure (however otherwise advantageous), which could be justly chargeable as a breach of public faith. His Majesty laments that some means cannot be devised of imposing upon the fundholders a portion of those burthens which are borne by the landholders and the industrious classes of his subjects. Earl Grey will also have learnt that, in anticipation of this occurrence, His Majesty had considered that a less reduction might be taken in the duty on tobacco, and he has learnt with satisfaction that this expedient has been resorted to.

The communications from Lord Anglesey, which Viscount Melbourne has submitted to the King, are extremely gratifying to His Majesty, sensible as he is that his Government could not ever possibly have hoped for a more decided confirmation of the correctness and wisdom of their proceedings than that which the course adopted by Mr. O'Connell has afforded; and His Majesty entertains sanguine expectations that their proceedings will have a very beneficial effect upon the general state of Ireland.

WILLIAM R.

No. 84.

The King to Earl Grey.

Brighton, Feb. 19, 1831.

The King has received Earl Grey's letter of yesterday, enclosing one from Lord Anglesey, which he returns, and which His Majesty has read with much satisfaction. His Majesty will be glad to communicate with Earl Grey, in London, on the subject of the Representative Peers of Scotland and Ireland. He has long been of opinion that they should, under any contingencies, be distinct, namely, sixteen for Scotland and twenty-eight for Ireland; and that the Representative Peers of either country should vacate their seats *as such*, upon becoming Peers of the United Kingdoms.

His Majesty's view rests upon the general principle of what is fairly due to both countries under their union with England, and has no reference to the feelings or politics of the individuals who may be benefited by it; but he trusts, with Lord Anglesey, that his Government would be strengthened by the adoption of it; and at any rate it would relieve His Majesty from some claims from Scotch and Irish Lords for promotion to the English Peerage.　　　　　　　　　　WILLIAM R.

No. 85.

Earl Grey to Sir H. Taylor.

Downing Street, Feb. 21, 1831.

My dear Sir,—As a letter from hence could only have added to your trouble, by reaching you at the moment you were leaving Brighton, I deferred acknowledging those which I received from you yesterday till to-day. I shall be obliged to you, therefore, to state to the King the reason of my not having sent an answer to His Majesty's letter of the 19th, and, having nothing material to communicate to His Majesty, of my now taking this mode of acknowledging it.

I felt equal pain, however, on being informed of the painful impression which Lord Althorp's communication with respect to the proceedings of the Civil List Committee had made upon His Majesty. I am not surprised at these feelings, acknowledging, as I do without reserve, their justice, and thinking that the reductions proposed on these parts of the expenditure of the Civil List now under consideration are consistent neither with true policy, nor with the grateful sense which ought to be entertained of what is, on many accounts, so justly due to His Majesty. Lord Althorp will have explained to His Majesty, that he meant, in no sense, to offer any justification of the proceedings of the Committee. But it is too true that public opinion, even amongst the most respectable classes, has acquired a force on matters of this nature which it will be very difficult, if not impossible, to resist. I feel myself bound, however, not more by duty than by my own feelings and opinions, to give it, on those points which are connected with the comfort and dignity of His Majesty, and with the permanent interests of the Crown, all the resistance in my power, though the result should be the necessity of tendering to His Majesty my resignation of the office which he has so graciously committed to my care, and my humble services which he has received with so much favour and indulgence. I have not yet seen the dispatches which have of course accompanied the private letter which I enclose, and which, though His Majesty will be in possession of all the information which has reached the Foreign Office, I thought might not be uninteresting to him.

I met Prince Talleyrand and Madame de Dino at dinner yesterday, at Prince Esterhazy's: they seemed both very low at the present state of affairs in France; and well they may; for, if the War-party succeed to the government, their immediate recall is certain, and their safety in returning to France, perhaps, somewhat doubtful.

You will have seen that an indictment has been preferred against Cobbett by the Attorney-General, and a bill found by the Grand Jury. It is for a very infamous excitement to burning, which was anterior to the number of the Register sent to me by the King.

This would have been done sooner, had it not been for the absence of the Attorney-General at the time of the Special Commissions, and there having been no Old Bailey Sessions since.

Will you have the goodness to ask of the King permission for me to wait upon him at any hour to-morrow, that may be most convenient to His Majesty. If I may venture to make such a suggestion, the time that would best suit my business here would be from half-past two till the hour when the House of Lords meets.

GREY.

No. 86.

The King to Earl Grey.

Windsor Castle, March 3, 1831.

The King forgot to mention to Earl Grey, when he saw him yesterday, a doubt which had occurred to him, whether the Committees of the House of Commons upon the Civil List and Salaries are justified, by the principles and the spirit of the Constitution, in their usurpation of functions which appear to His Majesty *constitutionally* to belong to the Government of the State alone. His Majesty is confident it will be found, that the history of this country has never before exhibited an instance wherein a Committee of the House of Commons has presumed to dictate to the Sovereign *how* he is to conduct his Civil List in all its minute details, and the amount of the salaries which he is to grant to each and every one of his own personal servants; and it appears to the King very desirable that the opinion of the

Crown Lawyers and the Lord Chancellor should be taken privately, whether the House of Commons is invested by the laws and the constitution of the country with the powers of doing that which they (their Committees) are now doing, in order that when the question and the resolutions of the Committees come to be discussed in the House, the Ministers of the Crown may be prepared to maintain its rights against any attempt to invade them, which may be shown to be illegal and unconstitutional.

His Majesty may possibly feel increased anxiety on this subject, from observing in the report of the debate of Tuesday evening, that one of the avowed objects of the proposition for the Reform in Parliament is to give to the People an *exclusive* influence over the House of Commons. If such be its effect, the authority which the Committees appear to His Majesty to be usurping, will be transferred from the Crown to the people.

The King, having learnt that the Earl of Roden has resigned the situation of Lord of the Bed-chamber, has appointed Lord Saye and Sele, and has directed the Groom of the Stole to cause the appointment to be gazetted to-morrow.

WILLIAM R.

No. 87.

The King to Earl Grey.

Windsor Castle, March 3, 1831.

The King acknowledges the receipt of Earl Grey's letter of this day, and is very sensible of his attention in sending him so early a report of the continued debate upon Lord John Russell's motion, in the satisfactory result of which His Majesty takes so warm an interest, fully sensible as he is of its importance to the peace and tranquillity of the country, and to the stability of his Government.

His Majesty rejoices to learn from Earl Grey that, according to all the information that has reached him, the measure has been received with general approbation out of doors, and that it has had the effect of checking the cry in favour of Ballot, Universal Suffrage, and Annual Parliaments, to which his Majesty had so distinctly declared that he *never* would consent. He earnestly hopes with Earl Grey, that this important measure may tend to the peace and prosperity of his people, which have been the objects of his earnest solicitude since Providence has committed them to his rule.

WILLIAM R.

No. 88.

Earl Grey to the King.

Downing Street, March 4, 1831.

Earl Grey has the honour humbly to acknowledge your Majesty's most gracious letters of yesterday.

In obedience to your Majesty's commands, Earl Grey will lose no time in submitting to the Lord Chancellor and to the Law Officers of the Crown, the point on which it is your Majesty's wish that their opinion should be privately taken. In the meantime, Earl

Grey craves leave humbly to observe, that he does not conceive that the Committee of the House of Commons can have raised a pretension to dictate to 'the Sovereign, how he is to conduct his Civil List in all its minute details, and the amount of the salaries which he is to grant to each and every one of his personal servants.' Such a pretension, Earl Grey would be one of the first to resist; but he humbly submits that the inquiry of the Committee with respect to the expenses of the Civil List, in order to ascertain the amount which may be required for the maintenance of the dignity of the Crown, may be defended on other grounds: and though Earl Grey is prepared to resist the reductions which have been proposed, he feels that he would be wanting in his duty to your Majesty if he were to conceal his opinion, that it might not be for your Majesty's interest that this should be done on the ground of right.

* * * * *

Earl Grey is duly sensible of your Majesty's condescension in complying with the request which he made some time ago, that Lord Saye and Sele should be appointed one of the Lords of your Majesty's Bedchamber; and he has to ask your Majesty's pardon for his forgetfulness, amidst the many important matters which have been pressing on his attention, in not informing your Majesty that, in consequence of some change in his family arrangements, and his wish to pass the greatest part of his time in the country, Lord Saye and Sele did not feel that he could, consistently with a proper discharge of his duty to your Majesty, accept this appointment. Earl Grey ought, therefore, to have withdrawn an application which your Majesty had received with so much favour, for which Lord Saye and Sele is, on his part, most grateful. Under these circumstances, Earl Grey has been under the necessity of desiring the notice of the 'Gazette' to be suspended, and humbly hopes that he may be allowed to recommend to your Majesty some other peer, whose appointment may mark the support given by your Majesty to your confidential servants at this important crisis.

All which, &c.   GREY.

No. 89.

Sir H. Taylor to Earl Grey.

Windsor Castle, March 4, 1831.

My dear Lord,—I have had the honour to submit your Lordship's letter of this day to the King, who observed at once that he was not at all surprised that, when your mind was so much engaged by matters of the utmost and most vital importance, you should forget that Lord Saye and Sele had requested that his application for the situation of Lord of the Bed-chamber should be withdrawn. Your Lordship will learn from His Majesty's reply, that he leaves to you the nomination of Lord Roden's successor, and that you are at liberty to declare and publish the appointment without waiting for His Majesty's confirmation of it, it being the King's earnest desire thereby to mark his determination to support his Government in the most unquestionable and unqualified manner *at this crisis.* It is on this ground chiefly that His Majesty regrets the delay in gazetting the appointment, which had occurred to His

Majesty as being very opportune for that purpose; but he orders me to say that you are at full liberty to make any use you please of this communication.

After this, I need hardly say that the King looks with anxiety to such a termination of the present struggle on the Reform Bill, as shall avert the danger which your Lordship justly apprehends from the effects upon the country of a successful opposition to it. His Majesty has not ceased to be steady and consistent upon this subject. He had wished, as your Lordship wished, that the introduction and the agitation of this 'perilous' question could have been avoided at this period; but being satisfied, by the reasoning submitted to him, of the paramount objections to its postponement, His Majesty entered into the consideration of it with a determination to weigh without prejudice all that should be submitted to him. He was satisfied that the question had, in all its bearings, been fairly brought before him; that, to be effectual, and to prevent its continuing a source and subject of constant agitation, it ought to be introduced upon the principle recommended by your Lordship; and His Majesty gave to it a deliberate and well-considered sanction, accompanied by observations on some of the details which it embraced; and, above all, by a declaration that, having done so, he would not shrink from the avowal and the assertion of that sanction and support. No pledge has ever been more religiously kept and redeemed, nor has a word ever escaped His Majesty which could weaken its effect.

I had not intended troubling your Lordship with these remarks when I began this letter, but the warm interest which I naturally take in the King's proceedings has produced them, and they may perhaps not be unacceptable to you.

I have, &c.   H. TAYLOR.

P.S.—I have read this letter to His Majesty.

No. 90.

The King to Earl Grey.

Windsor Castle, March 4, 1831.

The King acknowledges the receipt of Earl Grey's letter of this day, reporting the proceedings in the Houses of Lords and Commons last night, which appear to be of deep interest in every respect; for it is impossible not to view with anxiety even the notice of a motion which will have the effect of bringing into discussion in the House of Lords the question of Reform in the representation.*

His Majesty would hope, from the number and character of the speakers, that the debate on this stage of the proceedings would not be much protracted; and he is confirmed, by Earl Grey's observation, in his belief that there would be no division on it.

His Majesty is sincerely impressed with the honest and unreserved character of Earl Grey's reports to him upon this anxious question; and assures him that they afford to him, in that respect, ample confirmation of the

* This refers to a notice given in the House of Lords by Lord Wharncliffe, on Thursday, March 3rd, that he would, on the following Monday, move for returns of the population of certain counties, with the view of raising a discussion on the Reform Bill then before the House of Commons.

opinion His Majesty has not ceased to entertain of Earl Grey's honourable and correct course upon every subject which has been matter of communication between them, which has been truly satisfactory to him, and has established, upon solid foundation, that confidence which ought ever to exist between the Sovereign and his Minister, and which, perhaps, was at no period more essential than at the present.

The King is not surprised that Lord Saye and Sele's communication should have escaped Earl Grey's recollection. No apology for it was necessary, and His Majesty regrets only the delay in the notification of a successor to Lord Roden, of Earl Grey's selection. His Majesty approves of his having suspended the notice in the 'Gazette,' and desires he will name and *publish* the nomination of any Peer whom he may wish to recommend, without waiting for His Majesty's confirmation of the appointment.

The King will reply later to the other part of Earl Grey's letter. WILLIAM R.

No. 91.

Earl Grey to Sir H. Taylor.

Downing Street, March 4, 1831.

My dear Sir,—I think it necessary to say, in order to its being communicated to the King or not, as you may think best, that I have heard from others a less favourable account of the state of the Reform question than that which I communicated to His Majesty in my letter of this morning.

Mr. Baring, I hear, produced a good deal of effect, though the last half of his speech was an answer to the first; and the general impression upon the whole was, that he will vote decidedly against the question. Others, however, still think that he left this in some degree of doubt.

I was anxious to make this communication, that I may not be thought to have stated the case too favourably. It is very difficult to form a satisfactory opinion upon the reports of others, and I am quite unequal to the fatigue of attending the debates in the House of Commons myself.

* * * * *

The accounts of the general feeling of the country are more and more favourable to the measure; and but for the timidity of some of those who ought to have more courage, I should have no fear of the ultimate success. If it should fail, there is nothing with which I have to reproach myself; and my only concern is for the difficulty into which the King may be brought, who, after all the kindness I have experienced from him, must be the first object of my solicitude.

I am nearly worn out, and write this under the effect of the annoyance I have experienced from the causes I have referred to; but we have still our best speakers left for to-night's debate (by the way, many people think there may be another adjournment), and I hope to have a better report to send to-morrow.

I am, &c. GREY.

No. 92.

The King to Earl Grey.

Windsor Castle, March 4, 1831.

The King deferred replying to that part of Earl Grey's letter which relates to the proceedings of the Committees of the House of Commons upon Salaries and Civil List, because he did not wish to delay the transmission of his communication respecting the nomination of the Earl of Roden's successor, and as he felt desirous of giving due consideration to what he had to say upon a subject, to which it must have been evident to Earl Grey, from his communications to Viscount Althorp, and also from his letter to Lord Holland of a recent date (which His Majesty concludes Earl Grey has seen), that he attached extreme importance. Although the communications from Lord Althorp, and more especially those from Earl Grey, have satisfied the King that they disapprove the proceedings of the House of Commons and its Committees in many of the questions arising out of the discussion on the Civil List, and the spirit in which some of the reductions are urged, and that they are prepared to resist those reductions, His Majesty has considered it his duty to watch those proceedings, and to call the attention of Earl Grey and Viscount Althorp to the systematic determination they betray to reduce the influence of the Crown, and to lower the dignity of the Monarchy. It is natural that his solicitude upon this point should acquire additional force, at a period when he has been induced to consent to the introduction of a measure which must have the effect of giving a more popular character to the House of Commons, and, therefore, the effect also of increasing the disposition of its Members to oppose the influence of the People to that of the Crown and the Aristocracy.

The King does not shrink from the avowal, in this stage of the question; nor will he, in any future stage of the question, shrink from the avowal, that such are his anticipations of the effects of the measure, and that such they were when he sanctioned its introduction. His Majesty felt that it became him to consider and to weigh well the spirit of the times, its influence upon the people of the country; and whether the apprehensions he entertained for the influence of the Crown and the interest of the Monarchy, from yielding to the clamour for a Reform of so popular a character, were such as to justify a resistance which might greatly increase the public excitement, and produce a degree of discontent and agitation fatal to the peace and the tranquillity of the country, and internal struggles, at a moment when the united energies of the people might be required in the support of the honour and the security of the country against external enemies. His Majesty was satisfied that the welfare of this country, the peace and happiness of his subjects, and consequently the interests of the State and of the Monarchy, called for the concessions which he was advised to make; and he has not since, at any time, repented the decision to which, as God is his judge, he came from a sense of his duty. But while the King has yielded to these imperious considerations, it behoves him not to forget what he owed to the dignity and the honour of the Crown, and to the maintenance of those constitutional rights which had been transmitted to him by his ancestors.

He has considered that it was incumbent upon him to assert and to endeavour to protect these, while he increased the privileges of the people; and to watch with jealousy the attempts to invade them, which the temper of the times, and the revolutionary spirit which unfortunately so generally prevails, had promoted. It appeared to him, and he continues of opinion, that a strong disposition had been shown by the House of Commons and by its Committees to take advantage of this temper and of this spirit (so decidedly opposed to elevated rank and station and to their attributes and supports), to reduce the influence and to lower the dignity of the Crown, and to usurp the authority which had been administered by the State and the Government, under the influence of the Crown, according to the principles upon which the Constitutional Monarchy of this country is established.

Hence the communications which His Majesty has, from time to time, made on this subject to Earl Grey, to Viscount Althorp, and to Lord Holland: hence, also, his desire that they should be considered as communications made to his confidential servants in general, who ought to be in possession of his sentiments upon it; and hence also his suggestion to Earl Grey, that the opinion of the Crown Lawyers and the Lord Chancellor should be taken, whether the recent proceedings of those Committees to which His Majesty has adverted are legal and constitutional?

In reply to Earl Grey's letter of this date, the King has to observe, that he considers the number of, and the amount of salary to, his Lords and Grooms of the Bed-chamber and his Equeries, to the Treasurer and

Comptroller of his Household, &c. &c., to be minute details of his Civil List, and that he considers these his *personal*, though of course not his menial, servants. His Majesty does not believe these details and appointments to have been heretofore subjected to the scrutiny and dictation of a Committee of the House of Commons; and he is anxious to ascertain whether such interference with what His Majesty had viewed as the prerogatives of the Crown be legal and constitutional, in order that he may feel assured that he is justified, on principle, in objecting to it, and in desiring that it may be resisted. If His Majesty's objections be not maintainable on the ground of right, he conceives that it will be more consistent with his dignity, and with the interests of the Crown, not to contest the point with Committees which have shown so little regard for either.

* * * * *

WILLIAM R.

No. 93.

Sir H. Taylor to Earl Grey.

(Private.)   Windsor Castle, March 5, 1831.

My dear Lord,—I did not hesitate to read to the King the letter which I had the honour to receive from your Lordship this morning, as it afforded another proof of your desire to communicate without reserve the state of the Reform question, and all that you can collect upon this anxious subject.

His Majesty learns with regret, that there are any grounds for apprehension of a failure, the serious consequences of which he does not disguise from himself; but His Majesty is quite prepared to encounter them, and to contend against the difficulties which may result from the unavoidable agitation of the measure; and your Lordship may feel quite at your ease upon this subject, as His Majesty has not been drawn unadvisedly, or inconsiderately, into any step he has taken. It is impossible indeed, for any person, to be more sensible than His Majesty is of the fair and straightforward course you have pursued.

I have, &c. H. TAYLOR.*

Pray excuse haste, as it is desirable the messenger should be in town early.

No. 94.
Earl Grey to the King.

Downing Street, March 5, 1831.

Earl Grey has the honour of acknowledging your Majesty's most gracious letter of this morning.

Earl Grey does not think it necessary to trouble your Majesty further with respect to the proceedings of the Committees on the Civil List and the Reduction of Salaries, till he shall have received the answer of the Lord Chancellor and the Law Officers of the Crown on the point which, by your Majesty's command, has been referred to them, except to state that he did not understand it to be the intention of the Committee to limit in their report the salaries of your Majesty's household individually, but to apportion, upon a fair consideration of what they might think necessary in that respect, a sum generally applicable to each branch of the Civil List, leaving the distribution of it to your Majesty's decision.

* * * * *

All which, &c. GREY.

No. 95.

Sir H. Taylor to Earl Grey.

Windsor Castle, March 6, 1831.

My dear Lord,—You may perhaps have been struck with His Majesty's persevering jealousy of the proceedings of Committees and of the House of Commons, in matters regarding the Crown. It really is quite free from personal object or feeling; and his constant remark to me is, 'How will Lord Grey, how will any other Minister, be able to carry on the business of the country?'

The King's horses are ordered at half-past ten to-morrow, and he will probably be in town about one.

I have, &c. H. TAYLOR.

No. 96.

The King to Earl Grey.

Windsor Castle, March 6, 1831.

The King has received Lord Grey's letter of yesterday, and is perfectly satisfied with his reasons for not entering further than he has done into the questions of the proceedings of the Civil List and the Reduction of Salaries Committees, until he shall have received the answer of the Lord Chancellor and the Law Officers of the Crown upon the point referred to them.

The intention of the Committee, as stated in Earl Grey's letter, had not escaped His Majesty's observation, and he will find it noticed in His Majesty's letter to Viscount Althorp of the 18th ult., in reply to that from him of the 16th, in which he stated that the Committee proposed to reduce the present amount of salaries issued for the Lords and Grooms of the Bedchamber from 13,171*l*. to 10,000*l*.; upon which His Majesty observed, that 'Although the Committee had condescended not to express any opinion.' (or rather not to urge the former proposal of reducing the number of Lords and Grooms, in opposition to Lord Althorp's remonstrance), 'they would propose a reduced sum for the object, thereby giving His Majesty the power, or, in other words, driving him to the alternative, of reducing the number at their present salaries, or of keeping up the present number at reduced salaries;' an alternative which the King freely admits not to be very palatable. His Majesty has so fully stated his feelings upon these proceedings of the Committees of the House of Commons, and his sense of the spirit which seems to govern them, in his letters to Lord Althorp of the 6th, 18th, and 22nd February, and in his letters to Earl Grey of the 3rd and 4th instant, that it is unnecessary that he should do more than refer generally to those communications, as conveying sentiments to which he is desirous of calling the serious attention of his Government. But His Majesty repeats what he has often expressed to Earl Grey, that his feelings upon this subject are excited, not only by the jealousy with which he does view, and ought to view, attempts to invade the prerogatives of the Crown, but by apprehensions that the effect of those proceedings will be so to lower the influence of the Crown, as to deprive the Government of the support which it may require towards carrying on the executive administration of the business of the State. Earl Grey, as a Minister of the Crown, and from his long experience of the general policy of the country, must be sensible that a House of Commons of a more *popular* character is not likely to *drop* the inclination to interference and control which had been gradually gaining ground, and has so rapidly increased of late, and is, therefore, well able to appreciate the difficulties any Government may have to contend with hereafter, if the means of making head against such overbearing interference and control be further reduced.

* * * * *

WILLIAM R.

No. 97.

The King to Earl Grey.

Windsor Castle, March 7, 1831.

The King has received with much satisfaction Earl Grey's report of the debate renewed last night on Lord John Russell's motion; and His Majesty congratulates him upon the favourable character of the discussion, and upon the improved prospect which it offers of a successful result. The general impression which the plan appears to have made upon the public is also very satisfactory, particularly as having had the effect of excluding the clamour for Universal Suffrage, Ballot, and Annual Parliaments.

His Majesty rejoices that Earl Grey had an opportunity last night of doing justice to the vigour and prudence of the Marquis of Anglesey's conduct, which is so well entitled to every expression of approbation which His Majesty and his Government can bestow upon it.

The King, in accepting Mr. Wynn's resignation of the Office of Secretary at War, may possibly relieve Earl Grey from hesitation and difficulty, in noticing his communication to Sir Herbert Taylor, which has been submitted to him. His Majesty is not disposed to object to Sir Henry Parnell, or any other individual, from personal feeling, or from any prejudice supposed to have been created in his mind by the part he may have taken in the discussion of arrangements which have more particularly attracted His Majesty's attention.

The King has always understood Sir Henry Parnell to be a very honourable man, and is therefore not inclined to think that he has acted upon any other principle than that which he believed to be correct, although to His Majesty it may appear to be erroneous, and to have produced feelings and measures to which he considered it his duty to object strongly, as hostile to himself. But those objections apply to the measures, not to the man; nor does His Majesty ascribe to others motives and prejudices as influencing their proceedings upon public questions, in which his immediate interests are concerned, for which he is not conscious that he has afforded any grounds. The only apprehension he would entertain from the appointment of Sir Henry Parnell to the Office of Secretary at War rests upon public grounds. He is known to have carried his plans of reduction and reform to great lengths, and to attach some importance to the reputation of being a great economist; and His Majesty does not disguise his dread of the application of these principles and notions, to which he may consider himself committed and pledged to the Military, and, *by sympathy*, to the Naval establishments of this country, in a degree so excessive and so unsparing as to destroy their efficiency, and the good effects of all that has been done towards placing them in their present useful and effective condition. If Earl Grey considers that there is no ground for this apprehension, and that he will be able to check any disposition shown by Sir Henry Parnell to cramp and curtail what His Majesty believes Earl Grey admits to have been sufficiently reduced, the King will approve of his recommendation of Sir Henry Parnell for the Office of Secretary at War. WILLIAM R.

No. 98.

The King to Earl Grey.

St. James's Palace, March 7, 1831.

Although the King has seen Earl Grey since the opinion of the Lord Chancellor and the Attorney and Solicitor-General, relative to the proceedings of the Committees of the House of Commons was submitted to him, His Majesty cannot refrain from expressing in writing his satisfaction that it so fully confirms the impression he had received, that these Committees had exceeded, and were exceeding, the powers which they are warranted to exercise. WILLIAM R.

The King returns the opinion, of which he has kept a copy, and he desires Earl Grey will communicate it to Viscount Althorp.

No. 99.

The King to Earl Grey.

St. James's Palace, March 8, 1831.

The King acknowledges the receipt of Earl Grey's letter of this day, from which His Majesty has learnt with pleasure that Lord Wharncliffe's intended motion has been postponed *sine die*, it being very desirable that the discussion on the Reform question should not be prematurely brought on in the House of Lords. The King also considers that his Government has acted wisely in deferring the second reading to Monday se'nnight, and rejoices that the opposition to it was defeated. WILLIAM R.

No. 100.

The King to Earl Grey.

St. James's, March 9, 1831.

The King acknowledges the receipt of Earl Grey's report of the proceedings in the House of Commons upon the Reform Bill last night.

His Majesty is not surprised that many should be tired of the prolonged debate, but He considers it very desirable that the measure should be fully discussed.
WILLIAM R.

No. 101.

Earl Grey to Sir H. Taylor.

Downing Street, March 19, 1831.

My dear Sir,—The newspapers will have informed you of the *untoward* event of last night.* It was produced by a most factious combination of various interests, who voted against it from very different motives: the effect, there is no concealing it, will be disadvantageous to the Government. I still feel assured, however, that there will be a considerable majority on Monday in favour of Reform. It must be considered, however, as creating some doubt as to the possibility of being able to carry the measure through a committee, where similar combinations may take place, without such alterations as would destroy its efficiency. The time is then come, when we must consider seriously of the course which the Government ought to take. For this purpose, as I have informed the King, I have summoned a Cabinet for this evening.

In the state at which we are arrived, one material point to be considered will be, the propriety of advising His Majesty to dissolve Parliament; and it is upon this point particularly that I shall be much obliged to you to inform me, with as little delay as possible, what you think is the state of His Majesty's feelings.

I have been so pressed this morning that I have hardly time for this hasty scrawl.

I am, &c. GREY.

---

* The defeat, in the House of Commons, of the measure for the reduction of the Timber Duties, proposed by the Government.

No. 102.

Earl Grey to the King.

Downing Street, March 19, 1831.

Though an account will have been sent to your Majesty by Viscount Althorp of the debate of last night, and of the result of the division in the House of Commons, Earl Grey feels that he would be wanting in his duty to your Majesty, if he were to omit stating the substance of what he has collected with respect to this event.

The opposition to a question which Lord Grey believes to have been founded on just principles, and which, if carried into effect, would have been eminently advantageous to the interests of your Majesty's dominions, consisted of an union of those who thought, as it appears to Earl Grey most erroneously, that their particular interests would have been injured by it, and of those who, being enemies to the measure of Parliamentary Reform, thought an advantage might be obtained over your Majesty's Government upon that question. Sir Robert Peel and others, who did not oppose a regulation which they said they had not had time to consider, and against which they made no direct objection, concurred in a vote, which can be attributed to no other motive, by which all further consideration of a measure on which they stated their wish to be further informed was precluded. The force thus united against the Government was further assisted by the absence of many of its supporters, who had left the House in the expectation of an adjournment.

Earl Grey will not attempt to conceal from your

Majesty the mortification and disappointment which he has experienced at this event. It is not, in itself perhaps, of any material consequence; but it undoubtedly will occasion an opinion of the weakness of your Majesty's Government, and may possibly have some influence on the question of Parliamentary Reform, which is to be debated on Monday next. Earl Grey's opinion still is, that there will be a considerable majority in its favour.

He has, however, thought it his duty to summon a meeting of your Majesty's confidential servants for this evening, the result of which he will have the honour of communicating to your Majesty to-morrow.

All which, &c. GREY.

No. 103.

The King to Earl Grey.

Windsor Castle, March 20, 1831.

The King is too sensible of the importance of the objects which may engage the attention of the meeting of his confidential servants, which Earl Grey informs him, in his letter of yesterday, that he has summoned for this day, not to feel anxious that His Majesty's answer to that letter, and to one addressed by him to Sir Herbert Taylor, and which has been submitted to him, should reach Earl Grey with the least possible delay.

The King assures Earl Grey, with the greatest sincerity, that he deeply regrets and laments any event which occasions to him mortification and disappointment is calculated, as observed by him, to occasion an opinion of the weakness of His Majesty's Government, and may possibly have a prejudicial influence upon the question of Reform.

His Majesty considers it unnecessary to advert at any length to what has passed upon that subject, or to his own sentiments so fully expressed in his letter to Earl Grey of the 4th February. He assures him that those sentiments are unchanged, and that they have not been influenced by any opposition to the measure, or by the arguments adduced in the course of that opposition.

His Majesty having been induced to waive his early objections to bringing forward the measure at this period, and having given his sanction to the introduction of a Bill which had been submitted by Earl Grey to him, in all its details, and with every explanation which he could require, His Majesty pledged himself to give his Government his utmost and unqualified support upon this occasion; and Earl Grey and his other confidential servants will, he is confident, do him the justice to admit, that this pledge has, in no respect, been forfeited or departed from; that nothing has escaped him, in word or deed, which could weaken its effect. That, on the contrary, the course he has pursued has been studiously that which was best calculated to impress upon the country and upon the public a firm belief of the sincerity of his support, and of the unreserved confidence which he reposed in those who had brought forward the measure.

That confidence continues unabated. His Majesty has taken many occasions to express his satisfaction with the conduct of his Government, and his approbation of the wisdom, the zeal, the firmness, and the energy with which they have discharged the arduous duties imposed upon them, from the moment they were called to his councils, under circumstances most trying and critical. And His Majesty is bound to notice, as having more particularly called for his approbation, the course which has been pursued with respect to the state of Ireland, and to the external policy of this country, which he considers to have insured the preservation of tranquillity at home and peace abroad.

The King would therefore seriously lament anything that could shake the stability of his present Government, and eventually deprive him of the services of Earl Grey and others, who have proved themselves so well deserving of his confidence; and he earnestly hopes, that his confidential servants will, in their deliberations this day, devise some means to avert a misfortune which His Majesty so anxiously deprecates, without coming to the resolution of submitting for his decision an alternative to which His Majesty cannot agree, namely, a dissolution of Parliament, to which it is his bounden duty most strenuously to object at this critical period, and in the present excited state of the United Kingdom, particularly of Ireland. Nor is the feeling which His Majesty is now called upon to express, one which has been recently admitted. It was impossible that he should not, in this view of the various bearings of the question, and of the proceedings upon it, have anticipated the possibility of such a proposition, even if such a result of any successful opposition to it had not been threatened, at an early period of the session, by one of his confidential servants; and it would have been strange, indeed, if the probable effects of such an alternative, in the present state of the country—England recently emerged from serious disturbance, Ireland still partially convulsed, the whole United Kingdom under the actual influence of increased excitement, produced by the legislative discussion of a question which had long been a source of agitation—had not engaged his serious attention and his anxious consideration.

This state of the country is, in His Majesty's firm opinion, a sufficient ground of objection : one which imposes upon him, as a sacred duty, the obligation of resisting any proposal for the dissolution of Parliament at this period ; and he will not now enter into many others which occur to him, although prepared to state them, if it should be necessary.

He cannot, however, close this letter, without repeating to Earl Grey the expression of his earnest, his sincere, his anxious desire, to secure to himself, by any means, by any arrangement, either of a general nature or more immediately connected with the provisions of the pending measure, which can be suggested or devised, and to which His Majesty's utmost aid and support will be given, the continued advantage of the services of Earl Grey and his colleagues, to which he justly attaches so much importance.

His anxiety on this point does not arise solely from personal feeling, from the satisfaction he has derived from the manner in which they have discharged their duties. It is strongly combined with a conviction of the serious prejudice which the interests of the country entrusted by Providence to His Majesty's sway must sustain from frequent changes in its councils and in the system of the administration: from a conviction also that the success of the efforts which have been so ably directed to the maintenance of the peace of Europe depends mainly on the confidence which is now reposed by Foreign Powers in His Majesty's Government; and which confidence must be weakened, if not destroyed, by frequent changes of men and measures.

WILLIAM R.

No. 104.

Earl Grey to Sir H. Taylor.

Downing Street, March 20, 1831.

My dear Sir,—The accompanying letter to the King states to His Majesty the determination taken by the Cabinet last night, to proceed with the Reform Bill as if the division on the Timber Duties had not taken place.

If the Civil List Bill and the Votes for the Supply of the year had been in a more forward state, it might have been a question whether it would not have been our duty to recommend an immediate dissolution, as it is quite clear that the opposers of Reform will scruple to use no means of embarrassing the Government, by uniting with any persons whose discontent on any particular question may give them an opportunity of making a successful attack. There could not be a stronger proof of this than was afforded on Friday night. A new regulation of the Timber Duties had been declared by Mr. Herries himself, last year, to be necessary; and there is every reason to believe, if he had remained in office, would have been proposed by him. To the measure proposed by us they (*i.e.* the late Ministers) offered no direct objection. Sir R. Peel complained that he wanted more time to consider it, and yet, when a motion was proposed which would have afforded him that opportunity, he voted for an amendment which, for the time, had the effect of stopping the measure altogether.

Ministers have frequently had votes with regard to taxes carried against them. It happened more than once to Mr. Pitt himself in the plenitude of his power. There is, therefore, no reason why the present occurrence should have any effect beyond the failure of the measure for the alteration of the Timber Duties. But, looking to the state of the House of Commons, and to the means which may be found during the progress of the Reform Bill through the Committee, of similar combinations to make alterations in it, which might be fatal to its efficiency, it is impossible to exclude from our consideration the necessity of resorting to a dissolution as I mentioned to you yesterday.

Upon our prospects with respect to the second reading my opinion remains unaltered; and as any resolution is therefore deferred as to the steps which it may be necessary to take hereafter, till the result of that question shall have been ascertained, it may, perhaps, be as well not to say anything to the King on the subject of dissolution. Indeed, what I wrote to you yesterday was only for the purpose of learning from you what you thought would be the probable effect of making such a proposition to him; but I believe I omitted, in the hurry in which I wrote, to express my wish that you should not bring this matter directly before him till you heard further from me.

I shall be much obliged to you to give me your opinion quite unreservedly upon this subject; as, in whatever it may become necessary for me to do, my principal object will be to save the King, as far as it may be in my power to do so, from all difficulty and embarrassment. All personal considerations with respect to myself will give way to this duty. Excuse all this trouble, and believe, &c. GREY.

As I write early, before my private secretary is come, and am unwilling to delay the messenger, may I request you to let me have these letters returned to me, upon your coming to town on Tuesday, that I may have copies taken of them.

I am, &c. GREY.

No. 105.

Earl Grey to the King.

Downing Street, March 20, 1831.

Earl Grey has the honour of informing your Majesty that a meeting of your Majesty's servants took place last night. After receiving all the information that could be obtained from the Members of the House of Commons, and considering very fully all that had passed in the debate on Friday night, the opinion of his colleagues confirmed that which Earl Grey had, yesterday, the honour of submitting to your Majesty, viz. that the late division does not materially alter the expectation which was before entertained, of a majority on the second reading of the Bill for a Reform in the Representation of your Majesty's subjects in the House of Commons.

It was agreed, therefore, to proceed in the course your Majesty's servants were pursuing previous to the late debate; and to advance the public business as much as possible, and particularly the Bill for the settlement of the Civil List, in the interval which must necessarily take place between the second reading of the Reform Bill, if it should be carried, and the Committee. The report from the Civil List Committee will be made, it is hoped, almost immediately; and no time will afterwards be lost in bringing in the Bill.

Earl Grey feels that, perhaps, he ought to apologise for troubling your Majesty with so unimportant a communication by a special messenger. He has done so thinking that, in consequence of his letter of yesterday, your Majesty might expect to hear from him sooner than by the ordinary post.

All which, &c. GREY.

No. 106.

The King to Earl Grey.

Windsor Castle, March 20, 1831.

The King received Earl Grey's letter of this day, just as he had signed and was about to dispatch his reply to that which reached him early this morning, and he was unwilling to delay its transmission.

His Majesty assures Earl Grey that he has derived great satisfaction from his communication of the result of the meeting of his confidential servants, and that he highly approves of their determination to proceed in the course they were pursuing previous to the late debate, sincerely trusting that it may be uninterrupted by any serious obstacle, and that their firmness and consistency will carry them through every difficulty. He is, indeed, not inclined to attach great importance to the defeat upon a bill of secondary consideration; nor does His Majesty think that, in the present state of the country, with the feeling of the people avowedly and manifestly in their favour, and having engaged in duties most arduous, and which, from their very nature and the spirit of the times, call upon statesmen and upon public men to contend against difficulties such as they might reasonably and honourably yield to in common times, his Ministers should allow themselves to be affected even by more serious and by repeated disappointments. He is convinced that, by perseverance, they will overcome opposition and combinations; and they may depend upon his utmost support in maintaining their ground, provided His Majesty be not called upon to dissolve Parliament at this period, his objection to which has been already stated. It appears, indeed, to have been prematurely stated; but he does not regret having been induced to put Earl Grey in possession of his sentiments upon this important point, before he was more formally called upon to express them to him.

WILLIAM R.

No. 107.

Sir H. Taylor to Earl Grey.

(Private.)　　　　　　　　Windsor Castle, March 20, 1831.

My dear Lord,—The King was so desirous that there should be no avoidable delay in dispatching his first letter to your Lordship this day, that it was out of my power then to write even a line in reply to that which you had addressed to me. Indeed His Majesty came to my room to sign the letter and to close the box. While so engaged, your second box was brought containing the letters for the King and for me, both which His Majesty immediately read. Your first letter contained no caution that I should not show it to His Majesty, or say any thing on the subject of dissolution; and I therefore did not hesitate showing it to him, as I have been in the habit of doing in all instances; to which I was further induced from the opinion I entertained, that it was of the utmost importance to your Lordship and to the deliberations (which I inadvertently imagined would take place this day, instead of yesterday, as I discovered afterwards), for which the meeting of Cabinet had been summoned, that you should, without loss of time, be possessed of His Majesty's sentiments. Other parts of your letter appeared to me to have been equally written for His Majesty's information; and, upon the whole, I flatter myself that you will not regret that this communication was made to His Majesty. Indeed, if I had not made it, I should have been placed under the embarrassment of departing from a principle I have hitherto observed, and I should still have been under the necessity of producing it, in consequence of His Majesty being with me when your second letter arrived, and desiring me at once to read it to him. Your Lordship will forgive my adding, that I should have been extremely sorry if the King had not read that second letter, as it gave him great satisfaction, and confirmed the opinion he entertained, and had strongly expressed, that votes carried against Ministers upon taxes, and indeed upon other measures not affecting the main principles and the system of the Government, ought not to be suffered to have any influence on the existence of that Government, while it possessed the support of the Sovereign and the confidence of the People.

Your Lordship will observe that His Majesty has expressed this sentiment very strongly in his letter to you; and, with reference to what you had written to me, I assure you that such has been his invariable language, and that he has stated that these extraordinary times call for extraordinary measures; and that those who have, from a sense of duty, and a feeling of patriotism, undertaken an arduous and invidious task, will best discharge that duty, and perform that task, by an *obstinate* perseverance in their course.

The King has stated so unreservedly, and so fully, his sentiments on the subject of a dissolution of Parliament, that it is unnecessary that I should enter further upon it. I imagined indeed, until I received your letter, that you had been aware of them, and that they had been expressed to you by His Majesty upon the occasion of his notice at Brighton of Sir James Graham's declaration in the House of Commons.

His Majesty has, on all occasions, expressed himself

truly sensible of the kind and affectionate feeling your Lordship has shown towards him, and of your anxious desire to save him, as far as it may be in your power to do so, from all difficulty and embarrassment, at the sacrifice even of your personal comfort, ease, and satisfaction. He would, I well know, dread and deeply lament the loss of your services; and he has, whenever the possibility of such an event has been stated, expressed in the strongest terms his desire to avert it by any means in his power. Indeed, the whole of his conduct must have proved this to your Lordship; and I hope you will forgive my expressing a most anxious hope and solicitude, that His Majesty's earnest wishes may not be defeated, and that circumstances may not impose upon you the necessity of proposing a measure to which His Majesty feels insuperable objection.

I will return your Lordship's letters to you. to-morrow. I would do so now, if it were not possible that His Majesty might wish to refer to them when I read to him the copy of this.

I have, &c. H. TAYLOR.

No. 108.

Earl Grey to Sir H. Taylor.

Downing Street, March 21, 1831.

My dear Sir,—In my hurry this morning, I forgot to say that the Duke of Devonshire being gone to Derbyshire, to attend the County Meeting, Lord Belfast will, of course, have to attend the King at the Opera to-morrow. If the debate in the House of Commons should be protracted beyond to-night, this may prevent his being present at the Division. Col. H. Cavendish is in a similar situation, being in attendance on His Majesty.

I don't know whether it will be possible to allow these two gentlemen to attend the House of Commons, by substituting two other officers of the household to attend upon their Majesties; but the loss of their votes would be much to be regretted, and I shall be obliged to you to let me know what can be done in this matter. I have just heard that a meeting has been held this morning at Sir E. Knatchbull's, at which it was determined to oppose the Bill now before the House of Commons, with a declaration of an intention to propose another of a more moderate character. Whose device this is I do not know; but it bears the character of a measure recommended by Sir R. Peel. It may procure a few votes, but its effect will be of the most mischievous, not to say dangerous, tendency. It is impossible that His Majesty's Ministers can yield to it as a compromise, without proving themselves to be unworthy of all confidence, either from the King or the People. It must be resisted, therefore, as a most disgraceful expedient to disguise a real opposition to all effectual reform by a false pretence. If it should succeed, I cannot answer for the consequences: they are, in my opinion, more to be feared than any that could result from direct opposition to the measure. The principle will be conceded, at the same time, that all the hopes and expectations of the public will be completely disappointed. What may be the result of such a state of things, I fear to calculate.

There is no practice, either fair or foul, of giving effect to the opposition we have not to encounter. An account has just been brought to me, that a report is industriously circulated, of a letter having been written to me by the King on Friday night, putting an absolute veto on dissolution. Whether any private information has been obtained of the fact, I know not; but if it is pure invention, as I believe, the inventor has certainly shown some sagacity in divining the truth.

In all this my only care is for the personal ease and comfort of the King, and my own course is plain and clear. I must abide the event, whatever it may be. There is no room left for compromise or retreat. It would not do, at the end of a long political life, to forfeit the character which I have obtained through many sacrifices.

I am, &c. GREY.

P.S.—I have just learnt that Sir T. Trowbridge told Capt. Elliott, that the fact of the King having written to declare that he would not consent to a dissolution, had been communicated to him by one of the King's household.

Lord ―― has also been offering large bets that the King has notified his refusal.

No. 109.

Earl Grey to the King.

Downing Street, March 21, 1831.

Earl Grey begs leave humbly to acknowledge your Majesty's two most gracious letters of yesterday, which he thought it his duty to communicate to the rest of your Majesty's confidential servants, at a Cabinet held last night.

The gratifying expression of your Majesty's approbation, with which your Majesty has been pleased to honour their humble efforts in your service, could not fail to afford to them, as well as to Earl Grey, the most heartfelt satisfaction; and the manner in which your Majesty, having been induced to waive your early objections, consented to their bringing forward the measure of Parliamentary Reform, and afterwards studiously pursued a course which was best calculated to impress upon the country and the public a firm belief of the sincerity of your support, and of the unreserved confidence which your Majesty reposed in those who had advised that measure, demands their most grateful acknowledgments, and must for ever command their sincerest devotion.

In what occurred at Brighton, when your Majesty was pleased to notice the allusion made by Sir J. Graham, in the House of Commons, to the possibility of a dissolution of Parliament, though no direct and positive objection was stated, Earl Grey could not fail to perceive your Majesty's repugnance to such a measure; and it was this recollection which made him anxious to learn from Sir H. Taylor what might still be your Majesty's feelings with respect to it, after the debate and division on Friday night in the House of Commons. That event unavoidably compelled Earl Grey to look to the possible necessity of making a proposition to your Majesty, which he had occasion to fear your Majesty could not receive without pain, and which nothing but a most imperative sense of public duty could make him think of after what had passed between your Majesty and him on that subject. He begs your Majesty also to be assured, that it was not without the most anxious thought and consideration of the state of this country, as well as of Ireland, and only after having received, in answer to an inquiry which he had addressed to the Marquis of Anglesey, the assurance that he should have no fear of the effect of a dissolution, that he had ventured even upon the preliminary step of writing in the manner your Majesty has seen to Sir H. Taylor.

This, as your Majesty must be aware, was the personal act of Earl Grey, without any authority from his colleagues, and intended not as a proposal, but merely as preparatory to a more direct communication which might eventually become necessary, but upon which he was unwilling to trouble your Majesty till that necessity became urgent.

The explicit declaration of your Majesty's opinions which has thus been obtained, and the open and candid manner in which it has been made, Earl Grey has the honour to assure your Majesty, both for himself and his colleagues, will command their most sincere deference and respect. It will be their most earnest wish to act in obedience to it to the utmost of their power; but they humbly hope that your Majesty's decision will not be considered by your Majesty as taking from them the privilege, which is essential to the discharge of their duty, of respectfully submitting to your Majesty such considerations as, upon a careful review of all the circumstances of the time, may compel them, as faithful servants to your Majesty, to recommend a course which nothing but the most painful necessity could induce them to urge in opposition to your Majesty's known opinions. This necessity, Earl Grey anxiously hopes may be avoided; and nothing can contribute more effectually to prevent it than the careful exclusion of every person not acting as one of your Majesty's confidential advisers from all knowledge of what had passed on this occasion. Perhaps Earl Grey ought to apologise for this remark, after the experience he has had of your Majesty's constant observance of the greatest caution and reserve upon all matters under discussion between your Majesty and your confidential advisers.

Earl Grey cannot conclude without adding the grateful acknowledgments both of himself and his colleagues, for the gracious manner in which your Majesty has been pleased to express your anxious wish to prevent any change in your Majesty's councils. With the encouragement held out to them by your Majesty, they will shrink from no difficulty. No private considerations will be allowed to influence their conduct. From personal attachment to your Majesty, no less than from the public considerations so forcibly stated by your Majesty, they could not look to their eventual removal from the service of so gracious and so kind a master, without feelings of the deepest sorrow; and they trust, whatever may be the result, that your Majesty will be assured, that it will be their most anxious wish and endeavour to prevent injury to the public interest, and to save your Majesty from all difficulty and embarrassment.

Earl Grey hopes he may be allowed the honour of waiting on your Majesty after your arrival in town to-morrow, when he may be able to furnish personally any further explanations which may be desired by your Majesty, and which may become more necessary if, as seems not improbable, the division on the Reform Bill should take place to-night.

All which, &c.   GREY.

No. 110.

Earl Grey to Sir H. Taylor.

Downing Street, March 21, 1831.

My dear Sir,—I have written so long a letter to the King, that I have hardly a moment left to thank you for the long and kind letter which I received from you last night.

I never experienced greater pain than in the discussion which has taken place, and which I fear may not end here, on the subject of dissolution. You may be assured nothing, as I have stated to His Majesty, but the most painful necessity can induce me to press it further; but if that necessity should arise, to prevent the loss of character which would render me an useless servant to him, I hope His Majesty will not deny to me and to his Ministers the right of laying fully before him all the considerations which bear upon this question, before his decision can be viewed as absolutely final and conclusive.

I have ventured to suggest, in a manner which I hope will not be considered as implying any distrust or suspicion, the necessity of observing the most careful secresy as to His Majesty's opinions on the subject of dissolution. A belief that he would not consent to such a measure is already operating very injuriously in the minds of those who would be willing to vote against the Reform Bill, if they could be relieved from the fear of being sent back to their constituents.

I think it very probable that the Division may take place to-night, and then we shall be able to see more plainly the course we have to pursue.

I had almost forgot to add, that, if there was any harm in your communication of my letter to the King, it was my own fault for not having desired you to consider it as for yourself only. The only feeling I had upon the subject arose from a wish to spare His Majesty, as long as possible, the consideration of a matter which I feared would be unpleasant to him; but I think it is much better that it has been brought under his attention; and you may be assured that a knowledge of his opinions will have all the influence upon our conduct which the obligations of our duty both to the King and to the public will permit.

The absence of my private secretary on an election committee again obliges me to request you to return these letters, that I may have copies of them taken.

In haste, &c. GREY.

No. 111.

Sir H. Taylor to Earl Grey.

(Private.) Windsor Castle, March 21, 1831.

The King was out when your Lordship's messenger arrived, and did not come in until near six, when I immediately delivered the letter under seal for His

Majesty, and that you had addressed to me. Both were read by him with the attention they called for; and the answer which I have the honour to enclose was written under His Majesty's very full and precise instructions, given after mature consideration.

I have, however, been so hurried to write it before His Majesty went to bed, that I fear it is not so clearly expressed as it ought to be, especially as His Majesty wished me not to absent myself from a large dinner, lest it should excite observation. I observed also, in reading it over to the King before he signed it, that I had omitted to execute his instructions to reply to that part of your Lordship's letter, in which you claim for His Majesty's confidential servants the privilege of submitting such considerations, as upon a careful review of all the circumstances of the time may compel them to recommend a dissolution. I therefore consider it my duty to supply this omission (as I cannot return with the letter to His Majesty, who wished it to be sent early to-morrow morning), by acquainting you that His Majesty admitted, without hesitation, your right to the privilege and the propriety of its exercise upon this occasion.

There are other parts of your letter which would and ought to have been noticed, but from the hurry to which I have adverted, and His Majesty's anxiety that his grounds of objection to a dissolution, as he had often expressed them to me, and as he distinctly repeated them to me on this occasion, should be fully stated; but the time was short, and the thing has, I fear, been imperfectly done.

Above all, His Majesty has been most solicitous in

every communication, to express his sense of your attachment to his person, and of your devotion to his service, as well as of the high-minded and honourable principle which has distinguished your proceedings on this and every occasion. He has felt not less desirous that your Lordship's colleagues should be assured of the satisfaction he has derived from their conduct.

I should be wholly unworthy of the confidence with which your Lordship has honoured me, and make a bad return for the unreserved manner in which you have communicated with me, if I were to disguise from you my conviction, that the King's objections to a dissolution at this moment, and in the present state of the country, will prove final and conclusive. They are indeed grounded upon apprehensions of a convulsion in this country, and chiefly in Ireland, which have taken such a firm hold on his mind, that I am persuaded no argument will be able to shake them. I do therefore most earnestly and most fervently hope, that the success of the Bill may relieve you from the necessity of submitting the obnoxious proposal.

I am very happy to hear that your Lordship had, upon consideration, been satisfied with my having shown your letter of Saturday to the King. I can assure you that His Majesty has been most cautious in disclosing his sentiments on the subject of a dissolution.

I have never heard him name it, nor heard any one notice his having named it; and he is extremely reserved on all political questions, and careful of naming or alluding to any matter which is the subject of communication with your Lordship, or any other of his confidential servants, which is not avowedly of a public and ostensible nature.

I return your letters as you desire, and shall be obliged to you for them when you have no further occasion for them.

His Majesty will be in town before one to-morrow, unless detained by official business here, and will be glad to see your Lordship at any hour most convenient to yourself.

I have, &c. H. TAYLOR.

No. 112.

The King to Earl Grey.

Windsor Castle, March 21, 1831.

Although the King will have an opportunity of communicating personally with Earl Grey to-morrow, His Majesty conceives that it may be more satisfactory to him and to His Majesty's other confidential servants, that he should receive an answer in writing to the letter he addressed to him this day, especially as that letter expresses their joint sentiments in reply to the King's communication of yesterday, which Earl Grey very properly, and as His Majesty fully expected he would do, laid before them.

The King rejoices that the expression of his general approbation of their conduct, and of the satisfaction at the course they have pursued, has proved gratifying to Earl Grey and his other confidential servants. It has been conveyed with great sincerity, and he cannot too often repeat that their proceedings, at a most critical period, and under most arduous circumstances, have amply merited the decided support they acknowledge to have received from him.

His Majesty rejoices also to learn, that Earl Grey had not mistaken the general expression of his sentiments at Brighton, on the possibility of a dissolution of Parliament, although no direct and positive objection was then stated, as indeed it had not then been called for: still it appears to have been such as to cause Earl Grey to approach the subject with hesitation, and with the apprehension of giving pain to His Majesty by the introduction of it; and the King assures him that he does lament extremely that Earl Grey should, by a sense of public duty, by which His Majesty is confident no man can be actuated in a stronger degree than he is, be placed under the necessity of urging a measure upon which a difference of opinion can arise between them.

His Majesty is perfectly aware that the first intimation of a possible resort to the measure of dissolution was Earl Grey's personal act, not submitted with the authority of his colleagues, and in fact a preliminary to a more direct communication; but His Majesty does not regret that the communication has been made before the necessity for it became urgent, as he feels that, upon so important a point, his confidential servants should receive an early intimation of his sentiments, and that it is due to them and to himself that they should be stated so explicitly and so candidly as not to be liable to mistake. This course, indeed, is most consistent with the principle upon which it has been his determination to act in the station in which he is placed: it is that which Earl Grey has observed towards him; and it is that which is most becoming the honest man, and in his opinion best calculated to meet the difficulties with which these times are so pregnant.

The King does not deny that he has learnt with great pain, that the possible alternative of a dissolution has engaged the serious consideration of his confidential servants, as he cannot divest himself, nor hope to divest himself of the feeling, with which he contemplates that alternative.

He has already, in his letter to Earl Grey of yesterday, stated generally his ground of objection, and that he considers as imposing upon him, as a sacred duty, the obligation of resisting any proposal for the dissolution of Parliament at this period; but upon this occasion, and with reference to the general nature of Earl Grey's communication, His Majesty is induced to remark further, that it is his firm conviction, that if a general election were to take place at this moment, in consequence of his Government being defeated in the attempt to carry the Bill of Reform, thereby throwing back, upon an excited population, a measure which is considered by that population to have been brought forward in deference to the expression of its opinion; if what is called an appeal to the people be now made upon a popular question so strenuously advocated by those who have been supported by popular clamour, when a spirit of agitation which has been so long in progress has been so much increased by the introduction of the Bill and the discussion upon it, this country would be thrown into convulsion from the Land's End to John O'Groat's house: miners, manufacturers, colliers, labourers, all who have recently formed unions for the furtherance of illegal purposes, would assemble on every point in support of a *popular* question, with the declared object of carrying the measure by intimidation. It would be in vain to hope to be able to resist their course, or to check disturbances of every kind, amounting possibly to open rebellion, while the few troops which might be brought forward in support of a civil power, often timid and inefficient (as recently shown in Lancashire), would probably have been assembled in the neighbourhood of London, for the preservation of tranquillity in the metropolis, or embarked for Ireland. Here again the effects of dissolution at this period would probably be still more serious.

Earl Grey has indeed stated the assurance given by the Marquis of Anglesey, that he should have no fear of a dissolution. But with all deference for the Marquis of Anglesey's opinion, and the highest sense of the resources he has shown, of his activity, his firmness, and his energy, and of his well-grounded confidence in the application of these qualities, the King cannot help opposing actual circumstances and facts to the assurance given, and the confidence expressed.

In the recent election for the county of Kilkenny, the Government candidate, Lord Duncannon, was admitted to be very popular. Yet the accumulation of troops and of constabulary force was insufficient towards repressing disorders and outrage, and towards protecting the voters, against whom the agitators had stirred up the populace. An election is approaching in the county of Clare, serious disturbances are taking place there, all the troops that can be spared from other districts are sent to that county, a regiment has been ordered from England upon the occasion, others are to be spared from the slender force in this country and to proceed to Ireland if required by the Lord-Lieutenant.

If such be the state of Ireland, such the effect of an election in *one* county in Ireland, is it necessary to ask what would be the effect of a *general* election, every county, every district, every large and small town equally disturbed, all calling for the aid of the military and the police? There are not 20,000 men in Ireland; twice the number would be insufficient in such a case; and where are these to be found?

The English militia are not embodied, but if they were now called out, their ranks would be filled with men who are, or have been recently, the promoters of disturbance and of lawless acts, and who would not have been a sufficient time under the control of discipline to shake off the fancy for outrage when called upon to repress it in others. His Majesty does not think he has exaggerated the state of things, nor that he errs in apprehending that its result would be a revolution in Ireland.

But supposing these apprehensions of great disorder and outrage in Great Britain, and of more serious disturbance in Ireland (upon which the King grounds an objection, which he has stated to be paramount, and which, if he feels it to be such, he is in duty bound to maintain), to be unfounded. It must be admitted, at least, that no effort would be wanting on the part of the lower orders of the rabble, of those arrayed in support of a popular measure, to destroy the freedom of election, to carry every vote by the influence of violence and intimidation, as was shown at Preston, and has occasionally been shown elsewhere. Would they not call upon every candidate to pledge himself to the support of measures of a democratic and revolutionary tendency?—to vote for universal suffrage, election by ballot, annual Parliaments, further reduction of the Civil List, other popular measures levelled at the dignity of the Crown, the influence of the Aristocracy, and the political existence of both? Gentlemen, men of principle and honour, would indeed decline so to pledge themselves; but their refusal would exclude them from the representation, and would thus open the door of admission to the House of Commons to demagogues, agitators, and revolutionists, unprincipled adventurers, who would pledge themselves to *anything*, and would not scruple to vote for the destruction of the monarchy and of every existing establishment.

Those who talk of an appeal to the people in support of administrative measures should consider in what manner it becomes the King to view such an appeal, its occasion and its probable effects. His Majesty may and does give credit to those who are inclined to force on the measure of Reform, by such an appeal, for the best, the most patriotic, and the most constitutional motives; but it is His Majesty's duty to consider whether the benefits which are held out, and even greater eventual benefits, shall justify the risk at which they are sought, the disorder and the bloodshed through which they are in his apprehension to be obtained. He has stated this to be the paramount objection. He cannot, he must not, waive it. He cannot help returning to that which is, and which ought to be, uppermost in his mind.

His Majesty has nevertheless to urge another, which

cannot fail to strike forcibly those whom he addresses. Supposing a dissolution to take place, and the House of Commons to be so constituted as His Majesty apprehends, can it be expected that they will give such support to the Government of the country as will enable it to carry on its business? Can it be expected that the House of Lords will concur in the measures which such a House of Commons will introduce and pass? Will not their proceedings produce an early schism between the two Houses? The consequences of such a case have always presented themselves to the King in a most fearful light;. and he is naturally most anxious to avert all that can provoke them.

His Majesty will not add to this long letter further than by assuring Earl Grey, that no expression of his sentiments or feeling on the subject of a dissolution has escaped him, and that his notice of the subject has been confined to the communications he has made to him.*

WILLIAM R.

---

* This letter shows the extreme importance of the majority of one in favour of the second reading of the Reform Bill, which was obtained the night after it was written. It will be seen from the preceding letter that Sir H. Taylor believed that at that time the King's objection to a dissolution would prove final and conclusive; and this was, I know, also my father's conviction; nor do I think the King's subsequent assent to this measure under altered circumstances affords any reason for supposing that they were wrong. The defeat of the Bill on this stage must therefore, in all probability, have led to the resignation of the Ministers, since this must necessarily have followed the King's final refusal to dissolve. And their resignation would have had very different consequences with the House of Commons, as then composed, from those which ensued in the following year, when they resigned with a House of Commons in which there was so large a majority earnestly in favour of Reform. The real feeling of a majority of the House of Commons of March 1831 was quite the other way.

No. 113.

Earl Grey to the King.

Downing Street, March 22, 1831.

Earl Grey has had the honour of receiving your Majesty's letter of yesterday. Upon the important matter to which it relates, as he hopes so soon to have an opportunity of personal communication with your Majesty, he trusts that your Majesty will not think him wanting in due attention and respect, if he abstains from offering any further observations at present. It would ill become him to enter into anything approaching to a controversial argument with your Majesty; and he must naturally be anxious to postpone, till compelled to do so by an overbearing necessity, any expression of opinions not conformable to those which are so strongly impressed on the mind of your Majesty.

The debate on the second reading of the Reform Bill lasted till a late hour this morning, when an adjournment took place. It was opened by Sir Richard Vyvyan, who moved that the second reading should be put off for six months, declaring at the same time, in conformity with a resolution said to have been taken at a meeting held at Sir Edward Knatchbull's yesterday morning, that if he carried his motion he would

---

I have no doubt, therefore, that a Government might then have been formed from the Opposition, which would, for a time at least, have commanded a majority, as the fear of Reform would have put an end to the divisions in the Tory party that had been fatal to the Duke of Wellington's Government. Thus a fearful experiment would have been tried on the patience of the country, which would have had no legal and constitutional means of enforcing the passing of the Reform Bill, on which its desires were so strongly fixed.

himself bring forward a resolution pledging the House to *some* Reform; but he did not state anything to inform the House as to the extent or principle of the measure he might have in contemplation. The principle of Reform, indeed, is admitted by this statement, which is perhaps not quite consistent with a direct opposition to the second reading. But waiving this minor objection, the course pursued by Sir R. Vyvyan and his supporters appears to Earl Grey fraught with the most dangerous consequences. It concedes the principle, it admits the necessity, and having given this advantage to the advocates of Reform, disappoints all their expectations. If there be a plan tending more certainly than another to assist the views of those who would urge the public to the worst extremities, Earl Grey believes it to be this.

In the debate nothing remarkable occurred, except a most eloquent and powerful speech from Mr. Sheil. The speakers were

AGAINST.	FOR.
Sir Richard Vyvyan.	Mr. Sheil.
Mr. Cartwright.	Mr. Pendarves.
Mr. R. A. Dundas.	Mr. Charles Grant.
Lord Valletort.	Mr. Slaney.
Mr. William Bankes.	The Solicitor-General.
Lord Norreys.	
Mr. Villiers Stuart.	
Sir E. Sugden.	

Mr. V. S. declared he voted only in obedience to his constituents, that his opinion was in favour of the measure, and that he should resign his seat.

All which, &c.   GREY.

No. 114.

Earl Grey to Sir H. Taylor.

(Secret and confidential.)

Downing Street, March 22, 1831.

Dear Sir Herbert,—I send you the letter* which I mentioned to you this morning, and which does not, in my opinion, overstate the case in the slightest degree.

There are three things that I wish to impress upon the King's mind :—

1. That we did not cause the excitement about Reform. We found it in full vigour when we came into office; and the King told me that every one of the late Ministers, except the Duke of Wellington, when they took leave of him, acknowledged that some Reform was necessary.

2. That the excitement which now exists is directed to what, I think, a safe and legitimate object. In the event of a dissolution, it would act in support of the King and Government. If a contrary direction is given to it, you probably will see associations all over the country; and, when once they have felt their power, the history of the Catholic Question will show the consequences that may be expected.

3. That this Government is now without its natural support, the Parliament having been chosen by the late Ministers, and all the seats usually at the command of the Ministers being now filled by their bitterest opponents.

* From Lord Durham.

It is objected to the plan of Reform, that the Ministers will not be able to command seats for themselves and their supporters. It is now ten times worse, as they not only have not the seats but that they afford a power against them.

Ever yours, &c. GREY.

P.S.—Pray send back Lambton's letter as soon as you have done with it.

No. 115.

Sir H. Taylor to Earl Grey.

(Secret and confidential.)

St. Katharine's, March 22, 1831.

My dear Lord,—Your Lordship's letter, enclosing Lord Durham's, reached me shortly before I left St. James's, and I was unable to read them quietly until I got home; nor would I sit down to reply to them until my family had gone to bed.

I feel very sensibly your confidence in making this communication; and I own that I regret that you have restricted me from imparting it to the King, as there are many points which I should have wished him to see and consider before the subject shall possibly be brought before him in a more formal shape. I know also, from experience, that his mind is ever open to receive the opinions of those whose situations and duties justify the expression of them, with kindness and indulgence, and with due allowance for the warmth of feeling in which they may be offered, although *freely* given, and although they may, for the sake of argument, place the question in points of view which may not accord with his sentiments, or with the honest spirit in which those sentiments have been admitted and maintained.

I may add, and in fact repeat, that I have been in the habit of submitting to the King, without reserve, whatever reaches me, provided it shall not appear to me calculated to operate to the injury or prejudice of the person who addresses me, or to create impressions not intended to be conveyed; and no question has ever arisen in the course of which I have felt more anxious than on this, that His Majesty should be put in full possession of all that can be said in support of the opinions and feelings of men to whose continued services he justly attaches so much importance. I have carefully read your Lordship's letters and that from Lord Durham, which I return, and I see nothing in them which may not be freely submitted to the King. On the contrary, I feel that the circumstances of the moment, and the extreme importance which attaches to His Majesty's full and unbiassed consideration of them, and to the decision he may finally adopt, render desirable his cognisance of every word they contain.

I would close my letter here, if there were not in those letters a few points upon which I may offer remarks without indiscretion, and without committing His Majesty, and departing from the strict line of duty which a *very delicate* situation prescribes to me.

1st. The King has never, to the best of my knowledge, entertained the opinion, nor I believe expressed such, that his present Government caused the excitement about Reform. He has admitted that it *had* been the occasion of increasing agitation; and he has, I well know, stated to your Lordship and to others, that all but the Duke of Wellington had acknowledged to him that some Reform was necessary. The King has indeed observed that this excitement has become more extensive and serious, in consequence of the legislative discussion of the measure; and he has stated, without reserve, his apprehensions of the effects which the disappointment may produce.

I am not aware that His Majesty has ever taken the view stated in your Lordship's second proposition. He has stated fully the grounds of his objection to a dissolution. He has considered the period of general election to have been, at all times and under all circumstances, a period of disorder, of general relaxation, and more or less of outrage; and he has been strongly impressed with the fear that, from the spirit of the times, the disturbances and lawless acts which prevailed some months ago, the illegal combinations which are still in existence, though not at present in active operation, those disorders which attend a general election would be carried to extremes, without reference even to any extraordinary excitement produced by the agitation of the question of Reform and its failure. His Majesty has, however, not concealed his apprehension of associations for the purpose of forcing forward the measure, although there should not be a dissolution; but he has not considered that they would endanger the tranquillity and the security of the country in the same degree as large assemblages of the lower orders, in every part of the country, at one and the same moment, which would be held under the sanction of the law.

3. This is undeniable, and is the natural result of

every change of Government, not followed by a dissolution of Parliament. It is impossible it should not have struck His Majesty, but he had hoped that it would have been, in some degree, counteracted by the divisions which prevailed among the opponents of the Government, and by the pains which he took to mark and declare his support of his Government. I should, however, add that this also has been one of the reasons why His Majesty felt and wished that the introduction of the Reform Bill should, if possible, be delayed. He considered the experiment a hazardous one; and that it required not only a popular, but a strong, Government to carry the object.

Upon Lord Durham's letter I beg to observe, that, although the King has dwelt so much and principally on the consequences of a dissolution from the excited state of public feeling, he has not disguised from himself the probable effect of a rejection of the Bill, which he has contemplated with serious concern and apprehension, although for the reasons already assigned, His Majesty may not have entertained the same apprehension of a general convulsion and of extensive disturbance arising out of such failure.

Heretofore elections may not have produced occurrences unconnected with the electioneering objects of the moment; but His Majesty feels, and I believe there are few that do not feel, that it would not be safe or correct to judge of what may happen from what has passed. No one can deny that the country is, in many parts, suffering under the influence of the revolutionary proceedings in France, Belgium, &c., and I have already alluded to disturbances, &c., serious outrages of recent date, to illegal unions, &c. &c.

Admitting, to the fullest extent stated, the feelings of disappointment and discontent from the rejection of the Bill and the refusal of dissolution, the effect of them would not be concentrated, nor brought into action; and, at any rate, the results contemplated by Lord Durham rest upon the supposition that the feeling in favour of the measure of Reform is general and undivided, which I believe your Lordship will find, on reference to His Majesty's early communication on the subject, has never been his opinion, although he has admitted the feeling to be extensive and strongly expressed, especially by the lower orders.

I do not believe that the King has ever admitted a supposition that he could be accused or suspected of not being sincere in his support of the question. His sanction had been given so honestly and so avowedly; every step he has taken hitherto, and during the progress of the discussion, has been so well calculated to manifest the sincerity of that sanction,—all that could imply a doubt of the propriety of the measure or of its success has been so carefully concealed (for I must be allowed to treat as undeserving of notice the reports scandalously fabricated and raised for the purpose of throwing doubt upon His Majesty's good faith), that His Majesty may bid defiance to such a supposition, may challenge every possible investigation. I may safely assure your Lordship that, when your Lordship submitted the measure, the King partook of the confidence expressed by yourself and others of his Government, that the measure would be carried in the House of Commons, and that his chief apprehension (which, indeed, he expressed) was that of a schism between the Lords and Commons on this subject. He did not contemplate the possibility of a proposal to dissolve Parliament, and he had taken occasion to express his strong objection to it, under any circumstances, long before he was made aware of the nature and extent of the measure to be submitted to him. His Majesty has so fully stated the principal ground of objection, that it would be a waste of your Lordship's time to say more on that point; but I may declare to you my conscientious belief, that it is this dread of throwing this country into convulsion and Ireland into rebellion, which principally influences His Majesty, and that every other consideration is secondary to one which has made so deep an impression upon his mind.

If, as Lord Durham apprehends, the effect of His Majesty's perseverance in this decision should be distrust of him in the public mind, he will have to lament that which he does not merit. It is very late; I am almost exhausted; and I will not encroach further upon your Lordship's time, although there are some parts of Lord Durham's letter on which I could have wished to touch. At any rate, what I have said, or may say, *without authority*, must be very immaterial; but I do conceive it to be material that the King should be put in possession of your Lordship's and Lord Durham's remarks; and I can see no objection to the communication.

I have no copy of this letter, and if you should authorise me to make the suggested communication, I shall be obliged to you to return this letter,* that I may submit it also to His Majesty.

I have, &c. H. TAYLOR.

---

* The following is the letter from Lord Durham referred to in the preceding letters:—

(Private and confidential.)

March 22, 1831.
Tuesday morning, 12 o'clock.

My dear Lord Grey,—The letters are gone on in circulation. [The letters to and from the King on the question of a dissolution.] It is surprising that throughout all these arguments against dissolution, grounded on the excited state of public feeling, he never for an instant alludes to what will be the effect of a rejection of the Bill, if unaccompanied by a dissolution. From this omission one would imagine, that he fancies the country would quietly acquiesce in the rejection—a rejection effected too through the agency of the very parties who are thus forcibly acquitting themselves, in opposition to the declared judgment of the King, his Ministers, and the country.

In the event of a dissolution, the excitement would be directed into the harmless course of an enthusiastic action in favour of the King and his Government, directed, it is true, warmly against the defenders of the Borough system, but in an equally strong degree pronounced in favour of the prerogatives of the Crown; of the beneficial use of which, for their own interests, the act of dissolution must have convinced them.

Is there an instance of any excitement at elections, producing occurrences unconnected with the electioneering objects of the moment? So far from increasing popular excitement, a dissolution would be its best and safest vent. On the other hand, what appearances would attend the exhibition of public feeling if the Bill were rejected, a dissolution refused by the King, and the Ministry dissolved, as it necessarily must be?

Feelings of disappointment, of almost reckless despair, would be added to that excitement which is now existing. The people are quiet now because they repose with confidence on the support of the King, should the Borough faction be too strong for his Ministers in the House of Commons. Take away from them this last resource, on which they so confidently rely, and who will answer for the consequences? To this may be added the danger of creating a notion that the King has not been sincere in his support of the question. The country will naturally say: How could it be expected that such a question, altering the whole system under which the majority of the House of Commons has been elected, and by which they have thriven at the expense of the country, could be

No. 116.

The King to Earl Grey.

St. James's, March 23, 1831.

The King acknowledges the receipt of Earl Grey's letter of this day, respecting the result of last night's debate, which he has learnt from Viscount Althorp also. His Majesty would have been better pleased if the majority in favour of the second reading of the Reform Bill had been greater, but he sincerely rejoices that it has been carried even by one. He considers it of great importance, that time should be gained for considera-

---

carried except in a Parliament expressly summoned for the purpose of taking it into consideration? The King must then have contemplated the certain arrival of that period at which the sincerity of his determination would be put to the test.

The King has denied to his Ministers their legitimate right to the additional strength which would accrue to them from the dissolution of a Parliament elected under the influence and direction of their predecessors, and most undoubtedly not when the question, which renders it necessary, is one on which the whole country unanimously supports the measure recommended to Parliament, and refused by it. If, therefore, the King refuses his consent to that constitutional measure, which would, to the conviction of every sane man in the country, ensure the success of the Bill, the country will say that he never was in earnest, or thoroughly determined to carry it. In fact, it would be another mode of refusing the royal assent.

What feelings would then exist in the public mind? Distrust of the King, whom they would proclaim to be the only obstacle to the attainment of their wishes; hatred and vengeance against those who have refused their claims, and to whom, by the way, the King must unite himself for the purpose of carrying on the Government; and a conviction, of all others the most dangerous, that the existence of the present form of Government is incompatible with their attainment of those rights and privileges to which they feel themselves entitled. Are these feelings not more likely to produce the tumults, massacres, &c., and the downfal of institutions to which so much allusion is made, than noisy but transient exhibitions of popular

tion; and he hopes and trusts that, when the question is resumed, the effect of that consideration will realize the wishes of His Majesty and his Government. The King trusts it will be satisfactory to Earl Grey to know, that he has appointed Colonel Fox his equerry in the room of Mr. Kennedy Erskine, deceased.

WILLIAM R.

No. 117.

Sir H. Taylor to Earl Grey.

St. James's, March 23, 1831.

My dear Lord,—I hasten to acquaint your Lordship that I have submitted to the King your letter of this

---

enthusiasm which accompany, it is true, but always terminate with every election?

Now as to Ireland: it is ascertained, beyond the power of contradiction, that if a general election were now to take place, that agitation which has so lately existed on the subject of the Union would be, if not destroyed, certainly in abeyance, and that the one object held in view would be Reform. Is this no benefit? It is surely of great importance that the Irish people should be convinced that there is a subject, which even their own leaders consider of paramount importance to that of Repeal; so much so that they are content to waive it; and it is often found that a question once put by can never be resumed with the same effect.

It is evident, to conclude, that the excitement of a general election would only tend to the weakening the enemies of Reform, and strengthening its friends, and ought therefore to be dreaded by the one and desired by the other. In which class is the King to be ranked? His determination as to dissolution must decide this.

I have written these observations as you receive them, and have not time even to copy them. I dare say many of the thoughts, so badly expressed, must have suggested themselves to you, but I thought it better to state them to you as they arose in my mind, after reading the letters you sent me.

Ever affectionately yours,

D.

day, and that of yesterday evening, and that I shall be glad to show him Lord Durham's, as well as that which I wrote to you last night. His Majesty was pleased to hear that his letter of this day had given you satisfaction, as also the appointment of Colonel Fox. His Majesty had always intended to remove Mr. Horace Seymour and Mr. Meynell from their situations in the event of their voting against the Bill. The dismissal of Mr. Calvert will rest with the Duke of Devonshire, to whom I am writing, by His Majesty's command, respecting Mr. Seymour and Mr. Meynell.

I have, &c. H. TAYLOR.

No. 118.

Sir H. Taylor to Earl Grey.

(Private.) St. James's Palace, March 23, 1831.

My dear Lord,—The King has ordered me to thank your Lordship for the communication of the enclosed letters from Lord Durham, and to assure you that he is very sensible of your confidence, in allowing me to read them to him.

I shall be obliged to you to send me that which I wrote to you last night, that I may show it to His Majesty, after which I will return it if you wish it.

I have, &c. H. TAYLOR.

No. 119.

Earl Grey to Sir H. Taylor.

(Private.)   Downing Street, March 23, 1831.

My dear Sir,—In returning your letter of the 22nd, according to the desire expressed in that which I received from you last night, I cannot help troubling you with a few remarks.

1. By my anxiety to impress on the King's recollection the circumstances in which his present Ministers were called into his service, with a view to establish the fact that the excitement of the public feeling on the question of a Parliamentary Reform had previously existed, I did not mean to imply any belief that His Majesty had thought that it originated with them; but I did so from a wish to obviate any impression that might be made by assertions most assiduously disseminated, that such had been the fact. That the public feeling became more animated when the question was taken up by the Government, is indisputable. But this was a natural and unavoidable consequence; and if, on this account, it might become more difficult to resist it, it was attended, at the same time, with the advantage of being directed to a salutary object, and by constitutional means. It was this view that convinced me that it could not act dangerously on a general election.

2. If the above opinions are well founded, there would be nothing to be feared from the associations which assumed, some time ago, so formidable an appearance. They are now completely in abeyance, and would not be called into action by a measure recom-

mended by the Government, and supported by the King, which would be consonant to the wishes of the people. If, on the other hand, the present expectations of the public should be disappointed, there appears to me to be too much reason to fear, that, with the feelings which originally produced them, these associations will revive, that the peace of the country will be endangered, and that if they should unfortunately obtain power sufficient to force the Government to entertain anew the question of Reform, it will no longer be possible to confine it, as may now be done, within safe and constitutional limits.

3. It is undoubtedly true that this Administration experiences only the same inconvenience as must be felt by any Administration succeeding to office with a Parliament chosen by its predecessors. But this does not lessen the actual inconvenience, which has heretofore, as in 1807, obliged the Government to resort to a new election within a few months after the Parliament had been chosen. It is true the opponents of the Government, at its commencement, appeared to be much divided, as in fact they were; but this always left the Ministers exposed to the danger of an union against them on every occasion which might favour the views of those who, disagreeing in everything else, concurred in a desire to avail themselves of any opportunity to embarrass their measures. Of this a pregnant instance was afforded in the division on the Bill for altering the Timber Duties; and I am persuaded that, independently of the Reform question, it would be hardly possible for the Administration to act efficiently for the public service, with the present House of Commons.

The extent of the public feeling, as to the measure that has been proposed, will be differently estimated by different persons, according to their different opportunities of information, and their various interests and opinions. But I believe there never was a sentiment so general, or rather so nearly universal as that which now prevails. Let any impartial person look at the meetings in all parts of the country, the number and description of the persons attending them, and the unanimity of their decisions, to which scarcely, in any instance, an opposition has been attempted; and I think there can be little doubt of the opinion he must form. I confess I look with the greatest alarm at the consequences of an erroneous judgment on this part of the question.

I am sure you will acquit me of the most distant idea of insinuating any thing against the good faith and sincerity of the King. For those most essential qualities no man was ever more distinguished. In the whole of his conduct towards his present Ministers, as towards his last, they have been invariably displayed; and more particularly in every thing that has taken place on this important question. We all acknowledge this. We all feel grateful for it. We are all actuated by the truest sentiments of duty and attachment; and there is nothing we would not do to avoid any opposition to His Majesty's opinions, which that same sense of duty did not dictate, combined with the obligation of maintaining our own character and honour. By these sentiments nobody is more sincerely actuated than Lord Durham; and I hope, whatever may have been said by him with respect to any impression injurious to the King, which might be created by a refusal to dissolve the Parliament, could not be conceived to imply any suspicion of his own, than which nothing could be more remote both from his feeling and his intention, but merely an apprehension of what might be the effect on those who are led away by appearances, or by the representations of others who may wish, for purposes of their own, to pervert the public opinion. That such a suspicion would be most unworthy and most unjust, I can say, with confidence, is not more firmly my own conviction than it is that of Lord Durham. If ultimately this question should unfortunately come to a decision which might remove his present Ministers from His Majesty's service, I am sure there is not one of them who would not, both in public and in private, bear the fullest testimony to the pure and conscientious motives which had governed His Majesty's conduct. Nay, more; I should feel myself bound to acknowledge, though possessing strong opinions myself, grounded on the reasons which I have stated, that for the opposite view taken by His Majesty many strong considerations present themselves, arising out of the present circumstances of the country. I anxiously hope, therefore, that neither I nor Lord Durham can suffer in His Majesty's opinion, or be supposed to entertain a feeling inconsistent with the sincere respect which we feel for his character, and our affectionate attachment to his person, from any thing that may have been too incautiously or too freely expressed in a correspondence which was not intended to meet his eye.

I have been induced to dwell more upon this, because I have remarked that His Majesty's manner to

Lord Durham has not been marked with the same kindness that he has shown to his other servants. This may have been accidental, but I know it has been felt by Lord Durham; and I had once thought of desiring him to address directly to His Majesty, from himself, a statement of his feelings and opinions on the question we have been discussing, which few people could do so ably, and which I hoped might bring about more confidential communications between His Majesty and a most useful and attached servant. You will see a printed list of the Division, an examination of which will afford no bad ground for estimating the state of public opinion. The activity, the intrigue, the falsehood that was used to influence votes is not to be described. What hurt us most was the report so industriously propagated, that the King had put a positive veto on a proposal to dissolve the Parliament. Several Members, representing popular constituencies, who had before declared their intention of voting, changed on this assurance. Among other authorities for it, that of Lord Mansfield is stated. It was said that he had had an audience of the King, at which he had represented the dangers of the present crisis; and that, on his return, he had publicly said, that, whatever might happen, he could confidently assert that no dissolution would take place. This may be as false as many other reports that have been circulated, but it certainly had its effect.

This letter has extended to an unreasonable length, and, before you come to the end of it, I fear you will be even more tired than I have been in writing it.

I am, &c. GREY.

No. 120.

Sir H. Taylor to Earl Grey.

(Private.) St. Katharine's, March 24, 1831.

My dear Lord,—I took the earliest opportunity this morning of submitting to the King the letter I had the honour of receiving from your Lordship, returning mine of the 22nd instant, which I then also read to His Majesty; but it has not been in my power to reply to it until this evening.

I had the satisfaction of learning that His Majesty did not object to any part of my letter of the 22nd, and that he admitted that I had correctly stated his views and sentiments, so far as I had ventured to advert to them; and His Majesty was also pleased to say, that he rejoiced that what had been said had clearly shown that there had been no misapprehension on either side, as to the origin or the cause of the excitement, to which such frequent allusion has been made, whatever may be the impression as to the advantage or prejudice that may result from the direction it may assume and its general effects. His Majesty cannot divest himself of the apprehensions he has expressed, that the feelings which had recently produced disturbance and outrage, although at present suppressed, would again be called into action; and that assemblages, which might avowedly take place in support of a measure recommended by the Government and supported by the King, and consonant also to the wishes of a large portion of the people, would be taken advantage of to give to that support a character of violence and intimidation extremely dangerous to all whose opinions had been declared, or were otherwise known to be opposed to the measure, and therefore tending to affect seriously the peace of the country, especially as the violence thus exercised has of late been levelled at the property as well as the persons of all who have resisted popular clamour.

That, independently of the Reform question, the Administration must experience great difficulty in acting efficiently for the public service, has been shown not only on recent occasions, but before the present Administration had experienced that difficulty, although, upon the occasion to which your Lordship principally alludes (the division on the Bill for altering the Timber Duties), it was admitted that various interests, not usually opposed to the Government, were, from the peculiar nature of those interests, united to what may be considered as constituting the Opposition. Supposing a dissolution to take place before the Reform Bill is carried, it is natural to conclude that, from the pledges required from the candidates, the returns would produce a strong majority in favour of that measure; but other pledges would probably be required also; and the question is whether, with a House of Commons so constituted, it would be more possible than at present for the Administration to act efficiently for the public service. At any rate, the effect of the dissolution would be the re-production of the House of Commons in its present unreformed character, and another must take place within a very short period to afford the benefits anticipated from the measure. And if the sentiment in favour of Reform be so nearly universal as stated, the clamour for a second dissolution will be again pleaded as a reason for hastening its period. With regard to the meetings that take place, it may be questioned whether those who attend them express the opinions of the most respectable or most influential portion of the community. They are almost invariably the advocates and supporters of the object for which they are called together; and, upon a popular occasion, the great majority are of the very lowest class. The opponents, those who know that they will not be suffered to raise their voices, seldom attend, and unanimity is thus placed beyond the power of dispute.

I have taken the liberty of stating what I have reason to believe to be the King's opinions; but if, when I have the honour of reading this letter to him, it should not obtain his sanction, I shall withhold them.

His Majesty, however, ordered me to express, in the strongest terms, the satisfaction he has derived from the acknowledgment conveyed in your Lordship's letter, and indeed upon every other occasion, of the good faith and sincerity with which he has acted, more particularly in everything that has taken place on this important question. His Majesty, indeed, has never doubted that such was your feeling: that such were the sentiments of his other confidential servants, he could not doubt it. His Majesty is not less convinced of the sincerity of your duty and attachment, and of your disposition to avoid any opposition to his opinions, which a sense of duty and the obligation of maintaining your own character and honour did not dictate; and His Majesty is the last man who would expect deference to his opinions and wishes not so qualified, or who would attach any value to it. The King desires your Lordship will be assured that there is not an expression or a word in Lord Durham's letter which you have communicated to him that has, or could, excite any other feeling than that he has ordered me to express, than that which you are desirous they should have impressed upon him. The King wishes on all occasions to receive the free, the honest, the unreserved opinions of those who address him, more especially upon the present important question; nor can those suffer in his estimation who feel it to be their duty to utter and to maintain opinions which may not accord with his own. I think I may venture to say, and indeed I have the King's authority for saying, that your Lordship has mistaken the cause of His Majesty's manner towards Lord Durham, and that the appearance has been purely accidental. He observed, indeed, when I read that part of your letter to him, that Lord Durham appears shy and reserved, and that his manner did not encourage free intercourse. He ordered me to assure your Lordship, that he would be very glad to see Lord Durham whenever it might suit him, and that he should receive with attention and interest the statement of his feelings and opinions on the question under discussion.

I have had the honour of submitting to the King the printed list of the Division your Lordship sent me, which he examined with great interest.

His Majesty is not surprised at the means which have been used to influence votes, believing that upon those occasions such means have been usually resorted to, though certainly not creditable to those who adopt them. With regard to the report propagated, that the King had put a positive veto on a proposal to dissolve, your Lordship knows, from a comparison of dates, that it could not come from Windsor; nor had the King's feelings on the subject been mentioned, or even whispered, until he replied to the question put in your letter to me, received on *Sunday last*, and which I submitted to him; nor has it been otherwise broached. Lord Mansfield had been with the King on the preceding Tuesday. He wrote to me from the Castle Inn at Windsor to request an audience of His Majesty, to which he was admittted. I did not see him, but His Majesty told me that he had been with him some time, and had stated fully his view of the general question of Reform, without endeavouring to elicit His Majesty's sentiments, and without learning what they might be. I asked the King on that day, whether any mention had been made of a dissolution, or any allusion to that contingency, and His Majesty assured me that he had not committed himself upon it. No secret was made of Lord Mansfield's visit; and if His Majesty omitted to notice it to you, the omission must have been accidental.

With regard to what was stated to Captain Elliott, as having been said to Sir Thomas Trowbridge by one of His Majesty's household, I beg to repeat, that if the King could learn who the individual was who presumed to make so unjustifiable a use of his name, and so groundless an assertion, His Majesty would not hesitate to remove him from his situation; and I beg to remind you also that I requested your permission to write to Captain Elliott to request he would state to Sir Thomas Trowbridge that the individual in question had made an assertion to him for which he knew that he could offer no proof.

Your Lordship mentioned to me another person, whose language had been violent and indiscreet, and calculated, from his peculiar situation and habits of constant access to the King, to make great impression. That person has been seriously cautioned to be more guarded. He declares positively that he had not written a line from Windsor, and indeed he was not there at the date assigned to the asserted communication; nor, further, had the King ever expressed any opinion to him on the subject of dissolution. I do not mention this to remove impressions or doubts, which I am quite satisfied do not exist, but to show how impossible it is to guard against reports raised and circulated on presumption.

I have, &c. H. TAYLOR.

No. 121.

Earl Grey to Sir H. Taylor.

Downing Street, April 5, 1831.

My dear Sir,—There is nothing new that will not have reached the King by the usual communication of the dispatches. The French Government have taken up the advance of the Austrian troops to Bologna with more moderation than I had expected. Indeed the whole tenor of the late communications from Paris are encouraging to our hopes of preserving peace. The truth is, that not one of the Continental Powers, including France herself, is in a condition to go to war; and this consciousness must have a powerful effect in keeping them all quiet. The thing to be avoided is anything that might excite, beyond the control, either of the Government or of reason, the too susceptible spirit of the French people.

Count —— has been here for some days. He was in the battle of 25th February, and his account of it corresponds exactly with that which you may remember to have read in one of Lord Cowley's dispatches. He states the Polish regular army to amount to 60,000 men, and to be in good order; the irregular force, 40,000. This is probably an exaggeration. On the other hand, you will see in Mr. Chad's dispatches, the estimate of the Russian force. Making reasonable deductions on both sides, the party is too unequal to suppose that the resistance of the Poles can be ultimately successful; but there is still too much reason to fear a dreadful effusion of blood before the end of the contest. —— speaks with great praise of the new general, and there must be a good deal in a man who has raised himself in the field of battle above all the old generals with universal consent.

The accounts from Ireland to-day are very satisfactory; they came from Sir John Byng, Lord Anglesey being gone to Clare. He states, there will be no opposition to Sir Henry Parnell, and that he should have no fear of the new election in the event of a dissolution. These accounts come from Sir J. Byng and Mr. Spring Rice.

I had hardly finished this, when a box was brought

to me from the Home Office with letters of the 31st March, from Ennis, from Major Warburton, giving a very different account of the state of things.

Major Warburton is, I believe, a very good man, but his accounts always appear to me to be dictated by the worst view of the state of affairs. Lord Anglesey is however, by this time, in the south of Clare, and I am sanguine in my expectations of the good effect of his visit.

The papers will give you an account of the dinner at the Mansion House yesterday. The Lord Mayor introduced more of the politics of the day than I think advisable on such occasions; but nothing could be more favourable to his Majesty's Government, or more gratifying, than the expression of patriotic feeling on this occasion.

I am, &c. GREY.

No. 122.

Earl Grey to Sir H. Taylor.

Stoke Farm, April 6, 1831.

My dear Sir,—Did you see in the 'Morning Chronicle' of yesterday, the copy of a letter written by me, in 1814, to General Kosciusko? The purpose for which it is published, not quite fairly perhaps, is sufficiently obvious, and may expose me to some attacks. My defence, however, is not difficult. It is one thing to state certain political opinions with a view to arrangements which are not completed, and another to urge the same views in order to set aside these arrangements after they have been sanctioned by treaties. The opinions I then entertained, I see no reason to retract; and if the independence of Poland had been established on those principles which might have best secured the permanent settlement of Europe at the general peace, most of the difficulties and dangers which have since occurred, and which still embarrass us, might have been prevented. Everybody must wish the present contest in Poland terminated; and, if possible, in such a manner as may at once insure to the people of that unhappy country a good government, and to the neighbouring states, and to Europe generally, a sufficient security against the farther aggrandisement of Russia on that side.

I am, &c. GREY.

No. 123.

The King to Earl Grey.

Windsor Castle, April 10, 1831.

The King returns to Earl Grey the private letter from Lord Ponsonby to Viscount Palmerston, which he sent to him yesterday, and which appears to His Majesty to embrace several points of deep interest to the policy as well as to the character of His Majesty's Government and this country, and therefore requiring serious consideration, which His Majesty does not wish to *embarrass* by the communication of his opinions, although it may not prove unsatisfactory to Earl Grey and Viscount Palmerston.

Lord Ponsonby has, in this letter, stated so strongly

and unequivocally his conviction, that no advantage could result from further exertion in favour of the Prince of Orange, or from any attempt to re-establish the authority of the House of Nassau in Belgium; that, admitting this opinion to be correct, there appears no reason why this country should not endeavour to conciliate the party and the individuals now exercising authority in Belgium, whose cooperation may possibly have been withheld chiefly from the apprehension that the restoration of that obnoxious sovereignty was the object for which England would contend. It is essential that this country, being freed from this clog, should look to the issue of the general question, and endeavour to establish an influence which shall balance, and if possible outweigh, that of France; and His Majesty considers that, if this object can be promoted by receiving M. d'Arschott, this step might be taken, and that a sufficient *ostensible* plea might be found for it in the *recent* proceedings of the Belgian Government, which have shown a greater disposition to conciliate this Government, and to observe the conditions of the armistice, and in the assurances given by the Regent and M. Lebeau to Lord Ponsonby, of a more friendly feeling.

The next point is the suggested election of Prince Leopold to the sovereignty of Belgium; and His Majesty cannot deny that he has felt very strong objections to the Prince Leopold being brought forward with the concurrence of England, since England took so warm and so decided a part against the election of the Duc de Nemours. It is impossible that Prince Leopold, circumstanced as he is with respect to this country, should not be in some degree under its influence; and, at any rate, he will be considered to be so. It will be said that England contended for the House of Orange so long as no Prince immediately connected with or dependent upon itself was brought forward, but abandoned that cause for a selfish object. This will be urged or insinuated by France in any future stage of the discussion: it will excite a feeling of jealousy and suspicion in the other Powers: above all, it will produce a most unfavourable impression upon the House of Nassau, and all that are allied and connected with it; and will place His Majesty and his family in a very painful and invidious position towards a family with which they have so long been connected in bonds of strict union and friendship.

The King considers that the credit of this country, his own credit, and that of his Government, are concerned in maintaining the high and disinterested principle upon which this Belgic Question has hitherto been dealt with; and that it will be abandoned if their exertions should be used in favour of a candidate for the sovereignty of Belgium, who is brought forward under their influence. Nay, His Majesty cannot help suspecting that France may now be encouraging this measure, in order thereby to cast a reproach upon the fair character of this country, and to weaken its *moral* influence in Europe.

The King agrees with Lord Ponsonby, that the pretensions of the Belgians to the possession of the canal from the Sass de Gand to Terneuse, and the sluices by which it is in the power of those who hold them to inundate a large portion of the country, is reasonable;

and he thinks that means should be taken to secure Holland and Belgium reciprocally against the possibility of injury of this description.   WILLIAM R.

No. 124.

Earl Grey to the King.

Downing Street, April 11, 1831.

Earl Grey presents his humble duty to your Majesty, and has the honour of acknowledging your Majesty's letter of yesterday, with the very important communication of your Majesty's sentiments on that which had been transmitted to your Majesty by Earl Grey from Lord Ponsonby.

Earl Grey has now the honour of enclosing for your Majesty's information (Viscount Melbourne not being returned to London), some communications respecting the state of Ireland, which he has received from Mr. Stanley this morning.

Earl Grey deeply regrets the melancholy condition of that country, as it is described in these papers. It will require the immediate and anxious attention of your Majesty's servants as soon as they can be reassembled; and Earl Grey anticipates, with great pain, the unfortunate necessity which the next accounts from Lord Anglesey will too probably establish, of submitting to your Majesty a proposition for extending the powers of the Government to control a spirit of violence and outrage which has risen to so formidable a height.

Earl Grey humbly solicits the honour of being admitted to your Majesty's presence to-morrow as soon after two o'clock as may be convenient to your Majesty.

All which, &c. GREY.

No. 125.

The King to Earl Grey.

St. James's Palace, April 11, 1831.

The King returns the letter from the Lord-Lieutenant of Ireland and others addressed to Mr. Stanley, which accompanied Earl Grey's letter of this day, and from which His Majesty has learnt with great concern, that Lord Anglesey considers the state of the county of Clare to be such as may render necessary an extension of the powers of the Government towards repressing the spirit of violence and outrage, not to say insurrection, which prevails in that and neighbouring districts.

The King will be glad to see Earl Grey at any hour before or after two that may suit him to-morrow.

WILLIAM R.

No. 126.

Earl Grey to the King.

Downing Street, April 19, 1831.

Earl Grey has the honour of enclosing for your Majesty's information, a letter which he received yesterday from the Marquis of Anglesey. The account given in it, of the state of the disturbed parts of Ireland, leaves little doubt that it will become necessary for your

Majesty's servants to propose to your Majesty measures for increasing the powers of the Government.

The debate in the House of Commons last night is represented to Earl Grey as having been very satisfactory; and it is also stated to him that there is every reason to expect, that the division on General Gascoigne's motion* will be favourable. But Earl Grey thinks that it would not be right for him to conceal from your Majesty, that the decision upon this question, considering the manner in which it has been brought forward, must necessarily have so important an effect with regard to the future success of the Bill, as to require, in the event of its being adverse, the immediate and anxious consideration of your Majesty's servants with a view to their future procedings.

All which, &c. GREY.

No. 127.

Earl Grey to Sir H. Taylor.

(Secret and confidential.)

Downing Street, April 19, 1831.

My dear Sir,—In writing to-day to the King on the subject of Lord Anglesey's letter, I have thought it necessary to call his attention to the present state of the Reform question in the House of Commons.

* General Gascoigne had moved, as an amendment on the motion for going into Committee on the Reform Bill, the following resolution, 'That it is the opinion of this House, that the total number of knights, citizens, and burgesses, returned to Parliament for that part of the United Kingdom called England and Wales, ought not to be diminished.' The debate had been adjourned.

Though I could have consented to such an addition to the Members of the House of Commons as would have filled the deficiency left by our plan, the mode in which the proposition has been brought forward raises a difficulty which, if the motion should be carried, will be of a very serious nature. It has been done, artfully enough, to take upon a collateral question a division which, in its consequences, as has been obviously the intention of Sir R. Peel and its supporters, must be decisive of the fate of the Bill. For if carried it will prevent any addition being made to the number of representatives of Ireland and Scotland, unless an addition to the same extent should be made to the present numbers of the House of Commons. I need not tell you how inconvenient this would be with the declared opinions of the King's Ministers, with the views which have influenced them in framing the Bill, and how impossible for them it would be to consent to such an alteration.

A decision of so adverse a nature would necessarily deprive them of all hope of being able to carry the Bill without such further alterations as would altogether destroy its character in the present House of Commons; and we shall then have arrived at the crisis in which the expediency, or rather the necessity, of a dissolution must be seriously considered. The calculations of those who know the House of Commons best encourage us to expect a favourable division; but still the event is too uncertain to allow me to expose His Majesty to the chance of its coming upon him without some previous preparation for the emergency which may follow.

I feel deeply the embarrassment in which he may be involved, and it is my duty to diminish it as much as possible.

I write this to you in the most unreserved confidence, that you may act upon it as you may think will be most conducive to His Majesty's ease and to the public interest, but without extending the communication to any other person.

I enclose a letter from poor Captain ———. It is a case of real compassion; but I know how circumscribed the means are which are possessed by His Majesty to meet this and other claims upon his benevolence. Had there been any fund at the disposal of the Government out of which I could have assisted this poor old man, you should have heard nothing about it; but as there exists no source from which I can afford him any succour, I could not help laying his own statement of his case before you. The Lord Mayor has been with me this morning, to state that the citizens have become very impatient for the visit of their Majesties, and that he has with difficulty prevented their calling a Common Council to vote a renewal of their former invitation. He was very properly anxious to learn their Majesties' wishes before such a step should be taken, and for this purpose came to me. I have told him that I would state what he had said to His Majesty, and communicate the result to him. This I shall do when I have the honour of seeing the King previous to the levee; but in the meantime I thought it useful that you should be enabled to prepare His Majesty for such a communication.

I am, &c.   GREY.

No. 128.

The King to Earl Grey.

St. James's Palace, April 19, 1831.

The King received, soon after his arrival in town, Earl Grey's letter of this day and the accompanying letter from the Lord-Lieutenant of Ireland; and Sir Herbert Taylor has submitted to His Majesty that which Earl Grey addressed to him. The King has given to those communications the consideration which their importance demands; and he laments to be under the necessity of admitting, that the state of the disturbed parts of Ireland, as it is described so clearly, ably, and dispassionately in Lord Anglesey's letter, appears to him such as not only to justify, but imperiously to call for the adoption of measures for increasing the power of the Government. His Majesty cannot express the opinion without stating also his anxiety to do justice to the wisdom and the efficiency of all the proceedings of his Government with respect to Ireland, and to the energy, the good sense, and the zeal with which Lord Anglesey has discharged the duties of his arduous situation.

This state of Ireland, as His Majesty has viewed it for some time past, and as it has been represented by Lord Anglesey, has caused His Majesty to receive with additional concern the intimation conveyed in Earl Grey's letters, and more especially in that addressed to Sir Herbert Taylor, that the further proceedings on the Reform Bill in the House of Commons may be such as to place his confidential servants under the necessity of considering the expediency of a dissolution. The King does full justice to the honourable feeling and the manly candour which have prompted Earl Grey to call his attention thus early to this crisis; and he appreciates equally the consideration for himself which has influenced every part of his proceeding on the occasion. It is therefore, with sincere regret, that he is under the necessity of stating to Earl Grey that his objections to a dissolution of Parliament, at this period, have continued such as they have been described to him in former communications; and that, anxiously solicitous as he has felt to yield his opinions to those which have been urged by Earl Grey and Lord Durham, and to overcome impressions which had become so strong upon his own mind, he has not been able to reconcile the dictates of his duty, such as they offer themselves to him, to the adoption of a measure which he would readily sanction, if his objections to it could be said to rest on political grounds.

The King, therefore, most earnestly hopes that the division upon General Gascoigne's motion may be such as to relieve Earl Grey and his other confidential servants from the necessity of submitting for his decision a measure against which he has not ceased to state his objections; and that he may be thus freed from the embarrassment and the distress of entering with them into any discussion which would not accord with the spirit and the feeling which have hitherto governed the communications which have passed with them upon every subject, which have been truly satisfactory to him, and which he cannot notice without declaring also that the manner in which the business of the country has been carried on, whether as relating to its interior concerns or its exterior policy, at a period of almost unexampled difficulty, has, in his opinion, merited in the fullest degree that approbation which has been so unequivocally bestowed upon it.

The King has already alluded to the state of Ireland as increasing the concern with which he has received Earl Grey's communication, as the view he considers himself bound to take of it has added to his apprehensions of the convulsions which may result from a dissolution; nor does His Majesty contemplate without dread the difficulty which may be experienced in supplying Lord Anglesey with the additional military means for which he has applied.

His Majesty had hoped that the necessity of producing more correct returns of the population than those which the census of 1821 affords (a necessity which he had early contemplated) would, after his Government had carried the principle of the Bill and established the necessity for Reform, have afforded to them a sufficient and very reasonable plea for proposing that the discussion should be postponed until a more opportune period.

He may have entertained this expectation on false grounds, but he naturally seeks for any expedient which may avoid the proposal to which Earl Grey alludes.

WILLIAM R.

No. 129.

Sir H. Taylor to Earl Grey.

(Private.) St. James's Palace, April 19, 1831.

My dear Lord,—The King is so desirous that there should be no unnecessary delay in sending his answer to your Lordship that, after copying it, I do not find myself at liberty to reply at any length to that which you addressed to me; and I must reserve for another time, the answer to those parts of it which regard Captain —— and the Lord Mayor's communication.

I cannot, however, transmit His Majesty's letter without saying, that I hope I correctly understood that it was intended for His Majesty's eye; indeed, its purport seemed to point out the indispensable necessity of submitting it to him without delay; and I may add that as His Majesty received the box before I got to St. James's, the letter was opened in his presence and at once read to him.

His Majesty has replied to it so fully that I shall only observe, that he appeared extremely distressed by that part of it on which he has chiefly dwelt in his answer.

I have, &c. H. TAYLOR.

No. 130.

Sir H. Taylor to Earl Grey.

(Private.) St. Katharine's, April 19, 1831.

My dear Lord,—The King received most kindly the appeal which poor Captain —— has made to him through your Lordship, and has honoured me with his commands to acquaint you that he has, in consequence, directed his name to be placed upon his list for an annual allowance of two hundred pounds (£200), but that the extent of that list and the means applicable to it do not admit of His Majesty continuing to him the allowance which he received from the late King.

The fact is that, upon His Majesty's accession, he received from the late King's executors a list of pensions, allowances, and other payments made by his late Majesty, which it was recommended to him that he should continue from his Privy Purse. The amount was very considerable, and one item was the payment of 6000*l.* annually to Mrs. Fitzherbert; but it does not include *all* his late Majesty's pensioners, and among those excluded, as considered to have no particular claim upon his present Majesty, was Captain ——. Many of those have been replaced upon the list; others (including old servants of the late King and dependants upon their late Majesties George III. and Queen Charlotte) have been added, besides many who had immediate claims upon His Majesty; and these additions to the transfer of charges from the Privy Purse of His Majesty's predecessor on the throne, which had heretofore been provided for by grant from Parliament, absorb, with the latter, a very large portion of His Majesty's disposable funds; nor does a week pass that some claim is not preferred, either for a subscription, donation, or annual provision, which it is difficult for His Majesty to resist. I need not observe that the demands continually made, and in some instances without much consideration, are a heavy charge, to which has been added the payment of the Queen's outfit, which the King has taken upon himself.

It was therefore not extraordinary that His Majesty should have endeavoured, as far as possible, to limit his admission of the late King's pensioners to the list received from the Duke of Wellington; and this led to his having hitherto resisted the appeal of Captain ——, with whom there has been some correspondence, in the course of which he obtained the promise of a gratuitous commission for one of his grandsons.

The King ordered me to say, that he would speak to your Lordship when he has the pleasure of seeing you to-morrow, previous to the levee, on the subject of the invitation from the City.

I have, &c. H. TAYLOR.

No. 131.

Earl Grey to the King.

Downing Street, April 20, 1831.

Earl Grey has the honour of acknowledging your Majesty's most gracious letter of yesterday, with all the feelings of the most lively gratitude, for the expressions of confidence and approbation with which your Majesty has been pleased to honour the conduct of your servants in their endeavours to discharge the important duties confided to them, and with all the pain, which the prospect of their finding themselves under the necessity of offering to your Majesty any advice, in which your Majesty may not be able to concur, must necessarily occasion.

The Division last night has, contrary to Earl Grey's expectations, proved adverse to your Majesty's Ministers, the numbers being, for General Gascoigne's motion, 299; against it, 291. Under these circumstances, a meeting of your Majesty's servants in Cabinet has been appointed for this morning at eleven o'clock, the result of which Earl Grey will lose no time in communicating to your Majesty.

Earl Grey has the honour of informing your Majesty that the Civil List Bill passed the Committee of the House of Lords, and was reported last night, and will be read a third time to-day.

All which, &c. GREY.

No. 132.

The King to Earl Grey.

St. James's Palace, April 20, 1831.

The King acknowledges the receipt of Earl Grey's letter of this day, stating the Division of last night in the House of Commons, which His Majesty has learnt with great concern.

He will be prepared to receive Earl Grey at any time that may suit him before the levee.

WILLIAM R.

No. 133.

Minute of Cabinet.

Downing Street, April 20, 1831.

At a meeting of your Majesty's confidential servants held this morning, at the House of the First Lord of the Treasury, in Downing Street,—

PRESENT:

The Lord Chancellor,	The Lord Privy Seal,
The Lord President,	The Duke of Richmond,
Viscount Goderich,	Lord Holland,
Viscount Melbourne,	Viscount Palmerston,
The Earl of Carlisle,	Viscount Althorp,
Earl Grey,	Sir James Graham,

Mr. Grant,

it was agreed humbly to submit to your Majesty the following Minute:—

Your Majesty's confidential servants having taken into their most serious consideration the circumstances under which the Division of last night took place in the House of Commons, and the effect of that Division, have arrived at the painful conclusion, that there is no reasonable hope of the ultimate success of the Reform Bill in the present House of Commons.

Earl Grey having communicated to them your Majesty's letter of yesterday's date, they have been impressed with the most lively gratitude for your Majesty's most gracious approbation of their humble services; and they must necessarily feel the deepest regret at finding themselves compelled to offer your Majesty advice which possibly may not meet with your Majesty's concurrence.

But, under the circumstances in which they are now placed, they can see no alternative consistent with the duty which they owe to your Majesty and to the country, but that of humbly recommending a dissolution of the present Parliament.

Your Majesty's confidential servants beg leave to add that they have not come to the determination of humbly offering this advice to your Majesty without having anxiously deliberated on the state of every part of the United Kingdom, and particularly of Ireland; and without having convinced themselves, from the best information they could collect, that the measure which they recommended would be perfectly consistent with the public safety.*

No. 134.

The King to Earl Grey.

St. James's Palace, April 20, 1831.

Although the King has read, more than once, the Minute of Cabinet which Earl Grey has submitted to him, it involves matter of such deep importance to the interests of the country, and to His Majesty's character, that he cannot come to any decision upon it, without mature consideration.

His Majesty's answer shall, however, be sent to Earl Grey early to-morrow.

WILLIAM R.

No. 135.

Earl Grey to the King.

Downing Street, April 20, 1831.

Earl Grey presents his humble duty to your Majesty, and has the honour of acknowledging the receipt of your Majesty's letter of this day.

In discharging the painful duty of submitting to your Majesty the Minute of Cabinet agreed to by your

---

* This Minute was submitted to the King by Earl Grey in an audience before the levee.

Majesty's servants this morning, it was far from Earl Grey's intention, as it was from that of his colleagues, to press your Majesty for an earlier decision than was entirely consistent with your Majesty's convenience, and with the necessity of maturely considering the important matter submitted to your Majesty's determination, which your Majesty's servants respectfully await, with all the sentiments of gratitude and affection to which your Majesty is so eminently entitled.

All which, &c. GREY.

No. 136.

The King to Earl Grey.

St. James's Palace, April 21, 1831.

In the short letter which the King wrote to Earl Grey yesterday afternoon, in acknowledgment of the Minute of Cabinet submitted to him, His Majesty stated that the Minute involved matter of such deep importance to the interests of the country and to His Majesty's character, that he could not come to any decision upon it without mature consideration.

The question which has engaged his serious attention and his anxious reflection has been, whether he should subscribe to a proposal to which he has repeatedly stated objections which have not been removed, nor essentially weakened; or whether he should make up his mind to a second change of administration, within a very short space of time since his accession, at a period when so much of the welfare of this country, so much of the welfare of Europe, depend upon the stability of his Government, and upon the confidence which the adherence to a steady system of administration may inspire?

Such is the alternative upon which the King has had to decide; for, although it has not been presented to him in words in the Minute of Cabinet, His Majesty could not expect that his refusal to dissolve Parliament, when he had been so strongly urged to do so by his confidential servants, would not be followed by their resignation.

With this view of the question—with a mind happily unbiassed by any predilection for this or that party, and wholly free from political prejudice—with a deep sense of the obligations which the duties of the station in which Providence has placed him impose upon him to divest himself of every feeling, except that which is directed to the interests, the welfare, and the prosperity of the country entrusted to his charge, and to consider calmly and dispassionately the various contingencies under which his decision was to be made, and the consequences which might result from it—His Majesty has endeavoured, upon this occasion, to discharge correctly the duty which he owes to his God and to his subjects; and, although he may have erred in judgment, his conscience assures him that his intentions are pure and honest.

His Majesty's objections to a dissolution of Parliament at this period have been so fully stated in repeated communications to Earl Grey, that it would be quite superfluous to recapitulate them in this letter; but he cannot forget that, upon the first occasion in which the possibility of such a measure was brought before him, he stated that he had made up his mind not to sanction it; and in his letter of the 19th instant, as well as in the former part of this letter, His Majesty has declared that his objections have not been removed, nor weakened, although his confidential servants have assured him that they have not come to the determination of offering this advice to His Majesty without having anxiously deliberated on the state of every part of the United Kingdom, and particularly of Ireland, and without having convinced themselves, from the best information they could collect, that the measures which they recommend would be perfectly consistent with the public safety, To which statement, recorded in their Minute, Earl Grey has added the verbal assurance, that Lord Anglesey has pledged himself for the maintenance of the tranquillity of Ireland during a general election.

The apprehensions which His Majesty entertains must be strong indeed not to be removed, as indeed they have not been removed, by these assurances and opinions, submitted by individuals whose conduct, under the pressure of the difficulties in which they undertook and have continued to discharge the duties of their responsible situations, has so well merited His Majesty's confidence. He therefore owes it to his own character, he owes it to his claim to consistency, to state, fairly and without reserve, the considerations which have, upon due reflection, led him to waive his objections to a dissolution, or rather to subscribe to it, as the lesser of two evils.

The King does not deny that, in his general view of the situation and of the interests of this country, of its Foreign relations, and of the influence of the state of the Continent, by reaction, upon the tranquillity and the prosperity of this country, he attaches the greatest and an almost paramount importance to the stability of his Government, and to the maintenance of a fixed system of policy, which shall inspire confidence at home and abroad. He feels deeply the mischiefs which must result, the danger which may arise, from the frequent change of men and measures; and these considerations have induced him to abandon his objections to much which, in less perilous times, might, in his opinion, have justified his adopting and pursuing a different course.

Upon this principle His Majesty had, upon his accession to the throne, made no change in his councils; he gave his strenuous support to the Duke of Wellington's administration, and he sincerely regretted its dissolution. Upon the same principle, he determined to give his utmost support to the administration which Earl Grey was then called upon to form, and he cannot be said to have departed from that determination. His Majesty has more than once admitted that Earl Grey and his colleagues undertook this arduous task at a period of unexampled difficulty; he has more than once declared that they have executed their duties in a manner which entitled them to his unqualified confidence and approbation; and he would not have discharged his own duty, if he had not hesitated to give occasion to another change, and to their removal from his councils, by refusing to accede to a proposal which, in their opinion, was essential towards enabling them to carry into effect a measure which they were avowedly pledged to bring forward, and which, as was notorious to the whole country, had been a prominent feature of the principles on which they had accepted office.

The King does not disguise from Earl Grey and his confidential servants, that this apprehension of a frequent change of Government, so detrimental to the general interests of the country, has had a principal share in producing his determination to yield to the proposed measure of a dissolution of Parliament; and that, upon this occasion, he had considered very seriously whether the state of parties and the feeling of the country offered a fair prospect of making any permanent arrangement which might relieve him from the necessity of conceding that which is so repugnant to his feelings; and that he is satisfied, from the best attention he has been able to give to the subject, that he would not be justified in resorting to an alternative which, in his opinion, would not have secured him for many months against an event, the dread of which could alone have induced him to contemplate an arrangement so much at variance with the feelings he entertains towards his present Government, nor indeed have secured him against the recurrence of the alternative.

His Majesty has deemed it due to himself to make this candid declaration, and he trusts that Earl Grey and his other confidential servants will not view it as betraying any diminution of the confidence which he has not ceased to repose in them, or of his sense of their valuable services.

The King cannot close this letter without reminding Earl Grey, that one of his objections to a dissolution was, that, in the present temper of the people, those who should offer themselves for their representatives might be called upon to pledge themselves to the support of proceedings greatly exceeding any measure of Reform contemplated by his Government, or to which the King could have been induced, *under the pressure of any circumstances*, to give his sanction; and His Majesty having waived his general objections, expects that he may rely with confidence upon his Government for the most strenuous and firm resistance and opposition to any attempt to introduce and carry measures which would extend the principle of the present Reform Bill, or which should have the effect of impairing the influence and dignity of the Crown, and of curtailing the constitutional rights of the monarchy.

His Majesty indeed considers that, if the result of a general election should give to his Government a decided preponderance in the House of Commons, advantage should be taken of it, not to re-establish the Bill in its original shape, but to introduce such modifications as, without producing any essential departure from the principle of the measure, shall be calculated to conciliate the opponents of the Bill, and to reconcile the *general* opinion and feeling of the country to it. He considers the framers of the Bill to be pledged to those modifications of it which Earl Grey has stated to His Majesty, in detail, that they were prepared to introduce, and that he was willing to admit; and His Majesty conceives also that every attention should be paid to the production of correct returns of population, in order to remove the objections which have justly been made to the inaccuracy of calculations founded upon the census of 1821, which has, in many instances, been shown to be defective, and therefore inapplicable.

WILLIAM R.

No. 137.

Earl Grey to Sir H. Taylor.

(Private.)   Downing Street April 21, 1831.

My dear Sir,—I have this moment received the King's letter, with what feelings of gratitude for His Majesty's kindness, and of admiration of his noble and generous conduct, I will not attempt to describe. I feel, at the same time, very deeply for all the distress he must have experienced on this occasion. The Cabinet is to meet here at twelve, and I will either send an answer to the King immediately after it, or wait upon His Majesty with it. In the meantime will you have the goodness to explain to His Majesty the cause of my not sending a more immediate acknowledgment of his most gracious letter.

I am, &c.   GREY.

No. 138.

Sir H. Taylor to Earl Grey.

St. James's Palace, April 21, 1831.

My dear Lord,—I have this moment had the satisfaction of receiving and of submitting your Lordship's letter to the King, who appeared extremely gratified by its contents, and desires that your Lordship will be the bearer of the answer to his communications.

I had anticipated the impression which His Majesty's letter appears to have made upon you, and I cannot help taking this opportunity of stating, that it expresses most accurately the sentiments, nay, the *very words*, which His Majesty *uttered* to me in his instructions, which have not, upon any occasion, been conveyed with greater precision or consideration of their import.

I have, &c. H. TAYLOR.

No. 139.

The King to Earl Grey.

St. James's Palace, April 21, 1831.

The King has this moment received Earl Grey's letter* from Cleveland Row, and having appointed the

* This letter, of which no copy has been preserved, was written late in the evening of the 21st, from Lord Durham's house in Cleveland Row, where several members of the Cabinet had met at dinner.

The purport of the letter, as indeed is obvious from the King's answer to it, was to propose that the dissolution, to which the King had already assented, should take place the next day. The circumstances which led to this recommendation, and under which the letter was written, I can state from my own recollection, confirmed by that of Lord Halifax, who was my father's private secretary at the time.

Although a dissolution had been decided upon, it was not intended that it should take place until some votes of money had been obtained, which were wanted to carry on the public service till a new Parliament could be assembled. But, on the evening of the 21st, notice was given in the House of Lords, by Lord Wharncliffe, that he would on the following day move an Address to the Crown against a dissolution of Parliament; and on the same evening the Opposition, in the House of Commons, showed their intention to prevent any vote of money from being obtained by the Government. Before the report of the votes in the Ordnance estimates, which had been passed in Committee of Supply, could be brought up, a long debate was raised upon a resolution respecting the Liverpool election, in which the conduct of the Government was vehemently attacked, especially with reference to the supposed intention of dissolving Parliament; and at last a motion for the adjournment of the House, without having received the report, was made and carried against the Ministers on a division. This defeat prevented the money already voted from being available to the Government.

Prince of Cobourg to be with His Majesty to-morrow by eleven o'clock, will be happy to see Earl Grey

---

While the debate was in progress, and when it became evident with what object it was protracted, Lord Althorp, who was to have met my father and several of his colleagues at dinner at Lord Durham's, sent Mr. Wood (Lord Halifax) and myself, who were also to dine there, to tell my father from him what was going on, that the money votes could not be obtained, and that in his opinion the dissolution ought to take place at once.

In consequence of this message, and after some communication with those members of the Cabinet who were present, my father wrote to the King from Cleveland Row, proposing that the intended dissolution should take place immediately. The King approved, saying, as will be observed in his answer, that after seeing my father at half past 11 he would hold a council at 12 the next day.

The object of this meeting of the Council was of course to make the formal orders required for the dissolution. Mr. William Bathurst (now Lord Bathurst), the then Clerk of the Council, informs me in a letter that I have received from him, that, on the morning of the 22nd, he received orders to issue summonses immediately for a Council to be held for the dissolution of Parliament, and that he was directed to bring with him the usual papers which are required when Parliament is to be prorogued or dissolved by Commission.

In the meantime, and almost at the last moment, it was found necessary to make a further change in the mode of proceeding. By the law and usage of Parliament, the House of Lords is entitled to dispose of any business actually in progress, before it admits the Commissioners of the Crown; and it was ascertained that the Opposition Peers intended to avail themselves of this rule, so as to carry Lord Wharncliffe's proposed Address.

It is quite true that their doing so would no more have deprived the Crown of its constitutional power to dissolve Parliament, than the addresses of the same character which were carried in the House of Commons, after the Coalition Ministry had been dismissed and succeeded by that of Mr. Pitt in 1784. It was however thought desirable to prevent the House of Lords from coming to such a vote, lest it should have a bad effect on public opinion.

This could only be done by the King's going down to prorogue Parliament in person, the appearance of the King in the House of Lords putting a stop to all proceedings. This course was accordingly proposed to the King by my father, at the audience which the King had previously

at half-past eleven, and to hold a Council at twelve o'clock, everybody being in their morning dress.

WILLIAM R.

No. 140.

Earl Grey to Sir H. Taylor.

Downing Street, April 24, 1831.

My dear Sir,—The King expressed a desire that I would record in writing the substance of the answer

---

fixed for half past 11 on the morning of the 22nd and at which Lord Brougham was present.

The King at once agreed to what was proposed to him: indeed, my father told me at the time, and he more than once afterwards mentioned the same fact in the presence of myself and others, that notwithstanding his strong objection to a dissolution in the first instance, the King, when the measure had been decided upon, resented the attempt to impede it by an Address of the House of Lords, as an invasion of his prerogative, and was therefore not only ready, but eager to do what was necessary to put a stop to Lord Wharncliffe's motion. As till after my father and Lord Brougham had seen the King no orders had been, or could be, given for the usual preparations for his going in state, there was some difficulty in making them at such short notice. Lord Albemarle, who was in attendance upon the King as Master of the Horse, said that it would be hardly possible to get the state carriages ready so soon, and complained that there would not be time to plait the horses' manes. The King however insisted that any preparations which could not be completed in time should be dispensed with, and was reported to have said to Lord Albemarle that, if necessary, he would go down in a hackney coach. I believe that this story, which was generally current at the time, was true. I know that the King did express, in the strongest manner, his determination to go to the House of Lords, however incomplete the preparations for the usual procession might be. The orders for the attendance of the Life Guards were so late, that the regiment at Knightsbridge which was to have lined the road, though it was turned out as quickly as possible, did not arrive till after the King was gone, and could only keep the ground for his return. This fact I learn from Sir T. Biddulph, who was then an officer of the regiment. I believe that the escort for the King could only be obtained in time by sending to the Horse Guards for the troop on guard there.

which I gave to His Majesty verbally, with the authority of my colleagues, to the gracious communication of His Majesty's assent to the proposal for an immediate dissolution of the present Parliament.

This I have done in the accompanying paper, antedated on the day on which His Majesty's communication was received, and on which the answer ought to have been formally given. I do not know that any further explanation is required of the form in which the present Cabinet Minute has been framed, and which it has been my endeavour to make conformable to what I understood to be His Majesty's desire.

I am, &c. GREY.

(Enclosure.)

Minute of Cabinet.

Downing Street, April 21, 1831.

At a meeting of your Majesty's servants, held this day at the house of the First Lord of the Treasury, the following Minute, in answer to your Majesty's most gracious letter of this day, was agreed upon:—

PRESENT:

The Lord Chancellor.	The Viscount Melbourne.
The Lord President.	The Viscount Goderich.
The Lord Privy Seal.	The Lord Holland.
The Duke of Richmond.	The Viscount Althorp.
The Earl of Carlisle.	The Viscount Palmerston.
The Earl Grey.	Sir James Graham, Bart.

Right Hon. C. Grant.

Your Majesty's servants have received, with feelings of the most unbounded respect and gratitude, the gracious communication which your Majesty has been pleased to make to them, through Earl Grey, in answer to the Minute of Cabinet, which they had yesterday the honour of humbly submitting to your Majesty. Penetrated with a deep sense of the just views by which your Majesty has been influenced in all the communications which have passed between your Majesty and your servants on the momentous question of Parliamentary Reform, they beg leave humbly to assure your Majesty, that nothing but an imperative sense of duty could have impelled them to propose to your Majesty a measure to which they were aware that your Majesty felt strong objections.

But being at length convinced, by the divisions which had taken place in the House of Commons, that there no longer remained any hope that the Bill for a Reform in the Representation, which had been proposed by them, under the sanction of your Majesty's approbation, could be carried, their serious attention was necessarily called to the consequences of the rejection of that measure. The Bill had been generally approved, public expectation had been raised high, and the effect of a disappointment seemed greatly to be feared, as likely to disturb the peace of the country. To prevent, therefore, an agitation of so formidable a nature, your Majesty's servants felt themselves called upon humbly to advise your Majesty to dissolve the present Parliament.

Your Majesty's servants beg leave to tender to your Majesty their warmest thanks for the additional mark of your Majesty's confidence, evinced by your Majesty's adoption of this their humble advice; and they entreat your Majesty to be assured that your Majesty may rely with confidence on their determination, firmly and strenuously, to resist any attempt to introduce and to carry measures which would extend the provisions of the Reform Bill beyond those principles on which it has been framed, for the purpose of uniting in one common interest, by the safe and permanent settlement of this important question, the constitutional rights of the Monarchy, the influence and dignity of the Crown, and the liberties of your Majesty's people. The security of these, they are well aware, would be as greatly endangered by granting too much as by conceding too little; and it is therefore their settled determination steadily to adhere to that prudent course which has, up to the present moment, been sanctioned by your Majesty, and has gained the support of the great mass of the property, respectability, and intelligence of the country.

No. 141.

The King to Earl Grey.

St. James's Palace, April 24, 1831.

The King's sanction to the dissolution of Parliament having finally removed all doubts which the country in general, or individuals, might have entertained of his determination to support his actual Government in the prosecution of the measure of Reform of Parliament, His Majesty will not further delay the statement of his sentiments upon certain points which had engaged his serious attention during the late proceedings on the Bill, and which have become objects of his anxious solicitude with reference to the further legislative discussion of it.

This statement, which is intended for the consideration of his confidential servants, has been for some time contemplated by the King, and would have been made earlier, if His Majesty had not been apprehensive that it might produce a misconception of his intentions, and be received as resulting from the influence of collateral causes and of opinions which had not originally weighed, but which, having been recently admitted, were brought forward in support of the objections he had felt and urged against a dissolution.

The King's verbal sanction to the proposed measure of Reform was repeated in a written communication to Earl Grey, in which His Majesty entered at some length into the feelings with which he had anticipated the introduction of the measure and approached it, and into its leading features, as submitted to him in the documents which Earl Grey had left with him.

His Majesty considers it unnecessary now to advert to any other than two points, being those upon which his feeling and opinion had been most strongly expressed.

First, the expediency, policy, and possibility of delaying the introduction and legislative discussion of the measure which has been avowed to be contemplated in order to afford more time for calm deliberation and reflection, and to avoid its agitation while the feelings of the country were supposed to be excited by other causes which, combined with this, might produce a serious convulsion. Next, the propriety and necessity of taking a new census, towards carrying into effect a measure of which the principle and details and the local interests and contingencies must be obviously so much affected by the accuracy of the returns of population.

His Majesty's observations on both these points were met by objections to which he subscribed, but the result has shown that they were not undeserving of attention. The course which the discussion has taken, the serious objections made to some of the provisions of the Bill, and, finally, the interruption of the proceedings, have established the necessity of further and more deliberate consideration of the principle and details, while the general effect of all this has been the postponement of the discussion and the gain of time for better deliberation, which appeared to His Majesty so desirable. The validity of his objection to the imperfect census of 1821, as applicable to a measure introduced in 1831, and embracing local and individual interests, to be determined by the returns of population, has been fully established by the proceedings on the Bill, by the admission of those who framed it, and by the modifications on this head to which, in justice and equity, they have been obliged to agree.

The King has adverted to the feelings with which he approached the measure, as stated in his letter to Earl Grey of Feb. 4. It has been more than once characterised by Earl Grey as 'perilous,' and His Majesty feels the full weight of the responsibility which, as the Sovereign of this country, he has incurred by sanctioning it. This observation is not intended to convey an impression that he repents of the steps he has taken, or that he wishes he could retrace them. They were taken on mature consideration of the circumstances under which these realms were placed. These called for his decision, how far it behoved him to resist, or, to a certain degree, to yield to a torrent which had been increased by external causes. He had to weigh well, whether the tranquillity and the peace of the country were more likely to be preserved by the assertion than by the abandonment of the objections which he and others, whose principles he had early imbibed, entertained to measures of extensive Reform; and he was satisfied, from the best reflection he could give to this state of things, that the permanent peace and tranquillity of the country and its prosperity would be best promoted by the decision to which he has come.

As an individual, consulting merely his own feelings and prejudices, he would probably have taken and maintained a different position. As a Sovereign, responsible to God and his country for the welfare and happiness of millions, it was his duty to set those feelings and prejudices aside.

Still he cannot help considering this perilous measure as an experiment—as a fearful experiment, which the general circumstances and the general considerations to which he has alluded could alone have justified his risking; and it is incumbent upon him to urge upon the attention of his confidential servants all that can, in his opinion, tend to lessen that risk.

His Majesty has stated, in the concluding part of his letter of the 21st inst., that advantage should be taken of any preponderance which his Ministers may obtain in the House of Commons, by the results of the ensuing general election, to introduce such modifications in the Bill, as, without producing any essential departure from the principle of the measure, shall be calculated to conciliate the opponents of the Bill, and to reconcile the *general* opinion and feeling of the country to it; and he is induced upon this occasion to call the serious attention of his confidential servants to that recommendation.

Although His Majesty had, during the progress of the discussion, abstained from the communication of any sentiments to which it gave rise, and carefully avoided embarrassing his Ministers by suggestions arising out of his casual knowledge of the opinions of others, it cannot be supposed that he could be indifferent to any step, any feature of a question of such vital importance; or that much that passed in debate, or was otherwise published on the subject, should not have made some impression upon him; that he should not have noticed the difference of opinion which prevailed, and have observed that opinions, not in unison with those of the framers of the Bill, were entertained by many individuals of acknowledged ability and experience, and of sound judgment. It was impossible that these opinions should not have raised doubts in his mind as to the correctness of the position taken, that the Bill, the whole Bill, and nothing but the Bill, should pass.

This remark would not have escaped His Majesty pending the late discussion. He was aware of the extent to which the framers of the Bill and some of his Ministers had committed themselves in the assertion of its *integrity*. He felt how difficult it was to recede without making concessions which might seem to have been extorted; and he felt also how much an obstinate adherence to the measure as it had been introduced, had been provoked by the nature of the opposition, and by the spirit and temper in which it had been carried on; how difficult it is, under such circumstances, to admit the conviction which results from calm consideration; and generally he has felt (and has, indeed, had occasion to satisfy himself from *personal* observation), how necessary it had become, upon this occasion, to make allowance for the excitement and irritation produced by the agitation of a question on which the opinions of those who had been in the habit of legislating for the country appear to be so much divided.

But a respite has been obtained; time is given for consideration and for revision; the Bill has been withdrawn. It may be remodelled, and advantage may be taken, in this interval, of all that has been said and written, to correct whatever may have been shown to be objectionable, to amend the details without abandoning the principle of the Bill.

These concessions (if they can be so called when the question lays between the maintenance of opinions originally advanced, and the admission of conclusions deduced from a free and extended discussion of their merits) will not henceforth appear to have been wrung from the framers of the Bill by opposition and clamour. They must be considered amendments *voluntarily* introduced upon the most liberal principle, with the most patriotic views, free from irritation and prejudice, with the intention of conciliating those whose support is desirable, and of uniting the general feeling and sense of the people in favour of a measure which so deeply affects their general interests.

The King earnestly recommends this course. He does not, he cannot, take upon himself to point out in what manner, and in what respects, the Bill shall now be modelled and so framed as to effect the object in view; but he urges a calm and dispassionate revisal of it, with due regard to the objections which have been taken to it, whatever may be the source from which they spring. If this revisal shall satisfy the framers and the promoters of the Bill, that they have too highly or erroneously estimated the value of some of its provisions, His Majesty has too favourable an opinion of their good sense, and of the honourable and public-spirited feeling by which they are guided, to doubt their inclination to admit the necessity of correction, and act upon it, rather than encourage the continuance of opposition, and to forfeit the advantage of a more general concurrence in the measure by pertinaciously adhering to their own exclusive opinions, because they have been declared and hitherto maintained.

The sentiments which the King has expressed are not limited to the consideration of this question. They have been suggested by anxious reflection upon the general state of the country, and a firm conviction of the necessity and the importance of endeavouring to unite, at this crisis, all that are loyal and well disposed in support of its constitution and institutions, and in aid of measures which may insure its tranquillity and prosperity, maintain the established distinctions of rank and society, and give security to property.

The times are awful; and they seem to His Majesty to call upon those who love their country, and are attached to its constitution, to lay aside party feeling and prejudice, and to devote their talents and their energies to the preservation of the blessings which the various ranks and classes of this country have so long enjoyed. It is impossible not to view with alarm the character of the attempts which have for some time past been making to invade property and to destroy the gradations and the links of society, and the success which has attended those attempts in their effects upon the lower orders, not a little aided by the poisonous influence of a licentious and unobstructed press. It is impossible not to feel, that if the progress of this evil be not checked,—if, on the contrary, it be encouraged by disunion among those who are interested in preserving things as they are, the hands of Government and the laws will soon be powerless towards upholding rights and privileges, and towards securing persons and property.

The King considers this state of things the more lamentable and the more alarming, as it cannot be traced, in England at least, to any reasonable causes. It is, therefore, the more difficult to know where to find, and how to apply, the remedy. The sanguine advocates for Reform of Parliament, indeed, assure His Majesty that this will prove the great panacea. God grant it may! and His Majesty will bless the day on which he gave his assent to the measure. But he repeats: he views it as an experiment, and his anxiety to ensure, as far as possible, the success of that experiment, has induced him to make this full communication of his sentiments and feelings to Earl Grey and his confidential servants; and to urge, as he has done, the importance of taking every step that can tend to reconcile jarring interests and opinions.

WILLIAM R.

No. 142.

Earl Grey to the King.

Downing Street, April 25, 1831.

Earl Grey begs leave humbly to acknowledge your Majesty's most gracious communication of yesterday, which Earl Grey has just received.

The duty which Earl Grey owes to your Majesty, as well as the importance of the suggestions contained in your Majesty's letter, will command his most anxious attention to them; and Earl Grey will lose no time in bringing them under the consideration of your Majesty's confidential servants.

It was always Earl Grey's intention, and that of his colleagues, to avail themselves of the opportunity now afforded them, to revise carefully all the provisions of the Reform Bill, with the purpose of obviating any objections which may be reasonably opposed to it. Your Majesty seems to feel that it would not be right to do any thing that might detract from the principle and efficiency of the measure; and it cannot be necessary to call your Majesty's attention to the very unfortunate circumstances which might ensue, if any reasonable ground were given for suspicion and complaint, that your Majesty's Ministers had abandoned the pledges which they had given to the public. Of this the certain result would be, first, a loss of character to themselves, which would greatly impair their means of acting usefully for your Majesty's service; and, secondly, the greatest danger to the tranquillity of the country, and to the establishment of those feelings of confidence and contentment, which it has been the first object of your Majesty's Ministers to promote.

In stating this with the freedom which your Majesty has been so good as to allow Earl Grey to use in all his communications with your Majesty on every subject of public interest, Earl Grey hopes he will not be understood as expressing any unwillingness or hesitation in reconsidering the difficulties which have been found to exist in the progress of the Reform Bill, or to act in obedience to your Majesty's wishes to the utmost of his power.

All which, &c. GREY.

No. 143.

The King to Earl Grey.

St. James's Palace, April 25, 1831.

The King acknowledges the receipt of Earl Grey's communication of the Minute of Cabinet in reply to His Majesty's letter of the 21st inst., and rejoices that his sentiments, as therein expressed, have proved so satisfactory to his confidential servants.

WIILLIAM R.

No. 144.

Sir H. Taylor to Earl Grey.

St. James's, April 26, 1831.

My dear Lord,—The King did not return from Kew until six, and has detained me for some time since his arrival, which will account for the delay in replying to your Lordship's letter. His Majesty has honoured me with his commands to request you will accept the Lord Mayor's invitation for Friday, the 20th May.

His Majesty asked for you casually last night, and without having anything particular to say, and knowing how much you had been worn lately, was not at all surprised at your having left the Palace.

He hopes that you will now be able to get fresh air and some rest.

I have, &c. H. TAYLOR.

No. 145.

Earl Grey to the King.

Downing Street, May 2, 1831.

Early Grey presents his humble duty to your Majesty, and in consequence of the communication made to him by Viscount Melbourne of your Majesty's letter, signifying your Majesty's strong disapprobation of the conduct of the Lord Mayor, Earl Grey begs leave to express his deep regret at the occurrence which has incurred your Majesty's displeasure.

Earl Grey had no knowledge of the intention to illuminate on the dissolution of Parliament, till after a public notice had been given, which it was no longer in Earl Grey's power to prevent; nor was he informed of the placard which had been issued respecting the employment of the city and county police, till he saw your Majesty's letter.

Earl Grey trusts that it cannot be necessary for him to state how impossible he feels it to be to dispute the justice of your Majesty's observations on the Lord

Mayor's conduct, and will not endeavour to excuse it by imputing it solely to indiscretion. The steps that have been taken upon it will have been stated to your Majesty by Viscount Melbourne, and will, he trusts, meet with your Majesty's approbation. Earl Grey feels that too much reason has been given for the resolution which your Majesty has taken, to allow of his presuming to offer any objection to it, though he cannot but regret this second disappointment of the wishes and expectations of the citizens of London.

Earl Grey has the satisfaction of informing your Majesty, that from one or two hasty notes, written by the Lord-Lieutenant of Ireland, as well as from other information, the state of that country seems to be generally more tranquil.

Dispatches have been received to-day from Lord Granville stating that Count Guilleminet, in consequence of his unauthorised attempt to excite the Porte to declare war against Russia, will be immediately recalled from the Embassy at Constantinople.

All which, &c. GREY.

No. 146.

The King to Earl Grey.

Windsor Castle, May 3, 1831.

The King has received Earl Grey's letter of yesterday, and is glad to learn from its contents, as well as from Viscount Melbourne's letter, that they both concur in the view which His Majesty has taken of the conduct of the Lord Mayor, and of the character of the notice issued by him on Wednesday last, and which the King presumes no editor of a newspaper would venture to publish, unless it had been actually issued.

His Majesty regrets that the expectations of his visit to the City should be again disappointed, but, independently of these proceedings of its chief magistrate, which have appeared to him to offer sufficient cause for his declining the invitation, he has reason to apprehend that he might not, when the time came, be equal to the exertion.

His Majesty has received with great satisfaction Earl Grey's general report of the favourable accounts from Ireland, and he sincerely hopes that they will continue so, and the tranquillity of this country will not be disturbed, more than is usually the case at periods of general elections.

The information received from Lord Granville, of the complete disavowal by the French Government of the attempts of Count Guilleminet to excite the Porte to declare war against Russia, and of his consequent recall, is also satisfactory.

The King takes this opportunity of sending Earl Grey some numbers of a "Penny Paper for the People," which were put into his hands yesterday, many parts of which appear to His Majesty treasonable. They were marked before he received them, but he has himself particularly marked a passage in the 3rd page, of that of the 15th April, which contains a direct recommendation to the Poles, individually and collectively, to *assassinate* the Emperor of Russia.

WILLIAM R.

No. 147.

Sir H. Taylor to Earl Grey.

(Private.) Windsor Castle, May 3, 1831.

My dear Lord,—I take the liberty of addressing a few lines to your Lordship, to say that, independently of other reasons which certainly have influenced the King to decline the visit to the Lord Mayor, His Majesty is by no means well. This is the season at which his health is in general more or less affected; and he is suffering from gouty symptoms, which affect his whole frame and his nerves and spirits, which is in almost all cases the effect of the disorder when it does not fairly show itself. Mr. Davis also tells me, that there is a little return of the swelling in the neck, but he attaches no consequence to it: still all this together gives to him an appearance of weakness and helplessness and of dejection, which renders it desirable that he should not go to any public show if it can possibly be avoided; indeed it is with great difficulty that he gets in and out of the carriage, and he requires considerable assistance. His Majesty will probably, on the same account, give up the intention of going to Portsmouth.

I shall be obliged to your Lordship not to answer this letter, or notice it in any shape, and also to excuse the hurry in which I write, as I do not wish to detain the messenger, and have no assistance here.

I have, &c. H. TAYLOR.

No. 148.

Earl Grey to Sir H. Taylor.

Downing Street, May 3, 1831.

My dear Sir,—When I wrote to the King yesterday, I concluded, though I never heard of it, that the placard which had called for so strong an expression of his Majesty's displeasure must have been authentic.

By a letter which accompanies this from Lord Melbourne to the King, you will learn that the Lord Mayor entirely disclaims it, and, like me, was in total ignorance that such a paper had ever been published (if, indeed, it ever was published, except in the infamous columns of the ——), till he received Lord Melbourne's letter enquiring as to the fact. This, therefore, has evidently been a foul device of some of the violent anti-Reformers who stick at nothing. I cannot express my indignation at this or other similar proceedings. I have hitherto met all this violence with the greatest moderation; but they must not provoke me too far. Things are now exactly in the same state as when the King instructed Lord Melbourne to appoint to-morrow for receiving the invitation from the City, and it is our duty to await His Majesty's further determination of this subject.

I am sure you will be glad to hear that Mr. Bell has given up the contest for Northumberland, and that Lord Howick will be returned without further trouble. All the elections, except those of Schedules A. and B., prosper beyond our most sanguine expectations.

* * * * *

I am, &c. GREY.

No. 149.

Sir H. Taylor to Earl Grey.

(Private.)   Windsor Castle, May 3, 1831.

My dear Lord,—I read your Lordship's letter to the King, at the same time that I gave him Lord Melbourne's; and he at once expressed, in the strongest terms, the satisfaction with which he learnt that the Lord Mayor had not issued the placard which had given him so much displeasure; and his indignation at the fabricators of this calumny, who will, he hopes, not escape condign punishment. His Majesty read the paragraph in 'John Bull,' which he has always taken in, and its insertion looks very like a trick of the anti-Reformers, though a most unjustifiable one, if it be so.

Your Lordship will learn from the King's answer to Lord Melbourne, that he persists in declining the invitation, and he really is not in a state to go at present; and those about him think the gouty symptoms, &c., are more likely to increase than diminish at this season.

* * * * *

His Majesty was very glad to hear that Mr. Bell's retirement from the contest for Northumberland had secured that county from such a visitation, and insured Lord Howick's return without further trouble; also that the elections in general are proceeding so prosperously. I conclude that you have accurate returns distinguishing party; and I am certain that the communication of such would prove interesting to the King when you see him to-morrow.

I have, &c.   H. TAYLOR.

No. 150.

Sir H. Taylor to Earl Grey.

(Private.)   Windsor Castle, May 6, 1831.

My dear Lord,—I have had the honour to submit to the King your Lordship's letter of yesterday, and the accompanying memorandum of the returns of yesterday, which I have inserted in the book you gave His Majesty. The elections appear to be proceeding most satisfactorily, excepting at Cambridge, where the failure of Lord Palmerston and Mr. Cavendish seemed to be generally expected. There is, however, not the least foundation for the speech attributed to the King; on the contrary, the only observation His Majesty remembers making on the subject of the Cambridge election was, that he could not believe that it would go against the Government, as the Whig interest had always prevailed at Cambridge.

His Majesty has ordered me to say, that he fears your Lordship may have been led to infer, from what passed in London, that he might still be prevailed upon to go to the City; but he really does not feel equal to the exertion now, and fears he may be still less so when the time comes. He therefore wishes your Lordship to consider his decision not to go as final. He has, for the same reason, determined to give up his proposed visit to Portsmouth, and has ordered me to write to Sir James Graham to that effect.

The King presented the silver kettle-drums to the 2nd regiment of Life Guards here this morning in the Home Park. All went off very well, and luckily the rain kept off, although the early part of the day looked very threatening.

I am very sorry to hear that you have been suffering from pain in the head and face, than which nothing can be more wearying.

I have, &c. H. TAYLOR.

No. 151.

Earl Grey to Sir H. Taylor.

Downing Street, May 6, 1831.

My dear Sir,—I have just received your letter. I certainly understood the King to say that he reserved his final determination with respect to his visit to the City till after his return to town next week; and knowing the very great disappointment which will take place on its being entirely given up, I entertained an anxious hope that the state of His Majesty's health might then have been such as to admit of his accepting the invitation which was postponed on Wednesday last.

It is therefore, with the greatest regret, that I have now learnt His Majesty's final determination, and that it has been rendered necessary by his not feeling equal to the exertion. His health is much too valuable to allow any other consideration to be put into competition with it, and I trust this will be the prevailing sentiment even amongst those who will feel the greatest disappointment. It is to be considered in what manner the communication should be made to the Lord Mayor. It ought, I think, to go through the Home Secretary, as the proper official channel of communication. I shall expect His Majesty's commands on this subject.

The enclosed list will show you that the elections are going on better and better. The freeholders of Northampton have insisted upon putting up Lord Milton in conjunction with Lord Althorp, and declare that they will bring them in free of expense. Mr. Cartwright, the present member, and Mr. Knightley stand on the opposite interest.

A melancholy account has been received at the Admiralty this morning of the deaths of Sir J. Yorke, Captain Bradby, and Captain Young, R.N. They were drowned by the upsetting of a boat at Southampton.

I am, &c. GREY.

No. 152.

Sir H. Taylor to Earl Grey.

(Private.) Windsor Castle, May 7, 1831.

My dear Lord,—I have had the honour of submitting your Lordship's letter of yesterday to the King, who has ordered me to say, that he will feel obliged to you if you will convey to Lord Melbourne his decision not to accept of the Lord Mayor's invitation, and His Majesty's desire that he will communicate it to him, assigning as the reason that which I was ordered to state to your Lordship yesterday, and which, indeed, had been previously mentioned to him.

The lists which were enclosed in your Lordship's letter, and which I have had the honour of submitting to His Majesty, offer ample proof of the continued success of the elections; and, under the circumstances which you state, His Majesty has no doubt Lord

Althorp and Lord Milton will both be returned for Northamptonshire.

He regrets the failure of Captain Elliott at Plymouth.

The King was very much shocked to learn the sad accident which has proved fatal to Sir Joseph Yorke, Captain Bradby, and Captain Young, of the R. N. The report reached him loosely last night, and His Majesty was in hopes it would prove unfounded.

I have, &c. H. TAYLOR.

No. 153.

Earl Grey to Sir H. Taylor.

Downing Street, May 7, 1831.

Dear Sir,—I lost no time, after receiving your letter, in communicating the King's commands to Lord Melbourne. The Lord Mayor has been prepared for the determination, which will be now announced to him officially, by a letter which Lord Melbourne wrote to him yesterday; but I still fear that the disappointment will be very great.

I enclose the election returns of this morning. It is still said, that there is a fair chance of success against Lord Chandos, but the start he has got is much in his favour.

In Northamptonshire and Cumberland there will be troublesome and, I fear, expensive contests, which I think it would have been as well to avoid.

A letter from you to Mr. Spring Rice has been sent to me from the Treasury. I beg you will assure His Majesty, with my humble duty, that I shall have the greatest pleasure in executing His Majesty's commands for giving the Lodge in Richmond Park, lately occupied by the Countess of Pembroke, to Lord and Lady Erroll. May I be permitted, at the same time, to express my regret that this communication should not have been made directly to me, and my anxious hope that any similar commands may be so transmitted in future, and not through the Secretary to the Treasury.

I am, &c. GREY.

No. 154.

Earl Grey to Sir H. Taylor.

Downing Street, May 8, 1831.

My dear Sir,—I enclose this morning's return of the elections. We have just heard that Mr. Stuart has given up the contest in Bedfordshire. Bucks seems to me to be over. It was a foolish attempt, and though we lose nothing even there, there will be a great triumph on the success of Lord Chandos.

Lord Melbourne was gone out of town before I wrote to him yesterday, but returns to-morrow, when he will make the communication ordered by His Majesty to the Lord Mayor. In the meantime I hear the apprehension of what is coming creates the greatest dismay. In consequence of the pains taken to disseminate an opinion, that it is not on account of his health only that His Majesty declines the City invitation, a very unfavourable impression has been produced. The Lord Mayor feels himself peculiarly aggrieved, and is preparing, I am told, a long representation of the unpleasant consequences that will be produced by this second disappointment. I am very sorry that the King should be plagued about these matters, and I would not on any account take any part in urging him to risk an exertion which might be prejudicial to his health. But it is my duty not to conceal from him what is passing. The truth is that, notwithstanding all that can be said to the contrary, the conduct of persons supposed to be in His Majesty's favour, like that of —— at ——, the known opinion of persons composing Her Majesty's household, ——, and the declared hostility of the Princesses, have produced suspicions which every endeavour is used to propagate, that the King is in reality adverse to the measure of Reform. This you will say, with truth, is most unreasonable and most unjust; but you must make some allowance for the effect of the circumstances which I have described on the public feeling, and the apprehension which every unfavourable appearance is calculated to excite.

* * * * *

I have, &c. GREY.

No. 155.

Sir H. Taylor to Earl Grey.

Windsor Castle, May 8, 1831.

My dear Lord—The King, to whom I have had the honour of submitting your Lordship's letter of yesterday, and the accompanying statement of the election returns, quite agrees with you, that the expensive and troublesome contests in Northamptonshire and Cumberland might as well have been avoided.

The communication respecting the Lodge in Richmond Park was made to your Lordship through Mr. Spring Rice, by His Majesty's command, in consequence of Sir Henry Wheatley being informed, at the Office of Woods, that such had been the usual course on these occasions; and I did not submit that the direct communication should be substituted, as I conceived that to Mr. Spring Rice would give your Lordship less trouble.

I have now received His Majesty's commands, that all future communications of a similar nature shall be made direct to your Lordship.

I have, &c. H. TAYLOR.

No. 156.

Earl Grey to the King.

Downing Street, May 9, 1831.

Earl Grey presents his humble duty to your Majesty, and has the honour of enclosing two letters, which he received this morning from the Lord Mayor, with a copy of his answer to the last.

Earl Grey thought it better, on this communication, to confine himself to the fact of your Majesty's visit to the City having been prevented by the state of your Majesty's health, leaving it to Viscount Melbourne to enter more fully, if it should be deemed necessary, into the other circumstances adverted to by the Lord Mayor, when he makes the communication which your Majesty has ordered. This has been delayed by Lord Melbourne's having been, during the last two days, at Brocket; but this is perhaps rather advantageous than otherwise, as the Lord Mayor had not been led to expect a final answer till after your Majesty's return to town.

Earl Grey has also the honour of enclosing two letters from the Lord-Lieutenant of Ireland, expressing his desire, for reasons that appear to Earl Grey to be quite satisfactory, that your Majesty may be pleased to give your authority for the admission of the Duke of Leinster and Lord Cloncurry to your Majesty's Privy Council in Ireland. Presuming that your Majesty will not object to this measure, Earl Grey has given directions to the Home Office to have the necessary instruments prepared, and sent for your Majesty's signature, in order to save, if possible, to-night's post.

Earl Grey has added to the other enclosures, a list of the returns which have been received this morning. The Cumberland election appears to be quite safe, and it is expected that Lord Lowther would not persevere much longer in the contest.

Earl Grey will have the honour of attending your Majesty's pleasure between three and four, if he hears that your Majesty has arrived in town.

All which, &c. GREY.

No. 157.

The King to Earl Grey.

St. James's Palace, May 13, 1831.

The King having noticed the introduction of General Saldanha's name in Viscount Granville's dispatches as a Portuguese refugee desirous of obtaining permission to reside at Gibraltar, has been thereby reminded of his intention, some time entertained, of communicating to Earl Grey his decided opinion, that it is not consistent with the honourable character of this country, and the good faith manifested by its Government in every transaction with Foreign States, to allow individuals, either Spanish or Portuguese, who are excluded, whether justly or unjustly, from their respective countries on account of political opinions, or as known or supposed agitators, to take up or to continue their residence at Gibraltar.

His Majesty has indeed always felt that this indulgence is calculated to weaken the remonstrances made by this Government to that of France, upon the subject of the assemblage of Spanish and Italian refugees in the vicinity of the frontiers of Spain and Piedmont.

WILLIAM R.

No. 158.

Earl Grey to the King.

Holland House, May 14, 1831.

Earl Grey presents his humble duty to your Majesty, and begs to acknowledge your Majesty's most gracious letter of yesterday.

Earl Grey hopes that your Majesty will be assured of his entire acquiescence in the justice of your Majesty's opinion, that in affording to the unfortunate fugitives from other countries an asylum within the British dominions, it is necessary to prevent that protection from being made conducive to purposes which might cast upon your Majesty's Government the suspicion of acting inconsistently with the obligations of good faith and honour.

It is on this account that the Spanish refugees have lately been removed from Gibraltar; and, in obedience to your Majesty's commands, Earl Grey has communicated your Majesty's letter to Viscount Goderich, with a request that he will immediately send instructions to your Majesty's Governor at Gibraltar, not to allow any other persons, who may be supposed to have similar objects in view, to establish themselves within the jurisdiction of that place.

* * * * *

All which, &c. GREY.

No. 159.

The King to Earl Grey.

Windsor Castle, May 15, 1831.

* * * * *

His Majesty was persuaded that Earl Grey would concur with him in the propriety of excluding from residence at Gibraltar, or within its jurisdiction, all Spanish or Portuguese refugees who might be suspected of wishing to establish themselves there for the purpose of encouraging or carrying into effect projects hostile to the Government of those countries. Even if this country were at war with Spain and Portugal, encouragement given to individuals, whose object it might be to subvert their established Governments and to destroy their institutions, would be a system of warfare very repugnant to His Majesty's feelings, and to the principles upon which he has always considered that the contests in which this country may be engaged should be carried on by it.

His Majesty's attachment to these principles has been strengthened by the apprehension he entertains, that the spirit of revolution has, since the recent events in France and Belgium, found its way into this country, and has made such strides as may render its effects very formidable, without requiring aid from any plea which might be afforded to Foreign States, and particularly to France, for encouraging its progress.

WILLIAM R.

P.S.—The King cannot avoid, with reference to the observation made in the concluding part of this letter, calling Earl Grey's attention to the letter he will find in the foreign box addressed to him, and which offers one specimen of the *ulterior* views of the demagogues in this country. With these and many others, His Majesty fears that Reform of Parliament is a mere pretext. WILLIAM R.

No. 160.

The King to Earl Grey.

Windsor Castle, May 17, 1831.

The King has read Earl Grey's letter* of yesterday, with the attention which it so well deserves, and His Majesty does not regret that the brief expression of his feeling in his letter of the 15th should have induced Earl Grey to enter upon a subject which has long been with His Majesty one of deep solicitude.

Earl Grey is mistaken if he imagines that the King's apprehension of the introduction and the existence of a

* This and several other letters, which must have been addressed to the King by my father, between the 16th and 29th of May, 1831, are missing. I cannot account for their loss.

revolutionary spirit in this country has arisen from the agitation of the question of Reform of Parliament, or the excitement produced by it. His Majesty had not failed to notice, as had others, the progress which had been made in support of the cry for a Reform in Parliament. He felt that sooner or later it must be yielded to, to more or less extent; and he lamented the uncompromising declaration of the Duke of Wellington, which may be said to have hastened the agitation of the measure, and to have brought it on at a period by many other causes disturbed. This question of Reform was otherwise an abstract question: it embraced alterations and amendments in the representation; and to these features the introduction of it might possibly, in ordinary times, have been confined. As matters stood, the measure would, the King is satisfied, have been soon forced upon any Government, however unwilling it might have felt to introduce it; but it was natural and to be expected that Earl Grey, whose sentiments on the subject had so long been known, should, whenever called to the head of His Majesty's Councils, obtain the sanction of His Sovereign to the introduction of a Bill for the Reform of Parliament; and His Majesty is convinced that he did so, with the hope and expectation that it might be regulated by such principles as might quiet the agitation which had prevailed on the subject, and afford a ground on which all further change might be resisted.

The King admits that the effect produced upon the public by this measure, so far as the measure and its immediate effect are *alone* taken into consideration, appears to have justified Earl Grey's anticipation, that the excitement produced by it has not been hostile to the Government; that the extent of the measure has proved so satisfactory as to have excluded the renewal of proposals for Annual Parliaments, Universal Suffrage, and Vote by Ballot, and even (as far as it is possible as yet to judge) for the Repeal of the Union. His Majesty admits that the expressions of loyalty and attachment to his person have been very general during the late elections; but he cannot help ascribing these effusions of loyalty to the gratification of popular clamour by his sanction of a popular measure, rather than to any feeling upon which much reliance could be placed; and he cannot but apprehend that, if he had not yielded to this popular clamour, the most meritorious discharge of his duty, in other respects, would not have secured him from the fate of Sir Robert Wilson and Mr. Hunt. This may appear to Earl Grey a strong expression of the King's opinion of popular feeling and favour; but it will also serve to show the degree of value which he is disposed to attach to it *in these times.*

The fact is that the King had noticed, with extreme pain and alarm, the early effects produced in this country by the contagious example of the recent French Revolution. They followed close upon his accession to the throne, and preceded, by somewhat more than the same interval, the change of Government and the introduction of the Reform Bill. They have been very striking; and although the introduction of a popular measure by the Government, with the declared sanction of the King, has secured to both the support of the great mass of the people, and expressions of favour and attachment, it is impossible not to trace, in much that has taken place and manifested itself in the course of the elections and the popular demonstrations, the seeds of Revolution, a disposition generally hostile to the aristocracy of the country, a strong inclination to introduce a form of Government purely democratical, and other symptoms, which are calculated to raise the apprehension that those who may now appear, and express themselves satisfied with the measure of Reform introduced, have ulterior objects in view, towards which they trust this may prove a stepping-stone.

Although His Majesty may and does wish that the success of a measure to which he has given his unequivocal sanction, and which involves the existence of his Government and the tranquillity of the country, may be placed beyond the possibility of doubt by the results of the elections, it is impossible that he should view with indifference, and without apprehension for the future, the exclusion of that influence by which the Monarchy and the Executive Government of the country had been so long supported, and the dissolution of the ties and links which had produced an union of interests between the different classes of society, which His Majesty believes to have tended to the peace and prosperity of the country, not less than the existence of an influential and respectable Aristocracy and Gentry has tended to the maintenance of the Constitution and the support of the Monarchical form of Government.

It is impossible that His Majesty should not have noticed with regret that there has, upon this occasion, been in many instances no real freedom of election, that violence and intimidation have had the effect of excluding it, that pledges have been called for and given by the candidates for popular favour to an extent which may be productive of extreme inconvenience to the Government hereafter, as those pledges have not been confined to the measure of Reform. The King thoroughly agrees with Earl Grey in his view of the extreme importance of carrying through this measure of Reform, and in deprecating the endeavours of the opposers of the measure to place the House of Lords in opposition to the House of Commons and to the strong opinion of the Public. He feels the necessity of guarding against the excitement of suspicion, or distrust, by any appearance of a doubtful conduct in its supporters; and he is anxious that nothing, which may not be inconsistent with the principle on which the Bill was introduced, should be left untried, which can disarm and conciliate the opponents of the measure in the House of Lords.

His Majesty's sentiments upon this point have been already fully expressed in the letter of the 24th April, which he desired Earl Grey to communicate to the Cabinet; and they must show the sincerity with which he desires that his Government should arrive at such a result as may not only insure the success of the Bill, but secure to them the firm and cordial support of the respectable and generally well-disposed members of the two Houses of Parliament, and of the community at large; thus realising Earl Grey's expectations that this measure will afford a ground on which all further change might be resisted.

His Majesty is anxious that, in these trying times, his Government should be respectably supported by those who have a stake in the country and an interest in the maintenance of its established institutions. If this can be effected he will feel at ease; but he owns that, for the reasons he has stated, he contemplates with dread the difficulties which may arise after this Bill shall have been carried. His Majesty fears that, in the anxiety to collect ample materials for the repair and amendment of the foundation of the building, some timbers may have been introduced and substituted for others of sounder quality, which may prove defective at the core, and may, with the active aid of that dry rot, the press, endanger the safety of other essential parts of the fabric.

Such being His Majesty's apprehensions, he considers it his duty to communicate them to Earl Grey, upon whose able and vigilant survey of the work he confidently relies.

The King has learnt with serious concern the alarming state of the Earl of Donoughmore.

WILLIAM R.

No. 161.

Sir H. Taylor to Earl Grey.

St. James's, May 21, 1831.

My dear Lord,—I return the Lord-Advocate's letter, which I have had the honour of submitting to the King, who ordered me to thank your Lordship for the communication.

His Majesty quite agrees with you and the Lord-Advocate, that the over-eagerness of magistrates to call in the military force upon the occasion of elections is much to be deprecated.

The King's neck is doing extremely well; but he observed this morning, that it was fortunate he had put off his visit to the City, as he could not have kept his engagement, as he apprehended might prove the case.

I have, &c. H. TAYLOR.

No. 162.

The King to Earl Grey.

St. James's Palace, May 23, 1831.

The King returns to Earl Grey the letters he sent yesterday for his perusal, and His Majesty sincerely rejoices at the improvement which has taken place in the Lord-Lieutenant's health, the account of which has been confirmed by Sir John Harvey, who left Dublin on Friday afternoon. His Majesty, on the other hand, laments the melancholy state of poor Lord Donoughmore.

His Majesty avails himself of this opportunity of stating to Earl Grey that, desirous as he has felt to confer upon him a public mark of his approbation and favour, and sensible as he is of the importance of doing so at this crisis, His Majesty has determined not to delay further investing him with the Blue Riband. Earl Grey will receive it as a Supernumerary Knight, and will fall into the first vacancy in the Order, for which precedents are not wanting.

WILLIAM R.

No. 163.

The King to Earl Grey.

St. James's Palace, May 28, 1831.

It is impossible that Earl Grey should not have noticed the anxiety, not to say the apprehension, with which the King contemplates the approach of the period when the Reform Bill shall again become the subject of legislative discussion, and when it shall be carried to the House of Lords.

Of the decided preponderance which must be given, by the results of the late elections, to the supporters of the Bill in the House of Commons, there can exist no doubt: but His Majesty is grieved to say that, from all the information he has been able to obtain, this prospect and the popular feeling which has produced it have not weakened the disposition which had been shown by a majority of the House of Lords to oppose the Bill as it now stands; and that, notwithstanding every endeavour which has been and which may be used to prevent so serious an evil, there is too much reason to expect that collision between the two Houses which the King dreads as an event the most prejudicial to the interests of the country at this period, and the most embarrassing to himself which could possibly occur.

If Earl Grey will refer to His Majesty's letter of the 4th of February, in which he gave his sanction to this Bill, he will find in it a strong expression of the apprehension even then entertained by him, ' of a quarrel between these two branches of the legislature, to be viewed as a great national and political calamity;' and he will find it to have been more or less dwelt upon in subsequent communications, and more especially in his letter of the 24th of April. It has also been the subject of his conversations with Earl Grey, and has suggested steps taken by His Majesty, with his concurrence, to endeavour to moderate and disarm the opposition and the hostility which were anticipated.

His Majesty's reasons for agreeing to a dissolution of Parliament, in order to enable his Government to carry the Reform Bill, have been fully stated in his letter to Earl Grey of the 21st of April. These reasons retain their full weight upon his mind; and Earl Grey and his colleagues will do him the justice to admit, that every step he has taken, every act of His Majesty, has tended to offer proof of his determination to support his Government, and has given the lie to the reports which have been insidiously raised and circulated, that his opinions and intentions had undergone a change.

His Majesty's confidential servants ought therefore to be satisfied, that the stability of his Government and the success of its measures have not ceased to be the objects of his solicitude, and that the anxiety and the apprehension which now harrass his mind are produced by a deep conviction, that the security of any Government in this country, the peace and tranquillity of the country, and his own comfort and credit, depend mainly upon the success of his endeavours to avert that collision between the two Houses of Parliament which has, since the introduction of this perilous question, been the object of his alarm.

His Majesty cannot but feel how essential it is not to lose sight of the attempts which the demagogues are making to dissolve the connexion which has so long subsisted between the Monarchy and the Aristocracy of this country; and he does not deny that he looks forward with dread to the possible occurrence of circumstances which may have the effect of weakening that Aristocracy, and of depriving it of the influence in the state which the Constitution of the country has assigned to it.

The King has reason to believe, that there are few members of the House of Lords who do not admit the propriety and necessity of some measure of Reform; but the majority object, more or less, to the extent of the proposed Bill; and His Majesty fears they will persist in their opposition to it at every risk, unless they shall be encouraged to expect and hope for some disposition, on the part of the framers of the Bill and the Government, to endeavour to reconcile their objections.

His Majesty believes that they feel, as he does, as his Government doubtless feels, as *all* must feel who value the peace and prosperity of this country, and take an interest in the maintenance of that Constitution which has hitherto ensured both, amidst the convulsions and the desolation of other states, the extreme importance of preventing a collision between the two Houses of Parliament, and that they would readily consent to sacrifice much of their prejudice, and of what they may consider to be the interests of their body, collectively and individually, to the attainment of this end, provided they felt assured of meeting with a corresponding feeling. Earl Grey is perfectly aware of the King's sentiments with regard to the general state of the country, and of his dread of ulterior projects entertained by many who have eagerly embraced this measure of

Reform, not on account of its abstract merits, but as a stepping-stone to those projects. He is aware also of His Majesty's anxiety to unite the respectable and well-disposed portion of the community with his Government, in support of the Monarchy and of the established Constitution of the country; and he must feel how solicitous His Majesty must be, not to detach himself from the great body of the Aristocracy, and not to be reduced to the alternative of seeking, under difficulties which may arise, the precarious support of a democracy, of which the spirit and the principles are at variance with the existence of that state of things which it his duty to endeavour to transmit to his posterity unimpaired, so far as circumstances, which have borne upon him with so much weight and accumulation, may admit.

His Majesty is, therefore, induced again to call Earl Grey's attention to his letter of the 24th of April, and to urge his serious re-consideration, and that of his other confidential servants, of the earnest recommendation which it conveys, that they should endeavour to moderate the further opposition to the Bill by the introduction of such modifications as may, without abandoning the principle of it, show a disposition to conciliate and to remove the objections which may be considered to have been reasonably urged in the course of the previous discussion.

The King has sacrificed his own prejudices and scruples; he has abandoned objections which were deeply seated and had been strongly urged; and he claims from those whom it has been his study to support, throughout the perilous struggle in which they have engaged, that they will so shape their further course as to relieve him, if possible, from the serious embarrassment in which they may place him, by a too close and too rigid adherence to all the features of the Bill.

His Majesty, therefore, considers that, at this stage of the question, when they have, in consequence of the decided step to which His Majesty consented, obtained the certainty of a *sweeping* majority in the House of Commons, it should be the object of their utmost attention to avoid all that can afford a reasonable plea to the continued hostility of those whose concurrence is, *after all*, indispensable to the perfection and the eventual establishment of the measure for which this risk has been incurred. WILLIAM R.

No. 164.

Earl Grey to the King.

May 29, 1831.

Earl Grey has the honour of acknowledging the receipt of your Majesty's letter of yesterday, which was not delivered to him till late in the evening. He will immediately obey your Majesty's commands in submitting it to his colleagues, who were already appointed to meet for the purpose of continuing their deliberations on the Reform Bill to-day at two o'clock.

In the meantime, Earl Grey humbly begs your Majesty's permission to express individually some of his first impressions on reading your Majesty's letter.

He never can refer, but with sentiments of the most heart-felt respect and gratitude, to every part of your Majesty's conduct towards himself and his colleagues, since they had the honour of being admitted to your Majesty's councils.

The calm and patient attention given by your Majesty to the plan of Reform prepared by your Majesty's Ministers, when Earl Grey had first the honour of submitting it to your Majesty,—the fair exposition of your Majesty's early opinions upon the principle of that measure,—the anxiety with which your Majesty contemplated the possible effects of its being carried into execution,—the enlightened views taken by your Majesty of what was required by a due consideration of the state of public opinion, in a moment of great and pressing difficulty,—the clear and explicit manner in which your Majesty's consent, not unaccompanied with apprehension, was finally given to a measure on every part of which your Majesty had bestowed the most careful attention,—the steady and unequivocal support which your Majesty's Ministers received in every subsequent stage of the proceedings upon it; and, finally, the manner in which your Majesty acquiesced in the proposal of your Majesty's Ministers, when no other course was left to them, to dissolve the Parliament, as they demand Earl Grey's warmest acknowledgments, must also ensure to your Majesty, whatever circumstances may arise, his unchangeable attachment and devotion. Earl Grey has never ceased to bear in mind the recommendations, to which it was his bounden duty to attend, in your Majesty's most gracious letters of the 21st and 24th of April. In answer to the first, your Majesty's servants pledged themselves 'to resist any attempt to introduce and to carry measures which would extend the provisions of the Reform Bill beyond those principles on which it had been framed, for the purpose of uniting in one common interest, by the safe and permanent settlement of this important question, the constitutional rights of the Monarchy, the influence and dignity of the Crown, and the liberties of the People.' To this pledge they have adhered; by this pledge they continue to be bound, believing, as they then had the honour of stating to your Majesty, that these paramount interests 'would be as greatly endangered by granting too much as by conceding too little.' It therefore was, and is, 'their settled determination, to adhere to that prudent course which, up to the present moment, has been sanctioned by your Majesty, and which has gained the support o the great mass of the property, respectability, and intelligence of the country.'

In the same manner, upon the recommendation in your Majesty's letter of the 24th of April, they felt themselves bound to employ the interval afforded by the dissolution of Parliament in a careful revision of the provisions of the Reform Bill, for the purpose of correcting defects, and obviating objections, as far as this could be done, without making changes which might incur the risk of producing a strong reaction in the public feeling and opinion which might be destructive of all the expected advantages of the measure, and would not be compensated by any adequate benefit, to be expected from them.

Their attention to this matter was unavoidably interrupted and delayed by the occurrences of the elections, and by the absence of several Members of the Cabinet, on that account, from London.

Their deliberations on this subject have now been

resumed, and will be proceeded upon with all possible care and diligence, and at the same time with the earnest desire of removing from your Majesty's mind those causes of anxiety which are so strongly expressed in your Majesty's letter, and which Earl Grey grieves to find have given your Majesty so much uneasiness. Of the evils which would result from a collision between the two Houses, Earl Grey is deeply sensible. There is nothing he would not do to avert such a calamity, that would be consistent with his character and honour, and with the duty which he owes to your Majesty and to his country. He feels confident that it is only under the influence of these considerations that, on this or on any other public question, your Majesty would require him to act. But it would be inconsistent with that frankness which your Majesty has been graciously pleased to allow him to use in all his communications with your Majesty, if he were to withhold from your Majesty his firm and settled conviction, that no concessions that could be made, short of a total destruction of all the beneficial effects of the Bill, would satisfy those by whom it has hitherto been most violently opposed; and that the great and important object of uniting the two Houses of Parliament, and of obtaining for both the support of public opinion, would not be secured by any such changes as, materially altering the provisions of the Bill, and narrowing its principle, would disappoint the just expectations which it had raised, and appear to be a departure from the grounds on which it had received the public approbation.

Your Majesty's Ministers, should they deviate into such a course, could only expect to draw upon themselves general distrust and censure, by enlisting themselves on the side of those who have engaged in a dangerous and, as Earl Grey believes, an unavailing resistance to the strong current of public opinion.

Recurring, therefore, to what he has heretofore had the honour of stating to your Majesty, Earl Grey has only to repeat his sincere and anxious desire to introduce into the details of the Reform Bill, all such corrections as may at once give vigour to its principle, and render it convenient and safe in practice.

To any thing of a different character Earl Grey could not be a party, without depriving himself of all hope of having it in his power hereafter to render to your Majesty any useful service.

To popular clamour he never has yielded; he never will yield. To popular obloquy he has more than once exposed himself, when required to do so by a sense of duty; and he would not hesitate at any time to encounter the same risk for the real advantage of your Majesty's service.

For your Majesty's personal ease and comfort there is nothing short of a useless sacrifice of his character and honour to which he does not feel himself personally bound. But he could not place himself in opposition to the strongly expressed opinion of the sound part of the community, by forfeiting the pledges by which so general and so decisive a support has been obtained for your Majesty's Government.

Of such a conduct much more disastrous effects than those which would fall personally on Earl Grey and the rest of your Majesty's confidential servants would be the infallible result. All confidence in public men would again be destroyed, and the danger to the institutions of the country, and particularly to the House of Lords, would be incalculably increased.

To the risk of such consequences Earl Grey is confident your Majesty would do everything to prevent your Government and the country from being exposed.

But when it is stated to be the object of your Majesty's present communication to open a way for conciliating persons who, though now professing to acknowledge the necessity of conceding something on the principle of Reform, have hitherto obstinately resisted every the most trifling advance towards it; and whose conduct has afforded but too much reason to fear, that any attempt of this kind would only be used as affording advantage for future misrepresentation and attack, Earl Grey could not help fearing that some such extensive changes might be contemplated, as might lead to the consequences which he has described.

It is under this impression that Earl Grey, without waiting for the result of the communication which it will be his duty to make this day to the Cabinet, has felt himself impelled humbly to submit to your Majesty the expression of his individual feelings and opinions, for which he further solicits your Majesty's kind consideration and indulgence.

All which, &c. GREY.

No. 165.

The King to Earl Grey.

St. James's Palace, May 29, 1831.

The King was at chapel when Earl Grey's letter was brought here, and did not receive it until three o'clock.

Desirous as His Majesty, therefore, is to reply to it while the Cabinet may be sitting, he must confine himself to a few leading points of it, and notice even those briefly. But he cannot do so without assuring Earl Grey of the satisfaction which he has derived from the general character of this communication, and from the expression of sentiments as regarding the course pursued by Earl Grey, and the principles upon which he acts, to which no person is more disposed to do justice than is the King, or more highly to appreciate the value.

His Majesty has learnt with pleasure, that the attention of his confidential servants has been engaged, and continues to be engaged, in a careful revision of the provisions of the Reform Bill, for the purpose of correcting defects and obviating objections as far as this may be done, without infringing the principle of the Bill. The King readily admits that no changes should be made which might produce the risk of a re-action in the public opinion; and he owes it to himself to remind Earl Grey that he has not, upon any occasion, urged the introduction of any modification which could cause a departure from the *principle* of the Bill, sensible as he was that his Government was pledged to the maintenance of that, and had declared that it would stand or fall by it.

The King has too high an opinion of Earl Grey's character, and places too firm a reliance upon his integrity, to have admitted for a moment a thought that his conduct would, under any circumstances of difficulty and embarrassment, be influenced by considerations not strictly consistent with his character and his honour; and His Majesty would consider himself unworthy of the station in which he is himself placed, if he could wish those whom he employs ever to yield to such influence.

He is grieved to gather from Earl Grey's letter, that no concession short of a total abandonment of all the beneficial effects of the Bill would, in his opinion, satisfy those by whom it has hitherto been most violently opposed. But it is not those whose opposition it had been His Majesty's hope to moderate and conciliate.

Those whom he wished to endeavour to influence by conciliation, are that portion of the House of Lords which, feeling and dreading the effect of a collision between the two Houses, might be disposed to sacrifice their objections to the necessity of averting this evil, and thus give to Earl Grey and the Government that preponderance in the House of Lords, which they have already secured in the House of Commons; or, at least, such an accession of force as would render unavailing the attempts of the more violent opponents of the Bill to establish and keep up the dreaded collision.

This has been the tendency of the King's recent communications, and he had not despaired of attaining so desirable an end by what he has suggested, and particularly by what is suggested, in his letter of the 24th of April. The introduction of corrections and modifications in the details of the Reform Bill, which shall appear to have been made without prejudice, and with a desire to meet the reasonable objections of the opponents, so far as these shall not apply to the *principle* of the Bill, is all that His Majesty has ever contemplated.

WILLIAM R.

No. 166.

Earl Grey to Sir H. Taylor.

Downing Street, May 29, 1831.

My dear Sir,—Together with the Cabinet Minute herewith enclosed, I return His Majesty's letter, according to your desire, which you may give to me again to-morrow, when I hope to have the pleasure of seeing you at Windsor.

The King's second letter has afforded me a great relief. I never could imagine that His Majesty, whose high sense of honour and kind consideration I have experienced on every occasion, would expect from me anything that might appear to violate the pledges which I have given to the public; but I must confess that I was fearful His Majesty might contemplate changes in the Bill, as not inconsistent with the principle to which it might have been impossible for me to consent.

I am, &c.
GREY.

(Enclosure.)

Cabinet Minute.

Downing Street, May 29, 1831.

At a meeting of your Majesty's servants, held this day at the house of the First Lord of the Treasury, the following Minute was unanimously agreed upon:—

PRESENT:

The Lord Chancellor.	The Viscount Goderich.
The Lord President.	The Lord Holland.
The Duke of Richmond.	The Viscount Althorp.

The Earl of Carlisle.   The Viscount Palmerston.
The Earl Grey.   Sir J. Graham.

The Lord Privy Seal and Viscount Melbourne absent from illness, and Mr. Grant not yet returned from Scotland.

Your Majesty's servants having had before them your Majesty's letter to Earl Grey of yesterday's date, together with Earl Grey's answer, beg leave humbly to state their general concurrence in the sentiments expressed by Earl Grey, and more especially in renewing their acknowledgments of the debt of gratitude which they owe to your Majesty, for all the proofs of confidence with which they have been honoured.

Whilst engaged in considering the matters to which this communication referred, your Majesty's second letter in answer to Earl Grey's was laid before them. It is with the greatest satisfaction that they have received the assurance that your Majesty would not think it expedient 'to make any changes which might produce the risk of a re-action in the public opinion, and that your Majesty has never contemplated a departure from the principle of the Bill, to which your Government is pledged.'

Your Majesty's servants have, therefore, only to repeat what has already been stated by Earl Grey, that they consider any alterations in the detailed provisions of the Bill consistent with this limitation, which may be found necessary to correct defects, or to obviate objections, as open to consideration; and it will give them sincere pleasure, if, by the adoption of any such alterations, they should be enabled to conciliate ' that portion of the House of Lords which, feeling and dreading the effect of collision between the two Houses, might be disposed to sacrifice their objections to the necessity of averting this evil.'

It appears that Earl Grey had in some degree misunderstood that part of your Majesty's letter of yesterday, which referred to this matter, for which Earl Grey, for himself, begs leave to offer to your Majesty his humble apologies.

Your Majesty's servants have only further to repeat the assurance, that they will pursue the further consideration of this important subject with all the deference which is due to your Majesty's expressed opinions, and with a view, as is expressed in Earl Grey's letter, at once ' to give vigour to the principle of the Bill, and to render it convenient and safe in practice.'

No. 167.

Earl Grey to Sir H. Taylor.

Downing Street, June 6, 1831.

I send, for His Majesty's information, a letter which I have this morning received from Lord Belhaven, with the enclosed return of the new Scotch Representative Peers. The result is unfortunate. It has been produced by a good deal of bad luck, and, I am afraid, some mismanagement. As Lord Belhaven gives me no particulars, I can only guess as to his being elected, that he could not transfer his votes so as to secure a friend, and that he was obliged to come in himself to keep out an enemy. I am very much vexed at Kinnaird's defeat, and the whole return adds considerably to the majority against us in the House of Lords.

I learnt with great regret, that Lord —— as well as Lord —— are decidedly against the Government. I had hoped that, with respect to the former at least, it might have been otherwise. The truth is, that persons of this description, if they find that by voting against the Government they lose nothing, either in their official situation, or in the favour of the Court, will follow the dictates of their own feelings, or of their party attachments. I feel that it would be improper for me to urge His Majesty more on this head than I have already done, but I must also feel the greatest regret in contemplating the embarrassments which the conduct of these persons may produce, not only to the Ministers, but to the King himself.

In truth the Government is, at this moment, deprived of a great part of the support which it ought to command, or rather finds a considerable portion of what may be considered as its natural strength turned against it.

I enclose letters from Mr. Stanley with a very satisfactory account of the progress of the Special Commission in the county Clare, as well as in Limerick. The measure of sending the convicts immediately [to the transports], which had been previously determined upon, is much to be approved. It is much better, I am persuaded, as an example, than their execution could have been, which, where the number was so great, would have been cried out against as a butchery, and would have produced a very bad effect on the public feeling.

From Merthyr Tydvil, I am sorry to say the accounts continue to be of a very unpleasant nature: the town remained quiet, but there were still assemblages in the country with some arms among them, and a small corps of yeomanry, Mr. George Lamb has just told me, had suffered itself to be surrounded and disarmed.

I enclose also a letter which I received late last night from Lord Ponsonby. It was brought by a Mr. White, the gentleman who went with General Belliard to Antwerp, and with Mr. Abercromby to Maestricht.

He has been for some time resident in the country, and seems to be well acquainted with its circumstances. He confirms, to the full extent, all that Lord Ponsonby has said; and enforces strongly the opinion, that the choice now left us is between acquiescing in the election of Prince Leopold under all the circumstances attending it, and seeing the Netherlands immediately joined to France. I need not state to you all the difficulties arising out of the adoption of either side of this alternative. Mr. White adds that the Rhenish Provinces, belonging to Prussia, are quite ripe for revolt, if the Tricolor flag should be hoisted in Belgium.

I am, &c. GREY.

P.S.—I forgot to state, with respect to the dreadful state of distress described in Mr. Stanley's letters, that every thing that it was in our power to do has already been done by the Government: £17,000, a saving from the Commissary's department, has been placed at the disposal of the Irish Government; and Captain Hill, of the Victualling Board, a very intelligent person, who has been much employed in the Commissariat, goes tonight with instructions to freight a vessel from Liverpool for Westport (a steamer if possible), with meal and potatoes, and to make arrangements for a further supply by purchases, either there or in Ireland. He is to go from Liverpool to Dublin, and from thence to Westport, to assist in the distribution of this relief.

I have seen, since I began this letter, the accounts from Glamorganshire, which will be transmitted from the Home Office for His Majesty's information.

I this moment hear that there are accounts from Berlin, stating that in a battle which took place on the 26th and 27th, near Ostrolenka, the Poles were completely defeated, and that Skrzynecki had returned to Praga.

Excuse haste. GREY.

No. 168.

The King to Earl Grey.

Windsor Castle, June 7, 1831.

The King learnt with great concern, from Earl Grey's letter to Sir Herbert Taylor of yesterday's date, and the accompanying documents, that the result of the elections of the new Scotch Representative Peers has been so unsatisfactory, and that the accounts received from various other quarters are, generally speaking, so uncomfortable; and he assures Earl Grey that no person can be more alive than His Majesty is to the nature and extent of the difficulties with which those charged with the Administration of this country have to contend at this period; nor more anxious than he is to take every step, and to make every sacrifice, which can reasonably be expected from him, in aid of the measures which his Government has submitted to him.

His Majesty is induced to say this, in consequence of Earl Grey's remarks, that persons to whom his letter refers, 'if they find that, by voting against the Government, they lose nothing, either in their official situations or in the favour of the Court, will follow the dictates of their own feelings, or of their party attachments;' that Earl Grey 'must feel the greatest regret in contemplating the embarrassments which the conduct of those persons may produce, not only to the Ministers but to the King himself, and that in truth the Government is, at this moment, deprived of a great part of the support which it ought to command, or rather finds a considerable portion of what may be considered as its natural strength turned against it.'

The King cannot help noticing these remarks, as they would seem to imply that the Government is exposed to difficulty, is deprived of much of the support it ought to receive, and may be placed under serious embarrassment in consequence of His Majesty's continuing to admit to his private circles individuals with whom, or their families, he has been, during great part of his life, on habits of friendship and the most familiar intercourse, though never politically connected with them, His Majesty having ever avoided to attach himself exclusively to any party, or to yield to the influence of political opinion or feeling in the selection of his friends and associates. The King is perfectly sensible of the necessity of giving a positive and unequivocal support to his Government, and he had flattered himself that the whole of his conduct had been calculated to satisfy his Government and the country, that it had been fairly and honestly directed towards the establishment and the maintenance of this principle. He had not hesitated to discard from his household any individual, whether holding a superior or an inferior situation, who, being a member of either House, had withheld or stated his intention of withholding his support from the Government upon the question of Reform. He has endeavoured to convince the public, by other acts, of the sincerity of his own support, and of the estimation in which he holds those whom he has admitted to his councils, of the unbounded confidence he reposes in them, and of his earnest desire to carry them successfully through the measure which has been so essentially the object of their attention and their solicitude.

His Majesty, therefore, cannot believe, nor feel inclined to allow, that the non-interruption of intercourse which has been of long standing, and which contributes to his domestic comfort, which is quite unconnected with any political feeling, and never leads to the utterance of an opinion on politics, can be productive of those difficulties and embarrassments which Earl Grey describes as so serious; and he believes, on the contrary, that the course he has taken, while it has on the one hand marked his determination to support his Ministers, has, on the other hand, tended to encourage that conciliation to which he attaches so much importance.

Earl Grey observes 'that the Government finds a considerable portion of what may be considered as its natural strength turned against it,' and the King does not clearly comprehend to what he alludes.

It has been admitted that, in consequence of the dissolution of Parliament and the new returns, a very great majority has been obtained in favour of the measure of Reform in the House of Commons. Here, therefore, the Government has not been deprived of support, nor has any considerable portion of its strength been turned against it. The opposition which is apprehended must, therefore, be in the House of Lords. But this had always been contemplated; at least the King has never deceived himself by admitting expectations of ready or unqualified concessions from the majority of the Peers; and his hopes of obtaining a change of sentiment, or rather the abandonment of their opposition to the measure, have rested chiefly upon the effect which the dread of collision between the two Houses might produce upon them, and upon the possibility of influencing and conciliating them by such alterations in the details of the Bill and other modifications as might remove some of the objections *without affecting the principle of the Bill.* Had the Bill passed the House of Commons with a comparatively small majority, the opposition in the House of Lords would probably have been much more powerful than it is likely to prove, while so great a preponderance has been obtained in the House of Commons by the dissolution.

His Majesty having again adverted to the dread of a collision between the two Houses, as likely to influence many of those Peers who would otherwise persist in their opposition to the Bill, he cannot avoid reminding Earl Grey of the serious apprehensions which he has himself, by letter and in conversation, repeatedly expressed of such an event. His Majesty believes that Earl Grey takes an equally serious view of it and of its possible consequences; but he has not yet had an opportunity of gathering from his communications what may be his sentiments as to the nature and extent of the difficulties under which His Majesty may be placed by such a contingency, and as to the measures which it may be necessary to adopt under the existence and the continuance of such a state of things. And yet it may be advisable to be prepared for it; for the contingency may arise at once, possibly on the very first days of the ensuing session, when addresses to the Throne may be carried in the two Houses of a character diametrically opposed to each other, and when both will call for answers.

The King takes this opportunity of repeating to Earl Grey what he has so often said. It is his earnest, his anxious wish, that the Bill should be carried without the abandonment of an iota that can reasonably be considered as constituting the principle of the Bill; but it is this very wish and, connected with it, the desire, to avoid the dreaded collision between the two Houses, which induce His Majesty to urge, as he has done and still does, the introduction of any alteration or amendment in the details of the Bill which may tend to obtain for it the concurrence of those whose objections may be considered reasonable, and not to have arisen from factious motives and party prejudice.

WILLIAM R.

No. 109.

Sir H. Taylor to Earl Grey.

(Private.)   Windsor Castle, June 7, 1831.

My dear Lord,—Your Lordship's letter and the several documents which accompanied it, were delivered to me soon after the King rose from table, and I immediately submitted the whole to him. His Majesty entered very seriously into all their contents, and immediately dictated to me the letter which I have the honour to enclose, and which renders it unnecessary that I should reply to those parts which particularly engaged his attention.

The King, however, was greatly interested by the contents of the letters from Ireland and from Lord Ponsonby, and lamented extremely the sad distress which prevails in the county of Mayo, while he expressed his approbation of all that had been done, and is proposed to be done, towards affording relief to its suffering population. The accounts of the progress of the Special Commission in the counties of Clare and Limerick appeared to the King, as they do to your Lordship, very satisfactory; and he considers the course taken by the Commission and the Attorney-General very judicious and very humane.

His Majesty has been considerably annoyed by the further accounts from Glamorganshire, as indeed by the whole of the occurrences in that quarter, of which he considers the features very serious, and as bearing an appearance more formidable in the spirit which has produced them, than riots of this sort have done on former occasions.

His Majesty enters fully into your Lordship's views of the difficulties which attach to the Belgic Question, and the adoption of either alternative which it now presents; and His Majesty fears that the proposal to admit the unreasonable pretensions of the Belgians, although best calculated to avert a general war, the risk of which the King of Holland has no right to expect that the Mediating Powers shall incur on his account, may be productive of very angry discussion at the Conference, some members of which will, at any rate, consider it their duty to protest against the Dutch being despoiled of what never belonged to Belgium.

I have, &c.   H. TAYLOR.

No. 170.

Earl Grey to the King.

Downing Street, June 7, 1831.

Earl Grey begs very humbly to acknowledge your Majesty's most gracious letter of this day.

From what he wrote, probably with too much haste and freedom, yesterday to Sir H. Taylor, Earl Grey would deeply regret the possibility of its being inferred that he could have the presumption to object to your Majesty's avoiding all distinction of party in your Majesty's private society. Still more grieved would he be to have it supposed that he could wish to press anything that might interfere with your Majesty's domestic comfort.

He has repeatedly acknowledged, as he now again acknowledges, with heartfelt gratitude, the numerous marks which he has received of your Majesty's confidence and favour; but his duty obliges him to state, what he trusts is not inconsistent with the sentiments he has expressed, that the active and avowed hostility of persons connected by official situations with your Majesty's Court, has undoubtedly the effect of diminishing the strength of your Majesty's Government in the House of Lords. Having thus stated what truth and a sense of duty would not allow him to suppress, Earl Grey humbly begs your Majesty to pardon him for any uneasy feeling it may have occasioned.

The Reform Bill has engaged the anxious attention of your Majesty's servants both individually and collectively; they have had much discussion on the amount of the qualification, which is again to be brought under their consideration to-morrow, when it is hoped there will be a fuller attendance of the Cabinet than the last time they met. After looking at the matter in all views, and carefully examining the returns, Earl Grey is firmly of opinion, in which he believes a great majority of his colleagues to concur, that the inconvenience arising from the number of voters which the 10*l.* franchise would produce, would be confined to a very few places, that even in these it would not be of a serious nature, and that an attempt to raise it would be attended with the worst effect. This, however, is a matter still under deliberation; but having a very decided opinion upon it, Earl Grey thought it better that your Majesty should be apprised of it. With respect to any other alterations not inconsistent with the principle and efficiency of the measure, Earl Grey fears that they would have little effect in diminishing the opposition in the

House of Lords. It must necessarily be the wish of your Majesty's servants to relieve the Bill as much as possible from all reasonable objections, and Earl Grey trusts that there never has been on his part, or on that of his colleagues, any indisposition to measures of conciliation. But he candidly acknowledges his increased persuasion, that it is only from a decided support of the Reform Bill in the House of Commons, that the concurrence of the House of Lords can now be expected.

Earl Grey will to-morrow have the honour of putting into your Majesty's hands the lists which have been formed of the House of Lords. The majority which these will show on the side of the opponents of the Government is not so considerable as to deprive Earl Grey of the hope, which he still entertains, that an amendment of a hostile character will not be carried on the first day of the session. The possibility of such an event must necessarily be carefully considered, but so much will depend upon the nature of the vote which may be carried in opposition to your Majesty's Ministers, that it is hardly possible to determine beforehand what should be done upon it.

The accounts received to-day from Merthyr Tydvil do not appear to show any material change of the state of things in that part of the country. The population there is numerous and resolute, and in former disturbances, and particularly in 1815, a similar spirit appeared. As a considerable additional force will be by this time collected, Lord Grey trusts that the next accounts will state the restoration of tranquillity.

Lord Grey has seen letters to Mr. S. Rice from Ennis, giving most satisfactory accounts of the progress of the prosecutions before the Special Commission, and of the effect produced by them.

All which, &c. GREY.

No. 171.

Earl Grey to Sir H. Taylor.

Downing Street, June 7, 1831.

My dear Sir,—My first intention was to have deferred saying anything in answer to the King's letter of to-day, till I should have the honour of seeing him to-morrow. But I was fearful that this might not be consistent with the respect which is due to him; and I have been obliged to write the enclosed under a pressure of other business, and amidst frequent interruptions. This must be my excuse for any carelessness or inaccuracy which may appear in it; but I trust it will be sufficient to remove from His Majesty's mind any suspicion that I could contemplate anything that could interrupt his personal ease and comfort.

The truth is, that a most unfair use is made of His Majesty's kindness to those who, either by themselves or their connexions, hold places in the Court; and it was under the impression of the effect produced by this that I wrote perhaps too hastily and unguardedly. But having said what I have now said in the enclosed letter, I shall never revert to the subject.

I have no certain knowledge of the plans of our opponents, but I can have no doubt that they will employ all the means of which they can avail themselves, both against the Reform Bill, and to thwart and harass the Administration upon their other measures.

Believe me, &c. GREY.

I enclose a correspondence which, I think, will amuse you. It is a specimen of the manner in which *gentlemen* think themselves at liberty to press their demands when they think the Government in difficulty. I have many of the same sort, but none so complete as this.

No. 172.

Sir H. Taylor to Earl Grey.

(Private.) Windsor Castle, June 8, 1831.

My dear Lord,—I have not delayed to submit to the King the letter which I had the honour of receiving from your Lordship this morning, and to present that enclosed for His Majesty, who expressed himself quite satisfied with what you have said in both in reply to his of yesterday's date; and observed that, as he would see you in town this day, he would have the opportunity of noticing its receipt verbally. The King will probably tell your Lordship that, from what he has heard, he has reason to hope that the Bishops will not feel inclined to contend against a sweeping majority of the House of Commons.

I beg to return the letter from Lord ——, and your Lordship's answer, which I have submitted to the King, who was surprised that even so strange a man as he is should have so committed himself, and highly approved of your answer to his extraordinary letter.

I have, &c. H. TAYLOR.

No. 173.
The King to Earl Grey.
St. James's Palace, June 18, 1831.

The King now returns the draft of the proposed speech to Earl Grey, having again read it with great attention. His Majesty still objects to the introduction of the paragraph respecting the provision for the Queen, in the event of his demise, as being the only point which is not of public and general interest. He would therefore prefer, that it should be the subject of a distinct message to Parliament.

His Majesty considers the remainder of the proposed speech unobjectionable, and the only part upon which it occurs to him to make a remark is the introduction of the specific mention of the *War* in Poland, as he fears that offence may be given to Russia, if what is considered by that Power a *rebellion* (whether correctly or not the King has no wish to argue) be described as a war between parties having equal rights, in His Majesty's speech from the Throne. If Earl Grey should consider this apprehension to rest on good grounds, it might be advisable to omit the words in question, and to suffer the War in Poland to be included in the general catalogue of civil commotions which disturb Europe. WILLIAM R.

No. 174.
The King to Earl Grey.
St. James's Palace, June 22, 1831.

The King acknowledges the receipt of Earl Grey's letter of this day, from which His Majesty was glad to learn that no Amendment had been moved in the House of Lords on the Address. His Majesty approves of the proposed answer to the Address, the draft of which he returns. WILLIAM R.

No. 175.

Sir H. Taylor to Earl Grey.

(Private.) St James's, July 2, 1831.

My dear Lord,—The King has ordered me to acquaint your Lordship, that the communication made to you by the Duke of Cumberland has not surprised him, as His Majesty always expected that some one or other would start a question as to the necessity of a Coronation, or at least of taking the Coronation oaths.

The grounds of His Majesty's objection to the former are known to you, as being principally the great, and, in His Majesty's opinion, the useless and ill-timed expense, attending such a public ceremony and exhibition; next, the excitement and agitation which must attend and arise from that ceremony, at a period when it is so desirable to avoid all that can promote popular effervescence. It has occurred to His Majesty that he might take the prescribed oath in the House of Lords before the Lords and Commons assembled, and that this might satisfy all legal and conscientious scruples; at the same tim ethat it appears to him strange, that these should not have arisen equally as to the Royal Acts which preceded the Coronations of George III. and George IV., during the intervals of eleven and eighteen months respectively from the periods of their accession. This would, in His Majesty's opinion, prove the period of Coronation to be optional and indefinite, as, indeed, he has always understood it to be. The King expressed himself obliged to your Lordship for not delaying to apprise him of the communication made to you, and he approves of your taking high legal opinion on the subject. His Majesty will be glad to see you to-morrow, or Monday, as may be most convenient to yourself. He goes to chapel at twelve to-morrow, and immediately after luncheon (namely, at three), to the British Institution.

I have, &c.   H. TAYLOR.

No. 176.

Sir H. Taylor to Earl Grey.

St. James's, July 5, 1831.

My dear Lord,—The King has ordered me to thank your Lordship for your attention in sending him Mr. Wood's report of the debate in the House of Commons last night, which I beg to return. His Majesty appeared much pleased with the manner in which you met the question put to you on the subject of the Coronation; and he suspects that the Duke of Wellington took up the question, in order to get it out of more troublesome hands. The Duke of Cumberland has been talking *very eagerly* on the subject to Sir Henry Wheatley.

His Majesty is going to Lord Hill's breakfast.

I shall remain until six, in case anything should come that may require to be forwarded. I suspect that I am under the early influence of the influenza, as I can hardly hold up my head.

I have, &c.   H. TAYLOR.

No. 177.

Earl Grey to the King.

Downing Street, July 12, 1831.

Earl Grey has the honour of submitting to your Majesty, in obedience to your Majesty's commands, a sketch of the proceeding, which it is humbly recommended to your Majesty to adopt at the Council to be held to-morrow, for the purpose of issuing the necessary orders respecting the Coronation. If your Majesty should approve of this course, Earl Grey will take care to have a copy of the statement to be made by your Majesty to the Council, with such corrections as your Majesty may be pleased to order, made out in time for your Majesty's arrival in town to-morrow. Many representations have been made to Earl Grey on the inconvenience of having the Coronation fixed for the 22nd of September; and he has, in consequence, had a communication with Sir B. Stephenson this morning, for the purpose of ascertaining whether the preparations in Westminster Abbey, which alone will require much time, can be completed at an earlier period. The result is, that Earl Grey has reason to expect that everything may be ready by Thursday the 1st, or, at latest, by Thursday the 8th of September, if it should be your Majesty's pleasure to have the ceremony of the Coronation at that time.

Earl Grey has made the inquiry, directed by your Majesty, as to the number of the Knights of St. Patrick now vacant, and is given to understand that there are now four vacancies.

Earl Grey hopes he may be permitted to offer to

your Majesty his congratulations on the acceptance of the propositions of the Conference by the Belgian Government; an event which, together with the favourable result of the French elections, encourages an augmented hope of the preservation of peace.

All which, &c. GREY.

No. 178.

The King to Earl Grey.

Windsor Castle, July 12, 1831.

The King has read and entirely approves the sketch of the proceedings to be adopted at the Council to-morrow, which Earl Grey has prepared for him, and which His Majesty returns. He has not considered it necessary to make any alterations, and will observe the course which is therein suggested.

His Majesty has not the least objection to the Coronation being fixed for an earlier day than the 22nd of September, namely on the 1st or the 8th of that month, if the preparations in Westminster Abbey can be completed by that time.

The acceptance of the propositions of the Conference by the Belgian Government, and the promising state of the French elections, do appear to offer a better hope than existed a short time since of the preservation of peace, and His Majesty sincerely participates in the satisfaction with which Earl Grey indulges this hope.

WILLIAM R.

No. 179.

Earl Grey to Sir H. Taylor.

(Private.) Downing Street, July 16, 1831.

My dear Sir,—It was not till this morning that I had any knowledge of the proceedings that had taken place with respect to the expenditure in the department of the Lord Chamberlain.

The circumstances in which they originated have been already, as I am informed by Mr. Ellice, explained to you by him. The object, a very necessary one, was to check the irregularities which had been observed with respect to requisitions and orders for various articles, which tended to a great and unnecessary increase of expense, by evading the control under which every part of the expenditure of the Lord Chamberlain's department ought to be placed, and for the enforcement of which the officers of that department ought to be responsible.

In thus enforcing a system of economy and regularity, I am sure it cannot be necessary for me to say, that nothing could have been further from the intentions of the Treasury, or more opposed to my personal feelings, than any idea of limiting His Majesty's discretion as to any orders which he might be pleased to give, satisfied as every body must be that it is His Majesty's most anxious wish to prevent any unnecessary addition to the expenses required for the maintenance of his personal comforts and dignity.

I enclose a statement which I have desired to be made out at the Treasury, which will be found, I trust, to contain a satisfactory explanation of all that has been done with respect to this subject. But I cannot help expressing the strong feeling with which I have been impressed as to the impropriety of Mr. ———'s conduct. It was impossible for him to suppose, under any fair understanding of Mr. Ellice's notes, that it could be intended to interfere with His Majesty's pleasure, as to such expenses, insignificant as they were, as might be required for the intended ball at Windsor Castle; and if he could have had any doubt on that matter, the course which he ought to have pursued should have been that of applying to the Treasury, before he ventured to make a statement so improper and unfounded as that which he has laid before His Majesty on this occasion. This conduct, added to that which came some time ago under the consideration of the Treasury, with respect to the articles furnished to Brighton from the King's stores, prove the necessity of a vigilant control over this officer; and may lead to his removal if he should persevere in endeavouring to evade or to defeat the regulations which are required in the Lord Chamberlain's department.

* * * * *

I have, &c. GREY.

No. 180.

Sir H. Taylor to Earl Grey.

(Private.) Windsor Castle, July 17, 1831.

My dear Lord,—I have not delayed to submit your Lordship's letter of yesterday and the enclosures to the King, who orders me to assure you that, before he received them, His Majesty had been fully satisfied by the interpretation which I had given to the instructions issued to Mr. ——, when he spoke to me on the subject on his way to St. James's on Friday last, and by my report of Mr. Ellice's subsequent verbal communication to me, that those instructions had become necessary to check irregularities and a want of due vigilance and control which had long existed in the Lord Chamberlain's departments. The King was equally satisfied that it had never been intended that these instructions and checks, of which His Majesty admits the full necessity, should have the effect of limiting His Majesty's discretion as to any orders which he might be pleased to give, and which His Majesty has shown that it is his anxious wish to keep within due bounds.

The statement which your Lordship has enclosed of all that has been done with respect to this subject, is perfectly satisfactory to the King; and it is His Majesty's earnest desire that the business of the Lord Chamberlain's departments should be conducted upon the principle therein laid down; nor can there now be any plea for departure from it, although much of what had taken place in this and other departments of the household, and which has been very properly objected to by the Treasury, arose from circumstances which those who are held responsible may not have been able to obviate or control.

This must, in His Majesty's opinion, have produced irregularities in the mode of conducting their business, and confusion in their accounts, which have very naturally attracted the attention of the Treasury, and, having done so, have as naturally called for the enforcement of very popular checks.

With regard to Mr. ——, I should state to your Lordship that he first brought me the papers, and desired me to submit them to the King; and that I declined to do so, observing that I had not received any instructions from His Majesty connected with the subject, and that it was no concern of mine; further, that His Majesty was in the habit of issuing his orders *directly* to the responsible officers of his household. That I had no doubt, however, that this question would find its way into my hands. It did so, as stated in my letter to Mr. Ellice, to whom I thought it best to write at once *privately* on the subject.

I have, &c. H. TAYLOR.

No. 181.

The King to Earl Grey.

Windsor Castle, July 17, 1831.

The King returns the letter which Earl Grey enclosed to him from Prince Leopold, respecting the disposition which it is his intention to make of the annuity secured to him by an Act of Parliament on his marriage with the late Princess Charlotte.

His Majesty concurs with Earl Grey in considering these intentions liberal and just; and he gives Prince Leopold great credit for the additional mark of the kind attention he has invariably shown to the Duchess of Kent, in allowing her to make use of Claremont as her residence whenever she might wish to do so.

His Majesty approves of Earl Grey communicating this determination of Prince Leopold to the House of

Lords on Monday; but he cannot help suggesting the propriety and reasonableness of it being accompanied by an understanding, that His Royal Highness shall be replaced in the receipt of *the whole* of his annuity, in the event of his being dispossessed of the precarious Sovereignty, his election to which has led to the voluntary surrender of a principal portion of that annuity. His Majesty is sensible that there may be objections, on the ground of policy, to Earl Grey's stating to the House of Lords any doubts of the permanency of this Sovereignty, however common sense may suggest them to all those who may receive the communication; but His Majesty considers it due in justice to Prince Leopold, that he should be secured by some stipulation, or admitted understanding, against the chapter of accidents, and should not be placed at the mercy of the House of Commons for such consideration as they may think fit to give to his case, if the contingency to which the King has adverted should arise. The King had hoped to learn from Earl Grey that Prince Leopold had resigned the Colonelcy of the 5th regiment of Dragoon Guards, of which he cannot with propriety retain the emoluments under this change of circumstances, though there can be no objection to his retaining the nominal rank of Field Marshal in His Majesty's service.

WILLIAM R.

No. 182.

Earl Grey to the King.

Downing Street, July 18, 1831.

Earl Grey has the honour of acknowledging the receipt of your Majesty's letter of yesterday.

Nothing can be more considerate and just than the desire expressed by your Majesty, that the possession of his annuity should be secured to his Royal Highness Prince Leopold, in the event of his being deprived of the situation which he is now called upon to fill. This, Earl Grey apprehends, will be done in the manner in which the trust for distributing the income settled upon him by Parliament is to be created, as the Prince does not surrender his right, but merely gives authority for the use and distribution of the revenue derived from it.

Nothing passed between His Royal Highness and Earl Grey on the subject of the regiment of which His Royal Highness is colonel, and Earl Grey regrets extremely that it did not occur to him to mention it, as he feels quite confident that Prince Leopold would at once have taken the course of resigning all emolument derived from it : indeed this is to be inferred from an expression used by Prince Leopold in his conversation with Earl Grey, that it would be improper for him, as Sovereign of another country, to derive any portion of his income from this.

It is with the deepest concern that Earl Grey has to inform your Majesty, that the accounts of the state of Earl Spencer's health are of the most alarming nature. The interest which everybody who knows him must feel with regard to so excellent a man, supersedes every other consideration ; but your Majesty cannot fail to perceive the embarrassment which may be occasioned to your Majesty's Government by his loss at this moment. Since writing the above, Earl Grey has been informed by Lord Hill, that a communication has been made to his Lordship this morning by Colonel Cust, to this effect,—that it was Prince Leopold's intention to resign his regiment, and that his not having formally done so is to be ascribed to the various important considerations by which his mind was engrossed previously to his departure from this country.

Earl Grey has the honour of informing your Majesty, that accounts have this morning been received at the Admiralty, stating that actual hostilities had taken place between the French squadron and Portuguese at Lisbon. A Portuguese merchant ship having been chased under the guns of Cascaes, the fort opened a fire on the French ship, which was endeavouring to take possession of her. The fire was returned by a French line-of-battle ship, and after two broadsides, from which the fort sustained considerable damage, and about 30 Portuguese soldiers were killed and wounded, the merchantman was taken. The French squadron, reinforced both from Brest and Toulon, is stated to consist of six or seven line-of-battle ships, five large frigates, and several smaller vessels, making in the whole about twenty-one pendants.

All which, &c.   GREY.

No. 183.

The King to Earl Grey.

Windsor Castle, July 19, 1831.

The King acknowledges the receipt of Earl Grey's letter of yesterday, and is perfectly satisfied with the assurance it conveys, that the possession of the annuity should be secured to the Prince Leopold (in the event of his being deprived of the sovereignty of Belgium) by the manner in which the proposed trust is to be created. His Majesty had received, yesterday evening, from Lord Hill, a communication of what had been stated to him by Colonel Cust, respecting the 5th Dragoon Guards, which removes all doubt of Prince Leopold's previous intention of resigning that regiment, and enables His Majesty at once to act upon it.

The King has been so long in habits of the most friendly intercourse with Earl Spencer, and feels so sincere a regard for him, that he has not learnt, without sincere concern, the alarming state of his health, though these accounts have not surprised His Majesty. He has indeed, for some time, thought that Earl Grey would have to be prepared for the event from which he apprehends embarrassment to the Government.

His Majesty hopes that the collision in the Tagus, between the French and Portuguese, so disgraceful to the arms of the latter, may have the effect of bringing them to their senses. The accounts received this morning of the safety of Donna Maria de Gloria have given the King the greatest satisfaction.

WILLIAM R.

No. 184.

Earl Grey to the King.

Downing Street, July 19, 1831.

Earl Grey has the satisfaction of informing your Majesty, that the accounts received this morning of Lord Spencer are much better.

The Archbishop of Canterbury's Bill respecting the Collection of Tithes, after some debate, in which the Earl of Eldon intimated his intention of opposing it if not greatly altered in the third reading, passed a second reading without opposition; and Lord Dacre's Bill for a Commutation of Tithes was withdrawn.

The communication made by Earl Grey, of Prince Leopold's intentions for the future disposition of his annuity, and the resignation of his regiment, appeared to be received by the House with great satisfaction. Earl Grey has the honour of enclosing a list of the Peers present.

All which, &c. GREY.

No. 185.

The King to Earl Grey.

Windsor Castle, July 29, 1831.

The King does not delay to return to Earl Grey the Messages to the two Houses of Parliament, recommending an increased provision for the Duchess of Kent and the Princess Victoria. His Majesty rejoices that the Bill for the Queen's Dower has been read a second time without opposition, and he approves of the manner in which Earl Grey met the Marquis of Londonderry's intemperate speech, and of his having forborne to notice his questions.

The King has learnt with satisfaction that Lord Ponsonby considers the selection of the new Ministers in Belgium an extremely good one.

WILLIAM R.

No. 186.

Earl Grey to the King.

Downing Street, July 30, 1831.

In obedience to your Majesty's commands, Earl Grey has made the necessary inquiries as to the manner of passing the Bill for Her Majesty's Dower. It appears that the Royal Assent to a similar Bill was given by His Majesty George III. in person, Her Majesty Queen Charlotte being present, as appears by the accompanying extract from the Calendar of the House of Lords, which Earl Grey received last night from Mr. Courtenay. The Bill will pass to-day, and be ready for the Royal Assent on any day in next week, on which it may be convenient for your Majesty and the Queen to attend, if it should be your Majesty's pleasure to follow the precedent of King George the Third.

All which, &c.
GREY.

No. 187.

Earl Grey to the King.

Downing Street, Aug. 5, 1831.

Earl Grey has the honour of enclosing a letter, which was left at his house at three o'clock this morning, from the King of Belgium. Your Majesty has already been informed by Viscount Palmerston, of the orders sent for Sir Edward Codrington's squadron to assemble in the Downs. Nothing more can be done on the part of your Majesty's Government till this squadron arrives at its destination; and it is also necessary, before any more direct measure is taken, that the Conference should come to some decision on this very unexpected and difficult state of affairs. The Conference met yesterday, but did nothing more than make a record of all that had passed, wishing for time for further consideration: they are accordingly to meet again to-day.

As Viscount Palmerston may have been prevented, by his attendance in the House of Commons, from sending to your Majesty an account of the meeting of yesterday, Earl Grey encloses for your Majesty's information, a letter which he received from him late last night. That Prince Talleyrand, in the state of uncertainty in which he is, as to the intentions of the new Government in France, and indeed as to its construction, should hesitate, is not much to be wondered at; but Earl Grey cannot help thinking the disposition shown by Baron Bulow and Count Matuscewitsch rather extraordinary. Indeed, the whole transaction is calculated to excite suspicions that there has been, somewhere, some unfair proceeding, which time only can develop.

Earl Grey saw Mr. Abercromby last night, who, though he appears to be the bearer of the accompanying letter, did not mention it. The account he gives of the state of the two armies is very unfavourable to the Belgians. Their whole force, as stated by him, does not exceed 35,000 men, badly composed and worse officered. They were animated, however, by a good spirit, which prevailed throughout the country.

All which, &c. GREY.

No. 188.

The King to Earl Grey.

Windsor Castle, Aug. 5, 1831.

The King has received Earl Grey's letter of yesterday, on the subject of the Crown and Circlet, which are deposited at the Tower, as being those to be worn by the Queen at the Coronation, and which, from the description of them which His Majesty has received, are certainly unsuited to the occasion. His Majesty entirely approves of the steps which Earl Grey has taken upon the subject.

His Majesty takes this opportunity of calling Earl Grey's attention to a letter which he has this day written to Viscount Melbourne, with reference to the general state of the country, and the necessity of taking early measures for the augmentation of its military means. He is confident that Earl Grey will concur with him in his feeling at this crisis, and that every step taken by him and his colleagues, will be commensurate with its importance, and in accordance with the firmness, vigour, and prudence, which have distinguished his administration.

WILLIAM R.

No. 189.

The King to Earl Grey.

Windsor Castle, August 5, 1831.

The King is sensible of Earl Grey's attention in the communication which he has this day made to him, and in transmitting to him the letters addressed to him by Viscount Palmerston, and by the King of the Belgians, upon the subject of the hostile course adopted by the King of the Netherlands, and the circumstances connected with it.

His Majesty must repeat to Earl Grey, what he has already expressed to Viscount Palmerston, that he has so long been impressed with a conviction of the obstinacy of the character of the King of the Netherlands, and of the ungracious mode in which he concedes, when he discovers that obstinacy can no longer avail him, that he is not surprised that he should have taken this extraordinary step, although His Majesty laments that he should be so short-sighted as to allow the possibly well-founded expectation of early success to supersede the apprehensions of the ruin which such a course may entail upon himself and Holland.

The proceedings of some of the Powers whose representatives have been joined with His Majesty in the negotiations conducted in London, as they have given rise to suspicion of unfair dealing, would seem unaccountable, if the conduct of other Powers could be estimated according to the straightforward and honest policy which has happily directed the proceedings of His Majesty's Government; but His Majesty does not deny that it is a subject of regret rather than of surprise to him, that there should now appear to be cause for such suspicion, as he has, for some time past, been inclined to doubt the sincerity of some of them, and more especially of Prussia. It has, indeed, been very evident, that neither that Power, Russia, or even Austria, have cordially sanctioned the concurrence of their representatives in some of the protocols; while the French Government has, by its proceedings on more than one occasion, manifested its disavowal or dislike of some of the provisions contained in them.

It is natural enough that the Dutch Government should have perceived and have calculated upon this circumstance, as affording a hope that all the Powers joined in the negotiations would not unite in enforcing its results, as they affected the King of the Netherlands. It may also be observed that the speech of the King of the Belgians was of a character that was well-calculated to irritate a disposition already soured; and it is impossible not to lament that he should have been so ill-advised as to introduce in it expressions which were any thing but conciliatory, and which in the paragraph relating to Luxembourg were actually hostile.

These remarks have not recently occurred to the King; they were made by him as he read the various documents to which they apply; although he considered that they must be so obvious to others, having similar means of information, that he did not consider it necessary to communicate them.

But whether they be well-founded or not; whether other Powers be disposed to act fairly, or to confirm the suspicions to which some of their proceedings have given rise, England appears to His Majesty to be placed in a crisis in which it must take counsel from its own energetic and magnanimous character, and act with a determination, promptitude, and vigour, which shall maintain for it that moral and political ascendancy, to which the maintenance of peace, since the last French Revolution, may be justly ascribed.

His Majesty highly approves of the first step which has been taken, that of ordering Sir Edward Codrington's fleet to the Downs; and he is anxious that it should be followed up by a declaration, that the perseverance of Holland in its hostilities, *begun* pending a negotiation of which the declared object is pacific, and above all the barbarous measure of destroying Antwerp, and of ruining any part of the Belgian territory by opening the sluices, if such be contemplated, would be viewed by this country as a declaration of war, and would draw upon Holland acts of serious retaliation; that this declaration should be followed up by measures of preparation, showing that it is not an empty threat.

The King cannot but flatter himself that such a course would have the effect of checking the warlike disposition of the King of the Netherlands, and of inducing Russia, Prussia, and Austria, to pause before they further encourage it, directly or indirectly, especially as they would naturally apprehend that their refusal to co-operate with England might have the effect of uniting England with France, against any coalition formed to support Holland in its violent opposition to measures to which they had themselves been parties. On the other hand, France, aware of the unfriendly feeling entertained against it by these Powers, would probably feel disposed to unite in enforcing the acts of the Conference in the hope of producing that result, the fear of which might deter them from persevering in the apprehended course.

WILLIAM R.

No. 190.

Earl Grey to the King.

Downing Street, Aug. 5, 1831.

Earl Grey has the honour of acknowledging the receipt of your Majesty's letter of this day, respecting the providing a suitable crown and circlet for Her Majesty's use at the approaching ceremony of the Coronation; and suggesting the expediency of immediate attention to the measure proposed some time ago by your Majesty, for adding to the efficiency of the Army; which Earl Grey will not fail to bring under the consideration of your Majesty's confidential servants.

Earl Grey has the honour of enclosing a list of the Peers present this evening in the House of Lords, and of the speakers on the Earl of Aberdeen's motion for information respecting the occurrences which have taken place in the Azores. The Earl of Aberdeen's speech was distinguished by a general and bitter spirit of attack on the whole conduct of your Majesty's Ministers with respect to Portugal, very little of which was applicable to the particular motion before the House. It was supported by a short speech of the same character from the Duke of Wellington, and a short observation on a part of Lord Holland's speech by Lord Ellenborough. The motion was negatived without a division.

Earl Grey will not trouble your Majesty with a statement of the information contained in the dispatches received this morning from Lord Granville, as the dispatches themselves will, of course, be transmitted to your Majesty.

They are important, as conveying a hope that the

new Ministry may be of a pacific character, and even that M. Perrier may ultimately be induced to resume his office. But Earl Grey feels that much dependence cannot be placed on the most favourable appearances in the present state of affairs in France.

Since writing the above, Earl Grey has had the honour of receiving, and begs to tender his humble thanks for, your Majesty's gracious answer to his letter of this morning.

It is, as it always must be, a cause of the most grateful satisfaction to Earl Grey, to find his opinions on the important questions now depending, confirmed and sanctioned by the enlightened views of your Majesty. In all that your Majesty suggests, as to the course to be pursued in the present crisis, Earl Grey most entirely concurs; and he is happy to be able to add that, from interviews which he has had to-day, both with M. Van de Weyer and with M. Falck, Earl Grey has hopes, if hostilities have not proceeded too far, that an arrangement may still be effected between the contending parties. M. Van de Weyer promised Earl Grey to send a courier to-day with a dispatch, urging the necessity of recalling the determination so unfortunately announced by the Belgic Government, not to treat till the Eighteen Articles had been accepted by Holland.

The Conference have also agreed, on a representation to the King of Holland, to put an end to hostilities.

All which, &c. GREY.

No. 191.

The King to Earl Grey.

Windsor Castle, Aug. 6, 1831.

The King acknowledges the receipt of Earl Grey's letter of yesterday, from which he learns with very great satisfaction, that there exists so entire a concurrence of sentiment between them upon the present state of affairs, and the course to be pursued by this country; and His Majesty rejoices also that Earl Grey entertains hopes, which appear so well justified, that an arrangement may be effected between the contending parties, before they shall be so seriously committed as to endanger the preservation of general peace.

Lord Palmerston has sent to the King the 30th Protocol and the Annexes, which His Majesty highly approves; and although he regrets the seizure of Java by the Belgian part of the garrison, as likely to produce future embarrassment, and as actually distressing an old ally, His Majesty cannot but view this event as calculated to promote the success of the negotiation now at issue, as it must convince Holland of the necessity of *leaning upon England*.

The more His Majesty reflects upon all that passed, the more he is satisfied of the wisdom and propriety of the decided steps taken by his Government upon this occasion. It must naturally occur that London, being the seat of the Conferences in which it had been agreed that no infraction of the armistice by either Holland or Belgium should be admitted by the Mediating Powers, England would be the contracting party earliest appealed to, and therefore first called upon to interfere, and to carry into effect the engagements by which she is bound equally with the others.

It therefore became her, under the faith of such engagements, to act as she has done; and it is to be hoped that her influence and example will prevail with those who might have hesitated had the first appeal been made to them. It may be further observed, that the hostilities in which the King of the Netherlands has engaged under such circumstances are directed against all the Powers whose interposition and mediation he had subscribed to, although he might not have finally subscribed to conditions which it was clearly understood should be the subject of further negotiation.

His Majesty agrees with Earl Grey in his remarks upon the more satisfactory complexion of the last dispatches from Lord Granville, which Viscount Palmerston has submitted. He regrets that Lord Aberdeen should have betrayed so much bitterness in his speech respecting the occurrences in the Azores, and should have made it the vehicle of attack upon the conduct of His Majesty's Government with respect to Portugal, which, whenever all that relates to it can be disclosed, cannot fail to receive, as in the King's opinion it well merits, the approbation of the country.

WILLIAM R.

No. 192.

Sir H. Taylor to Earl Grey.

(Private.)   Windsor Castle, Aug. 6, 1831.

My dear Lord,—I am not at all surprised that your Lordship should be knocked up with all your business, and the attendance in the House of Lords, in which you have the labouring oar upon all occasions. I hope that you have been able to pass this day quietly at Sheen.

His Majesty had desired me to say that, if you could spare time, and the request should not appear unreasonable when you are so much engaged, he would be glad to see you here to-morrow at any time that might suit you; but this day His Majesty ordered me to add, that he desired you would not think of coming if you had calculated upon being undisturbed at Sheen.

You will judge from His Majesty's communication, how highly he approves the decided course your Lordship takes; but I cannot help saying, that I have not upon any occasion seen him better pleased, and his feelings are quite alive to the importance of the stake. I regret that those who oppose you do not feel that this is not the moment in which the Government of the country should be embarrassed by unnecessary annoyance.

* * * * *

I have, &c. H. TAYLOR.

No. 193.

Earl Grey to the King.

Downing Street, Aug. 9, 1831.

Earl Grey presents his humble duty to your Majesty, and has the honour of enclosing lists of the Peers present, and of the speakers in the debate on Lord Londonderry's motion, which he introduced in his usual manner, in a loose and desultory speech, full of confident assertion, and violent invective against every part of the conduct of your Majesty's Ministers, with respect to the affairs of Belgium and Holland. The whole drift and tenor of the arguments and topics which he used, went evidently to a war with France, which must have taken place long ago, if the course of policy which he recommended had been pursued. In a word, he could not have done more, according to his means, to increase all the difficulties with which the present negotiations are embarrassed. Earl Grey followed, opposing the motion on the obvious grounds of the inexpediency of producing information, with a view to the discussion of matters now in suspense, and avoiding, therefore, any particular examination or defence of the details of the negotiation. He was answered by the Duke of Wellington, who attacked with great vehemence the course which had been pursued by your Majesty's Government, as inconsistent with the ancient policy of this country to maintain and support the interests of Holland, and inconsistent with good faith in violating the engagements which had been contracted towards that country.

The Lord Chancellor spoke next and most admirably, exposing all the danger and impropriety of the course taken by the Opposition, and lashing, with no little severity, the Marquis of Londonderry. The Earl of Aberdeen followed: he went at great length into the details of the protocols and negotiations, and indulged in the same violent vituperation of all the measures that have been taken.

The Earl of Carnarvon spoke next, in the same tone as had been fashionable during the night, reverting to the former debate on Portugal, and both with respect to that country and to Holland, arraigning the whole conduct of the Administration, but concluding with a declaration which was, in itself, an answer to his whole speech, that he could not vote for the motion.

He was answered most powerfully and effectually by Lord Holland, in an able and argumentative speech, followed by an explanation from Lord Carnarvon; and Lord Londonderry concluded the debate in a short speech, withdrawing his motion in consequence of Earl Grey's declaration, that it could not be acceded to without inconvenience to the public service. This did not, however, prevent the mischief of the discussion, which, perhaps, it would not be very uncharitable to suppose, was the real object of a motion which it was found impossible to maintain. The House adjourned at half-past eleven.

Earl Grey cannot conclude without begging your Majesty's indulgence for any inaccuracies which the lateness of the hour at which he writes, and the fatigue experienced in a very heated House, may have occasioned.

All which, &c. GREY.

No. 194.

Earl Grey to Sir H. Taylor.

(Private.) Downing Street, Aug. 12, 1831.

My dear Sir,—I yesterday evening received your letter of the same date, enclosing one from Sir J. Macgregor, which I return.

I beg you will express, with my humble duty to His Majesty, my full acknowledgment of Sir J. Macgregor's claim to the distinction which he solicits; and I only wait to send the necessary directions to the Home Office, to learn whether it is His Majesty's pleasure that Sir J. Macgregor's baronetcy should be granted immediately, on the special circumstances of the case, or that it should be included amongst those which it may be His Majesty's pleasure to confer on the occasion of the Coronation.

In allusion to that event, you will have observed that a conversation took place last night in the House of Lords on the manner in which the homage is to be performed by the Peers. Strong objections were urged by Lord Strangford and Lord Londonderry, and, to my surprise, supported by the Duke of Wellington, to its being done by the senior Peer of each rank.

An official communication has been made to-day by Falck and Zuglen to Lord Palmerston, that orders had been sent to the Prince of Orange to retire within the Dutch frontier. It has, therefore, been agreed upon in the Cabinet, that Sir Edward Codrington should be immediately ordered back to Portsmouth. This will give us an additional right to enforce the immediate return of the French army.

As I am much pressed for time, and do not wish to give the King the additional trouble of reading a letter from me, may I request you to inform His Majesty, that I have proposed the vacant office in the Bed-chamber to the Marquis of Queensberry, who will think himself much honoured by being appointed to it, if it should meet His Majesty's approbation.

I hope I did not do wrong in advising Lord Durham to send a letter from Baron Stockmar for His Majesty's perusal, thinking that the information it contained could not fail to be interesting to him.

I am, &c. GREY.

No. 195.

Sir H. Taylor to Earl Grey.

(Private.) Windsor Castle, Aug. 13, 1831.

My dear Lord,—I have had the honour of submitting your Lordship's letter of yesterday to the King, who is glad to learn that you consider Sir James Macgregor to have a fair claim to the distinction he solicits; and His Majesty thinks it will be most advisable to defer conferring it until the occasion of the Coronation.

His Majesty had noticed the conversation which took place the night before last, on the manner in which homage is to be performed by the Peers, and he considers Lords Strangford and Londonderry and the Duke of Wellington all wrong. His Majesty observed, that their objections might be met by stating the precedent of George III., as being the rule taken; and he wishes your Lordship would take an opportunity of doing so, and calling the attention of the House to the nominations of *Bearers, Supporters,* &c. &c., which have been made for the ensuing Coronation, which will show most clearly that there has been a total absence and disregard of party and political feeling on this occasion. Indeed His Majesty apprehends they will find the greater number in the ranks of the Opposition.

The King considers the communications from the Hague, both from Sir Charles Bagot and from Mr. de

Verstolk, through the Dutch Plenipotentiaries here, very satisfactory; and His Majesty highly approves of the instructions sent by his Government to Sir Edward Codrington, to return with his fleet to Portsmouth.

He orders me to assure your Lordship, that the appointment of the Marquis of Queensberry to the vacant office in the Bed-chamber is very agreeable to him, and that he gives your Lordship full credit for the kind and considerate feeling which influenced the selection. His Majesty expressed himself much pleased with Lord Durham's attention in communicating Baron Stockmar's letter to him, and ordered me to thank him for it.

* * * * *

His Majesty has ordered me to send you a letter from the Hanoverian Resident at Vienna, received this morning, which is rather important, and may interest you.

I have, &c. H. TAYLOR.

No. 196.

Earl Grey to Sir H. Taylor.

(Private.) East Sheen, Aug. 14, 1831.

My dear Sir,—I had the pleasure of receiving your letter of yesterday in the evening.

It gave me the greatest pleasure to hear that the appointment of the Marquis of Queensberry to the vacant office in the Bed-chamber had met with His Majesty's approbation. He is obliged to return to Scotland on account of the illness of his mother, who is eighty-six and in a dying state.

He begged me to offer this as his excuse to His Majesty for not attending the levee on Wednesday next.

I return the letter of the Hanoverian Resident at Vienna, which His Majesty was so good as to desire you to send me. It contains a very interesting account of the state of Hungary, and adds to the reasons for preserving peace, if the French Government will allow us to do so. Their professions are fair, and their acquiescence in the 31st Protocol gives us a hold over them, from which they cannot easily escape, without outraging the public feeling of all Europe. Personally too, as the enclosed letter from Lord Granville will show, the disposition of the King of the French seems to be favourable. But, however willing I may be to trust to these appearances, I do not feel it to be the less necessary to insist upon the retreat of the French army from Belgium, as soon as that of the Dutch shall have left them without a pretext for staying there.

The precedent of the Coronation of George III. is, I am sorry to say, in favour of the statements of those who insist upon personal and individual homage. In the ceremonial on that occasion it is stated, that, to save time, the senior Peer of each rank read the form of words, and that then each Peer did homage. This precedent was followed at the last Coronation, and must, I fear, be followed at that which is now to take place, if His Majesty does not positively object to it. The disposition to raise difficulties upon every the most trifling occasion is very vexatious, and I have reason to suspect that what has been done upon this subject arises from a scheme of taking from the solemnity of the Coronation, by the non-attendance of Peers who are opposed to the Government. It will be as well therefore, whenever it can be avoided, not to furnish ground for conduct so little consistent with the respect which is due to the Sovereign.

Will you have the goodness to inform the King that, in consequence of His Majesty's permission, I have proposed to the Marquis of Cleveland to carry the sword, which was intended for the Marquis of Queensberry, and that he will undertake this duty with gratitude for the honour that it confers upon him.

I am, &c. GREY.

No. 197.

Sir H. Taylor to Earl Grey.

(Private.) Windsor Castle, Aug. 15, 1831.

My dear Lord,—I have had the honour of receiving your Lordship's letter of yesterday, and of submitting it to the King with that from Lord Granville, for the communication of which His Majesty orders me to thank you, and which I beg to return.

His Majesty would regret extremely that the Marquis of Queensberry should defer his journey to Scotland until after Wednesday, under the circumstances stated in your letter. He has no objection to the observance at his Coronation of the precedent of the Coronation of George III., viz. that the senior of each rank should read the form of words, and that then each Peer should do homage. His Majesty is sensible of the disposition to raise difficulties upon every the most trifling occasion, and of the length to which it has been carried by those who, under other circumstances, would probably have been advocates for the course which has been decided upon; but His Majesty is disposed to treat with great indifference, and the contempt it would merit, any scheme for taking from the solemnity of the Coronation by the non-attendance of Peers who are opposed to his Government, and he anticipates from it greater convenience of room and less heat. He was glad to hear that the Marquis of Cleveland is so pleased with being selected to carry the sword.

His Majesty will not require the Knights of the Garter to be in court-dresses at the chapter on Saturday the 20th, as their frocks will be covered by their robes, but they will of course wear swords with their robes.

The King sincerely hopes that the French Government will be true to its professions, and that the feelings of the French people, and the spirit of their army, will not force it into a different course, nor lead to a change of Government. His Majesty is deeply impressed with the absolute necessity of insisting upon the withdrawal of the French troops from Belgium as soon as the Dutch troops shall have re-entered their own limits, in order to remove all plea for measures which might produce a general war, and to satisfy the feelings of this country; and he considers it also most important, that it should be manifested to Europe, that France does not consider that she could recede from engagements contracted with this country, or in which the two countries are *principal* parties, without compromising her own interests. Under such circumstances the King is most anxious that the language held by every representative of this country should be consistently firm, although cautiously abstaining from anything like a threat, or that could irritate:

I have, &c.   H. TAYLOR.

No. 198.
Earl Grey to the King.

Downing Street, Aug. 18, 1831.

Earl Grey has the honour of sending for your Majesty's information two letters, which he has this morning received from the King of the Belgians.

The other communications, both from Paris and Brussels, will of course be transmitted to your Majesty by Lord Palmerston. The Cabinet has been in deliberation on them this morning, and it has been determined to instruct Lord Granville to represent to the French Government, in friendly but in firm and decisive terms, the necessity of the evacuation of Belgium by their army in conformity to the positive assurances given by them to that effect. The dispatch which has been prepared with this view, Earl Grey trusts will meet with your Majesty's approbation.

Earl Grey has just had a communication from the Duke of Bedford's medical attendant, that the state of His Grace's health will not permit him to have the honour which was graciously intended for him by your Majesty, of carrying the sceptre at the approaching Coronation. Earl Grey humbly awaits your Majesty's pleasure as to the Duke who should be appointed to supply his place.

All which, &c.   GREY.

No. 199.

Sir H. Taylor to Earl Grey.

(Private.)   Windsor Castle, Aug. 21, 1831.

My dear Lord,—The King has ordered me to say, that he forgot yesterday to speak to your Lordship on the subject of a Brevet promotion in the Army and Navy at the period of the Coronation, upon which, however, it is necessary to come to an immediate decision.

There was a Brevet on the occasion of the late King's Coronation, but there was not any at his accession; whereas there was a Brevet promotion upon His present Majesty's *accession*.

It appears from what Sir James Graham said to me last night, that he does not consider a Brevet promotion in the Navy at this period necessary or desirable, but that he is anxious that this opportunity should be taken of conferring upon the officers of the Navy and the Royal Marines some boon which, at the same time that it may improve their means and their comfort, may give effective promotion, and be conducive to the advantage and the efficiency of the service.

There is reason to believe that neither Lord Hill nor the Master-General of the Ordnance are greater advocates for a Brevet promotion than Sir James Graham; but *all* are agreed, that it would not be just or politic to make any arrangement upon this occasion, in favour of the officers of the Navy, without admitting those of the Army to corresponding benefits; and His Majesty is decidedly of the same opinion, and conceives that there would be no difficulty in placing this question upon a footing which shall consult the feelings and the interests of both services, if the heads of the respective departments will meet, discuss, and concert measures, and submit them for your Lordship's consideration, in order that you may be enabled, as soon as possible, to take His Majesty's pleasure upon the subject. Whatever may be agreed upon will be the occasion of some expense; and so indeed would be a Brevet promotion; but it is probable that the charge will be greater for the Navy and Marines, although the corresponding arrangements which may be proposed for the Army may be productive of advantages which will leave no room for grievance or jealousy; and as your Lordship will doubtless take the same view of the question, and of the propriety of dealing with the two services upon a principle of impartiality which is so well calculated to maintain the cordial union which so happily subsists between them, His Majesty is persuaded that you will not suffer any objections which may be made by the Secretary-at-War, upon grounds which are peculiar to his office, to operate against the admission of Lord Hill's proposals, if they shall appear to you reasonable and conformable to the principle which should guide the adoption of the *general* measure.

With reference to all this, His Majesty wishes your Lordship would desire Lord Hill, Sir James Graham, and Sir James Kempt to meet and to concert what they may think advisable to propose upon this occasion.

I have, &c.   H. TAYLOR.

No. 200.

Earl Grey to the King.

Downing Street, Aug. 22, 1831.

Earl Grey has the honour of informing your Majesty that having, in obedience to your Majesty's command, made the necessary inquiry, he finds that, on the Coronation of King William III., the communication to the House of Commons that seats had been provided for them was made by the Speaker, and that there was no message from the King. It is proposed, therefore, with your Majesty's approbation, to follow this precedent.

Earl Grey has referred to the records of the Treasury, on the subject of the settlement made on her late Majesty Queen Charlotte, and finds that the trustees are all appointed by name, and not in virtue of their offices; as will appear by the enclosed extract.

In obedience to your Majesty's command, signified to Earl Grey in Sir H. Taylor's letter of yesterday, he will lose no time in communicating with Lord Hill, Sir J. Graham, and Sir J. Kempt, on the subject of a Brevet promotion in the Army and Navy, at the period of the Coronation.

Earl Grey had already desired Lord Palmerston to prepare a dispatch to Sir C. Bagot, on the subject of the delay which had taken place in sending the necessary orders for the retreat of the Dutch army, and of the very unpleasant circumstances which occurred in consequence of it. Viscount Palmerston having been out of town yesterday, and not yet returned, Earl Grey has not had an opportunity of a further communication with him on this subject; but no doubt your Majesty's wishes have already been fulfilled. In the meantime, as nothing further has been heard from Brussels, Earl Grey entertains a sanguine hope that no unpleasant consequences have resulted from what took place in the interview between the Duke of Saxe Weimar and Lord W. Russell.

Earl Grey has the honour of submitting to your Majesty's consideration, a list of Lords-Lieutenants for the Irish counties, to be appointed by the new Bill which will be ready for the Royal Assent to-morrow. Those which are under the head of 'doubtful' may be reserved for further consideration; and the appointment of the others, if they meet with your Majesty's approbation, may immediately take place.

In the list of 'doubtfuls,' those marked with a cross, Earl Grey believes to be the names which should be preferred.

All which, &c. GREY.

No. 201.

The King to Earl Grey.

Windsor Castle, August 23, 1831.

The King does not delay acknowledging the receipt of Earl Grey's letter of yesterday, and assuring him that it is perfectly satisfactory on all points. His Majesty approves of the precedent in the Coronation of King William III. being followed with regard to the communication to the House of Commons. He heartily joins with Earl Grey in the hope that no unpleasant consequences have resulted, or will result, from the

Duke of Saxe Weimar's unjustifiable behaviour towards Lord William Russell.

His Majesty returns the list of the Lords-Lieutenants for the Irish counties to be appointed under the new Bill, which he highly approves; and, if Earl Grey will bring it to him to-morrow, he will determine with him upon the selection of those inserted under the head of 'doubtful.'

WILLIAM R.

No. 202.

Earl Grey to Sir H. Taylor.

Downing Street, Aug. 26, 1831.

My dear Sir,—I had yesterday an interview with the Duke of Wellington on the subject of the Fortresses, and he left a paper with me, expressing his opinion of their necessity for the defence of Belgium. I intended to have sent it for His Majesty's perusal, but Baron Bulow has just been with me, and I put it into his hands for his consideration, and that of the Baron de Wessemberg. They are to be with me at Sheen on Sunday for the consideration of this matter, after which I will transmit for His Majesty's information, the papers which may be material for this purpose. The Duke adheres to his opinion of 1815, as to the means of defence required for the security of Belgium.

I enclose a letter which I have just received from the Archbishop of Canterbury, upon which I shall be obliged to you to take His Majesty's pleasure. I conceive it to have been His Majesty's intention, that the homage of the Bishops as well as of the Peers should be made according to the precedent of George III. and George IV.

Considering the importance of the services, I think His Majesty would approve of the creation of two Peers, one for the Navy and one for the Army, amongst those which it may be His Majesty's pleasure to make at the Coronation. For the Army, I would propose Lord Howden, who has, as I understand, great claims of service, is strongly recommended by Lord Goderich, and has a fortune to support a title.

I mentioned Sir J. Saumarez to the King some time ago, as an officer whose rank and distinguished services appeared to me to give him the strongest claim. He commanded a line-of-battle ship in Rodney's victory of the 12th April. At the beginning of the French war, he fought a distinguished and most successful action in a frigate; was afterwards in the battles of the 1st of June and Cape St. Vincent, and of the Nile, and destroyed a French and Spanish squadron of four sail of the line, which he pursued from Algesiras, getting under way before the rigging of his ship was completed. He afterwards commanded in the Baltic, and took two Russian ships of the line from a fleet which he chased into Cronstadt. There afterwards occurred a melancholy loss of several ships of his own fleet, in a storm which caught them on their return from the Baltic. This I know has been thought to have been attended with some blame to him; and His Majesty seemed to have this impression. But, as far as I can learn, even if there exists any doubt as to this matter, it is more than counterbalanced, in the opinion of the Navy, by his long career of brilliant service; and that any mark of his Royal favour bestowed on him would give pleasure to the profession. I dont know whether I ought to have pressed this matter after what passed between His Majesty and me on this subject, but I could not feel satisfied in not again submitting to His Majesty's gracious consideration, the claims of this old and distinguished officer.

I have addressed all this in a letter to you, being much pressed for time, and being able to write more expeditiously in this form than in a letter addressed to His Majesty. GREY.

No. 203.

Sir H. Taylor to Earl Grey.

(Private.) Windsor Castle, Aug. 27, 1831.

My dear Lord,—I have had the honour of submitting your Lordship's letter of yesterday to the King, as well as that from the Archbishop of Canterbury, which I return, and which will have been answered by a communication I received His Majesty's commands, through Sir William Houston, to make to you yesterday afternoon, namely, that Sir George Naylor had mistaken the King, who does not object to the Bishops doing homage in the same manner as the Peers, but to the *salutation* at the altar. His Majesty told me this morning that this was exactly what he meant, and he ordered me to repeat it.

The King entirely approves of your Lordship's having at once put into the hands of the Baron de Bulow and M. de Wessemberg, the Duke of Wellington's paper expressing his opinion on the necessity of the fortresses for the defence of Belgium. His Majesty does not dispute the value of such a barrier against France, if they were in the hands of a power which could place and maintain in them sufficient garrisons, and provide for their security even against a coup de main, or at least until Allies, or those interested in the preservation of such a barrier, could come to the aid of the country in which those fortresses are situated. But this was not the case even when Holland and Belgium were united; and unless the arrangement made had provided for the permanent pay and maintenance of adequate garrisons as well as the construction of the fortresses, it was to be foreseen that the greater part of them would fall into the hands of France in the first week of the renewal of hostilities; and this contingency is yet more to be apprehended when the resources applicable to the maintenance of this supposed barrier are so diminished. Under such circumstances, the fortresses would be kept up for the benefit of France, which might occupy them when she pleased; and His Majesty has therefore often observed that of all the Powers concerned in this question, they should be the last to propose and urge the demolition of these fortresses. He has also regretted that so many of them were restored or re-constructed, and that a portion of the funds applied to this object was not vested for the payment and maintenance of garrisons for a smaller number. These are the King's opinions on this subject, which His Majesty has authorised me to communicate to your Lordship; adding, however, that he does not think that either *Ath* or *Courtray* can be considered as coming into the line of fortresses constructed for any other purpose than one strictly defensive.

His Majesty readily concurs in your Lordship's proposal, that two Peers should be created, one for the Army and the other for the Navy; and he considers the selection of Lord Howden for the former unexceptionable. With regard to the Navy, I did not fail to read to him all that your Lordship has said with respect to Sir James Saumarez; but I am sorry to say that His Majesty persists in his objections to his receiving that honour and mark of his favour; and his sentiments upon this point have been so strongly expressed upon many former occasions, and repeated upon this, that I am convinced that it would be quite hopeless to effect any change in them.

The question was not new to me, as I had had more than one very painful interview with Sir James Saumarez, who is deeply distressed by His Majesty's unfavourable disposition towards him.

I have, &c. H. TAYLOR.

The King is going to breakfast at Chiswick, where His Majesty may possibly meet you.

* * * * *

No. 204.

Earl Grey to Sir H. Taylor.

(Private.) East Sheen, Aug. 28, 1831.

My dear Sir,—I last night, on my return from the breakfast, received your letter of yesterday.

The King spoke to me about the Naval Peers, but did not mention Sir J. Saumarez. His silence gave me the impression which your letter confirms. I regret it, but there is nothing more to be said.

* * * * *

The sentiments of His Majesty so entirely correspond with my own respecting the Belgic fortresses, that I necessarily felt the greatest pleasure in reading your statement of them. The principle seems to me to be this: to preserve the fortresses, which could be easily supported by England, Holland, and Prussia; and to abandon those which, from the contiguity of her frontier, France could be able to carry before support to them could be given.

* * * * *

After my interview to-day with Barons Bulow and Wessemberg, I purpose transmitting for His Majesty's information papers which I before mentioned respecting the fortresses. Ath certainly must be preserved. Courtray is no longer a fortress.

No. 205.

Earl Grey to Sir H. Taylor.

Downing Street, Aug. 20, 1831.

My dear Sir,—I now transmit, for His Majesty's information, the papers relating to the communications which have lately passed between me and the Barons Bulow and Wessemberg and the Duke of Wellington on the subject of the Belgian fortresses.

You will observe, in the letter given to me yesterday by Baron Wessemberg, there is a very material difference from his former statement, Mons and Tournay being now amongst the fortresses which he thinks ought to be preserved. This I attribute to his fear of placing himself too directly in opposition to the opinion of the Duke of Wellington. But whatever may have been the cause, it may be productive of considerable embarrassment. On the one hand, it may be difficult to decide against all these authorities; and, on the other, I strongly suspect that the retention of Mons and Tournay would not be consented to by France. France, you will say, can have no just pretence for complaint in consequence of a measure purely defensive. But it unfortunately is not by a sense of justice that questions of this sort are influenced; and when you consider the means possessed by the French Government of throwing insurmountable difficulties in the way of any settlement between Belgium and Holland, by simply refusing to concur in the measures that may be proposed by the Conference for that purpose, you will see at once how much it is for the interest of all, and for the security of the peace of Europe, that France should be conciliated by such concessions as may be made, without being either in substance or in form derogatory from our national honour. We discussed these matters in the interview which I had yesterday with the Barons Bulow and Wessemberg; and they concurred in thinking that, Mons and Tournay being preserved, Ath might be given up; or that Ath being retained, that fortress, with Tournay, might sufficiently cover Brussels without Mons. The latter arrangement I should think the best, and perhaps, in one or other of these modes, a sort of *mezzo-termine* may be found, that might lead to a satisfactory arrangement.

* * * * *

I enclose the Duke of Leinster's answer to the offer, which I was authorised to make to him by His Majesty, of one of the Irish Ribands. I trust that His Majesty will not see in it any mark of a want of gratitude for the kindness which offered him the distinction which he has declined. GREY.

No. 206.

Earl Grey to Sir H. Taylor.

Downing Street, Aug. 31, 1831.

My dear Sir,—I am happy to find that in the view which His Majesty has taken of the two kingdoms of Belgium and Holland, with some very unimportant exceptions, and of the question of the fortresses, His Majesty's opinion corresponds so nearly with that which I had formed. The difficulty of defending Belgium against an attack from France is much increased, by the bitter animosity which now exists between that country and Holland, and which must prevent our looking to the latter for the means of assisting in the defence of the Belgian fortresses, any further than as that object might be promoted by the maintenance of their own line of defence.

I have this morning had a long interview with General Baudrand, the first aide-de-camp of the Duke of Orleans, who has been with him in Belgium, and is now sent here by the King to explain to Prince Talleyrand, and through him to this Government, the situation of things both in Belgium and in France. To make a long story short, the result is, that the insecurity of King Leopold, both from external and internal dangers, and the critical situation of the French Government from the state of parties in France, make it necessary that a portion of the French army should remain in Belgium. I met all his expressions of good will, of a desire to maintain peace, and of the disposition of the French Government to act cordially with this, with corresponding sentiments; but I told him plainly that it would only be deceiving him, if I could allow him to go away with an impression that this country could, after hearing all the reasons which he could urge for it, allow the French troops to remain where they now are.

* * * * *

I am bent double with lumbago, which made it impossible for me to go to the levee to-day; indeed, I can hardly move, though I intend going to-night, if possible, to Sheen, in the hope of being able to nurse myself for two or three days.

I shall then have occasion to write to His Majesty on various subjects which begin to press, unless there is a prospect of my being able to have the honour of seeing His Majesty at the beginning of the next week, if he should come to town previous to the Coronation. I shall then be prepared to submit to His Majesty's consideration my ideas with respect to the promotions which it may be His Majesty's pleasure to make at that period. In the meantime I would throw out for His Majesty's consideration, whether the best promotion for the Navy would not be that of Lord Duncan to an earldom.

I must also very shortly submit to His Majesty a full consideration of the state of things existing in the House of Lords. I hear, from what I believe to be good authority, that the Opposition have come to the resolution of making a stand against the Reform Bill on its first introduction into the House of Lords. If this resistance is successful, it may lead to difficulties of the most formidable nature, which I could not, without a culpable dereliction of my duty, abstain from laying fully before His Majesty.

I am, &c. GREY.

No. 207.

Sir H. Taylor to Earl Grey.

(Private.) Windsor Castle, Sept. 1, 1831.

My dear Lord,—I was extremely concerned to learn from the King on his return from town last night, that your Lordship was suffering so much from lumbago (of which I know the inconvenience from experience), and to find a confirmation of it in your letter of yesterday, which I have had the honour of submitting to the King. I hope you will have shaken it off long before there is any occasion for your waiting upon His Majesty, who goes to town on Saturday, and will remain there until the 13th, after the levee.

His Majesty rejoices that your Lordship concurs in general in the opinions which he ordered me to convey to you on the subject of the future limits of Belgium and Holland, and the fortresses. In making these communications his only object was to put you in possession of his sentiments, without any desire to give you the trouble of discussing them, His Majesty being sensible that your time is otherwise amply engaged.

The animosity which unfortunately now exists between those two countries must, as you justly observe, increase the difficulty of defending Belgium against any attack from France, as we cannot hope for any combination of efforts and means between them.

The whole question is one of extreme difficulty, and His Majesty is sensible of the necessity of this country steadily objecting to the continuance of the French troops in Belgium, notwithstanding the consequent embarrassment of the French Government.

* * * * *

His Majesty highly approves of your Lordship's proposal that Lord Duncan should be raised to the rank of an Earl, and considers it by far the best arrangement that could have occurred for the Naval Peerage. In His Majesty's opinion no man was ever better entitled to the honour and reward conferred upon him than the late Lord Duncan, not only on account of the splendid victory he gained, but from his firmness, devotion, and perseverance in keeping the sea with his fleet in a state of mutiny, and the general excellence of his character.

The King has learnt with sincere regret, that your

Lordship apprehends so decided an opposition to the Reform Bill in the House of Lords; but he cannot help observing that he had anticipated it, and had more than once expressed to you his expectation of such an event, and of a collision between the two Houses of Parliament upon this critical question. His Majesty apprehended this event, not only on account of the collision, but on account of the difficulties and embarrassments which it must produce. He is well convinced that your Lordship will, at no time and under no circumstances, hesitate to bring fully and fairly under his notice the state of things, however it may be involved in difficulties of the most formidable nature. His Majesty feels it to be his duty to meet the difficulties attending the station in which he is placed, whatever they may be; and he trusts you will give him credit for the friendly feeling with which he will always be disposed to receive whatever you may be under the necessity of submitting to him.

I have, &c.   H. TAYLOR.

No. 208.

Sir H. Taylor to Earl Grey.

St. James's, Sept. 10, 1831.
Quarter-past 8 p.m.

My dear Lord,—I have *very great* pleasure in obeying His Majesty's commands to send your Lordship the enclosed letter.

Your Lordship's, &c.   H. TAYLOR.

(Enclosure.)

The King to Earl Grey.

(Private and confidential.)

St. James's, Saturday Evening, Sept. 10, 1831.

The King permits the Peerage of a Baron to go on with respect to Sir James Saumarez, Bart., and G.C.B., and Admiral of the Red. Lord Grey, therefore, need not be at St. James's to-morrow unless his Lordship has fresh matter for the King.   WILLIAM R.

No. 209.

Earl Grey to the King.

Sept. 11, 1831.

In acknowledging your Majesty's most gracious letter of yesterday, Earl Grey begs leave to offer to your Majesty his humble but sincere thanks for the kind and considerate attention which your Majesty was pleased to give to the statement which, at the earnest request of Sir James Saumarez, he felt it to be his duty yesterday to submit to your Majesty. Lord Grey will lose no time in communicating to Sir J. Saumarez your Majesty's decision in his favour.

It must be a gratification to your Majesty's benevolent feelings to know that, by this decision, your Majesty will have relieved an old and meritorious officer, whose services extend over a period of more than 60 years, and who, in that time, has borne a conspicuous share in the most glorious actions by which the two last wars have been distinguished, from an acuteness of distress such as Earl Grey has seldom witnessed.

All which, &c. GREY.

No. 210.

Earl Grey to Sir H. Taylor.

East Sheen, Sept. 27, 1831.

My dear Sir,—You will have heard of the affliction which has fallen upon my family.* We had but too much reason to expect it; but no preparation can mitigate the severity of such a blow. My poor daughter and Lord Durham are now at Sudbrook. Our first interview was dreadful, and I am still quite overpowered by it. I am afraid I shall not be able to divert them from their intention of going to Lambton to attend the funeral, but as they will not set out for this purpose till next week, I am anxious to be near them as much as I can during the remainder of this.

May I request you, therefore, to lay before His Majesty my humble request, that he will have the goodness to excuse my attendance at the levee to-morrow.

I see Lord Londonderry insists upon my being in the House on Thursday, but I shall avoid it if possible. In the meantime, if His Majesty should have any commands for me, I shall trust to your acquainting me with them.

Sir James Graham informed me of the strong expression of the King's displeasure at what had been

* The death of Lord Durham's eldest son.

said with respect to the passing of the Reform Bill in the House of Lords, by ———. It cannot, I trust, be necessary for me to say how much I disapprove of anything so intemperate and indecent. Having myself this feeling of the language used by ———, it must be with the greatest diffidence that I express an opinion differing from that of His Majesty. But with all humility I must crave permission to state my concurrence in the opinion adopted by the Cabinet, at which I was not able to be present, that it would not be expedient on such an occasion for the King to resort to the exercise of his royal prerogative in depriving ——— of his commission. What was said in the House of Commons, unless taken up by the House itself, and made the subject of an address to the Crown, clearly could not be acted upon as the ground of such a measure. It seems, besides, to have been intended as an explanation and apology, whether satisfactory or not, for the language used in the City. What this was could be ascertained only by some species of inquiry, the mere authority of a newspaper being obviously insufficient, in which ——— must have been allowed an opportunity of offering matter in defence or explanation of what he had done; and this would have led to discussions which, to say the least of them, would have been extremely embarrassing and inconvenient at the present moment. This would inevitably have increased the excitement already prevailing, which threatens, I fear, very dangerous consequences if the Bill should be rejected by the House of Lords, and would have increased tenfold any power which ——— possesses of doing mischief.

But into whatever intemperance the excitement of the moment may have betrayed him, I hope His Majesty will pardon my expressing my sincere belief, that he is actuated by no intentions inconsistent with his duty as a loyal subject, or with the respect which he owes to the Crown and the other institutions of our Government.

I am, &c. GREY.

No. 211.

Sir H. Taylor to Earl Grey.

(Private.) Windsor Castle, Sept. 27, 1831. 11 P.M.

My dear Lord,—I had the honour of receiving your Lordship's letter of this day between 9 and 10 this evening, and immediately submitted it to the King.

His Majesty had learnt with extreme concern the death of poor Lord Durham's son, and is anxious that you should be assured how sincerely he sympathises in his feelings and those of poor Lady Durham, and all your family, upon this melancholy occasion; and how much he laments that they should have been thus prematurely deprived of so hopeful a son. His Majesty readily conceives how much you must be overpowered by this sad event; and he desires that you will not think of coming to him to-morrow, nor of quitting your seclusion for some days if you can possibly avoid it, sensible as His Majesty is of the comfort which Lord and Lady Durham must derive from your being near them. He is not surprised that they should intend to attend the funeral, but fears it will prove a severe trial.

The King was glad to learn that Sir James Graham had communicated to your Lordship the feeling which His Majesty had expressed to him upon the subject of ———'s indecent and unwarrantable language; and he hopes that, by the time this reaches your Lordship, you will have seen also his further communication of this date to Sir James Graham upon the same subject, in which you will observe that His Majesty, feeling that ——— could not be called to account for expressions used by him as a Member in his place in the House of Commons, had noticed the expressions *used by him at a meeting of the Corporation of London*, and repeated in the House of Commons; and that His Majesty expected Sir James Graham would confine the attention of the Board of Admiralty to the speech made in the Common Hall, to which the privilege of Parliament does not apply, and approved of Sir James Graham having done so; but that, judging from the report of two papers, His Majesty had viewed what ——— said in the House of Commons as confirmatory of the threat addressed to the House of Lords, rather than as apologetic.

As your Lordship may have seen, and at any rate will see, His Majesty's letter to Sir James Graham, he considers it unnecessary to repeat any more of its contents, except that he has admitted the advice of his confidential servants and the opinion of the Board of Admiralty, that it would not be expedient to exercise his prerogative upon this occasion by removing ——— from his service, however he may differ with the Board of Admiralty as to the doctrine which they introduce in their minute.

The King felt well assured that your Lordship would highly disapprove of the intemperate and indecent language used by ———; but His Majesty is not disposed to give him that credit which your good-nature prompts you to allow to him, for respect for the Crown and the other institutions of the State, it appearing to His Majesty that he has for years past distinguished himself by very industrious endeavours to subvert the existing institutions. Of his disposition to do so whenever the occasion should offer, he could not, in His Majesty's opinion, have offered a stronger proof than by suggesting the possibility of the Peers, who are opposed to the popular opinion, finding themselves placed in Schedule A.; and considering also how essential it is at this moment to avoid all that can tend to increase the prevailing excitement, and how desirable, therefore, to conciliate and to endeavour to disarm opposition, it appears to His Majesty that ——— could not possibly have been betrayed by his revolutionary feeling into a step more injurious to the result of the question he supports, than that of holding out to the high and respectable body which is about to discuss it, a threat that the maintenance of opinions hostile to it might produce the annihilation of that body.

I have, &c.   H. TAYLOR.

No. 212.

Sir H. Taylor to Earl Grey.

Windsor Castle, Tuesday Night, Sept. 27, 1831.

My dear Lord,—I cannot send the accompanying letter by His Majesty's command, without taking the liberty of adding this to express to you how sincerely I condole with you, and Lord and Lady Durham, and the rest of your family, upon the sad event which has plunged you in such deep and great affliction. I was aware from what you said to me in London, that you expected it; but it is impossible to be prepared for so severe a blow; and its effect, whenever it does come, is perhaps not the less serious because it has been long contemplated. On the contrary, the nerves have been shaken by the apprehension and the painful observance of its approach.

Your Lordship may depend upon my apprising you of anything which it may be desirable that you should know. His Majesty goes to Sandhurst on Thursday, and expects the Grand Duchess Helen on Friday. He is well, but easily excited; and I have never seen him take up anything more warmly than that *escapade* of ———. It is indeed very provoking that such language should be held at a period, when it is particularly desirable to avoid all that can irritate feelings already too much excited.

I have, &c. H. TAYLOR.

No. 213.

Earl Grey to Sir H. Taylor.

(Private.) East Sheen, Sept. 29, 1831.

My dear Sir,—I beg you will offer to His Majesty my humble thanks for his gracious compliance with my request, to be allowed to remain here for a few days; and I trust His Majesty's service will not suffer by it.

I communicated your letter to Lord Durham, and it had the effect which I hoped from it, of proving extremely gratifying to his feelings. He desired me to express to His Majesty his gratitude for the kind interest expressed by His Majesty in his deep and irreparable affliction; and he reverted with pleasure to an inquiry which the King had been pleased to make after his poor boy, during the ceremony of the Coronation.

I thought the Board of Admiralty wrong in their opinion, if it was meant to go the length of saying that an officer on full pay, and absent on leave, was not liable to martial law for a military offence; and Captain Barrington who was here, and had not been present at the board, concurred with me in thinking so. The only question in the present case will be, whether the words used by —— at a political meeting would constitute a military offence, cognisable by a court-martial. This point, however, will be satisfactorily settled by the opinion of the Law Officers of the Crown, and no entry will be permitted to remain on the records of the Admiralty which can be construed prejudicially to the discipline of the Navy. Of the absolute power possessed by the King to dismiss an officer by virtue of his royal prerogative, there can be no doubt whatever; but no Sovereign ever sat on the throne of this country who would less wish to exercise that power, except on just grounds, than His present Majesty.

Will you be good enough to tell His Majesty, that the living of Halesworth in Suffolk, worth about £400 per annum, becomes vacant by the appointment of Dr. Whately to the Archbishopric of Dublin. Dr. W.

has represented to me that Mr. Badeley the curate has for many years executed the duty of that situation in the most exemplary manner, and that his appointment to the living would be of the greatest benefit to the parish. A representation has come to me from the principal parishioners to the same effect. I would therefore propose, if His Majesty sees no objection, that Mr. Badeley should succeed Dr. W.

I am, &c. GREY.

No. 214.

Sir H. Taylor to Earl Grey.

(Private.) Windsor Castle, Sept. 30, 1831.

My dear Lord,—I have had the honour to submit your Lordship's letter of yesterday to the King, who was pleased to learn that Lord Durham's feelings had been gratified by the expression of His Majesty's sympathy in his affliction, which has indeed been very sincere.

His Majesty orders me to assure your Lordship how highly he approves of your recommendation of Mr. Badeley for the living of Halesworth in Suffolk, and of the principle on which you have brought him forward.

The King saw Sir James Graham yesterday, and understood from him that the Board of Admiralty wished to cancel their minute respecting ———, which was certainly not borne out by the rule and practice of the service, as their opinion was broadly laid down therein. Had they stated that the offence was one which could not be brought under the cognisance of a courtmartial, and that they considered that it would not be advisable or expedient to visit it by the exercise of the prerogative, they would have met His Majesty's opinion on the first point, and received his concurrence on the second; but they stated broadly, and without qualification, that an officer, absent on leave from his division, cannot be held amenable to martial law; and they proceed, after making this observation, to say that they cannot advise His Majesty to exercise the extreme power of the prerogative by striking the name of —— from the list, &c., without a trial, without a conviction, and even without a hearing, forgetting that the exercise of the prerogative applies to cases in which no trial, and therefore no conviction, take place.

These are the grounds upon which His Majesty objected to the minute, and desired that a reference might be made to legal opinion; but he had no wish or intention that such opinion should be taken, whether the words used by —— at a political meeting would constitute a military offence, cognisable by a courtmartial, His Majesty being sensible that they could not, unless they had been treasonable, or spoken against the King or the Royal Family, which case is specially provided for in the Mutiny Act.

I have, &c. H. TAYLOR.

No. 215.

Sir H. Taylor to Earl Grey.

Windsor Castle, Oct. 4, 1831.

My dear Lord,—The King has ordered me to acquaint your Lordship, that Lord Waldegrave waited upon His Majesty this day to tender to him his resignation of the situation of Lord of the Bed-chamber, as he could not make up his mind to vote for the Reform Bill in its present state.

His Majesty has accepted his resignation.

I have, &c. H. TAYLOR.

No. 216.

The King to Earl Grey.

Windsor Castle, Oct. 4, 1831. 10 a.m.

The King has received Earl Grey's letter, dated at half-past one this morning; and he is very sensible of Earl Grey's attention in making so early a report to him of the first proceedings in the House of Lords, upon a question which so deeply engages his interest; from which however, as stated by him, it does not appear that any judgment can be formed as to the issue of the discussion.*

His Majesty was aware, from what Lord Hill said to him before he left this residence yesterday morning,

---

* The Reform Bill had been passed by the House of Commons on the 21st of September and carried to the Lords on the 22nd, when it was read a first time without opposition. The 2nd reading was moved on the 3rd of October.

that he had felt under considerable difficulty as to the line he should take, his feelings and his opinions being decidedly opposed to the measure of Reform which has been introduced, although, as he had never felt inclined to take a warm part upon any question, and had not considered the situation which he holds a political one, he had not at any time expressed his opinions. If Lord Hill had attended this discussion, he would have appeared there as an opponent to the Bill; and he considered it to be more consistent with the duties of his official situation and its character, as it was more in accordance with his general disposition towards the King's Government, and with his inclination to support them in every other instance, to adopt the alternative of staying away.

His Majesty is glad to hear from Earl Grey that he has prevailed upon Lord Durham to abandon the intention of attending the melancholy ceremony on Friday next, for which the state of his health so little fits him. His Majesty hopes that he will soon get better, and that his spirits will gradually recover the severe shock they have received. He trusts he need not add, that he takes also a sincere interest in the state of Lady Durham and the other members of the family.	WILLIAM R.

No. 217.

The King to Earl Grey.

Windsor Castle, Oct. 6, 1831.

The King acknowledges the receipt of Earl Grey's letter, dated at two o'clock this morning, containing the report of the debate on the Reform Bill in the House of Lords last night and its further adjournment. His Majesty hopes that Earl Grey's health will not suffer from these continued late sittings.

WILLIAM R.

No. 218.

The King to Earl Grey.

Windsor Castle, Oct. 7, 1831.

The King acknowledges the receipt of Earl Grey's letter, dated one o'clock a.m. this day, transmitting the list of the Peers present and speakers on the Reform Bill last night, and the further adjournment of the debate.

WILLIAM R.

No. 219.

The King to Earl Grey.

Windsor Castle, Oct. 8, 1831.

The King does not delay acknowledging the receipt of Earl Grey's letter, dated at half-past six this morning, reporting the Division which has taken place in the House of Lords upon the motion for the second reading of the Reform Bill.*

His Majesty would deceive Earl Grey if he were to

---

* The Division had been,
  Contents present, 128; Proxies, 30—158.
  Not-contents, 150;   „   49—199.
  Majority against the Bill, 41.

say that the result is not such as he had long expected; that even the majority is not larger than he had expected, notwithstanding the accession of strength by the new creation of Peers at the Coronation; and it would be idle, after all His Majesty has said and written on the subject, more especially after the urgent representation contained in his letter of the 24th of April, written immediately after he had consented to a dissolution of Parliament, to admit now that he had not anticipated such a result, if the Bill should be carried to the House of Lords without such essential modifications as should render it more palatable to its opponents, or to admit that he had not then, or had not ever since, ceased to apprehend this result, and the consequent collision between the two Houses of Parliament.

The King considers it unnecessary to recapitulate the reasons which have been already so fully stated by him, why he should have deprecated, and why he should now lament, a state of things which, if it should continue, must be so fatal to the interests of the country. He considers it equally unnecessary to say, that the evil cannot be met by resorting to measures for obtaining a majority in the House of Lords which no Government could propose and no Sovereign consent to, without losing sight of what is due to the character of that House, to the honour of the Aristocracy of the country, and to the dignity of the Throne.

But His Majesty does not hesitate to say, that he would view as one of the greatest evils resulting from what has passed, the retirement from his Councils of Earl Grey and his colleagues, both as it would affect the interests of the country and those of Europe in general, at a period when so much is at stake, which a change of men and measures might interrupt and defeat.

His Majesty, therefore, trusts that a proposition to that effect will not be the result of the meeting which Earl Grey has summoned for this day at three o'clock.

WILLIAM R.

No. 220.

Earl Grey to the King.

Downing Street, Oct. 8, 1831.

Earl Grey has the honour of acknowledging your Majesty's most gracious letter, which he laid before your Majesty's servants at their meeting this morning.

They feel most grateful to your Majesty for the expressions of confidence with which your Majesty has been pleased to honour them, and for the wish which your Majesty has signified to them, that they should not retire from your Majesty's service. With so gracious a desire, every sentiment of duty and affection would naturally urge them to comply; and Earl Grey is authorised to state to your Majesty their unanimous resolution to suffer no personal considerations to interfere with the obligation by which they feel themselves bound to do everything in their power to contribute to your Majesty's personal ease and comfort; and to the general peace and security of your Majesty's dominions. But the circumstances in which the Government is placed are critical and difficult, and they hope for your Majesty's indulgent permission to take a few days for a careful consideration of all the circumstances of the country and of the times, before they come to a decision from which may result consequences of such serious importance to your Majesty, to themselves, and to the public.

In the meantime Earl Grey would be happy to be allowed to wait upon your Majesty as soon as may suit your Majesty's convenience, to explain to your Majesty his views on the present situation of affairs, with respect to which it is only necessary for him at this moment to add, that he feels himself bound, both by his own conscientious opinion and by the declarations which he has repeatedly made in the House of Lords, again to bring forward, if he continues in your Majesty's service, a measure of Parliamentary Reform which, though that which has now been rejected may require some alterations, will not be less efficient for all the objects which it was hoped to attain by it.

All which, &c. GREY.

No. 221.

Earl Grey to Sir H. Taylor.

Downing Street, Oct. 8, 1831.

My dear Sir,—I add a single line with the letter which I have sent to the King, to say that if it should be equally convenient to His Majesty, Monday would be the day on which it would best suit me to be allowed to wait on His Majesty; and *not at a very early hour.* I mention this, being quite knocked up by the fatigue of the week, and under the necessity of confining myself to-morrow under the orders of my doctor. I wrote the accompanying letter to the King from the Cabinet amidst the interruptions of such a meeting. But I do not know that anything more is required to be said, than that the amount of the majority puts all notion of an attempt to counteract it by a further creation of Peers quite out of the question. Indeed, I should not have been willing, under any circumstances, to resort to such a measure, and certainly not unless a very small addition would have been effectual for the purpose. I have also omitted to say anything respecting the modifications which I was well aware it was His Majesty's desire should be introduced into the Bill. There was a sincere desire to have acted in this matter according to His Majesty's wishes; but it was found impossible to do so without exposing the Government to certain defeat; and you may be assured, whatever professions they may now make, that no concessions, though they would have been ruinous to our own character, would have conciliated our opponents. You may be assured that carrying a measure not less efficient than this, though altered in its provisions, is absolutely necessary for the preservation of the public peace. With the expectation of such a measure, I trust no violation of it will ensue; but there are already very strong indications of the effect which the unfortunate decision of the House of Lords last night has produced upon the public feeling.

I am, &c.

GREY.

No. 222.

The King to Earl Grey.

Windsor Castle, Oct. 8, 1831. 11 p.m.

The King has received, with great satisfaction, the assurance conveyed in Earl Grey's letter of this afternoon, that he and His Majesty's other confidential servants have been gratified by the desire expressed by him that they should not, under the circumstances which have occurred, retire from his service. And His Majesty is too well aware of the critical state in which the country is placed, and of the difficulties under which his Government may labour, not to admit the propriety and reasonableness of their desire to be allowed a few days for careful consideration before they come to a decision.

His Majesty will be prepared to receive Earl Grey on Monday, at any hour that may best suit his convenience. WILLIAM R.

No. 223.

Sir H. Taylor to Earl Grey.

(Private.) Windsor Castle, Oct. 8, 1831.
Half-past 11 p.m.

My dear Lord,—I have had the honour to submit to the King the letter from your Lordship addressed to me, which accompanied that for His Majesty; and I can assure you that both have been received by him with great satisfaction, and that His Majesty looks forward with confidence to the continued exertions of your Lordship and your colleagues in the administration of the affairs of this country at this critical period.

The King highly approves of your laying by to-morrow and endeavouring to recruit your strength after so arduous a trial of it; and as you mention that not a very early hour would best suit you on Monday, I would suggest *three* o'clock, which will be perfectly convenient to His Majesty. I shall despatch the messenger at seven to-morrow morning, to prevent your being unnecessarily disturbed by his return in the night.

I have, &c.   H. TAYLOR.

No. 224.

The King to Earl Grey.

Windsor Castle, Oct. 9, 1831.

The King thinks it necessary to transmit to Earl Grey for his perusal before he sees him to-morrow, the 'Globe' paper of the 7th inst., in the last page of which he will find the report of Colonel Napier's* speech at

---

* It is not without much hesitation that I have allowed this letter to remain in its place in the correspondence, in consequence of the very strong language used by the King with respect to Colonel Napier. But as this language applies only to Colonel Napier's political conduct, while his merits as an officer are acknowledged, I have on the whole thought it better not to suppress a letter which affords a striking illustration of the manner in which the difficulties encountered by the Ministers in passing the Reform Bill were aggravated by the violence of some of its supporters, and the bad effect this had on the mind of the King. It also, I think, deserves to be noticed to the credit of the King, that although on this and on some other occasions, when his feelings were strongly excited, he urged his Ministers to adopt measures to which it was their

the Devizes meeting. If the sentiments therein recorded were really uttered by that officer, if expressions tending to excite the people in general of this country, and more particularly the lower orders who flock to those public meetings, to sedition and rebellion, and to acts of extreme violence in support of a question which is the subject of legislative discussion, have been addressed by that factious individual to the people then and there assembled, it becomes, in the King's opinion, a matter for serious consideration, whether such conduct should not be visited by the most severe mark of His Majesty's displeasure, which can be applied to the case of an officer who has shown so total a disregard for that duty and loyalty, which the obligations of his profession and his allegiance as a subject alike prescribe. Colonel Napier is an officer of acknowledged ability and talent, and of great resource; and he has served with great gallantry and distinction; but those circumstances offer no excuse, or justification, for the wild, the mischievous, the senseless, the revolutionary course he is now pursuing; and His Majesty cannot but apprehend, that if such course be overlooked, if those who set all government and all legal authority at defiance be permitted to do so with impunity, this passiveness will be ascribed to fear, and not to forbearance or

---

duty to object, he never failed to give the fairest consideration to their reasons for not doing what he had suggested, and to take in good part the advice they offered him. The subject of Colonel Napier's speech not being again adverted to in the correspondence, it may be presumed that when he saw Lord Grey the next day he was satisfied of the inexpediency of the extreme measure he had proposed.

contempt; and that those who may derive advantage in the discharge of arduous duties from the unqualified support of the Sovereign, will not reap the full benefit of that support if any impressions be suffered to prevail that he shrinks from the exercise of his prerogative when so much is done to provoke it, or that he fears to meet the expression of popular feeling in behalf of the individual who has become a candidate for popular favour by preaching sedition and violence.

If Earl Grey should view this question in the same light, he will consider whether Lord Hill should not be required to communicate the published report of his speech to Colonel Napier, and to desire he will state whether it be correctly reported; and if he should admit that such were the sentiments uttered by him, His Majesty thinks that Colonel Napier ought, without delay, to be struck off the half-pay list.

Earl Grey will observe that Colonel Napier is a very *sweeping* enemy to all government and established authority. WILLIAM R.

No. 225.

Sir H. Taylor to Earl Grey.

(Private.) Windsor Castle, Oct. 10, 1831.

My dear Lord,—The King has honoured me with his commands to acquaint your Lordship, that Lord Howe has, in consequence of the communication which His Majesty agreed to make to him, resigned the office of Lord Chamberlain to the Queen, and that Her Majesty has accepted his resignation.

His Majesty has further ordered me to say, that he forgot to mention to your Lordship that it is not his intention to prorogue Parliament in person.

I have, &c. H. TAYLOR.

No. 226.

Earl Grey to the King.

Downing Street, Oct. 11, 1831.

Earl Grey has the honour of submitting to your Majesty a Minute of Cabinet, unanimously agreed upon at a meeting of your Majesty's servants, held at the Foreign Office this morning. The Marquis of Anglesey, at Earl Grey's desire, also attended, and entirely concurred in the opinion expressed by the rest of your Majesty's servants.

Earl Grey begs leave to say for himself, how deeply and how sincerely he feels the condescending kindness and confidence with which your Majesty has been pleased to honour him. They have imposed upon him a debt of unalterable gratitude, and, as long as he can flatter himself with the hope of contributing to your Majesty's personal ease and comfort, or of acting usefully in the situation in which your Majesty has placed him, there is no personal sacrifice which can stand in the way of the duty which he owes to your Majesty and to his country.

Earl Grey had this morning the honour of receiving the communication which your Majesty had ordered Sir H. Taylor to make to him of Earl Howe's resignation. It was with great pain that Earl Grey found himself under the necessity of urging what might be disagreeable to Her Majesty, but he could not avoid what was essential to the support of your Majesty's Government under the trying circumstances of the present moment; and he begs your Majesty to accept his humble acknowledgments of your Majesty's gracious attention to the representation which he felt himself compelled to make on this distressing occasion.*

Earl Grey has the honour of informing your Majesty that, after examining the state of the public business, it was the opinion of the Cabinet that Parliament may be prorogued at the end of the present week. It is with great doubt and hesitation that Earl Grey ventures to offer a suggestion in opposition to your Majesty's declared intentions; but he is impelled, by an imperious sense of duty, humbly to express to your Majesty his anxious hope that your Majesty may be induced to reconsider your determination not to prorogue Parliament in person, which at this moment would be too likely to excite a feeling of distrust injurious in the highest degree to the interests of your Majesty's Government.

All which, &c.   GREY.

(Enclosure.)

Minute of Cabinet.

Downing Street, Oct. 11, 1831.

At a meeting of your Majesty's servants held to-day at the Foreign Office,

---

* The representation referred to was that Lord Howe's retaining his office in the Queen's household after his vote against the second reading of the Reform Bill would have a bad effect on public opinion. There are some further references to this subject in other letters which I have omitted.

PRESENT:

The Lord Chancellor,	Viscount Melbourne,
The Lord President,	Viscount Palmerston,
The Duke of Richmond,	Viscount Goderich,
Earl Grey,	Viscount Althorp,
The Lord Holland,	Lord John Russell,
Sir James Graham,	Mr. Stanley,
Mr. Grant,	

the following Minute was unanimously agreed upon:—

Earl Grey having communicated to your Majesty's servants the substance of what passed at the interview with which your Majesty was pleased to honour him yesterday at Windsor Castle, they beg leave humbly to express their unanimous feeling of gratitude and devotion to your Majesty for your Majesty's condescending expression of your continued confidence in their humble endeavours to promote your Majesty's service.

These endeavours will always be directed, as they have hitherto been, to the preservation of the honour of your Majesty's crown, and of the peace of your Majesty's dominions; and to secure these important objects, they cannot hesitate to express their entire concurrence in the opinion already submitted to your Majesty by Earl Grey, that it is absolutely indispensable that they should have the power of proposing to Parliament, at the commencement of the next Session, with the fullest indications of your Majesty's approbation and support, a measure of Parliamentary Reform founded on the same principles as that which has lately been rejected by the House of Lords, and of equal efficacy for the correction of those defects in the present state of the representation of the people in Parliament, which have become the subject of such general complaint.

Relying no less on their experience of your Majesty's uniform conduct towards them, than on the gracious assurances given by your Majesty to Earl Grey, they feel themselves bound, by every sentiment of gratitude and duty, to devote themselves to the support of your Majesty's person and Government under all the difficulties of the present crisis.

No. 227.

Earl Grey to Sir H. Taylor.

Downing Street, Oct. 11, 1831.

My dear Sir,

* * * * *

I cannot help adding how anxiously I hope, that what I have said in my letter to His Majesty may induce him to alter his intention of not proroguing the Parliament in person. Everything is at this moment viewed with so jealous an eye, that I greatly fear that His Majesty's absence, for the first time since his accession to the throne, on such an occasion would be liable to the most unfortunate misconception or misinterpretation. The opponents of the Government, above all others, who are always on the watch for anything that may assist their views, would not fail in this, as in many other instances, no matter how contrary to all truth, to argue upon it as an indication of His Majesty's not being satisfied with the course pursued by his Ministers.

I am sorry to say that there are accounts of serious

disturbances at Nottingham, and that the Castle had been burnt. In London everything appears to be perfectly quiet, and confidence greatly restored by the division and the declaration of Lord Althorp last night in the House of Commons.*

I am, &c. GREY.

* On Monday the 10th of October, when the House of Commons met for the first time after the rejection of the Reform Bill by the House of Lords, Lord Ebrington moved the following resolution:—

'That while this House deeply laments the present fate of a Bill for amending the representation of the people in England and Wales, in favour of which the opinion of the country stands unequivocally pronounced, and which has been matured by discussions the most anxious and laborious, it feels called upon to re-assert its firm adherence to the principle and leading provisions of that great measure, and to express its unabated confidence in the integrity, perseverance, and ability of those Ministers who, in introducing and conducting it, have so well consulted the best interests of the country.' This resolution was carried by a majority of 329 to 198. In the course of the debate which preceded the division Lord Althorp had declared that, unless he felt a reasonable hope that a measure as efficient as that recently passed by the House of Commons might be secured by the continuance of the existing Administration, he would not continue in office an hour. As showing the difficulties with which my father had to contend in keeping the Government together, and carrying the measure of Reform, it may not be uninteresting to mention that the above declaration made by Lord Althorp in the House of Commons, and the similar declaration made by my father himself in the House of Lords, were objected to by some of his colleagues, to one of whom he wrote the following letter in reply to one he had received on the subject:—

(Private.) Downing Street, October 10, 1831.

My dear ——, I received your letter late last night, and I must confess that it has given me great uneasiness. I thought when we talked the matter over in the Cabinet, that a declaration to the extent of what I had said in the House of Lords had been agreed upon; and that it was felt that we could not continue the Government with safety to the King and the public, and without loss of character to ourselves, if we did so without showing unequivocally that we considered ourselves pledged to bring forward another measure of Reform (though it might be necessary to alter many of the provisions of the last) equally efficient.

No. 228.

The King to Earl Grey.

Windsor Castle, Oct. 12, 1831.

The King will not delay acknowledging the reciept of Earl Grey's letter of yesterday, enclosing a Minute

---

By equally efficient, I certainly mean that the disfranchisement of nomination boroughs, the transfer of the members thus reduced to large towns and to counties, with such an improvement in the right of voting generally as should ensure a fair representation of the people in Parliament, and regulations for diminishing the expense, &c., attending the present mode of election, should form the essential principle and chief features of the measure. To this extent I thought we had all been agreed from the beginning; and if now, having fought the Bill through the House of Commons during a prolonged contest of six weeks or two months on these principles, we should appear to falter, I greatly fear that the consequences would be to us most ruinous in point of reputation, and absolutely fatal to the public.

For I am persuaded that nothing can preserve the public peace but the continuance of the present Administration in office, with the confidence of the people in the sincerity of their resolution to prosecute to a successful issue the cause which they have undertaken.

I am afraid you are greatly deceived in the state of public opinion, if you believe that anything short of this could prevent a very general adoption of proceedings throughout the country, which, though I trust they would not be attended with violence in the first instance, might lead to consequences of a most fatal nature. My information, and I do not think it is erroneous, leads me to believe that the middle classes, who form the real and efficient mass of public opinion, and without whom the power of the gentry is nothing, are almost unanimous on this question, and animated by a settled resolution to press it forward. Of the gentry too I am persuaded that a very large majority are now impressed with corresponding sentiments. That many of the Peers felt great apprehension of the extent of the measure, I am ready to admit. But I am equally persuaded that the majority was produced by a factious combination to overturn the Government; and I do not think it probable that an opposition of this nature can continue to prevail against so general and so strong an expression of public opinion, as has been and will be produced on this question. Indeed many of the opponents of the measure

of Cabinet unanimously agreed upon at a meeting of His Majesty's confidential servants yesterday, at which

---

have so far acquiesced in its principles, that it is not easy to reconcile their votes on the second reading with their declared opinions.

Of the disfranchisement of boroughs, of the transfer to large towns, of the addition to the representation of counties, says Harrowby, I approve; so say Wharncliffe and others. Why, really, this is the whole principle of the Bill; and, conceding this principle, it will not be easy to stop short, in applying it, of what we have proposed.

But I am getting more into an argument on the measure itself than the occasion requires. The question for us to decide is, whether we can continue in the Government on any other ground than that of a declared resolution to reproduce a measure of Reform, and to what extent that declaration should be made. Now, though I do not approve more than you do of prospective pledges, it appears to me not only that a declaration of our intention to propose an equally efficient measure would not pledge us further than our conduct in supporting the late Bill throughout all the discussion which it has undergone has already done, but anything less would naturally and justly excite a suspicion that we were shrinking from the principle on which we have been hitherto acting. The effect of this would be certain and decisive. The public confidence would be at once withdrawn from us. We should be compelled to retire in disgrace; and the best thing that could happen would be, that the Duke of Wellington, or whoever might be called upon to form a new Administration, would propose a plan, certainly not less extensive than ours. But the more probable event would be, that the people would take the matter into their own hands, and then God knows what might be the result.

I therefore remain of opinion, as I have already stated to the Cabinet, that our own honour and the public safety equally require that we should appear to continue in office, if we do so, with a sincere intention of redeeming the pledge which we have given to the public. To the terms of this declaration I am sure Althorp, with whom I hope you will have a full communication before you go to the House of Commons, will be disposed to obviate anything that might appear to engage you personally for more than you are prepared to assent to. The declaration, in my opinion, should be, that the Administration, if it continues, does so with the hope of being able to bring forward with better success an efficient plan of Reform, which may satisfy the just expectations of the public. That this will be carefully reconsidered after all the lights which the late discussions have thrown upon the measure, but that for himself individually he (Althorp) must declare that whatever variations may be

the Marquis of Anglesey also attended, at the request of Earl Grey.

The King assures Earl Grey that he has received with great satisfaction the expression which this Minute conveys of the sentiments of his confidential servants, and of the readiness to afford to him the continued advantage of their services at a period of almost unexampled difficulty; and that he entertains a just sense of the feeling which actuated them upon this occasion, and which so well entitles them to the confidence His Majesty has not ceased to repose in them. This assurance of His Majesty's sentiments is due above all to Earl Grey, who has, as the more responsible and the more prominent member of his Administration, devoted, with so much unvaried zeal and attachment, the powerful energies of his mind to the service of His Majesty and of the State, under circumstances most critical and

---

made as to the provisions of the late Bill, he cannot be a party to anything less efficient in principle and in substance. This I should hope would be satisfactory to you; but again, I say, pray see Althorp and discuss the matter with him fully before you go to the House of Commons.

If the matter cannot be thus arranged, and a division of sentiment amongst the Ministers should appear, it must be at once fatal to the Administration. As far as I am personally concerned, God knows this would not be *to me* an unpleasant result; for I should be glad to retire from a situation the duties of which are too much for my strength. But I fear for the peace of the country. To prevent the fearful extent of civil dissension which I foresee as the inevitable consequence of a change of Government at this moment, I feel to be my first duty; and I must at least secure to myself, in any event that may happen, the consolation of having done everything in my power to fulfil so sacred an obligation.

I was so unwell that I could not go to Windsor yesterday. I am going this morning and have written this in great haste, as you will perceive from its blotted appearance.

trying. Nor is His Majesty heedless of the sacrifice of domestic comfort, and even of health, which Earl Grey is making for the benefit of his country.

The same considerations which led the King to consent, in February last, to the introduction of a Reform Bill upon the principle then recommended by Earl Grey, must influence His Majesty now with respect to his assent to the earnest and urgent advice of his confidential servants, 'that they should have the power of proposing to Parliament, at the commencement of the next Session, a measure of Parliamentary Reform founded on the same principle as that which has lately been rejected by the House of Lords;' but His Majesty cannot give this assent without attaching to it an earnest recommendation, that they will consider well how important it is so to shape their course as to obviate, if possible, a recurrence of the result which has attended the recent discussion in the House of Lords—a result which His Majesty had so much apprehended, and anticipated, and deprecated. Upon this occasion the King cannot forbear again directing the attention of his confidential servants to his letter of the 24th April last. There will happily be full time for consideration and deliberation. The principle of the Bill, the necessity of Reform, appear to have been generally admitted and established; and it is hoped that henceforth the discussion may be considered as confined in great measure to the details, and that, in them, the modifications may be found which shall reconcile opinions which cannot be viewed as undeserving of attention.

The King feels that the times call for greater deference than at former periods to popular feeling and opinion; but he feels also that regard is due to the feelings and opinions of a great portion of the Aristocracy of the country—to a majority of the House of Lords; and he trusts, for the sake of the country and for their own credit, that while they hold these opinions they will never shrink from the avowal of them, nor yield to intimidation, although he hopes and wishes that they may yield to conviction.

His Majesty has learnt with satisfaction, that the state of the public business will admit of Parliament being prorogued at the end of the present week, and His Majesty will not persist in the intention he had expressed, not to prorogue Parliament in person, but will yield to the desire so strongly expressed by Earl Grey that he should do so. He does not deny, however, that his reluctance had arisen from his earnest wish to avoid all that could in any degree tend to increase the popular ferment at this period of extraordinary excitement; and that he dreads also that these frequent exhibitions might be construed into a disposition on his part to be put forth as a puppet to gratify the public inclination for opportunities of assembling and displaying its feeling on popular questions. But His Majesty would not upon any account, by his absence from such a ceremony, risk a construction so inconsistent with his sentiments as that which Earl Grey apprehends might possibly be given to it; and he has also, upon reconsideration, been directed by the example of his late father, who, until he was blind, always prorogued the Parliament in person.

WILLIAM R.

229.

The King to Earl Grey.

St. James's, Oct. 17, 1831.

The King having understood that a meeting of his confidential servants will be held to-morrow, to consider of the Speech on the Prorogation of Parliament, His Majesty considers it his duty, when the interests of the Crown, of the State, and of the people are involved in the issue of the question which must necessarily form a principal feature of that Speech, to express most earnestly his hope and his expectation, that the importance of avoiding all that can provoke opposition and increase the excitement of party and the effervescence of the people will engage the serious attention of His Majesty's Government.

He is, indeed, convinced that they must feel, with him, how great would be the difficulties in which this country would be plunged, how lamentable the embarrassments in which its Sovereign would be placed by a a second rejection of the Bill in the House of Lords, and how desirable, therefore, that, when they separate, and when the interval before they again assemble may be devoted to quiet and dispassionate consideration, the impression left upon their minds should not be that there is a determination to treat their opinions with contempt, and to hold out to the country as a *faction* 199 Peers, a majority of the great body of that House of Lords, which has been hitherto considered the faithful support of the Crown and the State.

It is His Majesty's most anxious desire that all that can irritate should in future be avoided; and he does not know that he can better express his feelings upon this occasion than by transcribing the words of Lord Bolingbroke, which appear to him peculiarly applicable:—

'As every new modification in a scheme of government and of national policy is of great importance, and requires more and deeper consideration than the warmth, and hurry, and rashness of party conduct admit, the duty of a Prince seems to require that he should render by his influence the proceedings more orderly and more deliberate, even when he approves the end to which they are directed.'

WILLIAM R.

230.

Earl Grey to the King.

Downing Street, Oct. 17, 1831.

Earl Grey has the honour of acknowledging your Majesty's letter of this day, which he received on his return from the House of Lords late this evening.

He hopes that no part of his conduct can have left an impression on your Majesty's mind, that he has not been at all times desirous of avoiding 'all that can provoke opposition and increase the excitement of party, and the effervescence of public opinion.' His best endeavours have been uniformly directed to prevent such effects; and he has this very day, in the House of Lords. made a statement with that intent.

But, as when he first accepted the situation which your Majesty was graciously pleased to offer him, he laid before your Majesty without reserve his humble but conscientious opinion of the necessity of bringing forward a proposition for Parliamentary Reform; so he has, in all that has subsequently passed, expressed to your Majesty his increased conviction that nothing could restore confidence to the Government, or secure the internal peace of the country, but a measure of that description, resting upon sound principles, and of sufficient efficacy to satisfy the just expectations of the public.

The Bill introduced with this view into the House of Commons, and carried through that House by a great and decided majority, has been, unhappily, rejected by the House of Lords; and, upon this unfortunate event, Earl Grey again stated to your Majesty, with the frankness which your Majesty had encouraged him to use, that he could not remain in your Majesty's service with advantage to your Majesty, or with honour to himself, except with the assurance of your Majesty's support on offering to Parliament another measure, varied in some of its provisions, where alterations might be found necessary, but the same in principle and of equal efficacy in substance.

A just confidence that such will be the conduct of your Majesty's Ministers, Lord Grey is persuaded has contributed, more than any other circumstance, to the preservation of the internal peace, under the severe disappointment experienced by the public. It is by this confidence also that the general feeling, of such unexampled extent and intensity, has hitherto been prevented from showing itself in such a manner as might have been productive of the most dangerous consequences; but, if anything should occur to diminish this confidence, and to awaken suspicion, still more, if a fear should be excited of the ultimate defeat of an object on which the wishes of the people are so anxiously set, Earl Grey could not answer for the continuance of public tranquillity.

With this conviction—in no degree arising, as he trusts your Majesty will believe, from any disposition to yield to popular violence or clamour, and in conformity with the views which he has so often stated to your Majesty—Earl Grey feels that it is necessary to hold out to the public an expectation that a measure of Reform, equally efficient with the last, will be presented to Parliament immediately after the opening of the ensuing Session.

In framing the Speech to be delivered by your Majesty at the Prorogation, and which will, of course, be submitted as soon as possible to your Majesty's consideration, it will be the anxious wish of Earl Grey, as he is sure it will also be that of the rest of your Majesty's servants, to express this in such a manner as may tend to allay, rather than to increase, the public agitation. But he would be guilty of an unworthy concealment if he were not to state, without disguise, his feeling of the absolute necessity that, to this extent, a public assurance should be given, that your Majesty's Government will not deviate from the principles on which they have hitherto acted.

In the quotation from Lord Bolingbroke, with which your Majesty concludes your most gracious letter, Earl Grey readily acknowledges that there is much wisdom. He trusts that the measures which, with the unanimous approbation of his colleagues, it has been his duty to submit to your Majesty, and which have been sanctioned by your Majesty's approbation, are not open to the censure of having been urged with the 'warmth, hurry, and rashness of party conduct.' Proceedings on all matters of public interest, and more especially with a view to any change in the institutions of the Government, ought, undoubtedly, to be 'orderly and deliberate;' but it is no less necessary that public opinion, which is so essential to the support of every Government, should be duly estimated, and that a course of policy, adopted after a careful consideration of what the interest and safety of the country required, and in which those ends, and the restoration of public confidence, were solely in view, should be pursued with consistency and firmness.

All which, &c. GREY.

No. 231.

The King to Earl Grey.

St. James's, Oct. 18, 1831.*

The letter which the King has this day received from Earl Grey is of too important a character to admit of His Majesty's passing it over in silence.

Earl Grey is quite mistaken, if he supposes that the observations which he quotes from His Majesty's letter of yesterday were meant to apply to any part of his conduct in the progress of the arduous task he has

* There appears to have been no answer to this letter, probably in consequence of Lord Grey having seen the King and spoken to him on the subject the following day.

undertaken, and of the important duties which he discharges so ably and so correctly. The King has never shrunk from the admission of his clear understanding of the principle and the contingencies under which he accepted, and has retained, the high office entrusted to him at a most critical period; and His Majesty gives him full credit for the consistency which he has shown in the pursuit of the measure which has chiefly engaged the attention and solicitude of his Government.

But Earl Grey is aware that the King has at all times expressed his apprehension of a possible collision on this subject between the two Houses of Parliament, and that His Majesty stated his anticipation of such collision, more especially immediately after he had yielded to the advice of his confidential servants, that he should dissolve Parliament with a view to secure a majority in favour of the Bill in a new House of Commons.

His Majesty has at no time required that the Bill should be essentially varied in principle, or rendered less efficient; nor has he in his letter of yesterday written aught that can reasonably bear that construction. But the recent issue of the discussion in the House of Lords having justified the apprehension His Majesty had expressed, and the Bill having been rejected by a larger majority of the Peers than his Government seemed to have expected, it is natural that His Majesty should contemplate as possible, the recurrence of such a result and its embarrassing effects. It is natural that this apprehension should be again expressed by him to his confidential servants; and it becomes his duty again to urge the adoption of that conciliatory course which appears to him best calculated to avert that result, without abandoning the main object in view.

His Majesty does believe, and has always believed, that a calm and dispassionate consideration of the proposed measure, and of the state and the feeling of the country as connected with it, is best calculated to promote the accomplishment of the object in view; and that this calm and dispassionate consideration, free from 'the warmth and hurry, and rashness, of party conduct,' would be most likely to be obtained from the *opponents* of the Bill, and would thus ensure in future 'proceedings more orderly and more deliberate,' by carefully abstaining from all that can provoke warmth and irritate feeling.

The King has already said that he does justice to the feeling and to the course pursued by Earl Grey in this respect; but Earl Grey cannot be surprised that his attention should have been called to the importance of inculcating this advice on others, and of preventing a reaction which might prove fatal to the measure, by the perusal of a public letter from one of His Majesty's confidential servants, in which the opposition of a large body of the Aristocracy of the country, and of a majority of the House of Lords upon a great constitutional question, which had been gravely and unreservedly discussed in that House, is called 'The Whisper of a Faction,'[*] and by observing the irritation thus pro-

[*] This refers to a letter of Lord John Russell's, which had just been published in the newspapers. A vote of thanks to Lords Althorp and John Russell had been passed at a great meeting held at Birmingham; and Lord John, in his letter to the chairman, acknowledging the vote, had said, 'I beg to acknowledge with heartfelt gratitude the undeserved honour done me by 150,000 of my countrymen. Our prospects are now

duced at the very moment when His Majesty had been so earnestly urging the necessity of conciliation.

The King readily subscribes to Earl Grey's sentiments, that the course of policy which has been adopted, after careful consideration, as best suited to the real interests and safety of the country, should be pursued with consistency and firmness; and His Majesty trusts that his conduct has given ample proof of his determination so to support the course which has been adopted by his Government, with his declared concurrence.

WILLIAM R.

No. 232.

Sir H. Taylor to Earl Grey.

St. James's, Oct. 20, 1831.

My dear Lord,—The King has made a slight alteration in the Speech, which your Lordship will find in the 4th page, as it appeared to His Majesty that the passage as it stood might be construed as pledging him to a reduction of *establishments* and not of *increased expenditure* on account of the present state of affairs in Europe.

His Majesty, therefore, sends the Speech back with the alteration, for your consideration, and desires you will return it as soon as possible.

Your Lordship's, &c. H. TAYLOR.

Words substituted:

'From which increased expenditure it will be my earnest desire to relieve the country.'

---

obscured for a moment, and I trust only for a moment. It is impossible that the whisper of a faction should prevail against the voice of a nation.'

No. 233.

The King to Earl Grey.

Windsor Castle, Oct. 26, 1831.

The King having, at the recommendation of his Government, agreed to the completion of Buckingham Palace as a private residence, and to abandon the plan of converting it into a barrack, His Majesty considers it necessary to call the attention of Earl Grey to the importance of not allowing any further delay in giving effect to the plan which had been agreed to, of building a barrack for the Foot Guards in the Birdcage Walk in St. James's Park, which His Majesty has reason to believe may be so constructed as to contain 1500 men. The site is the most eligible and the most convenient that can be fixed upon; and if arrangements can be made for increasing the accommodation in the Old Mews Barracks, without much adding to the expense of construction, the necessity for billeting a large proportion of the men in the worst of public-houses, and of placing them in constant association with the worst members of the lower orders, would be in a great measure obviated. It would be superfluous for His Majesty to dwell upon the advantage of withdrawing the troops from such associates at this period; and the question has become more urgent, in consequence of the approaching expiration of the lease of Knightsbridge Barracks.

His Majesty takes this opportunity of reminding Earl Grey of the measures which had been contemplated previously to his Coronation, in favour of the

Navy and Army, and in substitution for a Brevet. Earl Grey is aware of the King's anxiety to grant the proposed boon to the subaltern ranks of both services, and of his *unalterable* opinion that it cannot be granted to one and withheld from the other. It may be observed, possibly, that the time is gone by; but this would be taking a very unfair advantage of the delay arising out of objections made and not admitted as reasonable by the King, nor, His Majesty believes, by Earl Grey; and it ought not to be forgotten that the agitation of the plans at the Admiralty had produced an expectation on the part of both professions, the disappointment of which would be sorely mortifying.

Finally, His Majesty is desirous of knowing whether Earl Grey has come to any decision with regard to the pay of the Officers of the Blues.

WILLIAM R.

No. 234.

Earl Grey to the King.

East Sheen, Oct. 27, 1831.

Earl Grey has the honour of acknowledging your Majesty's letter of yesterday, which he received late yesterday evening.

Earl Grey, in obedience to your Majesty's command, will lose no time in taking the necessary steps for obtaining plans and estimates of the expense for erecting a new barrack in the Birdcage Walk; the advantage of which, in preventing the necessity of billeting the soldiers in public-houses, cannot be doubted: But Earl

Grey feels himself under the necessity of humbly submitting to your Majesty, that it may not be expedient to proceed further than preparing everything with a view to the least possible delay afterwards, without obtaining the consent of the House of Commons to an expense which Earl Grey fears may be considerable.

Earl Grey's opinion entirely accords with that of your Majesty as to the measure which, previous to the Coronation, was proposed as a substitute for a Brevet. But as this measure had not been provided for in the estimates of the present year, Earl Grey humbly represents that it may be expedient to defer it till it can be included in the estimates for the ensuing year, to be laid before Parliament at the commencement of the next Session. In the meantime, Earl Grey will call the immediate attention of Lord Althorp, after his return to town, to this matter, which has been too long delayed by the other important questions which have so largely occupied the time and attention of your Majesty's Government and Parliament.

With respect to the pay of the Officers of the Blues, Earl Grey is of opinion that it may be expedient to grant the advantage which is desired, though no strict claim of right can be urged in favour of it. But while there exists a case even of doubtful complaint, it is better that the Government take upon itself the burthen, especially when, as in this case, it is so inconsiderable, rather than incur even a suspicion of dealing hardly and unjustly. There is some difficulty, however, arising from the present arrangement having been made by Sir H. Hardinge and Lord F. Leveson. This matter also Earl Grey will consider on the earliest opportunity with Lord Althorp and Sir H. Parnell, and lose no time in reporting the result to your Majesty.

Earl Grey has just read, with the greatest satisfaction, dispatches both from Sir C. Bagot and Sir R. Adair, from which it appears that the question of accepting the 24 Articles of the Conference is likely to be carried in the Belgian Chambers; and that an order of the day was to be issued by the Prince of Orange, stating that it was not the intention of the King to order a renewal of hostilities, but that the army would remain in its present position to repel any attack that might be made on the Dutch territory.

All which, &c. GREY.

No. 235.

Earl Grey to Sir H. Taylor.

East Sheen, Oct. 28, 1831.

My dear Sir,—I enclose a letter from the Archbishop of Canterbury, proposing the adoption of a form of prayer on account of the cholera, also enclosed, which I shall be obliged to you to submit to His Majesty's consideration. I believe the order may be issued from the Privy Council without His Majesty being present.

By the Act for the Queen's dower, the King is empowered to appoint trustees. This appointment has not yet been made, and it is necessary that it should now be completed. I enclose a list of the trustees who were appointed for the late Queen Charlotte, and if you will be so good as to take His Majesty's pleasure, and let me know the names which he selects, I will give immediate directions for the preparation of the necessary warrant from the Treasury for His Majesty's signature.

* * * * *

My cold is as bad as ever, and I have not yet been able to stir out of the house.

* * * * *

I am, &c. GREY.

No. 236.

Sir H. Taylor to Earl Grey.

Windsor Castle, Oct. 29, 1831.

My dear Lord,—I have had the honour to submit your Lordship's letter of yesterday to the King, who has ordered me to return the Archbishop of Canterbury's letter and the proposed form of prayer on account of the cholera with his approbation. His Majesty trusts it may be issued by the Privy Council without his being present.

Upon the other points, namely, the appointment of trustees for the Queen's dower, and the nomination of a successor to Sir George Naylor (whose death has *already* produced five applications, and will probably produce one hundred), His Majesty will communicate with your Lordship from Brighton, for which he is on the point of setting out.

The King learnt with much concern that you continued to suffer so much from your cold.

I have, &c. H. TAYLOR.

No. 237.

Earl Grey to Sir H. Taylor.

Foreign Office, Nov. 1, 1831.

My dear Sir,—I came to town this morning, though very unfit to stir out of the house, for the purpose of attending a Cabinet on the melancholy events at Bristol.*

* On the news of these riots being received, Mr. Thomas Attwood of Birmingham wrote a letter to my father, earnestly pressing upon him 'the absolute necessity of not considering this great subject as a matter to be treated with strictness and severity,' on the ground that the mischief had arisen from 'the gross imprudence of the local authorities.' To this letter my father returned the following answer:—

East Sheen, Nov. 2, 1831.

Sir,—I have had the honour of receiving your letter of 31 October, and beg you to be assured that I am duly sensible of the humane feeling, and the anxious wish for the public welfare by which it was dictated.

I cannot, I hope, be suspected of a disposition to measures of severity or harshness, when not called for by an urgent and inevitable necessity. But as a member of the Government I am charged with the duty of protecting the peace and order of society, and from the performance of that duty I cannot shrink.

The late occurrences at Bristol are indeed but too justly described by you as 'lamentable.' They must be doubly felt to be so by those who, anxious to obtain for the people the advantages which they may justly claim, find all their endeavours for that purpose impeded and embarrassed by acts of violence and outrage.

It might have been desirable that Sir Charles Wetherall should not have appeared in Bristol at a time of so much excitement, but the Government cannot allow a judge to be prevented from proceeding to the discharge of his duty by popular opposition.

There may have been, too (I have no information that will justify me in saying that there were), both remissness at the beginning of these outrages, and imprudence afterwards in the conduct of the civil authorities; but this does not render it less necessary to proceed against the instigators and perpetrators of crimes from which so extensive a destruction of property and so dreadful a loss of life have ensued.

Justice under the benevolent and rational reign of his present Majesty

There is great reason to hope that the spirit which has broken out in such acts of violence and outrage at Bristol has been effectually checked, for the present, in that city; but not without a severe loss of killed and wounded amongst the rioters. More vigour and energy at the beginning might, it seems, have prevented this melancholy necessity.

It has appeared to the King's servants, that the first thing to be done was to issue a Proclamation, and a draft is enclosed herewith, with the Minute of Cabinet, which has just been agreed upon.

But we must look, if further outrages of this nature should occur, to the means of making some addition to the military force of the country; which I do not think can be so readily or effectually done as by calling out either the whole or a part of the Militia. But this would make it necessary to call Parliament together, which indeed might be required in any case if these dangerous proceedings should extend themselves. We must still hope that this necessity will not occur.

I do not like to urge the King to do what may be inconvenient to His Majesty, but some time would be saved by holding the Council in town, and besides would leave the Ministers at liberty to attend to any emergency that may arise upon the spot.

I write in great haste, that His Majesty may receive

---

will, I am sure, always be administered in mercy; but as a well-wisher to the peace and order of society, without which true liberty cannot exist, I feel confident that you, Sir, will be the first to acknowledge, that the violated authority of the law must be vindicated, and the lives and properties of His Majesty's subjects secured against future attacks of so destructive a nature.

I have, &c.   GREY.

this communication as soon as possible; and not having had time to take copies, either of this letter or of the Cabinet Minute, I shall be obliged to you to return them to me for that purpose.

I am afraid I should not be able to go to Brighton, but, if not worse, I shall certainly make a point of attending His Majesty, if he comes to town to-morrow.

I am, &c. GREY.

Be so good as to send your answer to Lord Melbourne, as he remains in town, and it will save the time which would be taken by the messenger's coming to Sheen and returning to town.

(Enclosure.)

Cabinet Minute.

Foreign Office, Nov. 1, 1831.

At a meeting of your Majesty's servants held this day,

PRESENT:

The Earl Grey,	The Duke of Richmond,
Viscount Melbourne,	Viscount Althorp,
Viscount Palmerston,	Lord John Russell,
Viscount Goderich,	Sir James Graham, Bart.,
The Right Hon. C. Grant,	

having heard the distressing accounts from Bristol read to them by Viscount Melbourne, it was unanimously agreed to submit to your Majesty the propriety of immediately issuing a Proclamation against outrages of so violent a nature, and expressing a determination to exert all the powers of the Government for their suppression.

A draft of the proposed Proclamation is herewith sent for your Majesty's approbation.

It was also further agreed, humbly to submit to your Majesty the necessity of issuing such Proclamation with the least possible delay, and therefore that a Council should be held to-morrow, at which it will be necessary for your Majesty to be present, either here or at Brighton, as may be most convenient to your Majesty.

In the meantime your Majesty's servants will be engaged in the consideration of such farther measures as may become necessary for the protection and security of the public peace.

No. 238.

Sir H. Taylor to Earl Grey.

Brighton, Nov. 1, 1831. 12 p.m.

My dear Lord,—I did not lose a moment in submitting your Lordship's letter of this day and the accompanying documents to the King, who fortunately was still up, and I am honoured with His Majesty's commands to return the draft of the Proclamation, which His Majesty has approved, and to say that he will be at St. James's by three o'clock, for which hour I wrote to Lord Melbourne to request he will summon the Council. His Majesty will return to Brighton after the Council.

Not wishing to detain the messenger, I will confine myself now to returning the Minute of Cabinet and your letter as you desire. These are sad doings, but the troops appear to have behaved admirably, and to be well deserving of the confidence which is reposed in them. God grant this example and the lamentable destruction of property may have the effect of checking these lawless proceedings, and uniting the well-disposed in support of the State.

I have, &c.   H. TAYLOR.

I shall attend His Majesty.

No. 230.

Earl Grey to Sir H. Taylor.

East Sheen, Nov. 3, 1831.

My dear Sir,—I return the Cabinet Minute and my letter of the 1st, having taken copies of them.

    *   *   *   *   *

The vigorous exertions of the military force at last appear to have been effectual in completely stopping the disgraceful outrages which have taken place at Bristol. The want of proper attention and vigour at the beginning, and some imprudence afterwards, are deeply to be lamented, as they led eventually to so extensive a destruction of property, and so melancholy a loss of human life. Nothing can have been more exemplary on this, as I cheerfully bear my testimony to its having been on every, occasion that has come within my observation, than the conduct of the troops; and if the severe punishment which the rioters have received shall have the salutary effect of preventing similar acts of violence in other places, it will be some consolation for what has happened.

The absolute helplessness of the civil authorities at the commencement of these disturbances, and the strange measure of sending away the squadron of the 14th, when the whole force, including it, was insufficient, appears to me to be perfectly unaccountable.

Immediately after the Council at St. James's we had a Cabinet on the information which Lord Melbourne had received respecting the meeting which is appointed to be held in the fields before White Conduit House on Monday next. The objects of the meeting, as described in placards posted in various parts of the town yesterday, are such as to render it questionable whether a meeting held with such purposes is legal; and the information received as to the language held, and the measures in preparation by the committee of management, are little short of treason. But as the evidence we have could not be made available for the conviction of the persons implicated in these proceedings, who appear to be of the lowest class, we have thought it better to wait till after Friday, when another meeting of the committee is to take place, when we may have further information to enable us to judge better of the measures to be taken. In the meantime all the accounts we have received are left with the Attorney and Solicitor-General, who attended the Cabinet, for their consideration. The Cabinet will assemble again upon this matter on Saturday morning.

I have just read the accounts which have been received to-day from Sir Richard Jackson and Major Mackworth. They are most satisfactory, and afford ample confirmation of the former testimonials in favour of the excellent conduct of the troops.

Major Mackworth appears to be entitled to the highest praise.

I am, &c. GREY.

No. 240.

Sir H. Taylor to Earl Grey.

(Private.) Brighton, Nov. 4, 1831.

My dear Lord,—I will not delay acknowledging the receipt of your Lordship's letter of yesterday, which I have had the honour of submitting to the King, who has also read the reports made from Bristol to Lord Fitzroy Somerset, which His Majesty considers, as you do, extremely satisfactory. He rejoices that the conduct of the troops has been so exemplary, and that it has been the means of averting the further destruction which must have resulted from the inefficiency and pusillanimity of the chief magistrate and the civil power in that city. His Majesty also concurs cordially in the opinion which you express, of the conduct of Major Mackworth; nor is this the first occasion upon which it has attracted His Majesty's notice and approbation.

His Majesty orders me to express to your Lordship his entire approval of the view you and his other confidential servants have taken of the preparatory measures and purposes of the meeting to be held before White Conduit House on Monday, and of your waiting until after the meeting of the managing committee this day, before you take such steps as the character of these proceedings and the opinions of the Attorney and Solicitor-General may suggest.

But His Majesty is by no means displeased that the measures contemplated by the meeting in question are so violent and in other respects so objectionable, as he trusts that the manifestation of such intentions and such purposes may afford the opportunity and the facility of checking the progress of the Political Unions in general, the introduction and establishment of which, the King orders me to say, he cannot too often describe as being, in his opinion, far more mischievous and dangerous than any proceedings of a more avowed and violent character, palpably illegal and treasonable. His Majesty has expressed his sentiments very strongly in his letter to Lord Melbourne on this subject, and orders me to refer you to these for them. He has, however, directed me on this occasion to call your attention more particularly to what has been reported of the influence exercised at Bristol by the Political Union there (of course in communication with that of Birmingham, from which place emissaries are stated to have been employed at Bristol). The interference of this said Political Union appears, during the riots, to have been confined to the issue of placards, and to an assumption of the authority of the civil power, which had unfortunately encouraged it by its inefficiency; but when the riots had been quelled by the small military force, the members of the Political Union came forward bodily to serve as special constables; and, as far as His Majesty can gather from the papers, they did so as a distinct body, and they claim especial merit for such exertion of their influence, as a body not connected with, nor under the control of, the Government or the local authorities. It is possible that His Majesty may have been misled by the papers to this view of their feelings and conduct; but, if it be correct, it would bear him out in the apprehension of the establishment of an *imperium in imperio*, and of the progressive effects of such a system.

The King observed in one of the reports from Bristol that Pensioners had been employed, and he is desirous of knowing to what extent; whether they came in readily, and whether employed as special constables or as soldiers? His Majesty is still inclined to think, that if any augmentation of our military force should be considered necessary, the increase of the rank and file of the regular Cavalry and Infantry, or the embodying of a proportion of the Pensioners with the Militia Staff, and with the aid of a few officers taken from the half-pay, would be preferable to calling out the Militia, and far less expensive. At this season, indeed, and in the winter, the process of drilling and exercising the Militia would be necessarily slow, and they would suffer inconvenience from want of good cover.

I have, &c. H. TAYLOR.

As you do not mention your health in your letter of yesterday, His Majesty hopes he may conclude that you are better.

No. 241.

Earl Grey to Sir H. Taylor.

East Sheen, Nov. 6, 1831.

My dear Sir,—As I had not time to write yesterday, after the Cabinet, before I left town, I deferred answering your letter of the 4th till my return to this place.

It was of less consequence that I should write, as Lord Melbourne would communicate to the King everything that it was material for His Majesty to know.

Of the measures taken by His Majesty's servants therefore, with a view to the proposed meeting of to-morrow, His Majesty will have been fully apprised. The notices by the Magistrates were issued under the advice of the Attorney and Solicitor-General; but though much information has been obtained indicating the worst designs on the part of many of those who appear to be most active in their endeavours to excite the working classes, His Majesty's law officers did not think the evidence, of which we are yet in possession, sufficient to render the arrest of any of these persons at present advisable.

I left town under the firm persuasion that no meeting would take place, and I see by the Sunday papers, not having yet received any more authentic accounts, that it has been abandoned. The alacrity and zeal shown by the middle classes in enrolling themselves as special constables for the preservation of the public peace, has been most satisfactory; and I feel great hope that the late events, distressing as they have been, will eventually be productive of good. Everything, however, depends upon the successful adjustment of the question of Reform; and it will be a most fatal mistake if those, by whom it has hitherto been resisted, should be encouraged in the belief, that the public feeling on this measure can be repressed.

It is by the fear of this opposition that the Political

Unions, which, as you know, had been formed at Birmingham and other places before the change of Government in November last, have been extended. In every sentiment expressed by His Majesty as to the nature and tendency of these unions, I entirely agree. It is impossible to shut one's eyes on the danger of their becoming permanently established. To discourage them, as much as possible, is equally the duty and the interest of His Majesty's Ministers. But as long as they keep within the limits of the law, it does not seem possible to take any measures for their suppression. I am not apprised exactly of the manner in which a body of this description appeared and acted at Bristol; but any offer of their assistance to the magistrates, I think, ought not to be accepted from them *as a body*; and they should be told that their services in preserving the public peace can only be rendered useful and available by their being sworn in as special constables under the provisions of the law. For this evil, the best and surest remedy will be the passing of the Reform Bill, and for this object all the influence of the Government must now be decidedly and vigorously exerted.

Lord Melbourne did not appear to be informed as to the number of Pensioners employed at Bristol, but will get the necessary information according to His Majesty's desire on this subject. I am inclined to think that the best way, when their services are required for the preservation of the public peace, will be to employ them separately in aid and under the direction of the civic power, an effectual organisation of which, more especially in the large towns, must be carefully looked to.

According to present appearances, I hope no addition to the military force will be required.

* * * * *

We agree to have a meeting of the Cabinet again to-morrow at one, to be ready for any emergency that may arise.

My cold is a good deal better, but I cannot shake it off altogether.

I am, &c. GREY.

No. 242.

Sir H. Taylor to Earl Grey.

(Private.) Brighton, Nov. 7. 1831.

My dear Lord,—The contents of your Lordship's letter of yesterday, which I had the honour of receiving this morning, and of submitting to the King, has proved very satisfactory to His Majesty.

The King had been fully apprised by Lord Melbourne of the proceedings and reported designs of the *soi-disant* working classes, or rather their instigators, as well as of the measures adopted by his confidential servants; and His Majesty had expressed to Lord Melbourne his entire approbation of all that had been done and was proposed by his Government. His Majesty has learnt this afternoon from Lord Melbourne, without surprise, that the meeting has been postponed; but he has no doubt that the promoters of mischief and violence will seek other opportunities to attempt to carry their plans into effect, and His Majesty hopes they may eventually so commit themselves as to justify their arrest. In the meantime the alacrity with which the middle classes have come forward to enrol themselves as special constables has been one very satisfactory effect of those proceedings to which the recent events at Bristol have probably contributed in some degree, as they had offered such lamentable proof of the destruction of *private* as well as public property, which might result from the absence of due zeal and exertion on the part of those who have any thing at stake.

The King hopes with your Lordship, that the successful and satisfactory adjustment of the Reform question may have the effect of quieting the country, and of repressing the disposition which has been shown to outrage and violence, and to revolutionary designs and acts; but His Majesty does not see in what degree these violent and illegal proceedings can be connected with either the support of, or the opposition to, the Reform Bill; nor that the Unions, which, as you observe, were formed before the change of Government, were directed exclusively to this object. The objects of the rioters at Bristol and other places were plunder and destruction; those of the assembly, which had been convened for this day, were revolutionary and treasonable; and Reform of Parliament must be considered as forming a very insignificant portion of such acts and projects; nay, its cause would be very little benefited by admitting that such could be its advocates, although they might eagerly avail themselves of this or any other plea for mischief. This may be applied equally to the Unions at Birmingham and elsewhere. Those which existed before the change of Government had been formed for purposes highly objectionable and illegal, namely, to raise the price and wages of work and labour in the manufacturing towns and districts. That at Birmingham, though dignified with the higher sounding title of Political Union, was connected with the former, and was understood to partake of their character. I have ventured to make these remarks, which have occasionally occurred in conversation with the King, to support the opinion that Reform in Parliament is not the sole object of those associations and unions; that it has been assumed and declared by some, in order to give a more correct and more legitimate colour to proceedings of which the purposes were illegal and partial; and that a similar direction has, with the same view, been given to the combination of those Unions. But they started with other intentions and purposes, and it does not follow that these will be abandoned when the Reform Bill shall have passed into a law.

These are some of the reasons which cause His Majesty to look with so much jealousy and uneasiness to the proceedings and designs of these political and other unions, abstractedly from the question of Parliamentary Reform, which he considers to be advanced by them as a plea for projects decidedly revolutionary, entertained before any expectation had been indulged of the introduction of the Reform Bill, and not likely to be abandoned when that Bill shall have been carried. His Majesty was therefore very happy to find that your Lordship and Lord Melbourne concurred in the sentiments he had expressed on their nature and tendency, and on the danger of their becoming permanently established, though he admits the difficulty of dealing with them so long as they keep within the limits of the law. The King rejoices also that he has called your attention to the circumstance of the Political Union of Bristol having (as stated in the newspapers) given their assistance to the magistrates *as a body*, which had struck His Majesty as a strong indication of the spirit in which these Unions are formed.

The King was glad to learn from Lord Melbourne, that the attention of the Government had been directed to the establishment in great and populous towns of a body of peace officers similar to the Metropolitan Police.

I have, &c. H. TAYLOR.

No. 243.

Earl Grey to Sir H. Taylor.

Downing Street, Nov. 7, 1831.

Dear Sir,

* * * * *

I came to town, as I believe I told you was my intention, to be prepared for any thing that might occur in consequence of the proposed meeting at White Conduit House. Up to this moment everything is quiet. Major Mackworth was on the ground about twelve, when there appeared to be an assemblage of about 500, which he thought rather diminished at one. A subsequent report, however, at the Horse Guards, from Colonel Brotherton, represents the numbers as being then (between two and three) about 3000, but scattered about, and not engaged in any proceeding. Of course the Police and the Military are prepared for anything that may occur after dark; but I feel very little doubt that everything will pass off without any serious interruption of the public peace.

We have accounts of language and conduct of a highly seditious, if not treasonable nature, which I am anxious to visit by a prompt application of the powers of the law, the moment we are in possession of evidence on which we can act with a certainty of conviction; but nothing does more harm than an abortive prosecution.

I called the attention of the Cabinet to the Unions, and we agreed unanimously that every possible discouragement should be given to them by the Government; and that the suggestion, which I mentioned yesterday, of not accepting their services as a body, which would be a sort of recognition, should be acted on.

I had letters yesterday from Lord Durham, whose presence at Brussels has been very fortunate, as he dissuaded Prince Leopold from giving a conditional assent, under certain reserves, to the 24 Articles, which would have embroiled everything anew. His acceptance will now be simple, accompanied by a separate note requiring explanations on certain points, which, perhaps, are left subject to some amendments, from the manner in which they are worded in the 24 Articles.

The letters to-day from Sunderland mentioned another case, but clearly one of common English cholera.

I think we may now feel great confidence that the present alarm may pass away.

I hear nothing more, so I conclude everything remains quiet, and I am just returning to Sheen.

Your account of the King's health gives me the

greatest pleasure. I certainly am better, though I lay awake coughing the greatest part of the night.

I am, &c. GREY.

No. 244.

Earl Grey to Sir H. Taylor.

East Sheen, Nov. 8, 1831.

My dear Sir,—I hasten to acknowledge your letter of yesterday. That the King's Government partake, in their fullest extent, in the sentiments entertained by His Majesty, on the subject of the late disturbances, and on the character and effect of the Political Unions, has been sufficiently proved both by their conduct and by what I have already written on these subjects. Neither do I dissent from the opinion that the Political Unions have been originally instituted with views directed to other objects besides a Reform of Parliament; and that many of their leaders—making this, from the advantage of the moment, their pretext—would be desirous of keeping up these societies, after that object was attained, for the sake of maintaining their own influence and power.

But it is not the less true that these Unions have received a great impulse and extension from the rejection of the Reform Bill; and that many persons, not otherwise disposed to do so, have been induced to join them for the purpose of promoting that measure. It is also undeniable that the middle classes, who have now shown so praiseworthy an alacrity in supporting the authority of the Government, are actuated by an intense and almost unanimous feeling in favour of the measure of Reform.

It is in this way that these matters are connected. Agreeing that the cause of Reform can derive no advantage from measures of so objectionable a character as those which we have been discussing, and thinking it necessary that the Government should neglect no means of discouraging the Unions, I cannot shut my eyes to the danger which may result from a second rejection of the Reform Bill; the consequence of which would be a great increase of public discontent, particularly in these classes, whose present soundness affords the best security and defence to the Government of the country.

If this cause of dissatisfaction continues, I greatly fear not only that the Unions will be more generally extended and organised, but that they will receive great additional strength from being joined by a description of persons who have hitherto kept aloof from them. On the other hand, if the question can be settled, all the sound part of the community would not only be separated from, but placed in direct opposition to, associations whose permanent existence every reasonable man must feel to be incompatible with the safety of the country. Under such circumstances these Unions could not long continue to exist, and all the real influence and power of society would be united with that of the Government in putting them down.

It is in this way that the prospect of putting an end to these things appears to me essentially to depend upon the success of the Bill which must be introduced immediately after the opening of the next Session. If it succeeds, I shall expect to see the Government stronger, and the country more quiet and more prosperous than it has been for many years. If it should unhappily fail (I must speak plainly), I cannot be answerable for the public peace.

I write in great haste, having a multiplicity of business pressing upon me, but I could not help offering these remarks in answer to your letter.

I am, &c. GREY.

No. 245.

Sir H. Taylor to Earl Grey.

(Private.) Brighton, Nov. 8, 1831.

My dear Lord,

* * * * *

The King is much obliged to your Lordship for noticing the state of things in London yesterday, and rejoices that it passed without riot or disturbance, which other reports made to His Majesty have confirmed. He has no doubt that, sooner or later, the promoters of these unlawful designs and proceedings will commit themselves, so as to afford to you the opportunity of visiting their seditious and treasonable language and conduct as it deserves; and His Majesty concurs in the propriety of not acting without a certainty of conviction, and in the impolicy of instituting a prosecution which may prove abortive. It is extremely satisfactory to the King, that the strong objections which had so early occurred to him to the principle and tendency of the Political Unions, and to the possible encouragement which they might derive from the acceptance of their services *as a body*, even for the preservation of peace, have met with the decided and unanimous concurrence of his confidential servants.

The King had learnt, also, from Sir Robert Adair's private letter to Lord Palmerston, what your Lordship mentions of the good effect of Lord Durham's excellent advice to the King of the Belgians. His presence at Brussels at this period was indeed very fortunate, and all would do well if the King of the Netherlands were as ready to take good advice. Mr. Bathurst has sent me the last accounts from Sunderland, which are very tranquillizing. The King is very glad to hear that you are better.

I have, &c. H. TAYLOR.

No. 246.

Earl Grey to Sir H. Taylor.

Downing Street, Nov. 10, 1831.

My dear Sir,—I have been detained so long at the Cabinet, that I have only time at present to acknowledge the receipt of your letter of yesterday, enclosing the correspondence which has lately taken place between His Majesty and the Duke of Wellington, for which I beg you to offer His Majesty my humble thanks.

I hope to be able to return it to-morrow, with any observations upon it which I may think it necessary to submit to His Majesty.

In the meantime I have thought it necessary, sanctioned by the opinion of the Cabinet, to write the accompanying letter to the Duke of Wellington, as it seems of indispensable necessity, if the fact of a contract having been made for the purchase of arms by the Birmingham Union be true, that His Majesty's Government should have the means of ascertaining it.

I am, &c.   GREY.

I hear there can no longer be the slightest doubt that the real cholera is at Sunderland. Dr. Russell and Dr. Barry, who have been with the Cabinet this morning, are decidedly of that opinion.

(Enclosure.)

Earl Grey to the Duke of Wellington.

Downing Street, Nov. 10, 1831.

My Lord Duke,—I have had the honour of receiving from His Majesty a communication informing me, that your Grace had stated to His Majesty your belief, that a contract had been made for a supply of arms to the Political Union of Birmingham.

No such information having reached any department of the King's Government, I think it my duty to request that your Grace will have the goodness, if it is in your power, and if you see no objection, to furnish me with the means of ascertaining the accuracy of a fact, which is certainly of a nature to call for the most careful attention on the part of His Majesty's Ministers.

I am, &c.   GREY.

No. 247.

Sir H. Taylor to Earl Grey.

(Private.)   Brighton, Nov. 11, 1831.

My dear Lord,—I have had the honour to submit to the King your Lordship's letter of yesterday, and the enclosed draft of one you had addressed to the Duke of Wellington, in consequence of the statement made by his Grace to the King, that a contract had been entered into by the Birmingham Union for the purchase of arms.

His Majesty orders me to say, that he concluded you would so notice this statement, and that he thinks it very possible that it will turn out that some members of this and other unions may have supplied themselves with arms, though not to any extent, or by a contract, as stated by the Duke of Wellington. The fact is, and your Lordship may ascertain it by reference to the correspondence of Sir Henry Bouverie and Mr. Forster, which I saw at the time, that the Trades' Unions did supply themselves (in 1829, I think) with pistols, for the purpose of resisting the civil authorities and enforcing the objects of their Union.

His Majesty has received with great concern the accounts of the increase of cholera at Sunderland. I own I did not apprehend it would so soon find its way to this country.

I have, &c. H. TAYLOR.

No. 248.

Earl Grey to Sir H. Taylor.

Downing Street, Nov. 11, 1831.

My dear Sir,—This accompanies a letter[*] to the King, upon the communication from the Duke of Wellington, whose letter, &c., I return.

[*] Neither this letter to the King, nor the memorandum of the Duke of Wellington and his correspondence with His Majesty can be found.

I never was more surprised than at reading these productions, the object of which cannot be misunderstood, and the propriety and constitutional character of them appear to me more than questionable; at least, I think nothing could have induced me, under similar circumstances, to have had recourse to such a proceeding.

The memorandum itself is as meagre as need be, and evidently written in a spirit which would have induced the author to pursue measures here which would have proved as fatal to our internal peace, as his policy, if he had continued in office, would have been to the peace of Europe.

Trained and disciplined armed bodies, acting as such under appointments not made by the Crown, are, there can be no doubt, illegal. But the Duke seems to forget, when he speaks of disarming, that the privilege of having and using arms is reserved to Englishmen by the Constitution; and this constitutes one of the difficulties of the case, because if these Unions resolve merely to have arms individually, without being formed or organised as armed bodies, I know of no authority under the existing law by which they can be prevented.

But I have not time to say more upon this at present. Hereafter it is possible, if I can find time, that I may send you a more detailed answer to the Duke's memorandum.

I came here to attend a Cabinet, where I have been kept very late. Canada was the chief subject, and a very difficult one it is. We are to meet again on Monday on Portugal, Russian debts, &c.

I am sorry to say the accounts from Sunderland to-day announce seven new cases and four deaths. But I fear this is not the worst, as there is evidently a desire, both in the medical people of Sunderland and others, to conceal the progress of the disorder.

I am, &c. GREY.

No. 249.

The King to Earl Grey.

Brighton, Nov. 13, 1831.

The King acknowledges the receipt of Earl Grey's letter of the 11th instant, respecting the communication which he had made to him of a letter from the Duke of Wellington, and of a memorandum which accompanied it, as well as of His Majesty's reply to it.

It is not His Majesty's intention, nor is it necessary that he should, enter into the object or the merits of the Duke of Wellington's communication, as he conceives that his answer to it was so worded as to satisfy him that His Majesty considered his Grace to have very unnecessarily taken alarm at the idea that the intentions of forming National Guards, &c., which had been declared by some of the Political Unions, would not be discountenanced by the King and his Government, or that His Majesty and his Government were not as much alive, as the Duke of Wellington could possibly be, to the dangerous tendency of such establishments, and to the necessity of counteracting them.

The King flatters himself that every passage of his letter to the Duke of Wellington was calculated to convey this impression, as well as to show that he relied with confidence upon the vigilance and energy of his Government to watch and repress such unconstitutional and mischievous designs, and upon its inclination to exert the power and the means which it possesses to afford protection to the lives and property of his subjects.

Such were the character and the intent of His Majesty's reply to the Duke of Wellington. He was not sorry to have this opportunity of doing justice to the proceedings of his confidential servants; and he rejoices to learn from Earl Grey, that he and his colleagues have correctly interpreted his meaning. After this, it appears almost superfluous to say that His Majesty had never suspected his confidential servants of 'inattention or indifference to the formation of armed bodies, incompatible with his prerogative and with the acknowledged laws and constitutions of his dominions;' and that, while he is sensible that these designs have not yet assumed a character which would justify the open and active interference of his Government, he is convinced that there will be no relaxation of their vigilance; and that, whenever the obvious necessity of measures of severity shall occur, they will be adopted with promptitude and pursued with energy and firmness. Such, indeed, is the course which His Majesty has a right to expect from individuals whom he has called to his councils, and who are responsible to him and to the State 'for the maintenance of his royal authority, and for the protection of the peace and safety of his people.'   WILLIAM R.

No. 250.

Sir H. Taylor to Earl Grey.

(Private.) Brighton, Nov. 13, 1831.

My dear Lord,—I submitted your Lordship's letter to me of the 11th instant to the King, with that which came in the same box for His Majesty.

I can easily conceive that you would be surprised at the Duke of Wellington's communications, which the King has, I think, correctly described as *unnecessary*. I hope you were satisfied with His Majesty's reply to them, and that you will be so with his letter of this date to yourself. His Majesty observed, when he read the Duke's letter, that, as a Peer and a Privy Councillor, he had a right to address to him by letter that which he might have communicated in a private audience if he had thought fit to ask for it. That in any other case His Majesty might have sent the letter, &c., to your Lordship, and confined himself to an acknowledgment of the receipt, and to informing the writer that it had been so disposed of; but that it appeared to him desirable that the Duke of Wellington should learn directly from His Majesty, and without any interval from which previous communication with his Government might be inferred, that the circumstances which had alarmed his Grace had not escaped the attention and solicitude of His Majesty and his Government, and that there existed a cordial union of sentiment on the subject between His Majesty and his Government.

The Duke, as your Lordship observes, seems to

forget, when he speaks of disarming, that Englishmen possess, by the Constitution, the privilege of having and using arms, and that this constitutes one of the difficulties of the case. I imagine, however, that he applies the expression to the actual existence of ' self-constituted armed *bodies*,' and has taken it for granted that such would be tolerated, for his Grace could not have forgotten, what I noticed to you in my letter of the 11th, that many members of the Trades Unions had supplied themselves with pistols. They were, in fact, known to have attended the meetings so armed, and it was not considered that this could be prevented by search or seizure so long as the arms were not produced or used.

The King orders me to say that he views the Canada question, as you do, as very embarrassing. His Majesty has not the least desire to come into collision with the United States; at the same time that he feels that our character and our interest would suffer from tamely submitting to the insolence and the encroachments of the State of Maine. He hopes that the general Government will interfere effectually. If it should not, it will be desirable to gain time until the ensuing spring, before which our means of resistance cannot receive any reinforcement from hence. It would, in His Majesty's opinion, be highly impolitic, especially with reference to Americans, to show our teeth without being prepared to bite.

There appears to be ample matter for deliberation; the cholera not the least uncomfortable, for, distressing as it is while confined to one unfortunate spot, we cannot, I fear, hope that it will not extend to other parts of the kingdom.

* * * * *

I have, &c. H. TAYLOR.

No. 251.

Sir H. Taylor to Earl Grey.

(Private.) Brighton, Nov. 15, 1831.

My dear Lord,—I have had the honour to submit to the King your Lordship's letter of yesterday and that from the Duke of Wellington to you enclosed, which I return.

His Majesty agrees in the view which your Lordship takes of the communication which has occasioned so much alarm to His Grace, and is surprised that he should dwell upon the subject of 'these armaments' as likely to be 'tolerated,' or to produce 'the serious operation of disarming six thousand men,' and 'much loss of life:' this, too, after receiving His Majesty's letter.

This induces His Majesty to feel still better pleased that he did not hesitate to answer His Grace's letter, without the delay of reference, as the Duke of Wellington might have inferred from it that this caution had become necessary, and that but for it the danger would have arisen.

Your Lordship will learn from the Lord-Chancellor and from Lord Holland what has passed here on this subject, as well as the assurance given by His Majesty, that His Majesty's reply to any communication from

His Grace relating to such matters will in future be limited to a simple acknowledgment. You will also learn from them what has passed here on the subject of the Political Unions, and will of course see the letters which His Majesty ordered me to write to Lord Brougham and to Lord Holland, in consequence of, and with reference to, these communications to him.

His Majesty concluded you would send Dr. Russell, or Dr. Barry, or both, to Sunderland, to ascertain the exact nature of the disorder; and he hopes their report will confirm the opinion which prevails there, that the alarm has been a false one.

I have, &c. H. TAYLOR.

No. 252.

Sir H. Taylor to Earl Grey.

Brighton, Nov. 16, 1831.

My dear Lord,—I beg to return Mr. Baker's report of the inquiry made of Mr. Riviere respecting the reported contract for firearms, which I have had the honour to submit to the King with your Lordship's letter of yesterday. His Majesty fully expected, as you did, that such, or something like it, would be the result of the inquiry.

You will, however, be surprised to learn that His Majesty received this morning another letter from the Duke of Wellington, written, as it would seem, for no other purpose than to send him the copies of his correspondence with your Lordship; and he has ordered me to enclose it to you with a copy of my acknowledgment of it, which will, he presumes, close the correspondence.

* * * * *

His Majesty has repeatedly remarked, in conversing upon the provisions of the Reform Bill, that it appeared to him very desirable that, instead of giving representatives to certain large parishes or districts of London and Westminster, additional members should be given to the county of Middlesex in general, throwing these parishes into certain county divisions, and that he thought this might obviate many of the objections which are made to this part of the Bill. He has so often reverted to this point, that I have thought it best to name it to you, although he has not desired me to do so.

The further account from Sunderland is very satisfactory to His Majesty.

He is highly pleased with the communications from Lord Palmerston relative to the proceedings of the Conference, which reached him this morning.

I have, &c. H. TAYLOR.

No. 253.

Earl Grey to Sir H. Taylor.

East Sheen, Nov. 18, 1831.

My dear Sir,—I have to acknowledge your letters of the 15th and 16th. I should have answered both more immediately, if I had not been occupied the whole morning, and been detained both yesterday and the day before at the Cabinet, till it was too late for the post.

I am deeply grateful to the King for the kind considerations which have influenced His Majesty's conduct in his late correspondence. It certainly might in many cases produce inconvenience, if His Majesty were to express opinions to any but his confidential servants in matters which may come under their consideration, with a view to the advice to be submitted to His Majesty upon them. I cannot, therefore, hesitate to express my satisfaction at His Majesty's having resolved to confine his answers to such communications as those lately made by the Duke of Wellington in future to a simple acknowledgment of their reception. I must however, at the same time, state how sensibly I feel both the kindness and the advantage of His Majesty's first answer to the Duke, in expressing the entire concurrence of His Majesty's opinions with those of his Government, and his approbation of the course they were pursuing with respect to the Political Unions.

The plan for the constitution and organisation of the Birmingham Union is now before us. Of its dangerous and unconstitutional character there can be but one opinion. That it is illegal, I am also thoroughly persuaded; and that opinion has been confirmed by the Attorney and Solicitor-General, before whom I desired Lord Melbourne to lay a case, upon the information which we had already obtained as to what was intended, and which has proved correct in every particular. Still it is difficult to determine how this case should be dealt with, and a farther opinion has been required from the Law Officers of the Crown, as to what mode of proceeding would be possible or advisable. I would not commit myself by any communication with Mr. Attwood, nor should I think it advisable for any member of the Government to do so; but if the means could be found of privately communicating to him a representation of the mischief and the danger of the course in which he is engaged, to himself as well as the public, it might perhaps, by stopping the proceeding, which I see is adjourned till Tuesday next, be the best way of getting out of this very unpleasant business. If by a little management things could be kept in such a state as not to require the active interference of the Government, and the Reform Bill can be passed, I have a sanguine hope that, by enlisting all the sound part of the community in the support of Government against all such mischievous projects, they would be speedily abandoned or defeated. But every day's observation convinces me more and more, that if the Reform Bill cannot be brought to a satisfactory settlement, there can be no security for the continuance of the internal peace of the country. This leads me to what you say of the proposed representation of the Metropolitan districts; and I cannot sufficiently thank you for having communicated to me the opinion which His Majesty entertains on this part of the question. To that opinion you cannot doubt my disposition to pay the most dutiful and respectful attention. I know, too, that this is one of the difficulties which may have been felt with respect to the Bill. But I am afraid the evil of altering it would now be greater than that of suffering it to remain as it is; and, from communications which I have had with some very respectable persons from the district of the Tower Hamlets, which has been supposed to be the one in which this right of representation would be most objectionable, I have the best grounds for believing that, by a provision to limit the right of voting to those who are actually rated on their own account, the inconvenience of a too numerous constituency would be avoided, and the measure as respects these districts rendered perfectly safe.

I enclose the Duke of Wellington's letter with its enclosures, and beg you will offer His Majesty my humble thanks for his goodness in having ordered them to be communicated to me. It was rather an odd proceeding on the part of his Grace, as he might have concluded that I should make the same communication to the King. But I suspect his chief object in writing this letter was to record the assurance given by His Majesty, that he would not tolerate these Unions, and that the Government were pledged to the same determination.

It gave me great pleasure to hear that the King had been so perfectly satisfied with what has been done in the Belgian affairs, and I was gratified to the highest degree in reading His Majesty's letter to Lord Palmerston on this subject. May I be permitted to add, that nothing was ever more just than the praise with which His Majesty has been pleased to honour Lord Palmerston on this occasion.

The late accounts from Sunderland have been much more unfavourable, and I fear we must admit that the real cholera exists there. The mission of Dr. Russell or Dr. Barry has been delayed by the necessity of their attendance on the Board of Health in London. But I think it will be necessary to send either one of these gentlemen, or some other who may have authority, to control the conflicting opinions which prevail in Sunderland respecting the true character of the disease, which have assumed all the violence of party feeling, and are greatly opposed to the adoption and success of any effectual sanitary regulations.

There is one consoling circumstance attending this matter, which is the very limited progress of the disorder, as compared with its rapid and fatal extension wherever it has appeared on the Continent. This seems to warrant an opinion, either that the disorder is less virulent, or that it has been more successfully treated than in other countries.

* * * * *

I forgot in my former letters to say, that I had seen Lord Duncannon, Sir J. Kempt, and Sir W. Gordon on the subject of the barracks. I can have no hesitation in saying that I think the Birdcage Walk the best, perhaps the only fit, place for them. Sir J. Kempt is to have a plan and estimate prepared of a plain but handsome building, which will, of course, be submitted to His Majesty before anything is determined upon it. I am only afraid that we may find some difficulty in getting the expense assented to by the House of Commons.

My son, the Lieutenant-Colonel, arrived yesterday from Malta, having been, as I told you, with his brother at Constantinople. He came home in the Madagascar, Captain Lyons, a most excellent and intelligent officer, who, I believe, can give better information respecting Greece than any other person.

I am, &c. GREY.

No. 254.

Sir H. Taylor to Earl Grey.

(Private.)   Brighton, Nov. 19. 1831.

My dear Lord,—I have had the honour of receiving and of submitting to the King your Lordship's letter of yesterday, and His Majesty ordered me to assure you, that he was much pleased to learn that you view His Majesty's answer to the Duke of Wellington's letter in the light in which he was anxious it should strike you. His Majesty thinks it very possible that his Grace's chief object in writing again was to record the assurance given by His Majesty, that he would not tolerate the *armed* Unions, and that the Government was pledged to the same determination. But His Majesty does not see what he could by possibility gain by this, as the King's expression and his assurance of the entire and cordial concurrence of his Government applied distinctly to self-constituted, self-armed bodies of troops, and the formation of National Guards under the control of Political Unions, not to that of Political Unions; and this distinction is kept up throughout the letter, so much so, indeed, as to observe upon the existence of Unions before the change of the Government, and to their having been tolerated by his Grace's administration.

His Majesty had observed in the newspapers the plan for the constitution and establishment of the Birmingham Union, and it had struck him as highly objectionable, and as dangerous, not only from its being independent of the Government legal and executive authorities, but also from its being of such a character as would mislead many well intentioned persons. His Majesty, therefore, rejoices to learn that it is considered by the Attorney and Solicitor-General to be illegal, though he regrets the necessity of so much caution in dealing with this case; at the same time that he does not wish to deny it, as well as the advantage of getting out of the difficulty by management, so as to gain time until the Reform Bill shall have passed. His Majesty only fears that many of the sound part of the community, who might be disposed to enlist in the support of the Government, may in the meantime commit themselves with those Unions, being left in ignorance of the sentiments of the Government, and of the opinion entertained of the unconstitutional and illegal character of these combinations. Your Lordship does not allude to Mr. O'Connell's scheme for a National Union, which strikes His Majesty as yet more objectionable, coupled as it is with his explanatory letter; and there is a curious observation and admission about the Dublin Trades Union, on which he seems to have at first contemplated engrafting his National Union, though he has ended by stating his intention of escaping indictment by drawing its members into the new combination. His Majesty has also noticed a letter from Mr. Hume, in which, in declaring himself a member of some Union, he urges their directing their efforts to enforcing measures of general reform and reduction after the Reform Bill shall have been carried, thus betraying at once the *ulterior* projects.

His Majesty is glad to hear that your Lordship considers that, by a provision to limit the right of voting to those who are actually rated on their own account, the inconvenience of a too numerous constituency would be avoided, and the measure as respects the large parishes in the metropolis rendered safe.

His objection, however, applied more to the parishes of Marylebone and St. Pancras than to the Tower Hamlets.

The King rejoices, also, that you are so much pleased with his letter to Lord Palmerston, who certainly has not shown less zeal and assiduity than talent in his late laborious task, to which His Majesty knows also, from the report of Baron Bulow and others, that temper and patience may be added.

He agrees with you in the view which you take of the state of things at Sunderland, and His Majesty considers that it would be very desirable to send either Doctor Russell or Doctor Barry there without further delay, in order to counteract the conflicting opinions of practitioners there.

His Majesty had learnt from Gordon that a meeting had taken place on the subject of the proposed barrack in Birdcage Walk, and how kindly and considerately your Lordship had entered into the question; and he hopes that the House of Commons will see the propriety and necessity of this arrangement.

* * * * *

The character you give of Captain Lyons is, in His Majesty's opinion, well merited; and he rejoices that his Government has the opportunity of resorting to so good a source for the information respecting Greece.

I have, &c.   H. TAYLOR.

No. 255.

Earl Grey to Sir H. Taylor.

Downing Street, Nov. 19, 1831.

My dear Sir,—The Cabinet sat so late that I have only time to write a hurried line, to accompany the Minute which is humbly submitted to His Majesty.

Though my opinion, and that of the Duke of Richmond and Lord Palmerston, was against calling Parliament together before the first week in January, we felt ourselves bound to acquiesce in the decision of the majority of the Cabinet, which was founded (excepting the opinion of the Chancellor, who argued the necessity of an early meeting on the question of Reform, independently of every other consideration), on the present state of the country, and the danger of depriving ourselves of the power for so long a time, of applying to Parliament for its authority in support of any measures which might be required in the case of these Unions assuming a more extended and more dangerous form, or any other circumstances which might arise dangerous to the public peace.

The enclosed note, which I have just received from Mr. Greville, I am sorry to say, shows that it will be necessary for the King to come to town to hold the Council on Monday; and I need not say with what reluctance I make a communication which may prove inconvenient to His Majesty. But I fear there would be no possibility of having the notification in time for the Gazette, if the Council should be held at Brighton.

An opinion has been given by the Attorney and Solicitor-General, which is quite decisive on the illegality of the Birmingham Union, and measures must be taken in conformity with that opinion, if the organisation of that body should be completed in the way that has been proposed. I send a messenger with this, that I may have an answer as soon as possible; and if the King acquiesces in the proposal of his coming to town, perhaps you will have the goodness to send a letter to Mr. Greville to summon the Council, which the messenger may leave in his way to Sheen.

I have not ventured to trouble His Majesty by going to Brighton, having had nothing to say to him that might not be equally well communicated by letter, and concluding that if His Majesty had wished to see me, he would have signified his pleasure to that effect.

There is not time to take a copy of this letter before I return to Sheen, and I shall be much obliged to you to let me have it again for that purpose, or to send me a copy of it.

I am, &c. GREY.

Lord Melbourne will send His Majesty the opinion of his Law Officers.

(Enclosure.)

Cabinet Minute.

Downing Street, Nov. 19, 1831.

At a meeting of your Majesty's servants held to-day at the Foreign Office,

PRESENT:

The Lord Chancellor,   The Viscount Melbourne,
The Duke of Richmond,   The Viscount Palmerston,
The Earl of Carlisle,   The Viscount Althorp,
The Earl Grey,   The Lord John Russell,
The Viscount Goderich,   The Lord Holland,
   The Right Hon. C. Grant,

the question being, To what day your Majesty should be advised to prorogue the Parliament? it was decided humbly to submit to your Majesty the propriety of calling Parliament together on the 6th of December next; the Duke of Richmond, the Earl Grey, and the Viscount Palmerston, though they were of opinion that it would have been better to continue the prorogation till the beginning of January, acquiescing in the advice which is thus humbly submitted to your Majesty.

No. 256.

Sir H. Taylor to Earl Grey.

Brighton, Nov. 20, 1831.

My dear Lord,—I have not delayed to submit to the King your Lordship's letter of yesterday, and the accompanying Minute of Cabinet; and I am directed to acquaint you that His Majesty is perfectly sensible of the necessity of his holding the Council in London for proroguing Parliament, and that he has directed it to be summoned for half-past two o'clock at St. James's Palace. I have written accordingly to Lord Melbourne, Mr. Greville, and to the State Page, and shall of course apprise the Lord-Chancellor, who is here. His Majesty orders me to assure your Lordship that this arrangement puts him to no inconvenience, and that he has not the least objection to return in the evening, for which there will be a fine moon.

His Majesty desires your Lordship will believe that he will be glad to see you here at all times, or at any time you may feel desirous of communicating personally with him; but that, although much has occurred, and is occurring, which engages his serious attention and reflection, he has felt unwilling to call for your attendance here at this period of incessant and important business, especially as it might have retarded your recovery from the severe cold from which you have been suffering.

The King is very much pleased with the very clear, decided, and straightforward opinion given by the Attorney and Solicitor-General on the illegality of the Birmingham Union, and other similar combinations. It confirms in substance the opinion His Majesty had entertained of them, and which led to the urgent communications of the uneasiness they had occasioned to him, and he rejoices that the Government is so well *armed* on this point.

I have, &c. H. TAYLOR.

I return your letter as you desire.

No. 257.

Earl Grey to Sir H. Taylor.

East Sheen, Nov. 22, 1831.

My dear Sir,—I have to acknowledge your letters of the 19th and 20th, which I should have been glad, if it had been possible, to have had an opportunity of doing yesterday in person.

I hope to hear that the King got back to Brighton without having suffered any fatigue or inconvenience from his journey.

It will be necessary to hold another Council before the meeting of Parliament, for the King's Speech, which I hope to be able to submit to His Majesty a day or two before for his previous consideration. I mention this now that His Majesty may be enabled to make his arrangements for holding the Council either at St. James's or Brighton, as may be most convenient to him. If, as I hope, it is His Majesty's intention to open the Session in person, it perhaps would not be inconvenient to His Majesty to come to town on the 5th, and the Council might be held on that day.

With respect to the apprehension which you state the King to have expressed, that some of the sound part of the community may be induced, from the plausibility of the professed intention, to commit themselves in the Political Unions, I trust that the warning given to them by the Proclamation,* which His Majesty was

* This was a Proclamation pointing out the illegality of the organisation it had been proposed to give to the Political Unions, and commanding His Majesty's subjects to abstain from joining associations so constituted.

pleased to sanction yesterday, and which I am disappointed at not seeing in last night's Gazette, will put them upon their guard. You will observe that nothing has yet been *done* as to the organisation, the decision having been adjourned at the last meeting. No further step, therefore, could be taken at present, and I have great hopes that nothing more will be required, having reason to believe that the plan of the Birmingham Union will be abandoned, from a conviction of its illegality, which will, I trust, prove an effectual check to similar proceedings, if any such were in contemplation in other quarters.

Mr. O'Connell's scheme of union, and his letter in explanation of it, had not escaped my attention; but he is too cunning, and knows too well what he is about, to expose himself by any proceeding obviously contrary to law. Till it assumes, therefore, a more tangible shape, nothing more can be done than to watch it closely; and his being called from Ireland by the meeting of Parliament, will prevent his giving to this new association the consistency, and to the public feeling the impulse, which he alone can give them; so far the early meeting is advantageous. In other respects I still doubt whether it would not have been better to defer it till the beginning of January. But the great thing for the security of the Government (I dont mean the Administration, that is of very inferior moment), and for the peace of the country, is the speedy settlement of the question of Reform. I hope we shall be able to offer to Parliament an improved measure, though in no degree detracting from the principle or diminishing the efficiency of the last (which for me would be impossible), and which it will be my duty previously to submit to His Majesty's consideration. As far as anything can be done consistently with my conscientious opinion, and my honour, to conciliate those who have doubted upon this measure, or been more directly opposed to it, the best endeavours on my part will not be wanting. I am to see the Bishop of London tomorrow, and the Archbishop of Canterbury on Thursday, respecting this matter; and after what has already passed with Lord Wharncliffe, of which I enclose a memorandum for His Majesty's information, I am not without hope that the next discussion of this question in the House of Lords may have a more fortunate issue. But the thing is becoming of the most serious importance. I do not speak, as I have already said, with a view to the present Administration; with respect to them the course is clear. If the next Bill is rejected, it is impossible for them to remain in office, but with a view to the permanent interests of the Crown, and the peace of the country. These will be exposed to the greatest danger by another decision, opposed to the earnest wishes and opinions of the people; and I do hope the King will see the necessity of exerting all the influence he possesses to prevent such a result.

I am, &c. GREY.

I will thank you to return the memorandum,* as I have not a copy. You will perceive that it has been shown to Lord Wharncliffe, and some additions made by him. I also enclose my letter to you of the 19th.

* See Appendix B., p. 464.

No. 258.

Sir H. Taylor to Earl Grey.

(Private.) Brighton, Nov. 23, 1831.

My dear Lord,—I have had the honour of submitting your Lordship's letter of yesterday and the enclosed minute of what passed in your interview with Lord Wharncliffe to the King, and I have received his Majesty's commands to thank you for the interesting and satisfactory communication.

The King has not suffered the least inconvenience from his journey to London; and orders me to acquaint your Lordship, that he is ready and willing to open the Session in person, and that he will go to St. James's on Monday the 5th, will hold a Council there at three o'clock, and will return here on the following Friday. If the Speech should be prepared before the 5th, His Majesty will be glad to receive the draft of it here.

His Majesty observed, that the apprehension he had entertained, that some of the sound part of the community might be induced, from the plausibility of the professed intention, to commit themselves in the Political Unions, was expressed before he was aware of the intention of his confidential servants to advise him to issue the Proclamation which he sanctioned on the 21st inst., and that this measure has, of course, relieved him from that apprehension, and has given him the greatest satisfaction, not on that account only, but as giving proof of firmness and vigour in his Government, which appeared to His Majesty very desirable at this crisis upon general grounds, and calculated more than any other course that could be pursued, to rally the well-intentioned round the Throne and the Government, and to disarm the opposition to the measure of Parliamentary Reform.

The King is also satisfied that this step is sufficient for the present, and is well timed, and he trusts that the check will prove effectual.

His Majesty also concurs in all you say on the subject of Mr. O'Connell.

* * * * *

The King is sensible of the extreme importance which now attaches to the speedy settlement of the question of Reform, and he readily enters into all the anxiety which you manifest upon the subject. He orders me to say, that he has so repeatedly expressed his approbation of the manner in which your Lordship and your colleagues have discharged the arduous and important duties entrusted to you, and the confidence with which your administration of affairs, domestic and foreign, have inspired him, that it is necessary for him, upon this occasion, merely to assure you that these sentiments continue unabated, and that nothing has occurred which could diminish the satisfaction he derives from the character of his intercourse and communications with the members of the Administration. His Majesty would, therefore, deeply lament the occurrence of any event which should have the effect of depriving him and the country of services to which he attaches, and has shown that he attaches, so much value; and it is on this ground, as well as with reference to the peace and the security of the country, with which, indeed, the existence of an able and powerful administration is closely blended, that His Majesty hails the step taken by Lord Wharncliffe, with the assent of Lord Harrowby, and met by your Lordship in the same spirit of conciliation which appears to have suggested it, as tending essentially to promote the speedy settlement of the question of Reform, without detracting from the principle, or diminishing the efficiency, of the last Bill, to which it is, after all that has passed, natural, in His Majesty's opinion, that you should attach so much importance. The communication which has taken place between your Lordship and Lord Wharncliffe is, indeed, in strict unison with the wish, so long entertained, and at various periods so strongly expressed by His Majesty, that endeavours should be used to reconcile conflicting opinions, and to prevent angry discussion; and it has realised his hope that the interval between the prorogation and the re-assembling of Parliament might be usefully applied in that sense. All that passed between you, as stated in your Lordship's minute, appears to His Majesty very encouraging; and he trusts that it will be productive of further amicable communication, and insure that result which the state of the country has rendered so urgent. His Majesty hopes that your communications with the Archbishop of Canterbury and the Bishop of London may be equally encouraging, and I assure you that it is impossible for any one to feel more strongly than does His Majesty the importance and the necessity of an union of feeling and sentiment and of purpose in the Aristocracy and Gentry, as well as in all those who have character or property at stake, towards checking and defeating the designs of those who seek to raise themselves by the ruin of *all* that exists.

His Majesty considers it unnecessary to notice any points of the minute particularly, and will confine himself to the general observation that he rejoices to find, that on many the most essential features of the Bill, a disposition is shown by Lord Wharncliffe (and His Majesty concludes by those who act with him) to drop their objections, and that your Lordship's desire of maintaining the principle and efficiency of the Bill will not operate against the modification of some of the details.

Adverting to the date of this communication, and to that of the Duke of Wellington's letter, but, above all, to the tone and character of the latter, as it applied to the proceedings of the Government, it occurred to His Majesty that His Grace could not have been consulted by Lord Wharncliffe upon this step; and, at any rate, that he could not have been a party to it; and the King is inclined to think also that His Grace and Lord Wharncliffe may not take the same view of the feeling of the country on the question of Reform : that it is possible also that the Duke of Wellington's communication was, in some degree, prompted by a knowledge obtained of Lord Wharncliffe's intention, and of the feeling of Lord Harrowby and others. If such be the case, the advantage which His Majesty's Government would derive from the immediate answer given, which so strongly expressed His Majesty's confidence in his Government, appears to the King still more evident. He conceives also, that if there had been any delay in the communication, the Duke of Wellington might have concluded that the Proclamation issued and the repression of the Political Unions had resulted from his representations.

By His Majesty's order I have taken a copy of your Lordship's minute (which I return); but if you should not wish the paper to be out of your possession, I will send you the copy or destroy it.

His Majesty ordered me to say, that the Duke of Gloucester had mentioned to him that a —— is one of the great instigators of mischief at the Rotunda and elsewhere, and that he supplies funds. I am, however, ignorant whence His R. H. derives his information.

I have, &c. H. TAYLOR.

Three-quarters past 6 p.m.

P.S.—The King sent for me a few minutes ago to notice a letter from the National Political Union, dated from the Crown and Anchor, Nov. 22, in which it is stated that the Proclamation *does not apply* to them, nor to the great majority of Unions now in existence; and His Majesty wishes to know whether the exemption so claimed be well founded.

No. 259.

Earl Grey to Sir H. Taylor.

East Sheen, Nov. 25, 1831.

My dear Sir,—I must, in the first place, beg of you to offer my humble duty to the King, and express to His Majesty my deep sense of the confidence and approbation with which his present servants have been again honoured, by the gracious expressions repeated by His Majesty's command in your letter of the 23rd.

It gave me great pleasure to hear that His Majesty had approved of what I had done in my recent communication with Lord Wharncliffe. I can have no objection to a copy of the memorandum of what passed on that occasion being kept by you for His Majesty's use. I had yesterday evening a written communication from Lord Wharncliffe on the various points on which it is wished an agreement may be effected. This paper, I confess, diminishes my hopes of so desirable a result, as more is required than I fear it will be possible for me to concede consistently with the pledges I have given, and with my conscientious and firm opinion; the more especially as Lord Wharncliffe professes to have no authority to speak for any body but Lord Harrowby and himself, though he entertains sanguine hopes, if an agreement with them can be effected, that a sufficient number of Peers would be found to follow them, to carry the Bill through the House of Lords. But, after what passed at the City meeting, called by the Governor of the Bank, such general hopes become much less encouraging. We are to have a Cabinet on the Reform Bill to-morrow, when I shall submit Lord Wharncliffe's paper to my colleagues, and will inform His Majesty of the result. I saw the Bishop of London at Fulham, in my way to town on Wednesday. My conversation with him was most satisfactory. He regrets the course taken by the Bishops in the late Division, and expressed his intention of voting for the second reading of the new Bill, with a hope that several others of the Bishops might do so. He mentioned particularly the Bishops of Llandaff, Chester, Bath and Wells, and Gloucester; making, however, the just and natural reservation of full liberty to dissent from any of the provisions of the Bill, which might appear to them to require alteration in the Committee. I repeated to him, in substance and effect, what I had said to Lord Wharncliffe on the views of His Majesty's Government. From the Archbishop of Canterbury, whom I saw yesterday, I got nothing but an acknowledgment that the effect of the rejection of the late Bill, and of the part taken by the Bishops, had been much greater than he expected, and that he saw all the difficulty and danger of our present situation. To this he added, that he would himself carefully consider and consult others as to what was to be done upon this important question. I do not trouble you with all the particulars, nor is it necessary, of his doubts and fears and objections. I am convinced nothing would have so decisive an effect upon His Grace's conduct, and upon that of most of the other Bishops, if he had permission to communicate it to them as an expression of His Majesty's opinion of the danger that might result from another rejection of the measure upon the second reading of the new Bill. By the former unfortunate decision, the best opportunity, which the Committee would have afforded, of canvassing and removing objections has been lost. With the Bishop of Worcester, more especially, if His Majesty could be induced to express his wishes to him, they would be decisive; and there are also Lay Peers connected, though not holding offices themselves, with the Court, who would yield, I am persuaded, to a similar influence.

It gave me the greatest pleasure to hear that His Majesty had been so well satisfied with the Proclamation. Its effect has been excellent, and I think we shall hear no more of these plans of organisation. It is in this sense, I conclude, that the National Union of the Crown and Anchor have declared, that the Proclamation does not apply to them, as they have not taken any measures similar to those which had been proposed at Birmingham. These associations cannot, in any form that they may assume, be looked at with indifference; but nothing can be done against them whilst they confine themselves within the limits of the law; and I look to their speedy dissolution if the Reform question can be satisfactorily carried.

Mr. Ellice yesterday showed me what had passed respecting a bill due to Messrs. Rundell and Bridge, for plate ordered by the late King, and now added to the property of the Crown.

His Majesty, I trust, cannot doubt my anxiety to relieve him, as much as possible, from all claims of this nature; but I am afraid there might be a great deal of difficulty in this case, which I have desired Mr. Ellice to explain to you. I think there can be little doubt that the House of Commons, if such a demand were brought before them for payment by the public, would make inquiries as to what funds had been left by the late King which might have been applied to such purposes, and that very unpleasant discussions might follow.

I am very happy to hear that His Majesty has determined to come to town on the 5th, and to open the Session in person.

I shall hope to have the Speech in time to be submitted to His Majesty before he leaves Brighton. I enclose an application for a Peerage which I think will amuse you.

I am, &c. GREY.

No. 260.

Sir H. Taylor to Earl Grey.

(Private.) Brighton, Nov. 27, 1831.

My dear Lord,—I have had the honour of communicating your Lordship's letter, of the 25th inst., to the King, who read it with great interest, though with concern that part of it in which you state that the written communication made to you by Lord Wharncliffe had diminished your hopes of an agreement on the various points which had been the object of your personal interview with him. His Majesty considers it very possible that his Lordship may have no direct authority to speak for any body but Lord Harrowby; but he believes the influence of both, and particularly of the latter, to be such with many of the opponents of the Bill, that if it were practicable to secure their assent to the new Bill, a second failure in the House of Lords would not be to be apprehended. His Majesty, therefore, anxiously hopes that the endeavour to effect this agreement may not be given up by either party while there is the least chance of its success.

His Majesty was much disappointed by the result of the meeting in the City, on which occasion the Governor of the Bank does not seem to have experienced the support to which his good and judicious intentions entitled him. The unfortunate interference of ——— on the one hand, and the ill-timed and indiscreet violence of —— on the other, seem to have defeated the object; and it is to be lamented that the latter, otherwise an excellent man, could not command his temper upon such an occasion

Your Lordship's report of your conversation with the Bishop of London has proved very satisfactory to the King; and His Majesty hopes that not only the Bishops whom he named to you, but others also, and a majority of the Peers, may, upon re-consideration of the question, be induced to vote for the Bill going into a Committee, which would be a great step gained. Indeed, His Majesty could not understand why, upon the former occasion, those who considered some sort of Reform necessary, should have opposed the going into Committee on the Bill. He is indeed aware that they objected that this would be an acknowledgment of the principle; but His Majesty does not conceive that it would be an acknowledgment of any more than the *general principle* of reform, and that it would not commit them to the admission of any of the provisions of the Bill which might appear to them to require alteration in the Committee. His Majesty expected that the Archbishop of Canterbury would be cautious of committing himself; but he cannot doubt his being alive to the extreme importance of the approaching discussion, and to the possible consequences of another rejection upon the second reading of the new bill in the House of Lords; and His Majesty cannot hesitate to express his wish that this subject should be maturely and dispassionately considered in all its bearings, by His Grace and by others, before they determine upon a course which may be productive of danger in the present excited state of the country.

His Majesty regrets that he does not feel at liberty, and that he cannot reconcile it to the principles upon which he considers himself bound to discharge the duties of his station, to authorise any stronger expression of his feeling on this question; or to exert, directly or indirectly, his influence with Spiritual or Lay Peers (excepting those among the latter who are of his household, and with whom of course he may with propriety so communicate,) towards obtaining their assent to the Bill. He conceives, indeed, that his desire to aid and support his Government has been unequivocally manifested by his acts, and that his cordial disposition towards them cannot be mistaken by any class of his subjects.

His Majesty has received very great satisfaction from the effect produced by the Proclamation against Unions of a certain description; and he hopes, with your Lordship, that they will eventually all be dissolved, the same time that he acquiesces in the propriety of your Lordship's observations upon the impolicy of attempting any thing against those which may confine themselves within the limits of the law.

Mr. Ellice will have told your Lordship that we have had some further correspondence on the subject of Messrs. Rundell and Bridge's bill, &c., and I can assure you that His Majesty is quite satisfied of your anxiety to relieve him from claims of this nature, and to place more ample resources at his disposal; at the same time that he admits the difficulties urged by Mr. Ellice, and the objections to bring any matter of this nature before Parliament. Mr. Ellice will, I believe, to-morrow meet Sir Henry Wheatley, to whom I shall write on the subject.

The King was much amused with the —— application for a Peerage, which I return.

I have, &c. H. TAYLOR.

No. 261.

Earl Grey to Sir H. Taylor.

Downing Street, Nov. 28, 1831.

My dear Sir,—I write only a single line to acknowledge your letter of yesterday, to answer which, more particularly with respect to its most important subject, I wait till I have seen Lord Wharncliffe again, who is to be with me to-morrow.

In the meantime I enclose two letters, which I think may not be uninteresting to the King. The first is by much the most dispassionate and sensible account which I have seen of the cholera at Sunderland, and encourages a reasonable hope that it may not extend itself, or prove so fatal as it has been on the Continent. The writer is a Dr. Fenwick, who has left off practising as a physician, a very old friend of mine, and a most respectable, and, as his letter will prove, a most sensible man.

The other, from Lord Lismore, is very satisfactory as to the present state of Ireland. Stanley says that country never was more quiet. The question which agitates it most is that of Tithes, about which something must be done, as, in many of the counties, nothing is at present paid on this account to the clergy.

Excuse haste. I am, &c.   GREY.

No. 262.

Sir H. Taylor to Earl Grey.

Brighton, Nov. 29, 1831.

My dear Lord,—I have had the honour to submit to the King your Lordship's letter of yesterday, and the enclosures which I return. His Majesty is obliged to you for the communication of them, and very much pleased with Doctor Fenwick's very sensible letter on the subject of the disorder which has appeared at Sunderland, and has happily as yet not spread further. All that has come to His Majesty's knowledge is calculated to confirm Doctor Fenwick's theory; and I may add, from the remarks which His Majesty has frequently made, that he has at no time been inclined to give credit to those who wished to establish the contagious character of the Indian cholera, nor to believe that it had been imported from the Continent to Sunderland.

Lord Lismore's letter is very satisfactory, and yet more so Mr. Stanley's report of the present quiet state of Ireland, which may account for Mr. O'Connell's renewed anxiety to disturb it. The question of Tithes has at all times been one of more or less agitation; and I was aware, from some recent private applications from clergymen in Ireland for assistance, that Tithes have been in many parishes of Ireland wholly withheld. I fear that, ere long, this difficulty will occur in England also, unless some arrangement be made to *secure* a composition and to enforce its payment.

* * * * *

The King will be obliged to your Lordship for your advice as to what he should do respecting the application enclosed from Paisley, for his subscription for the relief of the operative weavers. He is ignorant whether his late Majesty subscribed from his privy purse, or to what amount. The King is anxious to learn what further progress may be made with Lord Wharncliffe.

I have, &c. H. TAYLOR.

No. 263.

Earl Grey to Sir H. Taylor.

Downing Street, Nov. 30, 1831.

My dear Sir,—I have this morning received your letter of the 29th; that of the 27th I had previously acknowledged; but there are some points referred to in it, on which I am anxious to offer some explanation for the consideration of His Majesty, but which I must still defer, probably till I have the honour of seeing His Majesty in town. You may easily conceive the pressure upon me at this moment. I had my appointed interview with Lord Wharncliffe yesterday, and went with him regularly through the various heads contained in the paper which he had before sent to me, and which I now enclose.* It is not easy to detail in

* See Appendix C., p. 471.

a letter all that passed in a conversation of this nature; I will therefore confine myself to those points on which the chief difficulties seem now to arise.

1. The exclusion of the freeholders in towns from the right of voting in counties.

On this Lord Wharncliffe lays great stress, but, after much and careful consideration, we think the proposition inadmissible. All who, having such freeholds, reside and have votes in the towns, lose their votes for the counties; the numbers therefore of those who, possessing such freeholds, are non-resident, are not probably very great. The object, therefore, does not seem to be a very important one; and it would be quite inconsistent with the reservation in the Bill of all existing rights in other cases, to take away from the possessor of a freehold the right which he actually enjoys, without any compensation or equivalent.

2. The representation of the metropolitan districts. I am persuaded that the danger of this addition to the representation is very much exaggerated. It is founded chiefly on the effects which have been observed latterly in populous districts; but these have had their origin almost entirely in the agitation of the question of Reform: when this is settled, the natural influence of property and station may be expected to be restored. In the Tower Hamlets and Finsbury the returns will probably be commercial; in Marylebone, probably of persons connected with the law, or of those who are supported by a better description of persons resident in that opulent and extensive quarter of the town. The danger, or rather the inconvenience, of too large a constituency will probably be obviated, I

think certainly, by requiring the paying of the rates as well as the taxes by the occupier of a £10 house, and by the required residence of one year previous to registration, which will in effect be a residence of nearly two. These considerations remove, I think, all fear of real danger, but at all events we feel that it is now impossible to alter this provision of the Bill.

3. The alteration of Schedule B.

By referring to the memorandum of my former conversation with Lord Wharncliffe, you will see the plan which I had in contemplation for that purpose. Upon the fullest consideration of it, we have given up the idea of transferring a portion of the boroughs in that schedule to Schedule A., being apprehensive that such an addition to positive disfranchisement would give rise to increased opposition. The union of some of the boroughs in the middle of Schedule B. we have also found to be attended with so many practical difficulties, that we have been obliged to abandon it; such as that, in many cases, it would, on account of local situation, be necessary to unite a large town with a small one; in which case the latter would be entirely absorbed. We have, therefore, confined ourselves to taking the eleven highest boroughs out of Schedule B. altogether: these would include all the county towns, to the disfranchisement of which great objections have been made. But as this would take so much from the popular part of the late Bill, I feel it to be necessary, in conformity to the pledges which I have given not to consent to a measure of less efficiency, to find an equivalent in the popular representation. For this purpose it has been proposed in the Cabinet to give ten votes to the largest towns, which by the late Bill had only one member, thus removing the objection which has been made, and in which I think there is much weight, to single representation: one to Chatham and one to the county of Monmouth, in all twelve, which would have the effect of restoring the numbers of the House of Commons (which has been much insisted upon by Lord Wharncliffe and others, amongst other reasons, for the purpose of shutting out the claim of Ireland to more members than were given by the late Bill) to what they now are,

Thus: Boroughs taken from Schedule B.	.	11
,, Chatham and Monmouth	. .	2
,, Second Members to great towns	. .	10
		23

which is the number left deficient in the late Bill.

To this, however, Lord Wharncliffe appears decidedly to object; and it is only right to add that Lord Palmerston and Lord Melbourne also dislike it. It will therefore, perhaps, be necessary to re-consider the decision of the Cabinet on this head. But I am persuaded no so good way can be found to supply the whole numbers of the House of Commons; and I am convinced that it will not have the effect of increasing the democratic character of the measure, but the contrary. By giving a second representative to the great towns, you will ensure the return of one by the master manufacturers and people of property in the towns; whereas if there was only one, there might be an apprehension that he would be returned by the class of operatives; though this danger, for the reasons I have before given, would, I think, be greatly diminished, if not entirely removed, by the settlement of this question. You could not without great inconvenience supply the deficiency by an addition to the counties, the present addition comprehending all which could be entitled to it by their extent and importance; and by restoring the return of the eleven boroughs taken from Schedule B., which would certainly belong to the higher orders, you secure to them such an advantage, as with the effect of the double representation in the large towns would decidedly increase the preponderance of that influence, which in destroying what is obnoxious and indefensible, both in theory and practice, it is the wish of us all to preserve.

These are the difficulties which remain: perhaps there may be some other, but they are of minor importance, and I have not at this moment the possibility of entering into them; and upon them there was not much approach to agreement between Lord W. and me, though he reserved the case for further consideration with Lord Harrowby, who was expected in town last night.

Upon the other matters which His Majesty has referred to my consideration, I hope His Majesty will be pleased to make allowance, on account of the pressure of the moment, for my not saying more at present than that I shall give them my most attentive consideration, and shall be prepared to take His Majesty's pleasure upon them as soon as possible. Upon the subject of the solicited contribution to the poor of Paisley, it will be necessary to make some inquiry as to what was done by the late King on the occasion referred to.

I am, &c. GREY.

P.S.—I have just received a note from Lord Wharncliffe, in which he says that 'the alterations which we propose to make in our new measure are not of sufficient importance to form a basis for any previous understanding between the parties' (I really don't know of what his party consists), 'as to the course to be pursued in the progress of that measure;' and then thanking me for the kindness which had been manifested in our late communications.

This of course puts an end to all hope of previous agreement.

I have already stated the alteration that had been proposed in Schedule B., and the reasons that would have made me prefer it. But as it fails as a means of conciliation, and as the question must be reconsidered in the Cabinet, I feel now inclined to give it up, and to leave Schedule B. as it is, subject only to the change which will be produced by altering the criterion of population for a combined one of houses and taxation, which by the way was originally proposed by me, though it appears in Lord Wharncliffe's paper as one of his conditions. I am the more inclined to this, as by this new test the county towns of Guildford, &c., will be taken out of Schedule B., and worse boroughs substituted for them. But His Majesty will be pleased to consider the whole of this part of the question as still open to revision.

I have this moment received the result of the inquiry which I directed to be made, respecting the contribution of the late King in cases of distress, which I enclose for His Majesty's information.

I have also just got the accompanying report made

by Lord Melbourne, on the inquiry which he ordered, in consequence of the Duke of Gloucester's information respecting ———. I really ought to apologise for these crude communications upon matters not yet sufficiently matured, but I trust His Majesty will at least see in them a proof of my earnest desire to put him in possession, without any reserve, of the motives and reasons under which I am acting.

No. 264.

Sir H. Taylor to Earl Grey.

(Private.) Brighton, Dec. 1, 1831.

My dear Lord,—I have not delayed to submit to the King your Lordship's letter of yesterday, and the enclosures; and I have received His Majesty's commands to defer replying to that part of it which relates to the Reform Bill and your communication with Lord Wharncliffe, until he should have re-perused them, and finally determined upon the observations he may feel desirous of conveying to you thereon.

His Majesty has ordered me to desire Sir Henry Wheatley to communicate with Mr. Ellice on the subject of Mr. Collins's memorandum, and to return the report made to Lord Melbourne, respecting the persons who exhibit at the Rotunda, in consequence of the communication from the Duke of Gloucester.

I have, &c. H. TAYLOR.

No. 265.

Earl Grey to Sir H. Taylor.

Downing Street, Dec. 2, 1831.

My dear Sir,—I last night had the honour of receiving your letter of yesterday.

I am so anxious to have the King's opinion as to the topics to be used in His Majesty's Speech at the opening of the Session, that I send with this a copy of the rough draft which I have prepared for the consideration of the Cabinet, which is to meet here to-night at nine. I am aware that it will require much correction, particularly in what is said about Portugal, which I think may be better stated; but the general views probably will not be materially altered, as we had already talked them over, and I may hope to receive any suggestions which His Majesty may wish to offer on Sunday morning, which will give me ample time for producing the Speech, in a more correct form, for His Majesty's final consideration on Monday.

I have had a long and interesting conversation with Captain Lyons, whom it might be well worth His Majesty's while to see.

* * * * *

I have determined, with Lord Palmerston's concurrence, to request the Admiralty to send him back to the Mediterranean.

I am, &c. GREY.

Pray look at the leading article in the 'Standard' of last night.

APPENDIX.

APPENDIX A.

Report on Reform, referred to in the Note, p. 91.

To the Earl Grey, etc.

In compliance with your directions, we have carefully examined into the state of the Representation, with a view to its thorough and effective Reform, and we now present to you, as the result of our labours, three Bills, amending the Representation of England, Scotland, and Ireland.

In framing them we have been actuated by the belief, that it is not the wish, or intention, of His Majesty's Ministers to concede only as much as might for the moment evade or stifle the general demand for a complete alteration of the existing system, or to propose the adoption of such a measure as could merely be considered a bare redemption of their pledges to their Sovereign and the country.

We have been, on the contrary, convinced that it is their desire to effect such a permanent settlement of this great and important question, as will no longer render its agitation subservient to the designs of the factious and discontented; but by its wise and comprehensive provisions inspire all classes of the community with a conviction, that their rights and privileges are at length duly secured and consolidated.

We have not been insensible to the great and appalling dangers which attend any further delay in effecting this settlement, or to the notorious fact that obstinate resistance to claims, just in themselves, leads not to their suppression, but to advancement of others infinitely larger; a forced compliance with which would produce consequences never contemplated by the petitioners in the first instance.

We have, therefore, been of opinion, that the plan of Reform proposed by His Majesty's Ministers ought to be of such a scope and description as to satisfy all reasonable demands, and remove at once, and for ever, all rational grounds of complaint from the minds of the intelligent and the independent portion of the community.

By pursuing such a course, we conceive that the surest and most effectual check will be opposed to that restless spirit of innovation which, founding its open claims to public support on the impossibility and hopelessness of obtaining any redress of acknowledged abuses, aims in secret at nothing less than the overthrow of all our institutions, and even of the Throne itself.

We propose in one instance to make this a measure of disfranchisement. In the case of Nomination Boroughs—that system is one so entirely at variance with the spirit of the Constitution, so indefensible in practice, and so justly odious to the whole empire, that we could not consider any measure of Reform as otherwise than trifling and nugatory which did not include the abolition or purification of these boroughs.

We propose, therefore, to disfranchise all boroughs the population of which amounts to less than 2,000 inhabitants. This will effect the extinction of the worst class; and we propose also to deprive of one member all those whose population amounts to less than 4,000.

The purification of this latter class of boroughs, as well as of those cities and boroughs where the right of voting is enjoyed by close corporations, will, we think, be ensured by the extension of the Elective Franchise in them to all householders within the town or borough and parish entitled by the late Act to serve on juries, those who are rated to the relief of the poor, or to the inhabited house tax, at £20 per annum.

We propose to grant Representatives to all large and populous towns of more than 10,000 inhabitants, of which there are unrepresented now in England about thirty.

The right of voting to be vested (as in the case of the purified boroughs) in householders of £20 per annum.

In adopting this rate, we have considered that we have granted the Elective Franchise to a constituent body including all the intelligence and respectability of the independent classes of society. If we had not felt ourselves called upon rather to extend than limit the Elective Franchise, we might perhaps have recommended the propriety of rendering it uniform by immediately merging in it all the multifarious and inconvenient rights of voting now in existence.

We have, however, provided for their eventual extinction, and, in the meantime, we trust, by the addition of an independent constituency, and other arrangements, we shall effectually prevent the recurrence of those scenes of corruption and political profligacy which too often occur where the right of voting is vested in those whose want of education and state of dependence render them quite unfitted for its exercise.

We propose to give additional members to counties whose population amounts to more than 150,000, dividing them into districts, leaving the forty shillings franchise as it now exists, but enfranchising leaseholders of £50 per annum, and copyholders of £10 per annum.

Having adopted the principle of the amount of population as the surest proof of the necessity of disfranchisement in some cases, and an increase in the number of members in others, we could discover no test more fixed and recognised than that of the last Parliamentary census of 1821; upon which, therefore, our measure, both with regard to counties and cities, is founded.

We next turned our attention to the necessity of diminishing the expenses of elections, and we propose to accomplish this, by

> The enforcement of residence;
> The registration of votes;
> The adoption of ballot;
> The increase of the number of polling booths;
> The shortening of the duration of the poll;
> And in taking the poll (in counties) in hundreds or divisions.

We finally propose that the duration of Parliament should be limited to five years.

We have embodied these arrangements and other measures of detail connected with them in three Bills, the heads of which we annex to this Report.

(Signed) DURHAM.
JAMES R. G. GRAHAM.
JOHN RUSSELL.
DUNCANNON.

APPENDIX B.

Minute of Conversation between Lord Grey and Lord Wharncliffe on Nov. 16, 1831. Referred to, p. 437.

[This Minute is in my father's handwriting. The passages in the margin were added subsequently to its being first written, and are also in his handwriting, as are the words 'added by Lord Wharncliffe.']

East Sheen, Nov. 16, 1831.

Lord Wharncliffe called on me this morning, in consequence of a communication which had passed through Lord Palmerston, to talk upon the subject of the Reform Bill. He began by stating the difficulty and danger arising out of the present circumstances of the country, to which I expressed my assent; adding that I was persuaded that the only way in which they could be averted would be by a speedy and satisfactory settlement of the Reform question.

The consideration then was how this was to be effected. He stated that he was aware of the pledge I had given, not to propose a measure of less efficiency than the last, and that he could not expect me to abandon that pledge. I added that my pledge was to a measure founded on the same principles as the last, and of equal efficiency; that I must adhere to this, not from any false pride of consistency—as I hoped I should have manliness enough to act differently if I should be convinced that I had been wrong—but because I thought, without a measure of equal extent, no settlement that would satisfy the public mind could be effected. He seemed not to dissent greatly from this opinion, and asked what the principles were to which I thought myself bound. I answered, the disfranchisement of the decayed boroughs, the giving members to towns whose population and wealth gave them a fair title to be represented and the £10 franchise, with such provisions as might be effectual in limiting it to the *bonâ fide* possessors of that qualification.

To this he thought many who had before voted against the Bill might be brought to consent, from a conviction of its necessity, though he deeply regretted that such a necessity had arisen.

He then asked an explanation of a phrase I had used in the House of Lords, which he did not clearly understand, viz. that 'I felt Schedule B. to be the weak part of the measure.' To this I answered at once that I thought so, because I felt the objection made by Harrowby to boroughs with so limited a constituency as many of those in Schedule B. would have, and also because I thought there was a good deal of force in the objection to a single representative in these and other towns now to acquire the right of representation; that, to obviate these objections, I felt much disposed to reduce Schedule B. as much as possible, by adding a part of the boroughs contained in it to Schedule A., by uniting others, and by taking some out of the schedule altogether. But I added that this must be considered as a project, which I imparted to him

[That with respect to the £10 franchise there certainly were great objections, even among the Reformers, as being too low, and not having the same effect of giving a respectable constituency in all places: it was possible, however, that the provisions mentioned by Lord Grey might remove these objections. — *Added by Lord Wharncliffe.*]

confidentially, to explain my ideas, but which I could not at present state would be carried into effect. I added also that whatever changes of this kind might take place, it must be understood that I felt myself bound to take care that the disfranchisement should not be reduced within narrower limits than those of the late Bill. From all this he expressed much less dissent than I expected.

There was some discussion as to the possibility of retaining some of the present rights of voting, there having been great objection to the sweeping change of all that now existed, for the purpose of introducing one uniform right. Upon this there was little agreement of opinion between us, but being a very subordinate point, it was not much discussed. The possibility of raising the qualification in large towns and of lowering it in small ones was also talked of; but upon this I could not give him any encouragement to hope that I could consent to any change further than that which might be required to render the exercise of the franchise derived from a £10 qualification effectual and safe.

Lord Wharncliffe expressed himself very strongly as having a decided opinion against the representation intended to be given to the Metropolitan Districts, and, as wishing, in conjunction with many others, that this provision of the Bill could be altered. I told him that I believed the apprehension respecting this part of the Bill would be found to have been much exaggerated, and that in a conversation I had had with some very respectable persons from the district of

[Lord Wharncliffe stated that he now quite understood what Lord Grey meant by that expression in the House of Lords; that certainly this was the part of the measure in which the greatest attention would be necessary to conciliate the opponents of the

the Tower Hamlets, they had expressed themselves as being quite satisfied that, providing that the £10 householders should not be qualified to vote unless they were *themselves* rated, would secure the constituency from being inconveniently large, and would render it perfectly safe; but I stated that, even if it would have been better originally not to have given this right of representation to these districts, it would now I feared be impossible to alter it.

He also stated an earnest desire that no right of voting for counties should be derived from any property within the towns to be represented, such as Leeds for instance. I told him this had been the original intention, but had been altered from a sense of the hardship of depriving persons actually possessed of freeholds within these towns and not residing there of their votes. But I did not exclude this from reconsideration.

He also objected to any diminution of the present number of the House of Commons, and to the additions to Scotland and Ireland. With respect to the first, I stated, though I thought a reduction of the number would be convenient, that I should not find much difficulty in consenting to its remaining as at present. With respect to the second, that it appeared to me absolutely necessary to make an addition to Scotland, and that doing so, a corresponding addition to Ireland could not be avoided. It was to the latter that I apprehended the chief objection was felt, and I was far from urging that it was unfounded, but that the necessity of it arose from the addition to Scotland, which was required by the Bill, but that with the disposition shown by Lord Grey to admit of discussion upon it, he hoped a way might be found to a satisfactory arrangement. — *Added by Lord Wharncliffe.*]

altered circumstances of the country, the growth of large towns, &c. This he had admitted, but thought the case might be provided for by disfranchising some of the smaller boroughs, or uniting them with others and transferring the representation to large towns.

Some subordinate points were also talked of—such as getting rid of the commissioners, which he thought would be a great improvement; and the division of the counties, to which, with the exception of Yorkshire, Lincolnshire, and Lancashire, great objections are made; and which I stated as one of the points I would give up, thinking it a doubtful question, though my own opinion is upon the whole in favour of the division, in which he agreed.

He then spoke of dividing the Bill; expressing an opinion, that if the measure could be so separated, confining the first Bill to the disfranchisement of the decayed boroughs, the enfranchisement of large towns, and the £10 qualification, that he believed a Bill founded upon these principles might be carried successfully through the House of Lords. I answered that the policy of dividing the Bills had been under the consideration of the Government; but that I thought it absolutely necessary that one Bill should contain all the provisions for settling the whole representation on the footing on which it was afterwards to remain (his division, as I understood him, would leave Schedule B. and the representation of towns now returning members which are in neither schedule for the second Bill), and that the other should apply only to the machinery of the measure; such as the registration, and

[Lord Wharncliffe also mentioned the objection to making up the number of voters in the places of Schedule B., by calling in the aid of voters from the neighbourhood, and suggested whether it would not be better to lower the franchise in those places so as to include a greater number of householders, and not to insist on any precise number of persons as an elective body, supposing that it consisted of a sufficient number to guard against nomi-

other enactments of that description. He seemed to attach, however, great importance to having those towns which are to retain their right in the second Bill, for the purpose of discussing the right of voting, which might be established in them for the future; wishing, as I have before stated, that many of the old rights, where they would give a sufficiently extensive constituency, should be preserved. The additional members for counties, I understood him to say, should be in the first Bill.

Many other things upon the subordinate details of the measure, which perhaps I do not very accurately recollect, and with which it is not necessary to encumber this statement, were mentioned in the course of a long conversation, which I must say was conducted by Lord Wharncliffe in the most frank and conciliatory manner.

The result is, that to a measure resting on the three great points of a disfranchisement co-extensive with that of the late Bill, of the enfranchisement of considerable towns, and of the £10 qualification, provided that with these regulations could be coupled which would obviate some of the objections that had been felt to the former Bill, he thought that the assent of the House of Lords might now be obtained.

He guarded himself, however, by stating that he spoke only for himself, and completely without authority from any other person, though he had communicated, as was natural, very freely with Lord Harrowby, whose opinions and feelings on this subject corresponded almost entirely with his own.

nation. — *Added by Lord Wharncliffe.*]

Everything that passed between us was understood to be under the seal of the strictest confidence on both sides; though he gave me permission to state generally to the Cabinet the grounds on which he thought it might be possible to obtain the consent of the House of Lords to a new Bill.

Towards the end of the conversation he mentioned the scheme of which I had been previously informed, for a declaration from the City, which has been brought forward chiefly by the Governor of the Bank—stating an opinion that such a declaration might be useful in facilitating an agreement between both parties: he asked mine, which I had no hesitation in giving as favourable to the project, reserving to myself only the right of a more careful consideration of the terms of the declaration than I could give it from memory only.

APPENDIX C.

Lord Wharncliffe's Plan for the Alteration of the Reform Bill, Nov. 23rd, 1831   Referred to, p. 451.

[The Memorandum is in Lord Wharncliffe's handwriting; the remarks on the margin in my father's.]

THE basis upon which it is hoped that an arrangement may be made in order to bring the question of Parliamentary Reform to a satisfactory settlement, appears to be that of mutual concession, with an understanding that neither party is to be required to give up more than the other would, under similar circumstances, think consistent with their own honour and character as public men.

The points which the Government think indispensable for the efficiency of the measure are,

1. Enfranchisement of certain large and wealthy towns with a constituency founded upon an occupation of a house of *bonâ fide* £10 annual value.

2. Disfranchisement of small and poor boroughs and places to the extent of Schedule A. of the late Bill, or *thereabouts*.

3. An extension of the franchise where the right of voting is now confined to small and select bodies, so as effectually to put an end to the nomination and return of members to Parliament by individuals.

[It is not quite what I should state to be the basis of our communications. It was admitted in the first conversation, that I could not be expected to depart from the pledges I had given to maintain the principle and efficiency of the measure: all alterations, therefore, in the details or provisions of the Bill must be limited by that consideration.]

[At least.]

4. The extension of the franchise to copyholders of a certain amount in the counties, and the giving additional members to counties in at least an equal proportion to the number of members given to the large towns.

No notice is taken in this paper of that part of the late Bill which concerns the registry of votes, and the carrying on of the elections, those being points upon which, although there may be some difference of opinion, it will not probably be such as to make an agreement difficult.

It is advisable that each of the four heads should be discussed separately, and that the opposers of the Bill should point out the conditions and qualifications with which they would accompany their concession upon each.

Upon the first then, namely, the enfranchisement of large and wealthy towns, they admit the necessity of that measure; and they even hope that it may precede, in the Bill, the disfranchisement clause. They, however, feel great doubt whether this principle was in the late Bill carried into effect in the best manner. They object for instance, in common, as they believe, with a great proportion of the supporters of the Bill, to giving members to four additional districts adjoining to London and Westminster, thereby making up the number of representatives for, what may be called, one great city to sixteen. They also object to any of the places to which representatives are now to be given having one member only; and think it far better that, by some alteration, the number of those places should be so reduced, that generally, at all events, each place

[It was never professed that this was done on the principle of balance. It would in effect have given more influence to landed property than it now possesses.]

[I am persuaded that the danger of this is much exaggerated. But we feel it quite impossible to alter it.]

should return two members. They next object to Brighton and Cheltenham being considered as proper places to have the privilege of electing members; and, lastly, they object to the £10 franchise as being in some of those places far too low in amount, although they admit that, in some of them, that amount, with proper conditions as to residence, payment of taxes, &c., may be rendered sufficiently respectable.

[I really cannot see the reasonableness of the objection to these towns; they certainly would not add to democratic influence.]

Upon the second point, namely, the disfranchisement of the smaller and least opulent places, the opposers of the Bill, with great reluctance, and still impressed with a sense of the danger to the Constitution which may arise from the destruction of that part of the representation, cannot but see, that, after all that has passed within the last twelve months, and the decided judgment which has been passed against it by a vast majority of the people of almost all classes in this country, it cannot be retained with safety, and they therefore may, if satisfied in other particulars, give way to that extent. They require, however, in return for this concession, that a more correct mode of ascertaining the propriety of disfranchisement, in each case, should be adopted than that of the last Bill; and that, instead of the amount of population being the criterion by which to judge of the fitness or otherwise of any place to retain representatives, the number of houses and the amount of direct taxation in each place shall be that criterion.

[This was my proposal in our first conversation, and not Lord Wharncliffe's.]

Passing by the third head for the present, we now come to the fourth, which, inasmuch as the additional members for the counties must be taken from the fund created in consequence of the disfranchisement, comes more properly under consideration together with the first and second heads.

To giving additional members to counties, and admitting copyholders to vote for counties, it is presumed there can be no objection. But the opposers of the Bill think they have a right to ask that the object professed in the late Bill, of an effectual shutting out the direct influence of towns having representatives from the county elections, which that Bill failed in, should be secured. They, therefore, propose that no freehold within a town having representatives, should confer a right of voting for the county. They also require, that if the counties receiving members are divided, that division shall be declared in the Bill, and not be left to commissioners to be decided hereafter.

[This would be quite inconsistent with the principle adopted in the late Bill, of continuing persons now in possession in the enjoyment of existing rights.]

With respect to the division of counties, that is a matter upon which some difference of opinion exists, and therefore no stipulation either way is made upon it in this paper.

[May be done by an Act to be passed; so done in the Scotch and Irish Unions.]

It may be as well to consider, whether, if several additional members are given to towns in any county (as for instance Lancashire, Staffordshire, &c.), any additional county members shall be given to them, as it would appear that the object of giving additional members to the counties is to preserve the balance between the agricultural and the other interests, and in those counties and some other of the most populous, the *seats* of all the members must necessarily depend upon a manufacturing and commercial constituency; and, therefore, their having addi-

[Fact as to Lancashire; Yorkshire.]

tional members will, in no degree, add to the agricultural interest.

It would be desirable, if possible, to give two additional members to counties in every case, rather than one, as was proposed in some of the counties by the late Bill.

There remains to be considered the third head, which has reference to almost all the boroughs in Schedule B. of the late Bill, and to the rest of the city and borough representation as it exists at present; and here there will be found the greatest demand upon the part of the opposers of the late Bill for alteration.

The object of the Government appears to be to prevent nomination, and at the same time to secure, in every case, a sufficiently numerous and a respectable body of electors, and, with that view, the late Bill prospectively, after the lives of all persons now living who are or would be entitled to vote in those places, fixed a £10 householding as the universal qualification. To this there is the strongest dislike, and there does not appear to be any occasion for the object in view, to have recourse to so sweeping a destruction of franchise consequent upon corporate rights.

It appears to the opposers of the Bill that, admitting the advantage of a more extended right of voting in some of these places, all that would be necessary is to give to householders of a given amount a right to become members of the Corporation so far, at least, as to entitle them to vote for the members for that place. The bringing into the towns the householders of £10 residing within certain

[Keep birth, servitude and marriage; prevent new creations. This appeared satisfactory to Lord W.]

limits to be fixed by Commissioners, appears to be a very clumsy scheme, which is very likely to be distasteful to all parties; and there can be no doubt that, in many of the smaller of those places, the householder of £5, or even less, is at least equal in respectability to one of £10 in the larger and more populous towns. A £5 householder, for instance, in any of those towns which were included in Schedule B. is, without doubt, to the full as respectable a man as the £10 householder in Bath or Liverpool. And the mode of increasing the constituency here suggested savours somewhat more of a respect for old and established systems. A decided objection is also felt to there being only one member for any place where it can be avoided; and if there are some few of those places where a respectable constituency cannot be obtained within themselves, it would appear they ought to come within the description of those which it is proposed to disfranchise entirely. There does not appear to be any reason why there should be any schedule such as B. in the late Bill. If there should exist any fear that in the places where these corporate rights are preserved, corruption may still be systematically exercised, it should be well understood, either by an express provision to that effect in the Bill, or by a resolution of the House of Commons, that in every case of that sort, brought and proved before a Committee of that House, the corrupt place should be disfranchised entirely, or the right of voting in it so altered, as may prevent that corruption. Nor does there appear to be any necessity

[After repeated consideration, this has been thought impracticable. It would infallibly leave a cause of constant complaint in those towns which had the higher franchise.]

[To this it would be impossible for the supporters of the Bill to consent consistently with their opinions and their pledges. The proposed alteration of taking eleven from Schedule B. with a proportionate addition to the representation of the large towns, appeared rather to increase than to diminish Lord W.'s objections.]

for fixing 300, or any precise number, of voters, for each place as indispensable. If it should be thought right to alter the right of voting in places where it is now vested in those who are called potwallopers, there would be no objection upon the part of the opposers of the Bill to its being placed in more respectable hands.

Would there be any objection to give those persons who now enjoy the franchise in the disfranchised boroughs a right of voting for the counties in which they are situated during their lives? Such a regulation would be, in some degree, a compensation for the loss of that which they at present enjoy. [This would be contrary to the whole principle of county representation.]

Having now gone through all the four heads into which the subject was originally divided in this paper, it is suggested, as the best mode of carrying the whole into effect, and rendering the passing of the whole into a law more easy, that it should be done by three Bills instead of one. The first of these Bills to contain all that relates to the first, second, and fourth heads; the second, all that relates to the third head; and the third, all that relates to the proposed registry, and what may be called the machinery of the measure. There can be little doubt that the part of the measure, upon which the feeling in its favour is the most decided, and upon which the greatest excitement exists, is that which would be the subject of the first of these Bills, and that once carried, the other two would be discussed with comparative calmness. [In this there are found practical and technical difficulties which are almost insurmountable.]

There are two other matters which should be attended to as objections to the late Bill, viz. the necessary diminution of the whole present number of the House of Commons and the increase of the proportionate number of representatives for Ireland. At the same time there certainly appears to be considerable reason for some increase in Scotland; and if the whole number of the House is not diminished, the door may perhaps be shut against any further or future demands upon the part of Ireland, by there being in fact no vacant representations to dispose of.

It remains now only to add that, as in the arrangement thus proposed, great concessions are undoubtedly offered by the opposing party, they think they have a strong claim to call upon the Government to meet those concessions by all such as they feel they can make without compromising the principle to which they have pledged themselves.

East Sheen, Nov. 25, 1831.

Dear Lord Wharncliffe,—I have read your paper with great attention. It states, with great explicitness and clearness, the various points on which you are anxious to obtain alterations in the Reform Bill. With respect to some of them, I foresee great difficulties; but I should wish to defer entering into the matter more particularly till I shall have had an opportunity of consulting my colleagues upon it. This opportunity I shall have to-morrow, as we are to have a Cabinet expressly on the Reform Bill, and I shall be happy to see you on any day afterwards that may be most convenient to you. As I do not go to town till Monday, I would name Tuesday at twelve, if that day and hour suit you. I observe that you speak positively only for Lord Harrowby and yourself, though you have sanguine hopes that enough might follow your opinions, if an agreement can be effected, to carry the Bill through the House of Lords. I must confess, after the result of the meeting called by Mr. Palmer in the City, that such hopes are considerably weakened.

Ever, dear Lord Wharncliffe,

Most sincerely yours,

GREY.

END OF THE FIRST VOLUME.

LONDON
PRINTED BY SPOTTISWOODE AND CO.
NEW-STREET SQUARE

Milton Keynes UK
Ingram Content Group UK Ltd.
UKHW050847031124
2541UKWH00028B/139